Travel and Trav
in the
Early Modern

GW01017738

APPROACHES TO TRANSLATION STUDIES
Founded by James S. Holmes

Edited by   Henri Bloemen
                     Dirk Delabastita
                     Ton Naaijkens

Volume 26

Travel and Translation
in the
Early Modern Period

Edited by
Carmine G. Di Biase

Amsterdam - New York, NY 2006

The paper on which this book is printed meets the requirements of "ISO
9706:1994, Information and documentation - Paper for documents -
Requirements for permanence".

ISBN: 90-420-1768-6
©Editions Rodopi B.V., Amsterdam – New York, NY 2006
Printed in The Netherlands

alla memoria di

Luigi Monga

(1941-2004)

Contents

Section 3: The European as Other and the Other in Europe

Section 4: Towards Art and Parody

Introduction: The Example of the Early Modern Lexicographer

Carmine G. Di Biase

This collection of essays explores the various relationships between travel and translation during the early modern period, when both activities flourished. The many facets of this relationship are at times obvious, at other times elusive; its manifestations can be seen in the works of Martin Luther and Erasmus, of Petrarch and Shakespeare, and of lesser known writers such as Leo Africanus and Garcilaso de la Vega, who are among the subjects of these essays. It seems to me, however, and perhaps James Joyce would have agreed, that all of these writers have at least one thing in common: they were exiles. Such too were the early makers of bilingual dictionaries, who found themselves between worlds. In the lives and works of these lexicographers, in particular Michelangelo Florio and his illustrious son John, one can see that the act of translation is essentially like that of travel: both involve a certain moment of failure, and that moment, in both cases, leads directly to the creation of something new. In short, linguistic translation and its strange results may serve as an observable, illustrative instance of how travel generates culture.
Keywords: bilingual lexicographers, exile, Florio, identity, translation, travel.

What exactly is the relationship between travel and translation? Some answers suggest themselves readily. The traveler must translate in order to make sense of foreign places and foreign people. On the other hand, a knowledge of languages other than one's own might make one want to travel in order to put those languages to use in their native settings. And if what is meant by translation is the relocation of a message from one language to another, then is not all travel–the relocation of a person from one place to another–also a kind of translation? When such obvious answers left a group of scholars unsatisfied, they decided to look deeper into the matter. To study the relationship between these two human compulsions, however, is to enter into territory that is only now beginning to be charted. Michael Cronin has studied this relationship as it pertains to the work of modern and contemporary writers; a few other scholars, such as Loredana Polezzi and Mirella Agorni, have carried out more specialized studies. But the early modern period, during which both travel and translation enjoyed a spectacular flourishing, has not, until the appearance of this book, attracted an extended study. The goal of this book, then, is to examine how this relationship manifests itself in the works of early modern writers and thereby to continue closing the gap between the study of translation and the study of travel, or hodoeporics, the term coined recently by the late Luigi Monga (1996: 5), to whom this book is dedicated. True to the spirit of the form, the essays contained herein are investigations, experiments in inductive reasoning. They do not pretend to be conclusive, only to begin a dialogue that one hopes will continue for years to come. Nor do they pretend to be comprehensive in their coverage; the emphasis, with several exceptions, is on

English writers; the focus is on representative movements within the Old World. New World matters, however, have not been neglected.

These sixteen essays have been divided into four equal groups, each of which represents a different emphasis. The four in the first group take up, in one way or another, the matter of the European vernaculars and the languages of the Bible and the classics. When Martin Luther visited Rome, what he saw there intensified his disagreements with the Roman Catholic Church. How this journey might have affected his translation of the Bible is the subject of the first essay. Here, Russel Lemmons, using an illustrative passage from Romans 3:28, shows that the passion of Luther's convictions can still be felt in the particular lexical decisions he made as he translated. When he added the word *allein*, or 'alone', and thereby suggested that "faith alone" can justify one's life, he began an argument of profound significance. What Guido Latré (2002: 19) has said about William Tyndale and his translation of the New Testament applies equally well to Luther: "Behind what seems on the surface a philological quibble, there is a profound difference in the rendering of the ecclesiastical hierarchy, which eventually resulted in a change in the social and political order"[1]. Travel, then, as in the case of Luther, can inspire, can even compel, a writer to translate. This causal relationship is the subject of Erika Rummel's study of Erasmus, who, between 1511 and 1514, made six trips to England, all of which led to translations. Rummel, however, concentrates on the social and intellectual associations that Erasmus made during these trips–with Thomas More, William Warham, John Colet and others–and examines the effect these had on his translations.

Following Rummel's essay are two dedicated to John Milton, who, it is worth stressing, was under the spell of travel literature. In *Paradise Lost*, the geography of the world, of *our* world, is a concrete presence. When Adam, for example, guided by Michael, climbs up to the the highest hill in Paradise, a vast expanse of the world opens up to his view:

His Eye might there command wherever stood
City of old or modern Fame, the Seat
Of mightiest Empire, from the destin'd Walls
Of *Cambalu*, seat of *Cathaian Can*,
And *Samarchand* by *Oxus*, *Temir's* Throne,
To *Paquin* of *Sinæan* Kings, and thence
To *Agra* and *Lahor* of great *Mogul*
Down to the golden *Chersonese*, or where
The *Persian* in *Ecbatan* sat, or since
In *Hispahan*, or where the *Russian Ksar*
In *Mosco*, or the Sultan in *Bizance*,
Turchestan-born; nor could his eye not ken
Th'Empire of *Negus* to his utmost Port
Ercoco and the less Marítime Kings
Mombaza, and *Quiloa*, and *Melind*,
And *Sofala* thought *Ophir*, to the Realm
Of *Congo*, and *Angola* fardest South;
Or thence from *Niger* Flood to *Atlas* Mount

> The Kingdoms of *Almansor*, *Fez* and *Sus*,
> *Marocco* and *Algiers*, and *Tremisen*;
> On *Europe* thence, and where *Rome* was to sway
> The World: in Spirit perhaps he also saw
> Rich *Mexico* the seat of *Montezume*,
> And *Cusco* in *Peru*, the richer seat
> Of *Atabalipa*, and yet unspoil'd
> *Guiana*, whose great City *Geryon's* Sons
> Call *El Dorado* [...] (XI.385-411)

The source of this passage, as Robert Ralston Cawley (1951: 9-23) has shown, was Peter Heylyn's *Cosmographie*. The influence of such accounts was a powerful one, so powerful that Milton's Paradise and its first inhabitants begin to recall the New World and its naked Indians, and Milton's Satan begins to seem not unlike the European traveler, setting out to occupy and colonize, and ultimately to spoil, that world.

Milton, however, was himself a traveler. His journey to Italy in 1638-1639 is of central importance to Stella Revard's essay, in which she studies the role of Latin in the friendship between Milton and Giovanni Battista Manso, two intellectuals separated by different vernaculars. Milton knew Italian–he had written sonnets in it even before his journey–but when he wrote "Mansus" he would address his Italian friend in Latin. Milton's Italian journey deepened his appreciation of Latin as a traveler's language; also deepened was his understanding of the *questione della lingua*. Along, then, with a greater appreciation of Latin, came a more vital knowledge of Italian and, no doubt, a more comprehensive vision of the kind of English he would need for *Paradise Lost*. John Hale, in his penetrating study of Milton's multilingualism, has shown that, on the level of syntax and diction, Milton's English constitutes an ongoing, and multilayered series of allusions, to Italian, to Latin, to Greek, even to the sacred languages. For after his Italian experience Milton understood, says Hale (1997: 65), that English "could absorb more" than other languages could, that indeed "absorption suited it"; and so it was that, "in its egotistically sublime way", Milton's English "drew other languages to itself"–it was a kind of translation. Seen in this way, Milton's works are all translations, and not only on the level of syntax and diction but on the more elusive level of ideas.

It is on such a level that Anthony Cinquemani explores how, in *Paradise Lost*, Milton "translates" Petrarch's *Secretum*. Borrowing the terms of Karlheinz Stierle's important essay, 'Translatio Studii and Renaissance: From Vertical to Horizontal Translation', Cinquemani shows how, in the dialogue that unfolds between Raphael and Adam in Book VIII, Milton replicates the dialectical relationship between Petrarch's Augustinius and his Franciscus, between cultural verticality and cultural horizontality; that is, between a medieval world in which languages are in hegemonic relationship, with Latin at the top and the vernaculars below, and a Renaissance world in which Latin, having lost its primacy, coexists with the vernaculars on a level plane. "With Petrarch", says Stierle (1996: 65), "begins the dominance of the horizontal over the vertical axis of *translatio*". It is this new vision, says Cinquemani, that Milton adopts, or "translates", in *Paradise Lost*.

To the early modern English traveler, Italy and, to a lesser extent, Spain, were destinations of great importance. These two essays by Revard and Cinquemani could easily have been placed in the second section, which is dedicated to the English in Italy and Spain[2]. However, what brings this second group of essays together is that, rather than focusing on questions of language, they take up matters of politics and literary biography. Why, for example, did William Thomas, one of the earliest English travelers to Italy, translate Machiavelli for his young student, Edward VI? And what effect did Thomas's experience of Italy, and particularly of Venice, have on his translations? Thomas's translations were the products of a troubled, dangerous, and rebellious life. Having stolen money from his benefactor, Thomas fled to Venice, was promptly jailed and soon released, then spent the next four years in Italy. He returned after his benefactor's death, only to find himself caught up in the Wyatt rebellion, for which he was hanged, drawn and quartered, but not before he had translated Josafat Barbaro's account of his travels to Persia[3]. Such is the subject of Joseph Khoury's essay. Donald Beecher examines a similarly troubled life, that of John Frampton, an English merchant who became a victim of the Inquisition in Spain, where he was interrogated, tortured, and detained until he managed to escape and return to England. Having learned Spanish, Frampton then became a translator of great importance, giving English readers such books as the accounts of Marco Polo's travels and Monardes's study of medicines from the New World. What, asks Beecher, were Frampton's motives in undertaking such projects?

Thomas Hoby, the subject of the next essay, is best known, of course, as the translator of Baldassare Castiglione's *Il cortegiano*; but he is not often discussed as a traveler. When he went to Italy he recorded his impressions in a journal which has yet to be published in its entirety. This important document is now being edited by Kenneth Bartlett; here, however, Bartlett examines how Hoby's journal emerged from a combination of firsthand impressions of Italy and knowledge gleaned from books. Parts of his journal, in fact, amount to translations of Leandro Alberti's *Descrittione di tutta Italia*. Also influencing Hoby's account of Italy were his associations with other travelers, such as William Barker, who is the subject of Brenda Hosington's study. Hosington's focus is *A Dyssputacion off the Nobylytye of Wymen*, which is Barker's translation of Lodovico Domenichi's *La Nobiltà delle donne*. This translation, which Barker presented to Queen Elizabeth in 1599, resembles a travelogue. Like Hoby's journal, it integrates Barker's firsthand impressions with translations from his original; William Thomas had done much the same thing when he wrote the first English history of Italy (1549)[4]. Most interesting, however, about Barker's work is that it also includes passages that are entirely invented. Here one can see clearly how the act of translation serves as a stimulus to the imagination and leads to the creation of something new.

Following this group of essays are four that explore the question of otherness and its relationship to translation. In 1486, a German knight named Konrad Grünemberg embarked on a pilgrimage to the Holy Land where, to his dismay, he and his fellow pilgrims were treated by the Saracens they met there with unrestrained contempt. Grünemberg, moreover, spoke only German; his almost total dependence on translators and interpreters reduced him to a childlike state. Later, after he returned home, he recorded this experience in a narrative which, for the benefit of future pilgrims, stressed the role of translation and even included a glossary of Arabic terms. This remarkable narrative is the subject of the essay by Kristiaan Aercke, who, in addition to addressing all of the more obvious translation matters that preoccupied Grünemberg, also shows that this traveler wrote in order to transform, or "translate", his journey into an experience of redemptive Christian suffering, his own *via dolorosa*[5]. In Oumelbanine Zhiri's essay, in which she examines the peculiar Italian of Leo Africanus's *Descrittione dell'Affrica*, the situation is reversed: the struggle here is that of a speaker of Arabic who, taken to Italy by force, must make his Africa understood in an imperfectly acquired Italian. What made his task particularly difficult was that, because some fundamental African realities, which were quite alien to Italian culture, could not be rendered accurately in Italian, he had to search for rough equivalents in the new world into which he had been forced. "At the time", as Zhiri has said elsewhere (2001: 263), "no European language was equipped to express notions and concepts elaborated on in the Islamic civilization"; in his description of Africa, Leo Africanus can be seen "trying to create a language that is capable of such expression". This is cultural translation of a most vivid kind. Indeed, this famous account, which Ramusio included in his great compendium, bears all the signs of a linguistic translation–a translation, however, from an original that was never actually written down but that lived and died only in the head of this displaced writer, whose native language would no longer serve him.

The next two essays are both dedicated to Garcilaso de la Vega, who journeyed from the New World to the Old and, having mastered Spanish, was animated by the spirit of Renaissance scholarship. Why did Garcilaso, the son of a Spanish conquistador and an Incan princess, decide to translate Leone Ebreo's *Dialoghi d'Amore*? This is the question that concerns James Nelson Novoa, who suggests that in Leone Ebreo, Garcilaso found a consolation, a kindred spirit: both of them had given up their native lands, even their original names, and both of them–translators in every sense of the word–had to express themselves in acquired languages. What Garcilaso is best known for, of course, are his histories of his native Peru: the *Comentarios reales de los Incas* (1609) and the *Historia general del Perú* (1617). These histories, however, written originally in Spanish, achieved great fame through translation into other European languages. Most important was the French translation of Sir Paul

Rycaut, which spread the fame of this most unusual Renaissance humanist through France, the Netherlands and England. It is a case of a writer who traveled not only in life but also afterwards, through translation, and this is the subject of María Antonia Garcés's essay: 'The Translator Translated: Inca Garcilaso and English Imperial Expansion'. Nor are the travels of Garcilaso's works quite over yet. The *Historia general*, for example, only recently (2001) appeared in its first Italian translation, by Francesco Saba Sardi.

In ironic juxtaposition with these two essays on Garcilaso is the first essay of the concluding group: Randall Davis's 'Early Anglo-American Attitudes to Native American Languages'. Were Indian languages as copious and expressive as English? Were they capable of housing literary art? Such questions, all too often, were answered by Englishmen who had little or no knowledge of the strange new languages they were hearing. What happened, it seems, is very much what Eric Cheyfitz has described: a terribly imperfect, terribly distorted kind of cultural translation. In the mind of the early English traveler, he says, lived the idea that ownership of property was a distinguishing feature of humanity; early English travelers to the New World, seeing that the people they met there appeared not to own any property, soon began to consider them less than human. This, says Cheyfitz (1997: 41-82), made all sorts of offenses possible. What concerns Davis, however, is how this "translation" of reality, this conveniently imperfect perception, caused the Westerner's appreciation of the expressive qualities of Native American languages to be tragically delayed. This aggressive and damaging aspect of translation is also at the heart of Jack D'Amico's essay, '"Where the devil should he learn our language?"–Travel and Translation in Shakespeare's *The Tempest*'. Here D'Amico shows how, if Caliban spoke a language before he became Prospero's subject, that language was ruined, or "translated", when it was rendered into Italian (which of course is represented by Shakespeare's English). Thus by making Caliban speak Italian, Prospero takes possession of him. In the second half of his essay, D'Amico extends this idea–translation as taking possession–to the broader political sphere of this play, examining how travel between Tunis and Naples, between Prospero's island and Milan, is intertwined with the same sort of aggressive "translation", or struggle for power and possession. D'Amico's analysis is grounded at all times by Shakespeare's persistent references to language, which plays an active role in this struggle. Like Davis and D'Amico, Howard Miller is also concerned with the matter of literary art and the making of it. Specifically, how was it possible for Christopher Marlowe to create, in his Tamburlaine plays, a tyrant who so closely resembled the historical Timur? Miller's hypothesis is that Marlowe gained such knowledge during his time at Cambridge, where he might have met and studied with Jewish scholars who had traveled there, bearing knowledge of the legendary tyrant whom Marlowe would later immortalize in his art. Miller examines the Persian and other biographical documents and offers a compelling reconstruction of how these might have been translated for

Marlowe at Cambridge and become, during that formative time, the sources of his own Tamburlaine. Concluding this group of essays is Joanne Gates's study of John Taylor, whose life and works can be seen as constituting a long, hilariously funny parody of the English taste for the exotic, a parody indeed of travel and translation both. Of special interest to Gates is Taylor's parodic treatment of Thomas Coryate and his *Crudities*.

Each essay in this volume, then, is dedicated to the task of illuminating the different manifestations of this relationship between travel and translation in the works of early modern writers. What they all have in common, however, and what I shall try to clarify in the argument that follows, is that they were all, to one degree or another, exiles. The experience of exile, it seems to me, is related to the act of translation in a most profound way. It is a condition, of course, that has always been associated with the figure of the writer. It informs the works of Ovid as much as it does those of Joyce. But for the early modern writer, exile was a condition that could hardly be escaped at all. Bartlett Giamatti, writing about Petrarch, believed that exile was a defining feature of the Renaissance:

> The Renaissance, for all its assertive, expansive, cultural imperialism–its revival of the past, its new texts, institutions and perceptions–would never completely shake the sense that what it made was removed, not quite worthy of the original; if not second-rate, at least secondhand, just as beneath the oft-repeated boast of each people that their land had been colonized by a hero from Troy–Italy by Aeneas, France by Francus, Portugal by the sons of Lusus, Britain by Brutus–there would be the constant awareness that Europe was founded by the losers, that the European people were colonists who, for all their glory, were exiled from the homeland, that in the Westering of culture, much had been gained but something had also been lost. (1984: 14)

The task, for the Renaissance humanist, was to regain what had been lost, but it was not enough for Petrarch or any other genuine artist to imitate and pay homage to the ancients; one had to make something new, and in order to do so, one had to keep one's distance from one's origins. "This perspective", said Giamatti (*ibid.*: 16), "is what we may call 'the romance of early humanism'–the secondary culture's deep belief that, despite distance and loss, it might become primary; the conviction that, through effort and emulation, the copy might become an original, the removed might restore the beginning, the exile might–through purposeful wandering–become a point, or recapture the point, of origin". The "romance", then, "of early humanism" was a kind of game, whereby the student left, or pretended to leave, the master, and, in the freedom that travel affords, became or created something new. The student, however, could never entirely forget the master. "Petrarch", said Giamatti (*ibid.*: 16), "in his meditation on exile, is saying not that one will, or even should, come home, but that the hope of returning is ever alive–indeed, that the hope of returning home is as strong as the force that sends one away in the first place. The man who would not go home always had to believe he could".

This dialectical relationship, between nostalgia and contempt, is at once tormenting and generative. "Exile", says Edward Said (2000: 173), "is strangely compelling to think about but terrible to experience. It is the unhealable rift forced between a human being and a native place, between the self and its true home: its essential sadness can never be surmounted". Theodor Adorno (1974: 33) describes the condition rather more grimly: "Every intellectual in emigration", he says, "is, without exception, mutilated" and "lives in an environment that must remain incomprehensible to him". There can be no going home for the exile, and whatever the world offers in the way of an alternative is always a compromise. Life for the exile, then, can never be passive, for it is always attended by the threat that one's identity, which has been formed elsewhere, will be extinguished. If there is a "remedy" for this condition, says Adorno (*ibid*.: 33), it is the "steadfast diagnosis of oneself and others, the attempt, through awareness, if not to escape doom, at least to rob it of its dreadful violence, that of blindness". This diagnosis, for Adorno, is a verbal affair. "For a man who no longer has a homeland", he says, "writing becomes a place to live" (*ibid*.: 87). In this way exile, however tormenting it may be, becomes a generative condition, a condition that adds to or transforms or creates culture. The exile who becomes a writer must always negotiate between two worlds, and two languages, at least, leading a difficult life in the spaces between worlds; and it is in those spaces that the exile's main task–namely, to create an alternative, more habitable world–is carried out. "Much of the exile's life", says Said, "is taken up with compensating for disorienting loss by creating a new world to rule" (2000: 181). What Said has noticed here is the imperious character of the exile, who assumes the role of cultural curator, either of the world left behind or of the adopted world, or indeed of both, and then forges another world from materials both old and new. "It is not surprising", says Said (*ibid*.), "that so many exiles seem to be novelists, chess players, political activists, and intellectuals". To this list, I should like to add the lexicographer, who, like the imaginative writer or the writer of travel accounts, though perhaps in a more concrete way, finds a kind of home in language itself. For this reason, the experience of the early modern lexicographer, and particularly those who worked in more than one language, is, I think, exemplary of the experience of all the writers examined in this volume. My concentration, therefore, the essay that follows, will be on Michelangelo Florio and his son John. Like the lexicographers who came before and after them–such as William Thomas, Giovanni Torriano, and James Howell–the Florios rather vividly dramatize how and why travel and translation happen together. My particular interest will be the compulsion among such writers to translate, whether this involves languages or some more elusive cultural reality, and how translation becomes the means by which the traveler creates "a new world to rule".

In his "Apologia"[6], Michelangelo Florio says that his parents were born Jews but baptized "papists" (in Yates 1934: 2). Florio, who had been a

Franciscan friar, had grown contemptuous of Catholicism, and his outspokenness, a trait he would never lose, brought him considerable grief. He spent twenty-seven months in a Roman prison, after which he escaped and eventually made his way to London, where he was made preacher of the Reformed Italian church. Even there, however, he soon grew restless. His zeal for religious reform was apparently so great that the members of his congregation found it unseemly and began to defect. And there were private troubles as well. He was accused of fornication–which, incidentally, may have been the origin of his illustrious son John–and lost his post as preacher. Afterwards, he made a living as a language instructor, and even became Italian tutor to none other than Jane Grey. When Mary assumed the throne, however, she gave all Protestant foreigners twenty-four days to leave the realm. And Michelangelo Florio, exiled now for a second time, took refuge in the Grisons canton of Switzerland, where he resumed his preaching and spent the rest of his days in disputing religious matters, arguing over points of Italian grammar and spelling, and translating into Italian the documents that he felt were important.

Florio's passionate belief in the need for religious reform gave him a life characterized by rootlessness and loss. If anything redeemed this experience, it was his lifelong cultivation of his native language. In 1553, soon after he arrived in England, he compiled his Italian grammar, *Regole de la lingua Thoscana*. This work would be followed by a series of translations into Italian. Among these were Bishop Ponet's Catechism, to which he appended Edward VI's deathbed prayer; Jane Grey's surviving papers, which he seems to have gotten in Strasbourg during his journey from England to Switzerland; and finally, his most ambitious undertaking of all, Georg Agricola's *De re metallica*, a study of metallurgy[7]. Florio never fails, in these works, to express a preoccupation with the state of the Italian language and with what the critics will think of his handling of it. Indeed, aside from his desire for religious reform, this linguistic preoccupation is all that unifies an otherwise fragmentary life. Francis Yates, whose chapter on Michelangelo Florio constitutes the most lucid account of his life, is at a loss sometimes, despite her thorough and sensitive treatment of the documentary evidence. One shadowy area of Florio's life has to do with the charge of fornication. He had been given a good living as a preacher; but "unfortunately", says Yates (1934: 6), he "could not settle down in these comfortable circumstances". She suggests that he might have been "upset" by the influence of Ochino, who had defended polygamy and gone in other "strange directions" as well. Or "perhaps", she says, it was Florio's "recent sufferings in Italy" that "had disturbed his balance". What is certain, she says, is that "he seems to have spent a good deal of his time in England in getting into scrapes" and that his "moral failure at this point in his career was perhaps connected with his spiritual instability". All of this is plausible, of course, but it suggests perhaps too strongly that Florio's troubles were caused by matters of faith. An equally plausible explanation might be found in one of the most basic traits of the exile: an inability, or refusal, to respect the written or unwritten laws of any established culture. What Said says about the work and temperament of the exile–who "jealously insists on his or her right to refuse to belong"–seems to describe Florio, and for that matter his son as well, quite perfectly:

> Willfulness, exaggeration, overstatement: these are characteristic styles of being an exile, methods for compelling the world to accept your vision—which you make more unacceptable because you are in fact unwilling to have it accepted. It is yours, after all. Composure and serenity are the last things associated with the work of exiles. Artists in exile are decidedly unpleasant, and their stubbornness insinuates itself into even their exalted works. (2000: 182)

The exile's "vision", of course, is the exile's new home; it is a terribly lonely place, constructed, in the case of the writer, out of words[8]. To live in one's language is not at all easy when one has rejected, as Florio did, much of what might have sustained it. The danger, in short, is that the language one carries into a foreign place will gradually be drained of its power to mean. Confronted with this danger, Florio chose to translate documents that might replace, or somehow compensate for, what he had rejected. Ponet's Catechism, Edward VI's deathbed prayer, Jane Grey's papers–these documents were all connected to the living sources of the culture of Reformation England; in translating them, Florio must have seen a promise of healing the rift (as Said might say) between himself and the Italy he would never see again, of sustaining the life of the language in which he had first learned how to think and feel. This is not only translation in the ordinary sense of the word, but cultural translation as well, and of a very private kind.

If this activity, however, was to mean anything at all to Florio, the language into which he was bringing these documents would have to be made legitimate. That he was aware of this contingency, indeed anxious about it, is made clear in the prefatory material that he attached to his translations. In the "Proemio" to his *Regole,* Florio asserts that his language has been held in high esteem for a long time, and by the best minds, and that his manual will offer nothing less than the Italian language perfected (1954: 105-106). One manuscript of this work, dated 1553, bears a dedication to Henry Herbert. In this letter, Florio offers his manual, "knowing", as he says, that Herbert is "very studious" of the Italian language. The other manuscript of the *Regole*, which is undated, bears a dedication to Jane Grey, his most important student. Here he says that now, "many months" after he had promised to compile it, the manual is finally done, and he offers it to her, knowing how much she "desires to learn and to speak the Tuscan language" (1954: 203). Her regard for Italian, along with Herbert's and, later on, Elizabeth's as well, must have inspired Florio, and breathed new life into his handling of the language on which his sense of identity depended[9].

Of course, the humility and self-abasement that one finds in Florio's dedications are to some extent customary, but certain remarks do seem to have been made with genuine feeling. In claiming, for example, that his work is unworthy of Herbert, Florio rather frankly, and poignantly, admits to his unusual disadvantages: "I am a poor foreigner here", he says, "deprived of all the help, favor and succor that one might expect from one's homeland and friends" (1954: 104). This seems to me a quite authentic expression of Florio's anxiety that his language, or at least his mastery of it, might gradually deteriorate because of his separation from the Italy that had given life to it. If this is the case, then it helps to explain why Florio, who lived in exile for most of his adult life, was so preoccupied with the minutiae of language, even at the unlikeliest times. With regard, for example, to his translations of Ponet's Catechism and of Edward VI's deathbed prayer, Yates (1934: 12) notes how "curious" it is that Florio should have felt it necessary, or even appropriate, to defend his manner of translation, asserting that it is not necessary to translate literally and that words may be added here and there in order to clarify the original. What seems to have caused Yates the greatest wonder is that Florio, "even in these dangerous hours", should have given "his attention to the question of literary style" (*ibid.*: 11). To Yates, this linguistic preoccupation seems incongruous. "It is curious to note", she says, "how there is embedded in Michael Angelo's career as a left-wing theologian a quite different career of linguistic studies which found expression in his teaching and his *Rules of the Tuscan Language* and in translation" (*ibid.*: 24). My own explanation for this is that for Florio, who no longer had a homeland, writing, and translation in particular, became, as Adorno might say, "a place to live".

For his translation of Agricola, Florio wrote a letter to the reader that is highly revealing of the aggressive way in which he cultivated the Italian language while living at his mountainous Swiss outpost. Here, as in his previous translations, he is defensive, still worried that his handling of the language will not meet with the approval of the acknowledged custodians of Italian literary culture. He says, first of all, that he departs from what might be considered acceptable Italian because his translation is intended not only for those who are well versed in the prose of Pietro Bembo. Also, he says that he has used neither Boccaccio's diction nor "those long periods of his"; "my translation", he says, "will not have to be read by the age of Boccaccio but by the present one", and he stresses that "the difference between the speech of that time and that of today is like that between night and day", that "what was then considered purity of language" is seen today as "coarse ugliness" (1563: 6v). He reserves his final remarks for a commentary on the relationship between Italian spelling and pronunciation:

> If finally the spelling that I have followed does not seem to you the same that is followed by Bembo in his prose, I beg you not to curse me. This is something I have done on purpose so that it shall correspond to pronunciation, to speech. For to tell the truth, to do otherwise seems inconvenient to me. And why should one write a t where the pronunciation would call for a z? and two l's, where only the sound of one is heard? (1563: 6r)

Clearly, Florio is attempting to revive the Italian language, to make its written form, that is, correspond more closely to modern Italian speech. As Yates points out, this was an argument that Castelvetro, who was then in nearby Chiavenna, was also carrying on. But is this preoccupation of Florio's not also a measure of how urgent it was for him to cultivate a language that lived, and that lived, perhaps above all, for him?

Agricola's *De re metallica* was an important contribution to the new learning[10]. Florio, in his dedicatory letter to Elizabeth, says that this book will help England to appreciate its extraordinary mineral riches and to make the best use of them. Such knowledge, he says, will help, ultimately, to maintain domestic peace, to quell conspiracies, to provide for the poor, and somehow even to foster the study of literature. And he has translated the work into Italian, he says, not merely so that "the beauty of Agricola's mind" may be revealed, but "so as to accommodate those who understand my language, and not the Latin, and to give a reason to the intellects of every other nation to do the same, not only with this work but with many others, which are no less beautiful than they are useful, and especially with those that are divine and sacred" (1563: 3v). The worldly vision he expresses in this dedication is precisely what he admires in the English queen, whom he praises more unrestrainedly than he had praised Herbert or even Jane Grey. It is well known, he tells Elizabeth, that she is proficient not only in Italian but in all of the modern languages, and that when other nations send their representatives to her, she is able to address them in their own languages. Yates suggests that Florio's motive here was to prepare the way for his son John, who would soon be going to England, and this indeed seems likely; but the elder Florio's admiration for Elizabeth must have been genuine, more than mere flattery. To one who had lived so long in the spaces between worlds, the example of Elizabeth must have been a great inspiration; for if her own facility with languages did not allow her to travel widely, it did encourage travelers to come to her.

By the end of his life, perhaps the elder Florio achieved some peace of mind. The experience of exile, painful though it might be, is not without a certain spiritual or intellectual reward. To know more than one way of life, says Said, "gives rise to an awareness of simultaneous dimensions, an awareness that—to borrow a phrase from music—is contrapuntal":

> Thus both the new and the old environments are vivid, actual, occurring together contrapuntally. There is a unique pleasure in this sort of apprehension, especially if the exile is conscious of other contrapuntal juxtapositions that diminish orthodox judgment and elevate appreciative sympathy. There is also a particular sense of achievement in acting as if one were at home wherever one happens to be. (2000: 186)

This is rather like what George Steiner, in his majestic study of the subject, has said about translation: "To move between languages, to translate, even within restrictions of totality, is to experience the almost bewildering bias of the human spirit towards freedom" (1992: 498). In any case, there can hardly be a more concrete manifestation of this contrapuntal vision than the bilingual dictionary and, in particular, the many bilingual dialogues one finds in the early modern language guide.

The most important of these guides, with regard to English and Italian, were created by Michelangelo Florio's son John. His *Firste Fruites* appeared in 1578, his *Second Frutes* in 1591, and his most ambitious work, the *Worlde of Wordes*, in 1598. In all of these works, one can see that the younger Florio, who had been born in England but raised in Switzerland, must have felt just as alienated in England as his father had, just as insecure and restless, despite his mastery of both the Italian and English languages. At times, in the dialogues themselves, Florio expresses what seem to be his own misgivings about the English people. In the eleventh dialogue of *Firste Fruites*, for example, the question, "What do you thinke of the people of England, are they louing?" receives the following answer: "I wil tel you the truth, the Nobilitie is very courteous but the commons are discourteous, & especially toward strangers, the which thing doth displease me" (1578: 10v). It is hard to believe that such remarks are not autobiographical; Florio must have felt his foreignness keenly. In the dedicatory letter, he asks Robert Dudley to protect him from "such carping, blustering, and malignious tongues, which not onely doo perilously shake at, yea, and indeuour mainely to beat downe, and confute, not onely all kind of blossomes, and young budded fruites, but also those, which are already come to growth and perfection". He admits, or pretends to admit, that his learning is deficient: "consider, that little, or (to say truth,) none at all is the learning I haue". Here, again, the self-abasement may be customary, of the very same kind one sees in nearly all such dedications, but in the letter to his Italian readers he expresses an anxiety that makes all of his worries sound quite real. Calling them his friends, he asks these readers to defend him against those who would question his knowledge of Italian: "I know very well that some will say, How can he write good Italian? He was not born in Italy. My answer to them is that they should mind their own business".

Indeed, he seems to retaliate by criticizing the current state of the English language. "It is a language", he says in the twenty-seventh dialogue, "that wyl do you good in England, but passe Douer, it is worth nothing" (1578: 50r). And to the question, "what thinke you of the speech, is it gallant and gentle, or els contrary?" he gives the following answer:

> Certis if you wyl beleeue me, it doth not like me at al, because it is a language confused, bepeesed with many tongues: it taketh many words of the latine, and mo from the French, & mo from the Italian, and many mo from the Duitch, some also from the Greeke, & from the Britaine, so that if euery language had his owne wordes againe, there woulde but a fewe remaine for English men, and yet euery day they adde. (1578: 51v)

This observation, however, might very well be ironic, as Florio was of course among those who happily contributed foreign words to the English language. Florio's works do not, in any obvious way, suggest a stable or even coherent view of the English or their language. Here he is, for example, on the matter of translation, making a remark that suggests an admirable absence of bias: "marke", he says, "that an Italian prouerb, to say it in English, can not haue that grace, as it hath in Italian, and also an Englishe prouerbe, to say it in Italian, can not haue that grace as it hath in their natural language" (1578: 27r). Florio's remarks, in fact, are often contradictory. It is a quality that suggests the exile's difficult and constant movement between languages, the anxiety, perhaps, to redeem the old and familiar language and make peace with the new and alien language. As writers in exile have always done, Florio masters and in effect appropriates the new language, making new spaces in it and filling them with the culture that he has brought with him. Instances of this cultural translation can be found throughout Florio's work, which is nearly all bilingual. The "engagement with multiple worlds", says David Frantz (1997: 2), is "apparent on every page", but in certain places it happens in a particularly deliberate and transparent way. In the twenty-fourth dialogue, for example, the poets from whom Florio learned his Italian, such as Petrarch, Ariosto and Alciato, appear on the left in the original and on the right in their new English dress. And in this contrapuntal way, as Said might say, they are made to speak, both in Italian and in English, on such subjects as anger, jealousy, flattery and–one that must have been close to Florio's heart–patience.

By the time he wrote *Second Fruites*, Florio seems to have become much more critical of England and much more aggressive in his use of English. The dedicatory letter opens with a long passage in which he shows a thorough awareness of the kind of writing, such as that of John Lyly, Thomas Nashe and Robert Greene, which was popular at the time (Yates 1934: 127-129). It is a "stirring time", he says, a "pregnant prime of inuention when euerie bramble is fruitefull, when euerie mol-hill hath cast of the winters mourning garment, and when euerie man is busilie woorking to feede his owne fancie". As Yates points out, this passage is "slightly patronizing in tone" (*ibid.*: 129). This tone is heightened in the letter to the reader, where, as is so often the case with Florio, he is preoccupied with those who would criticize his work:

> Prints were first inuented for wise mens vse, and not for fooles play. These Prouerbs and prouerbiall Phrases, (hethertoo so peculiar to the Italians, that they could neuer finde the way ouer the Apenines, or meanes to become familiar to anie other Nation) haue onely been selected and stamped for the wise and not for thee.

Interesting here is that Florio employs a rather vivid travel metaphor in order to describe the passage that his Italian words and phrases have made. It is a metaphor of which he was quite fond; he would use it again in his dictionary, in the address to the reader: "this our paper-sea", he would call the whole business of publishing, and would look back to a "ship-wracke" he had suffered on one of his earlier "voyages"[11]. Most conspicuous about *Second Fruites*, however, is how Florio asserts his social superiority, a tendency that seems to have grown along with his fastidiousness about language.

Yates remarks on how Florio's tone in the *Second Fruites* has changed, from that of a moralist to that of a libertine, perhaps even an aesthete. She suggests that this development may have been caused by the influence of Giordano Bruno, or by changes in Elizabethan taste, but then concludes in a somewhat resigned fashion:

> The fact of the matter is that Florio had to grumble and he has transferred all his Puritan grumblings to the grumble about England as a place of residence in which Bruno had encouraged him. [...] There is something of the Italian courtesy-book in the *Second Fruits*, and Florio probably hoped that an Italian finish would refine away some of the English barbarism of mind and manners which he and Bruno found so trying. (*ibid.*: 138)

Desmond O'Connor (1990: 22), in his history of Italian and English bilingual dictionaries, seems to be equally at a loss. He notices that in *First Fruites*, Florio's use of northern Italian words, of Swiss regionalisms, and of Anglo-Italian constructions, gives way, "curiously enough", to a more conservative diction; so that of the many importations and inventions that Florio had included in the glossary of *Firste Fruites*, "only a very small proportion" find their way, twenty years later, into the *Worlde of Wordes*. Perhaps Yates is right in saying that Florio's motive was to "refine away" what he considered English barbarism; after all, in *Second Fruites* there is also a good deal of criticism about English table manners, which Florio found appalling.

This tendency towards purism, however, or at least towards an imagined purism, is also part of the more private condition of exile. Giamatti (1984: 14-15), writing about one of Petrarch's letters, in which the etymology of the word "exilium" is discussed, says that more interesting than the derivation itself is "the etymologizing habit, the philological cast of mind", which is "typical of the whole humanist effort to uncover and reconstitute meaning by returning to origins. Whether through single words or whole bodies of texts, philology reaffirms the humanist's exile from true meaning as he struggles to overcome it". But the condition of exile can also manifest itself in the opposite way, that is, in a tendency towards inclusiveness. These, it seems, are the two choices that the writer in exile must face. Some writers, such as John Florio, try them both, but either choice, no matter what the inclination of the writer, is part of an attempt, through language, to return home, or to return, as Giamatti puts it, to "true meaning"[12]. Of course, both choices reflect the broader concerns of enlightened early modern writers. Thomas Wilson, in *The Arte of Rhetoric* (1553), advocated a conservative approach to rhetoric and diction and was suspicious of novelty; Erasmus, on the other hand, in his *De copia* (1512) had promoted the charms of abundance and variety. This does not mean that these choices were historically determined, or that these lexicographers were merely following trends. One need only look at the gap that separates two of the most talented writers working today: V.S. Naipaul and Salman Rushdie. One is exclusive in the extreme and in every way; the other has taken the opposite path. Both are exiles.

What all of the essays in this volume show, in the end, is that there is hardly such a thing as a pure culture. Displacement always results in a collision between cultures. The aftermath of such collisions, I believe, is not merely *like* translation; it *is* translation, but of a broader, more comprehensive kind, which includes translation of the more concrete, linguistic kind. James Clifford, who believes that all new cultures are made on the borders between established cultures, uses "translation" in the title of his recent book, even though, to the exasperation of translation theorists[13], he barely touches upon the business of transferring meaning from one language to another. By "translation" Clifford means what happens when two cultures come together. It is an interestingly imperfect process, he says, whereby the ethnographer (or traveler), who can only understand (or translate) another culture subjectively, is involved in an encounter that leaves both cultures a bit altered, that results indeed in something new. Travel, he says (1997: 7), "is *constitutive* of cultural meanings"; that is, it does not simply move culture from one place to another but creates it, and this generative activity "takes place in the contact zones, along the political and transgressive intercultural frontiers of nations, peoples, locales. Stasis and purity are asserted–creatively and violently–*against* historical forces of movement and contamination". This resistance to cultural encounter and exchange is understandable because the attempt to understand each other, as Clifford observes, is always attended–and here the similarity to linguistic translation becomes clear–by a crucial moment of failure, crucial because it is also a moment of beginning:

> An awareness of what escapes the 'finished' version will always trouble the moment of success. I use the dramatic word 'failure' because the consciousness of being cut down to size, refuted by the constitutive 'outside,' is painful. It cannot be cured by revisions or by adding another perspective. If confronted consciously, failure provokes critical awareness of one's position in specific relations of power and thus, potentially, reopens the hermeneutic process. Such an awareness of location emerges less from introspection than from confrontation [...]. (1997: 183)

This awareness, this reopening of "the hermeneutic process", is what makes, and remakes, human culture. Willis Barnstone (1993: 262) arrives at the same conclusion, though by a different route, likening the experience of the translator to that of the mystic: "By passing through the night of aridity, by absorbing the ray of darkness, the translator, alone with sign and object, sees, and then shapes words into an appropriate creation. At that instant the translator becomes the interpreting creator". A truly intriguing similarity, however, lies between what Clifford says about cultural translation and what Lawrence Venuti says about linguistic translation. Venuti stresses that every translation is unique and, in very real ways, independent of its source. The translator, he says, must accept this reality, as it is inescapable, and must not pretend to be "invisible", hide, that is, behind a polished, fluent style, pretending to have deli original to a new readership intact. Such a translation, he says, which seems ... to be a translation at all, disguises the fact that the original has been happily violated, or domesticated, that it has suffered omissions and distortions and additions at the hands of a translator whose own cultural formation has been allowed to work freely on it, leaving no trace of its otherness. It is "highly desirable today", says Venuti (1995: 17-20), "to restrain the ethnocentric violence of translation"; indeed, the translator must allow the original to reshape–or "foreignize"–the language into which it is translated. In this way, not only does the translation constitute a new work but the language of the translation, altered now because it houses alien cultural realities, also becomes new[14]. Linguistic translation, then, begins to resemble the kind of cultural encounter described by Clifford. The essential link, it seems to me, between travel and translation, is precisely this moment of failure, the translator's awareness of it, and the something new that follows, urgently, as a consequence[15].

This awareness is what allowed Michelangelo Florio's translations to make the Italian language new and more alive; it is what allowed his son's translations–embellished with proverbs, euphuistic flourishes, and a great many new words–to transform English prose and exert a powerful influence on his contemporaries, even on the likes of William Shakespeare[16]. It is this awareness, indeed, that made possible the great translations of the English Renaissance, such as Edward Fairfax's Tasso, John Harrington's Ariosto, Thomas Hoby's Castiglione, and of course, perhaps the greatest of them all, Thomas North's Plutarch, without which the Greek and Roman plays of Shakespeare would not have been what they are. If by "travel", therefore, one intends cultural encounters and the resulting transformations that take place on both sides, then travel is indeed translation extended beyond the linguistic limits. To reject such a notion, it seems to me, is to encourage a kind of brutishness. Language, as Steiner (1992: 436-437) has put it, may be "a restrictive specialization, an evolutionary twist which has assured man's domination over the natural world but which has also insulated him from a much wider spectrum of somatic–semiotic awareness"[17]. To study translation, then, as it manifests itself on all of it various levels, may very well be to study how culture is made, even if culture is a notion that resists definition[18].

To conclude, I should like to mention one more kind of translation. As I have suggested, these early modern lexicographers, along with all of the other writers who form the subjects of the following essays, are, to one degree or another, exiles, bearing readily identifiable traits that recur with surprising regularity: the refusal to embrace any established way of life; the defensive, contrary, often insolent temperament; the inclination to appropriate language aggressively and to appoint oneself its curator; and, of course, the compulsion to translate, usually from their acquired languages into their native ones. Most often, the stated purpose of their translations, as one can see in document after document, is to advance the common good, even if that good is a political goal; but there is another purpose at work as well, though it is not often stated. "Language", says James Howell in his *Instructions for Forreine Travell*, "is the greatest outward testimony of Travell", but he hastens to add that "to be able to speake many Languages [...] is but vanity and superficiall Knowledge, unlesse the inward man be bettered hereby; unlesse by seeing and perusing the volume of the Great World, one learne to know the Little, which is himselfe" (1895: 69-71)[19]. This is what most stirs the mind of the displaced writer, the exile, who carries a world within that is forever colliding with the world without. Invariably, there is fragmentation on both sides, even if one of the two worlds is always more durable than the other. The task of such a writer, of course, is to reassemble the fragments and to create a new, coherent and unique world. It is a "forced" but "poetic 're-creation,'" as Monga (2002: 185) has put it, "of a spiritual *locus amoenus*, built on a feeling of not belonging". This experience, I would add, leaves the writer altered as well; the self that emerges is, if only for a moment, also new, coherent and unique, at once familiar and strange, for it too is a translation[20].

---

[1] In the case of Tyndale, travel made translation possible, for it was Antwerp that offered him, as Latré (2002: 13) says, the necessary "open-minded acceptance of ideological and religious changes". Also worth noting here is Willis Barnstone's excellent chapter, 'History of the Bible and Its Flagrant Translations', in which he makes the following observation regarding both Tyndale and Luther:

> In that Tyndale was connected with that other pestilent creature of the continent, Martin Luther, the dispute between More and Tyndale was no less than the struggle between Catholicism and rising Protestantism. Proof of Tyndale's Protestant heresy was the infamous translation. Indeed, never before nor since has translation enjoyed such passionate controversy as during the sixteenth-century German and English assays to bring the Hebrew and Greek Bible into the vernacular. (1993: 206)

[2] Cinquemani, in a recent monograph–*Glad to go for a feast: Milton, Buonmattei, and the Florentine Accademici*–has written eloquently on the subject of Milton in Italy. See also F.T. Prince's earlier study, *The Italian Element in Milton's Verse*.

[3] On Thomas's life see especially Sergio Rossi's article (1966).

[4] When George B. Parks edited this work in 1963, he excluded the passages that Thomas translated from other works.

[5] Aercke, it should be noted, has completed the first English translation of Grünemberg's narrative. It will soon be published by the Centro Interuniversitario di Ricerche sul Viaggio in Italia (Milan).

[6] Quoted in Yates (1934: 1-4). Here and elsewhere, all translations from Italian are my own.

[7] First published in Latin in 1556.

[8] On the temperament of the exile see also Monga (2002: 184-185).

[9] With regard to lexicography and cultural identity, see also Rajani Sudan's study of Samuel Johnson.

[10] Ironically, Agricola (a Latinized form of his real name, Bauer) was a staunch Catholic till the end of his life, a fact which caused him much grief, even until his death in 1555.

[11] That Florio described his efforts in terms of travel suggests more than a liking for quaint metaphors. Like his father, he was indeed a traveler, having made the journey from Switzerland to England; but more important was his close association with Richard Hakluyt, for whom he translated the two voyages of Jacques Cartier from Ramusio's Italian versions. Giuliano Pellegrini (1961: 21), in his introduction to Florio's translation of James I's *Basilicon Doran*, makes the observation that Florio "worked with an enthusiasm and fervor perhaps analogous to that which animated–in another field–the undertakings of a Drake, or even a Hawkins". Early modern lexicographers tend conspicuously to be travelers as well. Giovanni Torriano, who continued Florio's work on bilingual dictionaries, traveled a great deal and translated an important account of Rome. Like John Florio, he was the son of a Protestant refugee; but unlike Florio, he moved often between England and Italy, teaching Italian while in England and English while in Italy. In Torriano, who extols the virtues of each language in a more balanced way than either of the Florios had done, one finds perhaps a more complete manifestation of the exile's contrapuntal existence. On Torriano see Yates (1934: 322-333) and Rossi (1991: 36-50). James Howell, a consummate traveler, wrote a manual called *Instructions for Forreine Travell*, which appeared first in 1642 and again, in expanded form, in 1650. In this work one finds an English voice that is much more confident; at times it reaches the point of swagger. The exploits of Drake and Cavendish, after all, were behind him, and so of course was the defeat of the Armada. While William Thomas, writing in the 1550s, had been admiring of the Italian language, even at the expense of the English, Howell, writing in the middle of the seventeenth century, could compile a four-language dictionary–the *Lexicon Tetraglotton*, which appeared in 1659–in which English served as the main point of reference.

[12] See William Edward Engel's fine study of Elizabethan phrase-books and dictionaries, in which he makes the following acute observation on Florio and the significance of the dialogue form that characterizes so much of his work:

> [...] let us remember his effort to make a World of Words: Language *re-produces* reality. This is to be understood in the most literal way: reality is produced anew by means of language. The speaker recreates the event and his experience of the event by his discourse. The hearer grasps the discourse first, and through this discourse, the event which is being reproduced. Thus the situation inherent in the practice of language, namely that of exchange and dialogue, confers a double function on the act of discourse; for the speaker it represents reality, for the hearer it recreates reality. This makes language the very instrument of intersubjective communication. At this point some serious problems immediately arise which we shall leave to philosophers, notably the adequacy of the mind to express "reality". The linguist on his part considers that thought could not exist without language and that as a result the knowledge of the world is being determined by the expression it receives. Language reproduces the world, but by submitting it to its own organization. (1996: 520-521)

Similarly, David Frantz (1999: 121) says that "Florio's most telling practice [...] in attempting to bring Italian language and culture to the understanding of his English readers, is his penchant for giving a local habitation and name to a wide range of Italian words, practices and places". Thus he "presents himself not just as an expert on things Italian", says Franz, "but as an Englishman of immediate Italian descent who is acutely conscious of his complex status". It was this acute awareness, no doubt, that compelled Florio to build his new "local habitation" out of words.

[13] On this matter, see in particular Michael Cronin (2000: 102-104).

[14] This view is in sympathy with that expressed by Walter Benjamin (1969: 81) in his extraordinary essay on the subject: "The basic error of the translator is that he preserves the state in which his own language happens to be instead of allowing his language to be powerfully affected by the foreign tongue". Both suggest that the translator should yield to a certain cultural vulnerability. The reality of such a vulnerability, on the side normally seen as the more powerful, is confirmed by an observation made by Anthony Pym. Translators, says Pym (1998: 166), want "a position of relative prestige, the power to control and direct exchanges. Yet this power is very

temporary. The translators are so busy conveying someone else's words that they sometimes lose the capacity to speak in their own name. [...] Although translating initially looks like an act of power, the translating translator can become relatively powerless. Some people try it for a while then seek to recover their own voices".

[15] This similarity was, to my knowledge, first noticed by Kate Sturge in her review of *Routes*. Loredana Polezzi's recent study, however, seems to be the first extended synthesis of the work of ethnographers such as Clifford and translation theorists such as Venuti. Polezzi tries to clarify the important implications of Clifford's more inclusive use of the term "translation". In studies of travel literature, she says, there has been a "lack of attention to translation", and this she quite rightly calls "paradoxical"; for the obvious "metaphorical association" between translation and travel rests on very real "issues of language, power and representation", issues "which are central both to the production and reception of travel writing". Her approach is to see translation as "a material condition of the transfer of texts from one culture to another" but also as "a methodological and analytical framework which can highlight constraints and characteristics of the texts under examination (both originals and translated versions), as well as those of the audiences they address and the literary and critical traditions they enter" (2001: 1-2). Mirella Agorni also finds this analogy compelling. "Although the status of the foreign as the 'original' of travel writing is obviously debatable from the point of view of translation theory", she says, "the ethical commitment of the travel writer to find ways to reproduce an alterity, potentially conceived as incommensurable, is undoubtedly akin to the task of the translator" (2002: 91).

[16] Pellegrini (1961: 26) has observed that Florio's only substantial translation into Italian, James I's *Basilicon Doran*, shows the same compulsion to embellish: the euphonius doubling of words and phrases, the freely added brief interpretations, the occasional insertion of an opinion.

[17] Agorni (2002: 2) would agree: "By widening the limits of translation to include 'refracted phenomena' such as travel writing (together with adaptations, criticism and anthologizing, for example), translation studies may arrive directly at the heart of cultural history". Monga (2003b: 11-30), in an essay he completed shortly before his death, widened the limits of translation to include cartography. See also Monga (2003a: 7-45).

[18] Pym (1998: 190), for one, refuses to define what might be meant by "a culture"; adopting the language of the anthropologist, he prefers to speculate about "intercultures", which he believes come first, "just as nomads preceded sedentary cultivation".

[19] Howell goes on to make the customary appeal to patriotism: "Moreover, one should eventuate himselfe to bring something home, that may accrue to the publique benefit and advantage of his Countrey, and not to draw water to his Mill only [...]" (1895: 72).

[20] Pym (1998: 182) sees the translator as a "historical object", and "the historical object", he says, "always involves some kind of intersection"; indeed, looking at translators "bodies and all", he would go so far as to suggest, "as a more general hypothesis", that "translators *are* intersections".

References

Adorno, Theodor. 1974. *Minima Moralia: Reflections from a Damaged Life* (tr. E.F.N. Jephcott). London: Verso Editions.

Agorni, Mirella. 2002. *Translating Italy for the Eighteenth Century: British Women, Translation and Travel Writing (1739-1797)*. Manchester: St. Jerome Publishing.

Agricola, Giorgio. 1563. *Opera di Giorgio Agricola de l'arte de metalli* (tr. Michelangelo Florio). Basilea: Hieronimo Probenio et Nicolao Episcopio.

Barnstone, Willis. 1993. *The Poetics of Translation: History, Theory, Practice*. New Haven, CT: Yale University Press.

Benjamin, Walter. 1969. 'The Task of the Translator' in *Illuminations* (tr. Harry Zohn, ed. Hannah Arendt). New York, NY: Schocken Books. 69-82.

Cawley, Robert Ralston. 1951. *Milton and the Literature of Travel*. Princeton, NJ: Princeton University Press.

Cheyfitz, Eric. 1997. *The Poetics of Imperialism: Translation and Colonization from* The Tempest *to* Tarzan. Expanded Edition. Philadelphia, PA: University of Pennsylvania Press.

Cinquemani, Anthony M. 1998. *Glad to Go For a Feast: Milton, Buonmattei, and the Florentine Accademici.* New York, NY: Peter Lang Publishing, Inc.

Clifford, James. 1997. *Routes: Travel and Translation in the Late Twentieth Century.* Cambridge, MA: Harvard University Press.

Cronin, Michael. 2000. *Across the Lines: Travel, Language, Translation.* Cork: Cork University Press.

de la Vega, Garcilaso. 2001. *Storia generale del Perù* (tr. Francesco Saba Sardi). 2 vols. Milano: Rizzoli.

Engel, William Edward. 1996. 'Knowledge that Counted: Italian Phrase-Books and Dictionaries in Elizabethan England' in *Annali d'italianistica: L'Odeporica/Hodoeporics* 14: 507-522.

Erasmus, Desiderius. 1978. *De copia,* in *The Collected Works of Erasmus.* Vol. 24. Ed. Craig R. Thompson. University of Toronto Press.

Florio, John. 1578. *Florio His Firste Fruites.* London: Thomas Woodcocke.

–. 1591. *Florios Second Frvtes.* London: Thomas Woodcock.

–. 1598. *A Worlde of Wordes.* London: Arnold Hatfield.

Florio, Michelangelo. See Agricola, Giorgio and Pellegrini, Giuliano.

Frantz, David O. 1997. 'Negotiating Florio's *A Worlde of Wordes*' in *Dictionaries* 18: 1-32.

–. 1999. 'Florio's *Worlde of Wordes*: A Bridge Between Cultures' in Paolo A. Giordano and Anthony Julian Tamburri (eds) *Pluralism and Critical Practice: Essays in Honor of Albert N. Mancini.* West Lafayette, IN: Bordighera Press. 117-123.

Giamatti, A. Bartlett. 1984. 'Hippolytus among the Exiles: The Romance of Early Humanism' in *Exile and Change in Renaissance Literature.* New Haven, CT: Yale University Press. 12-32.

Hale, John K. 1997. *Milton's Languages: The Impact of Multilingualism on Style.* Cambridge: Cambridge University Press.

Howell, James. 1895. *Instructions for Forreine Travell* (ed. Edward Arber). Westminster: A. Constable and Co.

Latré, Guido. 2002. *Tyndale's Testament.* Eds. Paul Arblaster, Gergely Juhász, and Guido Latré. Turnhout, Belgium: Brepols Publishers, n.v.

Milton, John. 1957. *Paradise Lost* in Merritt Y. Hughes (ed.) *Complete Poems and Major Prose.* New York, NY: The Odyssey Press, Inc. 208-469.

Monga, Luigi. 1996. 'Hodoeporics?' in *Annali d'Italianistica–L'Odeporica/Hodoeporics: On Travel Literature* 14: 5.

–. 2000. '"Doom'd to Wander": Exile, Memoirs, and Early Modern Travel Narrative' in *Annali d'Italianistica–Exile Literature* 20: 173-186.

–. 2003a. 'The Unavoidable "Snare of Narrative": Fiction and Creativity in Hodoeporics' in *Annali d'Italianistica–Hodoeporics Revisited/Ritorno all'Odeporica* 21: 7-45.

–. 2003b. 'Translating the journey: a literary perspective on truth in cartography' in Jane Conroy (ed.) *Cross-Cultural Travel: Papers from the Royal Irish Academy Symposium on Literature and Travel.* New York: Peter Lang. 11-30.

O'Connor, Desmond. 1990. *A History of Italian and English Bilingual Dictionaries.* Firenze: Leo S. Olschki Editore.

Pellegrini, Giuliano. 1954. 'Michelangelo Florio e le sue *Regole de la lingua Thoscana*' in *Studi di filologia italiana* 12: 76-204.

–. 1961. *John Florio e il Basilicon Doron di James VI: un esempio inedito di versione elisabettiano.* Milano: Feltrinelli Editore.

Polezzi, Loredana. 2001. *Translating Travel: Contemporary Italian Travel Writing in English Translation.* Aldershot Hants (England): Ashgate Publising, Ltd. & Burlington, VT: Ashgate Publishing Company.

Prince, F.T. 1954. *The Italian Element in Milton's Verse.* London: Oxford University Press.

Pym, Anthony. 1998. *Method in Translation History.* Manchester: St. Jerome Publishing.

Rossi, Sergio. 1966. 'Un "italianista" nel cinquecento inglese: William Thomas' in *Aevum* 40: 281-314.

—. 1991. 'Giovanni Torriano: il primo insegnante di inglese in Italia' in *Journal of Italian Studies* 1: 36-50.

Said, Edward. 2000. 'Reflections on Exile' in *Reflections on Exile and Other Essays*. Cambridge, MA: Harvard University Press. 173-186.

Steiner, George. 1992. *After Babel: Aspects of Language and Translation*. Second Edition. Oxford: Oxford University Press.

Stierle, Karlheinz. 1996. 'Translatio Studii and Renaissance: From Vertical to Horizontal Translation' in Sanford Budick and Wolfgang Iser (eds) *The Translatability of Cultures: Figurations of the Space Between*. Stanford, CA: Stanford University Press. 55-67.

Sturge, Kate. 1998. Review of *Routes: Travel and Translation in the Late Twentieth Century* by James Clifford (Cambridge, MA: Harvard University Press, 1997) in *The Translator* 4(2): 375-379.

Sudan, Rajani. 1998. 'Lost in Lexicography: Legitimating Cultural Identity in Johnson's Preface to The Dictionary' in *The Eighteenth Century: Theory and Interpretation*. 39(2): 127-146.

Thomas, William. 1963. *The History of Italy (1549)* (ed. George B. Parks). Ithaca, NY: Cornell University Press.

Venuti, Lawrence. 1995. *The Translator's Invisibility: A History of Translation*. London: Routledge.

Wilson, Thomas. 1994. *The Art of Rhetoric* (ed. Peter E. Medine). University Park, PA: Pennsylvania State University Press.

Yates, Frances A. 1968. *John Florio: The Life of an Italian in Shakespeare's England*. New York, NY: Octagon Books, Inc. Reprint of first edition (London: Cambridge University Press, 1934).

Zhiri, Oumelbanine. 2001. 'Leo Africanus's *Description of Africa*' in Ivo Kamps and Jyotsna G. Singh (eds) *Travel Knowledge: European "Discoveries" in the Early Modern Period*. Houndmills, Basinstoke and New York, NY: Palgrave. 258-266.

Section I

Towards the Vernacular

1.1. "If there is a hell, then Rome stands upon it": Martin Luther as Traveler and Translator

Russel Lemmons

That Martin Luther was among early modern Europe's most important translators is undeniable. His 1522 German-language edition of the New Testament played a central role in disseminating the teachings of the Reformation. It also made an important contribution to the standardization of the German language. What is less widely appreciated, however, is that Luther traveled extensively throughout central Europe, his major journeys occurring at key moments in his development as a Christian, theologian, and reformer. Among Luther's most important excursions was the one he made to Rome in 1510-1511, presenting him with the opportunity to witness the moral and financial decay in the Renaissance Catholic Church. Luther often referred to his experiences in the "Holy City" in the years after 1517, when he wrote the "Ninety-Five Theses" and launched the Reformation. While scholars have had much to say about Luther's journey to Rome (the *Romfahrt*) as well as his translations of both the New and Old Testaments, no one has attempted to examine the links between the two. The following essay is a modest attempt to fill this gap in Luther scholarship.
Keywords: Bible, Catholicism, Luther, Reformation, Rome, translation, travel.

Martin Luther was undoubtedly among the most important translators in European history. Beginning with his first edition of his German New Testament, published in 1522, Luther, together with his associates, the humanist Philip Melanchthon and the Hebraist Matthäus Aurogallus, produced twelve volumes of Bible translation by 1541[1]. The first part of the Old Testament appeared in July 1523, and the first Luther translation of the entire Christian scriptures was published in 1534. Luther and Melanchthon revised the New Testament in 1529, and Luther and his team finished their final edition of the entire Bible (except the Apocrypha) in September 1541 (Raeder 1983: 270-274).

Because they were so determined to provide the best German edition possible, Luther and his associates put a great deal of effort into their translations, and this effort reflects the role that the scriptures played in their theology. The Bible was central to Luther's understanding of God's relationship with mankind, of Christian theology, and, ultimately, of his dispute with the Roman Catholic Church, an institution he aggressively criticized for abandoning Christianity's biblical roots (Stolt 1983: 242). The Bible, Luther believed, should serve the Christian as the essential guide in all matters relating to God. In 1522, while he was putting the finishing touches on his translation of the New Testament, Luther wrote, in "Avoiding the Doctrines of Men", that "Everyone must believe only because it [the Bible] is the word of God, and because he is convinced in his heart that it is true; even though an angel from heaven [Gal. 1:8] and all the world preached to the contrary" (1955-1976: vol. 35, 142). As Luther put it in his *Short Catechism*: "It [the Bible] is the word of

God, recorded by the prophets and apostles under the inspiration of the Holy Spirit, for the salutary knowledge of God and the acquisition of eternal bliss [*Seligkeit*]" (1862: 44). It was a Christian's primary duty to become familiar with the scriptures, to understand them, and to live by their precepts. Luther, says Heiko Oberman (1989: 305), sought through his translations to take the Bible, and hence the Reformation, into every corner of Germany. His translations not only made this possible, but also pointed out the errors of those for whom the Bible was not central to Christianity, those who adhered to the "Doctrines of Men"–Luther's opponents within the "Roman Church". The importance of his translations goes beyond their role in popularizing the Protestant precept of *Biblia sola*. His 1522 New Testament, for example, served as a model for the first Dutch translation, which appeared the following year, and the introduction to his German New Testament was the first of his works published in England. Further, the Luther Bible, playing much the same role as the Authorized King James version in the English language, was integral to the standardization of German that took place during the seventeenth century (Raeder 1983: 278; Daniell 1994: 119).

While scholars have long appreciated the importance of Luther's Bible translations, especially with regard to his disagreements with the established church, his experiences as a traveler and their influence on his translation efforts have been largely ignored. By sixteenth-century standards, Luther was an experienced traveler, and that travel played an important role in his personal, spiritual, and intellectual development is beyond dispute. Luther made the vow to become a monk, a necessary step on the road to becoming a reformer, on a return journey from his parents' home in Mansfeld to the University of Erfurt, where he was studying law. Fearing for his life in a severe thunderstorm, he promised God that, if He delivered him, he would become a monk. Luther, unlike so many others who have made similar promises to the Almighty, kept his vow and entered the Augustinian monestary in Erfurt in 1505, where he was ordained a priest on 4 April 1507 (Brecht 1985-1999: vol. 1, 48-49; Marius 1999: 48-49). All of these fateful steps were taken as a result of his experiences while traveling.

The most famous instance in which Luther traveled great distances was, of course, his trip to Worms under a guarantee of safe passage provided by Emperor Charles V. But Luther made other lengthy excursions that were almost as important as the trip to the Imperial Diet. Fearing papal and imperial assassins following his condemnation at Worms, he had to hide out for a year at the Wartburg, under the watchful eye of Duke Frederick the Wise. He made use of the isolation this secluded fortress provided, not only to write many of his most important early tracts, but also to translate the New Testament into German, an undertaking that might have been impossible without the young Reformer's willingness to journey into the Saxon hinterland[2]. The most interesting of Luther's trips, however, occurred a decade prior to his appearance before the Imperial Diet, in the fall and winter of 1510-1511, when he made his famous *Romfahrt* on behalf of the Augustinian monastery in Erfurt. This was the longest of the several extended journeys the German reformer made[3].

Scholars have universally recognized the importance of Luther's journey to Rome to his development as a theologian, but they have shied away from the subject because of problems with the sources available. First of all, very little can be said with any conviction about this journey. Luther specialists remain uncertain regarding the route that he and his companion–who remains unknown–took between Erfurt and Rome. Nor are they entirely sure when he went, how long he stayed, and what he did. Further, almost everything we know about the journey comes from his *Tischreden*, or "Table Talk", which some of his disciples began to record in 1531, twenty years after the events described[4]. Needless to say, this presents the scholar with serious problems. It is often impossible to say whether Luther's impressions of Rome developed because of his experiences there in 1510-1511 or if they were the product of later events in his life. The only scholar who has studied this journey in detail, Heinrich Böhmer, concludes–and most subsequent scholarship agrees–that Luther's experiences in the capital of western Christendom had no discernable immediate effect upon his stance concerning the established church, and that his reading of humanistic scholarship played at least as important a role in his later animosity against Rome's institutions (1914: 159-160). At first, Luther remembered Rome as the city of the catacombs and great Christian martyrs, not as the home of a morally corrupt and biblically ignorant clergy, a city populated by decadent sensualists. This is not the same, however, as saying that his experiences on the *Romfahrt* played no role in his dispute with the church and his subsequent decision to translate the Bible into the vernacular.

What it does mean is that anyone who attempts to link Luther's experiences in Rome to his decision to translate the Christian scripture must proceed cautiously, ever aware of the fact that any conclusions drawn must be tentative. One must be conscious of the uncertainty, inherent in the sources available, regarding when Luther formed his opinions. This is not to suggest, however, that the table talk is of no use to our understanding of Luther's trip to Rome and its influence on him as a Bible translator. We cannot simply dismiss his account from the 1530s and 1540s as hindsight growing out of his ongoing dispute with the "Roman Church". Other accounts of sixteenth-century Rome, most famously that of Desiderius Erasmus, related experiences similar to Luther's. Regarding his trip to Rome, Erasmus recorded that:

> With my own ears I heard the most loathsome blasphemies against Christ and his apostles. Many acquaintances of mine have heard priests of the curia uttering disgusting words so loudly, even during mass, that all around them could hear it.[5]

Another prominent sixteenth-century Humanist, Alfonso Valdès, writing after the 1527 sack of the city, put it even more bluntly:

> How blind all you people of Rome were, and how little you understood God! Every hour you met in the streets men who had already turned their souls into stables for vices, and yet you thought nothing of it. But when a stable was needed for horses and they were sheltered in the church of St. Peter, you tell me that it was a great evil and that it breaks your heart to think about it. You weren't heartbroken at the sight of the many souls so full of ugly and abominable sins that God, their Creator, was shut out! A fine religion![6]

In January 1523, the pope himself, Hadrian VI, admitted that Rome faced a serious moral crisis: "We know that for years there have been many abominable offenses in spiritual matters and violations of the Commandments committed at this Holy See, yes, that everything has in fact been perverted" (in Oberman 1989: 149).

If Luther's account of his trip to Rome was cruder, this was not the product of dissimilar experiences, nor entirely of having a different axe to grind, but of a distinct personality. Luther was subject to all of the prejudices of a sixteenth-century Saxon–witness his notorious antisemitism–which included an animosity against all things ultramontane. This may very well have colored his response to what he saw in Rome, but it is clear that there was no need for him to manufacture incidents of clerical immorality and ignorance.

What is known concerning the circumstances that led to the journey can be quickly summarized. The Augustinian monastery at Erfurt, which housed around fifty monks, was one of seven in Saxony that followed an extremely strict version of the Augustinian Rule. The leadership of the Augustinian order in Saxony, however, was far less rigorous in its application of the Rule than the more ascetic monks of Erfurt and these six other monasteries. As a result, these seven houses sought permission to form a union with the stricter houses located in Lombardy, but the leader of the order in Saxony, Johann Staupite, opposed these efforts. This dispute had been going on for several years when Luther and a companion were sent to Rome to appeal to the general of the order, Giles of Viterbo (Brecht 1985-1999: vol. 1, 98-101; Böhmer 1914: 36-75).

Augustinians could only leave the monastery with the abbot's permission, which was seldom given. Hence, for Luther, a young monk who had only been in the order for around five years, to be sent on such a journey was an honor, and undoubtedly he was the junior of the two monks, serving as *socius itinerarius*, or companion for the journey. The name of the other monk is not known, but clearly he was the leader of the excursion. The Augustinian Rule established that monks could not travel alone. The custom was that Luther, as the junior monk, would have walked behind his companion. In all probability, as Robert Fife points out, "Martin's contact with the affair in Rome can only have been slight" (1957: 165). While Luther says nothing in his table talk about the results of the journey, it is apparent that the leadership in Rome rejected Erfurt's proposal (Marius 1999: 79; Brecht 1985-1999: vol. 1, 98-100).

Exactly when Luther made the journey is uncertain. Böhmer concludes, based upon the circumstances surrounding the journey, as well as the weather conditions that Luther later described, that the monks left Erfurt sometime in November 1510 and returned in January 1511. The trip lasted approximately six weeks, around four of which were spent in Rome. What route Luther and his fellow monk took also remains obscure. It is probable, however, that they took different roads each direction. Luther would provide, later in life, detailed descriptions of both Innsbruck and Milan, each of which lay on a different road between Saxony and Rome. If, as Luther claims, he passed through Innsbruck, this means that they went through Tyrol in one direction. His account of Milan establishes that they traveled through Switzerland in the other direction[7]. They walked between Augustinian monasteries, which guaranteed them food and shelter. In spite of this advantage, the trek was undoubtedly a vigorous one, since the Alps had to be crossed in both directions, indeed, during the winter on the return journey (Böhmer 1914: 76-87; Fife 1957: 165-167; Marius 1999: 79-80).

As Luther himself admitted in his *Tischreden* (1912-1921: vol. 3, 432), he was excited at the prospect of visiting Rome with all of its holy places. Hoping to make a full confession of his sins while in Rome–as was the custom–he anticipated that the visit to the Holy City would be a life-changing experience. Upon first catching sight of the city, he fell to the ground and cried "*Salve, sancta Roma!* Sanctified in truth by the holy martyrs with whose blood you were drenched". Like the thousands of pilgrims who visited Rome every year, he eagerly looked forward to the opportunity to visit all of the holy sites in the city. The four weeks he spent in Rome would provide ample opportunity for him to do so, and he would prove to be an enthusiastic pilgrim[8].

Luther never recorded where he and his companion stayed while in Rome. In all likelihood, it was one of two places: either the reformed Augustinian monastery of St. Maria del Popolo, which was just north of the city, or St. Agostino's, where the head of his order resided. In either case, he was assured of room and board while in the city (Brecht 1985-1999: vol. 1, 101).

Sixteenth-century Rome was not the magnificent city that it is today. The population was only around 40,000, and, at the time, Italians had little appreciation for the heritage of the ancient world. The first floor of the Coliseum was filled with garbage, and the *Circus Maximus* was a vegetable garden. Entire quarters of the ancient city were overgrown with weeds. Luther, as was common at this time, assigned the condition of the ancient ruins to God's just punishment–meted out by the Goths–of the decadent pagan Romans. But even the sections of the city occupied with church matters were, by today's standards, a disappointment. St. Peter's lay unfinished, and the streets, peopled by prostitutes and thieves, were filthy (Brecht 1985-1999: vol. 1, 101; Fife 1957: 170). Luther claimed in his *Tischreden* (1912-1921: vol. 2, 49) to find the air in Rome unbreathable, and he and his fellow monk, after leaving their windows open for the night, awoke with their "heads full of fumes [*Dunst*]" that affected them so severely that they "could only travel a mile the whole day". It is small wonder that Luther never said anything regarding the city's legendary beauty.

But Luther did not go to Rome to visit pagan shrines or to employ the services of prostitutes. He came as a Christian pilgrim, and he intended to make the most of the opportunities afforded him. He engaged in all of the activities of a typical pilgrim, as well as those reserved for the clergy. While the order in which he visited these places is uncertain, Luther left detailed accounts of his experiences at the major sacred sites. Such experiences would have been life-changing for any devout Christian. The effects upon Luther–as a Christian, as a theologian, and as a reformer–would prove, in the long term, especially profound.

Since what he did in Rome is not of primary interest here, Luther's activities in the Holy City can be related quickly. Among the places he visited were the catacombs, which made a dramatic impression upon him. Anyone who passed through a catacomb five times, the tradition of the time contended, would release a soul from purgatory (Brecht 1985-1999: vol. 1, 104). His later rejection of the doctrine of purgatory, however, would have no effect upon his heartfelt admiration of those Christians who gave their lives for the church. This remained the case in spite of the fact that he discovered that there were sixteen burial sites ascribed to the twelve apostles[9]. Apparently, as was the custom, Luther also visited the seven principal churches of Rome in a single day, saying mass in each. He also tried to say mass on a Saturday in the church of St. John Lateran. Luther made this attempt, in keeping with sixteenth-century custom, to bestow special divine favor upon his mother and assure her a place in paradise. He discovered, to his chagrin, that the church was so crowded with other priests also trying to say mass that it was impossible for him to fulfill his wish (Brecht 1985-1999: vol. 1, 102-103).

Perhaps the highlight of Luther's activities in Rome was his visit to the *Scala Sancta*, supposedly the steps by which Christ approached Pilate. According to tradition, anyone who climbed up this stairway on his knees, saying a *Pater noster* on each step, would release a soul from purgatory. He would later point out that "I was sorry at the time that my parents were still alive for I should have liked to free them from purgatory [...]" Instead, he sought to redeem the soul of a deceased uncle. As he pointed out in a sermon delivered in November 1545, even at the time he had his doubts: "But when I got to the top I thought, who knows if it is true?"[10]. The German historian Leopold von Ranke (1996: vol. 1, 146) tells an apocryphal story, based upon an account related in 1582 by one of Luther's sons. According to his account, as Luther was performing the painful task of mounting the steps one at a time, he heard an internal voice quote the words of St. Paul: "The just shall live by faith"[11]. If Luther had such an experience, he would certainly have related it to his friends and associates himself, and, in all likelihood, it never happened.

Such experiences were typical for a sixteenth-century pilgrim, especially for one as devout as the young priest. In and of themselves they are of little interest. What is much more important about the *Romfahrt* are the impressions Luther took home with him: his opinions of the clergymen with whom he had contact, his reaction to the numerous abuses he witnessed in Rome, and his views regarding the Italian people. These would, over the years, have an effect upon Luther as a theologian, reformer, and, ultimately, Bible translator. He apparently did not have much to say, at first, regarding his negative impressions of Rome, but his opinions must have taken root during those four weeks he spent in the city. Otherwise, he probably would not have been able to remember his experiences so vividly and to relate the abuses he witnessed in such detail.

Luther was appalled at the shortcomings of the Italian clergy, who were incompetent priests. Since he knew no Italian, and the Italians were unfamiliar with the German language, he tried to communicate with his fellow priests in Latin. To his shock he discovered that most did not know this language. He would later point out that "they write nothing, [and] they read nothing [...]" (1955-1976: vol. 54, 330).

This ignorance of Latin helps to explain the Italian priesthood's attitude toward the mass. The Saxon monk heard and executed many masses, and he witnessed many abuses of this holiest of Christian rituals. In the time it took Luther to say one mass, for example, Italian priests performed "six or seven". They rushed through their masses, he says in his *Tischreden* (1912-1921: vol. 5, 181, 451), not so that they could say more of them to the glory of God, but rather because to do so earned them more money. Roman priests not only misused the mass, but also abused it, exhibiting an appalling disrespect for the doctrine of transubstantiation. Luther claimed to have heard priests say mockingly that "Bread thou art and bread thou shalt remain; wine thou art and wine thou shalt remain"[12]. These men, who piled the crime of theft upon their blasphemies, "held a Christian to be nothing but a fool" (1912-1921: vol. 5, 181).

These problems were so severe because they began at the very top of the church, with the papacy and the *curia*. Although the pope, Julius II, was not in Rome at the time of his visit, in Luther's mind he bore ultimate responsibility. In 1539, referring to the anonymously published account of St. Peter's rejection of the sinful Julius II at the gates of heaven, Luther pointed out that:

> The dialogue of Julius is very true and deserving of immortality. With tragic words it describes the papacy, especially under Julius, who was a monster in power above all others and who was an ungodly, warlike, and fierce man. He presumed to venture everything so that he could be god on earth. [...] In short, he was the [...] final effort of the devil.

The pope, he continued, was a "shameless harlot, the stain of infamy [...]. But if he's struck by the Word of God, the pope [*papa*] will be turned into a dandelion [*papus*], that is, the flower that rises with the sun and goes down with sun, like the yellow flower that turns in the evening into a stinking monk" (1955-1976: vol. 54, 347)[13]. Rumor had it that Julius even suffered from syphilis. In what would have been the ultimate insult to a sixteenth-century Christian, Luther insisted, as Marius points out (1999: 82), that the pope was no better than a Turk[14]. The cardinals and bishops, among whom homosexuality was supposedly rampant, were, in the Saxon's estimation, just as depraved[15].

Italian laymen with whom Luther came in contact fared no better than the priests and bishops, which is not surprising. A deep-seated prejudice against all things Italian was extremely common in sixteenth-century northern Europe, and there is every reason to believe that Luther was typical in this regard. He found the Italians dishonest and the streets of Rome unsafe. The depravity in Julius II's Rome was like "someplace in India [*einem Orte in India*]" (1912-1921: vol. 3, 219). Italians rarely attended mass and belittled the piety of their foreign visitors. "They laugh at and mock those of us who believe all of the scriptures". "Their fasts are just for show, and they eat better than we do at feasts". Italians assumed that they were the only "clever" people, yet they had no respect for one another, exhibiting no sense of community. They treated one another with contempt, showing no respect for the property of others. For example, urinating in public was such a common practice that many Italians painted the images of Saints Sebastian and Antonius upon the walls of their houses, hoping that this would discourage their neighbors from "peeing" [*pinkeln*] on them (1912-1921: vol. 2, 48-0). Even the Italian form of pederasty was more pernicious than the German variety. "To sum up, in Italy there is no shame but to be poor. Murder and theft are still punished a little [*wenig*], because they have to do so; otherwise no sin is too serious" (1912-1921: vol. 5, 181). "Rome is a dead ass". In short, "Roma basis inferni. Ist ein Hell, so sthet [sic] Rom drauf" (1912-1921: vol. 3, 218, 347).

In spite of all of the depravity he witnessed in the "Eternal City", Luther was glad that he went there. After all, his journey provided him with the opportunity to see the condition of the "Roman Church" with his own eyes. "I would not take a large amount of money not to have been in Rome. I wouldn't have believed it if I hadn't seen it for myself. For so great and shameless is the godlessness and wickedness there, that neither God nor men, neither sin nor shame is noticed" (1912-1921: vol. 3, 431-432)[16]. In Luther's estimation, Rome was the heart of all that was wrong with the Church, and later in life he would repeatedly harken back to his experiences there in his attacks upon the papacy and its institutions.

The problematical nature of the sources available, as mentioned above, has kept scholars from attempting a full analysis of Luther's account of his experiences in Rome and the influence they had upon his work as a Reformer or translator of the Christian scriptures[17]. Clearly, his reading of humanist texts also played a vital role in Luther's understanding of the Roman Catholic Church and its relationship to the Christian scriptures. But, if we keep in the mind that any conclusions drawn must be tentative, Luther's account of his *Romfahrt* can help us better to understand his decision to translate the Bible into German.

That the Bible was central to Luther's theology is beyond dispute. It was, therefore, also central to his disagreement with Rome. Luther, after all, assigned all of the problems within the "Roman Church" to its neglect of its biblical roots. If these premises are accepted, then it is clearly not going too far to contend that the *Romfahrt* had an influence on Luther as a Bible translator, especially later in his life, when a record exists concerning the importance of his experiences in Rome to his theology. After all, he believed that the scriptures were his most valuable tool in his dispute with Rome. As early as 1520, Luther referred to his opponents as "heretics and schismatics" because they had abandoned Christianity's biblical origins[18]. His decision to translate the Bible in 1521 was certainly, at least in part, made in order to convince German Christians that he was right and the pope was in error because the leadership of the Catholic Church had abandoned the Word of God. His experiences in Rome in 1510-1511 must have reinforced this conviction.

Luther's Bible translation naturally drew a great deal of criticism from his theological opponents, and his responses often incorporated echoes of his experiences in Rome decades earlier. This can be seen, for example, in his "On Translating: An Open Letter", written in September 1530. His adversaries had gone to great lengths to point out any and all of the deficiencies in his translation. One of the passages they concentrated upon most consistently was Romans 3:28, which reads in the Latin, "Arbitramus hominem justificari ex fide absque operibus", which Luther translated as "So halten wir nun dafür, daß der Mensch gerecht wird ohne des Gesetzes Werke, allein durch den Glauben", or "We hold that a man is justified without the works of the law, by faith alone". Hoping to undermine the cardinal Lutheran tenet of justification by faith alone, his adversaries were quick to point out that the word 'alone' (*sola* in Latin, *allein* in German) was present neither in the Latin that Luther had used nor in the Greek original. (1955-1976: vol. 35, 182).

Luther's response begins with a series of *ad hominem* attacks that often employ the same language and images that he would use, just a year later, to describe what he had seen on the *Romfahrt*[19]. He accuses his critics of ignorance, saying that they know neither Latin nor Greek yet have the audacity to question the accuracy of his translation. They are "asses", too ignorant to undertake such a task themselves. He sarcastically points out, as an example of their ignorance of Latin, that "I chose to use the word *sola*–though in Romans 3[:28] it was not *sola*, but *solum* or *tantum* that I used, so sharply do the asses look at my text!" Luther knew that the word *sola* was not in the original, "the papists do not have to teach me that". Yet, "those blockheads stare at them [the German words] like cows at a new gate. Their stupidity is impenetrable, for "a papist and an ass are the same thing". His opponents' ignorance of German, moreover, is even more complete than their ignorance of Latin, and they have no right to criticize him (1955-1976: vol. 35, 185-188). It is easy to posit that Luther was recalling the priests he had encountered in 1510-1511, whom he had seen as "asses" as well, appallingly ignorant of the *lingua franca* of western Christendom[20]. In his 1546 "Preface to the Epistle of St. Paul to the Romans", a reworking of his original 1522 Preface, Luther contends that Paul foresaw the degeneracy of the Roman Church when he warned against "the doctrines of men":

> It is as if he had certainly foreseen that out of Rome and through the Romans would come the seductive and offensive canons and decretals and the whole squirming mass of human laws and commandments, which have now drowned the whole world and wiped out this epistle and all the Holy Scriptures, along with the Spirit and faith itself; so that nothing remains except the idol, Belly, whose servants St. Paul here rebukes. God save us from them. Amen. (1955-1976: vol. 35, 379)

All of these problems were, to Luther's mind, the product of the Church's abandoning its biblical roots, and only by returning to the teachings of the scriptures could they be addressed. Luther's Bible translations were clearly an important component of his efforts to return Christianity to its scriptural origins.

Undoubtedly, the depravity and ignorance that characterized the sixteenth-century Roman Catholic Church were important to Luther's polemic against his critics. Even a casual reading of his writings makes it clear that these themes infused his work as a Reformer, including his efforts as translator. While there is no denying that his reading of humanistic works also affected his sentiments regarding Rome and the "Roman Church", as Luther put it himself, the degeneracy of Rome was so severe that "I wouldn't have believed it if I hadn't seen it for myself". This is, of course, neither to underestimate the troublesome nature of the sources concerning the *Romfahrt*, nor to ignore the uncertain nature of the judgments made here. Rather, this conclusion is merely a modest call for an understanding of Luther's actions as a Reformer and translator that more effectively incorporates his experiences as a traveler, especially his 1510-1511 journey to Rome.

---

[1] These twelve volumes are in the standard edition of Luther's works, the *Weimarer Ausgabe*, the first volume of which appeared in 1833. Melanchthon, whose Greek was far superior to Luther's, was integral to Luther's translations of the New Testament, especially the later editions. For a brief overview of his life see Wengert (1996: 119-120); see also the thorough study by Maag (1999).

[2] For a brief, if highly polemical, account of Luther's time at the Wartburg, see Bainton (1977: 149-151); see also Brecht (1985-1999: vol. 2, 47).

[3] Surprisingly, on this important episode in Luther's life there is only one major scholarly work, that of Heinrich Böhmer. After almost ninety years this remains the standard work on the subject, and the only major work written on Luther as a traveler.

[4] The standard edition of Luther's table talk is *D. Martin Luthers Werke, kritische Gesamtausgabe: Tischreden*. All English translations from this work will be my own.

[5] Quoted in Oberman (1989: 149). Regarding Erasmus's attitudes towards Rome, see *In Praise of Folly and Other Writings* (1989: *passim*, but especially 70-71 regarding the papacy).

[6] Quoted in Partner (1976: 158). In his *Tischreden* Luther mentions others who had experiences in Rome similar to his (1912-1921: vol. 2, 519).

[7] Regarding Luther's impressions of Switzerland, see *Tischreden* (1912-1921: vol.2, 484).

[8] On this episode see also Marius (1999: 80) and Fife (1957: 168-169).

[9] See *Tischreden* (1912-1921: vol. 5, 181); concerning Luther's abandonment of the idea of purgatory, see a tract he wrote in 1527, 'This Is My Body' (1955-1976: vol. 37, 369).

[10] Quoted in Fife (1957: 172-173).

[11] Concerning Paul Luther as the source of the story, see Oberman (1989: 150).

[12] Quoted in Oberman (1989: 149). As Oberman points out here, Erasmus had much the same experience regarding the mass while he was in Rome.

[13] For an English translation of this text, see Erasmus (1989: 142-173). Erasmus denied having penned it.

[14] See also *Tischreden* (1912-1921: vol. 3, 173).

[15] On the corruption in the episcopacy, see *Tischreden* (1912-1921: vol. 3, 218 and vol. 4, 257).

[16] The translation of the Latin portions of the original comes from Luther's Works (1955-1976: vol. 54, 237).

[17] Böhmer dedicates a mere two pages to the influence of the trip to Rome upon Luther's development as a theologian.

[18] On this subject, see Luther's "The Babylonian Captivity of the Church" (1955-1976: vol. 36, 24).

[19] One must keep in mind that, because his companions only began to record Luther's reminiscences of Rome in 1531, this does not mean that he had not developed any opinions regarding his journey to Rome before this date. He probably did, but unfortunately there is no evidence to confirm this.

[20] Luther does eventually get around to making a linguistic defense of his use of the word *allein*, but it is unconvincing, serving only as further proof that his theology governed his efforts as translator.

References

Bainton, Roland H. 1977. *Here I Stand: A Life of Martin Luther*. New York, NY: Mentor.

Böhmer, Heinrich. 1914. *Luthers Romfahrt*. Leipzig: Werner Scholl.

Brecht, Martin. 1985-1999. *Martin Luther* (tr. James L. Schaaf). 3 vols. Minneapolis, MN: Fortress Press.

Daniell, David. 1994. *William Tyndale: A Biography*. New Haven, CT: Yale University Press.

Erasmus, Desiderius. 1989. *In Praise of Folly and Other Writings* (ed. and tr. Robert M. Adams). New York, NY: Norton.

Fife, Robert. 1957. *The Revolt of Martin Luther*. New York, NY: Columbia University Press.

Luther, Martin. 1862. *Dr. Martin Luthers Kleiner Katechismus mit Erklärung*. Hamburg: Helmut Korinth.

–. 1912-1921. *D. Martin Luthers Werke, kritische Gesamtausgabe: Tischreden*. 6 vols. Weimar: Herman Böhlaus Nachfolger.

–. 1955-1976. *Luther's Works* (eds Jaroslav Pelikan and Helmut T. Lehmann). 55 vols. Philadelphia, PA and Minneapolis, MN: Muhlenberg and Fortress Presses.

Maag, Karin. 1999. *Melanchthon in Europe: His Influence Beyond Wittenberg*. Grand Rapids, MI: Baker.

Marius, Richard. 1999. *Martin Luther: The Christian Between God and Death*. Cambridge, MA: Harvard University Press.

Oberman, Heiko. 1989. *Luther: Man Between God and the Devil* (tr. Eileen Walliser-Schwarzbart). New York, NY: Image.

Partner, Peter. 1976. *Renaissance Rome, 1500-1559: A Portrait of a Society*. Berkeley, CA: University of California Press.

Raeder, Siegfried. 1983. 'Luther als Ausleger und Übersetzer der Heiligen Schrift' in Helmar Junghans (ed.) *Leben und Werk Martin Luthers von 1526 bis 1546*. Berlin: Evangelische Verlagsanstalt. 253-278.

Ranke, Leopold von. 1966. *History of the Reformation in Germany* (tr. Sarah Austin). 2 vols. New York, NY: Frederick Ungar.

Stolt, Brigit. 1983. 'Luthers Übersetzungstheorie und Übersetzungspraxis' in Junghans (1983): 241-252.

Wengert, Timothy J. 1996. 'Philip Melanchthon's 1522 Annotations on Romans and the Lutheran Origins of Rhetorical Criticism' in Richard A. Muller and John L. Thompson (eds) *Biblical Interpretation in the Era of Reformation: Essays Presented to David C. Steinmetz in Honor of his Sixtieth Birthday*. Grand Rapids, MI: Willliam B. Eerdmans. 118-140.

1.2. Fertile Ground: Erasmus's Travels in England

Erika Rummel

Erasmus visited England six times, including an extended stay between 1511 and 1514. Each of his visits resulted in translations, either directly or indirectly. His collaboration with Thomas More on translations of Lucian's dialogues was the direct result of a meeting of kindred spirits. Both men studied Greek and were attracted by Lucian's wit. The collaborative venture served as a tangible link and testimony to their friendship. By contrast, the translation of Euripides's *Iphigeneia* was born of irritation. When Erasmus presented William Warham, Archbishop of Canterbury, with a copy of his translation of Euripides's *Hecuba*, the reward was disappointing, and a friend explained the reason: the archbishop was wary of authors presenting their works to more than one patron. Stung by this insinuation, Erasmus completed a second translation, Iphigeneia, and published both works with a dedication to Warham. The archbishop eventually became one of Erasmus's most generous patrons, presenting him with a living in Kent in 1512. Several short translations from Plutarch's *Moralia* served Erasmus as New Year's presents during his next visit. Among the recipients were Cardinal Wolsey and Henry VIII. Travel to England provided Erasmus with fertile ground for his work as a translator.
Keywords: England, Erasmus, Euripedes, Plutarch, translation, travel, William Warham.

Editing and translating classical texts were quintessential humanistic activities, and Erasmus was no exception to the rule. In fact, he was one of the most prolific and widely read translators in the early sixteenth century, producing Latin versions of Libanius, Isocrates, Plutarch, Xenophon, Lucian, and Euripides as well as translations of Greek patristic texts–Origen, Chrysostom, Theophylactus–to name a few. Before making the connection between Erasmus's translations and his travels, a brief comment on his language skills is in order.

When Erasmus was a young man, knowledge of Greek was still an unusual accomplishment in Northern Europe. Complaints about the scarcity of Greek texts are a commonplace in the correspondence of humanists. Teachers were just as hard to come by. Lectures in Greek were instituted at the universities only in the second decade of the sixteenth century. For this reason the first generation of Northern humanists was largely self-taught. Erasmus's biographer, Beatus Rhenanus, tells us that he learned "the rudiments of both languages" as a pupil at Deventer. a school of the Brethren of the Common Life[1], but it was probably no more than the Greek alphabet and the meaning of individual words. Nor did he make significant progress in the Augustinian monastery at Steyn, which he entered as a teenager. Classical learning was regarded with hostility and suspicion at Steyn[2]. Looking back on his years at Steyn, Erasmus wrote to his superior in 1514: "My mind was attracted solely to literature, which is not practised in your community" (vol.2, 295). The same atmosphere prevailed at the Collège de Montaigu in Paris, where he was sent in 1495 to study theology. In the opinion of many theologians, Erasmus tells us, "[t]o know Greek is heresy; to speak like an educated man is heresy" (vol. 7, 115). He therefore was obliged to conceal his desire to learn Greek. When he "had the good fortune to come upon some Greek books", he tells us, he spent night and day in copying them", but he did so secretly (vol. 2, 25). Eventually Erasmus acquired a Greek teacher, the emigré Georgius Hermonymus, but he found him expensive and lacking in the requisite pedagogical skills. He describes him in disparaging terms as a man "who could not have taught if he had wanted to, and would not have wanted to teach if he had been able to" (vol. 9, 301)[3]. Accordingly Erasmus was obliged to teach himself. In this process he found translating a useful exercise, and we often find him engaged in this activity during his travels.

Today, an exchange program for university students in Europe is named after Erasmus–and appropriately so, since he traveled a great deal. He spent about five years in Paris, seven years in Leuven, and another seven years in Basel. He traveled in Italy, living for a year in Bologna and Venice. He visited England six times between 1499 and 1516, and this includes an extended stay from 1511 to 1514, when he taught at Cambridge. Thus Erasmus provides ample material for a study on travel and translation, but I will limit myself to his travels in England, which, as my title indicates, proved fertile ground.

I will divide Erasmus's translations into four categories, according to his motivation: first, translations intended for English patrons and offered in hopes of a monetary reward; secondly, translations based on manuscripts made available to Erasmus in England; thirdly, translations done on the invitation of or in cooperation with English friends. And, fourthly (a category that cuts across the other three), translations undertaken as exercises, that is, to hone his language skills or more generally to use his free time profitably.

In the first category, offerings to patrons, are the translations of two plays by Euripides: *Hecuba* and *Iphigeneia in Aulis*. These translations are a truly remarkable achievement. No humanist before Erasmus had produced a verse translation of a complete tragedy, let alone of two tragedies. The task was not easy. The lines of the chorus almost defeated Erasmus: They "are so obscure", he wrote, "[...] that they need an Oedipus, or a Delian prophet, rather than a commentator" (vol. 2, 108)[4]. But he persevered and in the end produced a lucid and elegant translation. In his introduction, he promised to stay close to the original. It was his aim, he said, "as far as possible to reproduce the shape and, as it were, the contours of the Greek poems, striving to render verse for verse and almost word for word, and everywhere trying zealously to adapt the force and effect of the meaning to Latin ears, with all fidelity" (vol. 2, 109). He succeeded admirably in this ambitious aim.

Strictly speaking, only one of the versions was done during his travels. The translation of the *Hecuba* was already complete when he arrived in England in 1506; the companion piece, that is, the translation of *Iphigeneia*, however, was substantially a product of that journey. This is what we know about the genesis and further fortune of the plays: Erasmus took a presentation copy of the *Hecuba* to William Warham, Archbishop of Canterbury, hoping for a generous reward from the prelate. Apparently the present he received fell short of his expectations. When he asked his companion, William Grocyn, who had introduced him to the archbishop, why the great man had turned out to be a stingy patron, he was told that he was up against the suspicion "that I might perhaps have dedicated the same work elsewhere to someone else". This was an unpleasant surprise for Erasmus. When he asked Grocyn what could have put that idea into the archbishop's head, he laughed and said, "It is the sort of thing you people do", suggesting that humanists made a habit of dedicating works to more than one person to multiply the profit (vol. 9, 298). Stung by this suspicion, Erasmus translated a second play, *Iphigeneia,* and dedicated both pieces to Warham, so that, in effect, the archbishop received two plays for the price of one:

> So as soon as I reached Paris [...] I gave the [*Hecuba*] to Bade to be printed, adding the
> *Iphigeneia in Aulis*, which I had translated more fully and freely while I was in
> England; and though I had offered the archbishop only one play, I dedicated both to
> him. Thus I took the sting out of that remark of Grocyn's, [...] such was my pride in
> those days, however empty my pocket. (*ibid.*)

Warham later became one of Erasmus's most important patrons and, in recognition of his learning, presented him with the living of Aldington in Kent, that is, gave him a permanent source of income to finance his scholarly activities. So Erasmus's strategy was successful in the long run. In a letter of 1514 he describes Warham as a father figure and praises his continued generosity, "even though I have never asked him for anything" (vol. 2, 298-299)[5].

In 1509, on the accession of Henry VIII to the throne, Erasmus returned to England on the advice of his friends who believed that Henry would turn out to be a generous patron of humanists. They raised Erasmus's expectations, describing the atmosphere at Henry's court: "[...] all is milk and honey and nectar. Tight-fistedness is well and truly banished. Generosity scatters wealth with unstinting hand" (vol. 2, 147-148). Royal support was slow in coming, however. In 1511 at last Erasmus obtained a lectureship at Queen's College, Cambridge. Having been forced to live on his own scant resources until this offer materialized, he was heavily in debt by that time and, as he himself said, in a letter to John Colet, "I entertain so little hope of any gain that I am sure I shall have to spend, here and now, every penny I can squeeze from my patrons" (vol. 2, 168)[6]. Accordingly he approached John Fisher, Bishop of Rochester, with a proposal to translate St. Basil's commentary on Isaiah. It was an early foray into translating patristic texts. He sent a sample version to Fisher, hoping to receive "a little something by way of emolument for the toil it causes me" (vol. 2, 171)[7]. The attempt was not very successful. Fisher, like Warham, had reservations about Erasmus. Warham, we have seen, suspected Erasmus of double-dipping; Fisher apparently suspected that he was cheating, that is, as Erasmus wrote to Colet, of "polishing up a previous version, and not translating from the Greek" (vol. 2, 183). He therefore sent him only a token gift.

In another effort to elicit money from English patrons, Erasmus translated several pieces from Plutarch's *Moralia*. Erasmus valued Plutarch for his moral philosophy. The act of translating Plutarch "contributed substantially", he wrote, "to the building of character [...]; for I have read nothing outside Scripture with such a high moral tone" (vol. 9, 303)[8]. He meant to present his translations as New Year's gifts to King Henry, John Yonge, Warham's chancellor, and to Cardinal Wolsey. Once again his hopes for a reward were disappointed. At first, ill health prevented him from presenting his translation to Wolsey during the New Year's celebrations (vol. 2, 275-276)[9]. Then, an outbreak of the plague kept him from pursuing this purpose. He made a third attempt to see Wolsey before leaving England in 1514, but received only splendid promises. However, he was nothing if not persistent. In 1520, he tried his luck again, this time presenting Wolsey with a paraphrase of the Catholic Epistles (vol. 7, 309-312). He sought an interview with the Cardinal at Calais, where Wolsey attended the meetings of the Field of the Cloth of Gold, but the Cardinal was too busy to give an audience to Erasmus. So much for Wolsey's patronage. The two other Plutarch pieces, which Erasmus had dedicated to King Henry and to John Yonge respectively, met with similar difficulties. When he first presented the translations in 1512, the King was preoccupied with the war against France and had no time for Erasmus; and John Yonge was in camp with the royal army. In this case, too, Erasmus was dogged in the chase. The Plutarch translations were printed and well received by readers. In 1517, Erasmus sent the king a copy of the third edition of the translations[10], reminding him of the original dedication and finally elicited a cash gift of 60 angels and the promise of a church living in the value of 100 angels *per annum*. The offer was, however, conditional on Erasmus's return to England. This was not feasible because, in the meantime, Erasmus had been appointed councilor to Prince Charles (later Charles V). That post, like Henry's offer, was contingent on his attendance at court. Erasmus therefore thanked the King for the cash gift but declined the offer of the living. To friends he explained that, unless the offer was sweetened, he was not tempted to change residence (vol. 6, 161).

In the second category, the use of local resources, we find that some of the translations Erasmus produced were the result of research opportunities created by his travels; in other cases he traveled in order to have those research opportunities. "Back to the sources" was the rallying cry of the humanists. Like many of his contemporaries, Erasmus actively searched for manuscripts during his travels, collated texts, and published editions or translations of them. While in England, he searched for Greek and Latin manuscripts of the gospels. He collated these texts and made them the basis of his revised translation of the Vulgate, published in 1516. In his dedication to Pope Leo X, Erasmus indicated that he had "call[ed] in the assistance of a number of manuscripts in both languages, and those not the first comers but both very old and very correct" (vol. 3, 222-223)[11]. We know that he used codices from St. Paul's in London, made available to him by John Colet. We know nothing, however, about their age because they are no longer extant. During his stay at Cambridge, Erasmus had access to the so-called Leicester Codex, a fifteenth century manuscript belonging to the Franciscan Richard Brinkeley. He continued his hunt for manuscripts during other trips, for example a trip to Basel in 1514, during which he consulted a number of Greek texts and commentaries belonging to the house of the Dominicans. These ranged in age from the eleventh to the fifteenth century. For later editions, he traveled in Brabant to consult manuscripts in the College of St. Donatian in Bruges, which according to Erasmus, were "more than eight hundred years old, as inscriptions in them testify". He furthermore used a codex belonging to Pieter Wichmans, his host during a vacation at Anderlecht in the summer of 1521[12]. As these examples show, travel was an important contributing factor in the production of a translation, which could not have been done without access to relevant manuscripts.

In the third category I have placed translations undertaken on the invitation or in collaboration with friends, and this was a significant factor in his choice of texts as well. Erasmus once noted that an author produces his best work when he writes on a subject "to which he is by nature suited, and in which his powers chiefly lie; all themes do not suit everyone. This I have never done; I have either stumbled on a subject unadvisedly or chosen one to comply with my friends' feelings rather than my own judgment" (vol. 9, 294). What he says here in general may also be adapted to the translations completed on his travels in England.

In many cases, these translations were not the result of a deliberate choice or preference on Erasmus's part. Rather, local availability of manuscripts or of a recently published edition were the determining factors. He turned to Euripides, for example, because he got hold of the *editio princeps* produced by the Aldine Press in 1503 and because he was encouraged to undertake the task by Jean Desmarais, at whose house in Louvain he was staying at the time (vol. 9, 297). His translations of St. Basil are another case in point. He proposed to translate Basil because he happened to have access to a manuscript in the library of his friend William Grocyn. He tackled the Greek satirist Lucian because his interest in that author was shared by Thomas More, at whose house he was staying during visits to England in 1505-1506 and 1509.

Lucian was a popular author in the Renaissance. Humanists admired his creative language, his wit, and his biting irony. But Erasmus noted that Lucian did more than produce "a civilized laughter"; he was both "useful" and "pleasant", (vol. 2, 291 and 114)[13]. for he criticized superstition and hypocrisy and satirized men's follies. In other words, Lucian provided moral lessons. Erasmus had tried earlier on to translate Lucian but was discouraged by the difficulty of rendering Greek compound adjectives into Latin. Here is an example of what he was up against. Lucian describes gout as "bandage-fancier, bedward-sender, gait-obstructor, joint-tormentor, ankle-burner, tender-stepper, pestle-fearer, knee-lamenting sleep destroyer, knuckle-chalkstone-devotee, knee-excruciator". "These words and others like them", says Erasmus, "are most attractive in Greek because of the scope they give for humorous imitation, but the Latin language [and, incidentally, the English] could not produce a pale reflection of them" (vol. 9, 300-301). It was only when Erasmus found a willing collaborator in Thomas More that he proceeded with the task. Together, their efforts resulted in nine translations: four by Erasmus, five by More. Both men translated Lucian's *Tyrannicida* (a speech in defense of a tyrant slayer) and wrote a retort to it. It is interesting to compare their translations. The two authors were at a similar level of proficiency and present a clear and idiomatically correct version, but the styles differ notably, obviously reflecting personal preferences. More tends to offer plain translations, staying as close as possible to the original; Erasmus tends to elaborate and expand on the original, giving his translation a more rhetorical ring. Or to put it another way: More presents a lawyer's plea; Erasmus a humanist's epideixis, a display of his rhetorical prowess.

The translations from Lucian fit into more than one category: first, Erasmus had monetary considerations. He meant to present his translations to patrons. For example, he offered one of the dialogues as a New Year's present to Richard Foxe, Bishop of Winchester (vol. 2, 101 and 103). During his second stay at More's house in 1509, Erasmus returned to the task of translating Lucian, and again it was partly in hopes of securing a monetary reward. As he explained candidly to his friend, Andrea Ammonio: "You see I am preparing something by way of bait in readiness for New Year's Day [...]" (vol. 2, 206). Accordingly, he dedicated one of the translations to Warham, and another to the royal physician Giovanni Battista Boerio.

That was one motive. But the translations were undertaken also as an agreeable pastime that allowed the two friends–More and Erasmus–to practice their language skills. That brings me to the fourth category: translation as an exercise. This motive applies to Lucian as well as to Plutarch and Euripides. In an annotated catalogue of his works, Erasmus said of his Plutarch translations that he "enjoyed the exercises". Similarly, he explained that he had undertaken the translations of Euripides's tragedies "in order to practise my Greek, for teachers were not to be had" (vol. 9, 308)[14]. He made this clear also in his dedication of the plays to Warham, where he said that the Euripides translations were a preliminary exercise, that is, a stepping stone to the more ambitious project of revising the Vulgate. Euripides, he said, afforded him good practice, but "any mistake I made would be at the cost of my intellectual reputation alone, causing no harm to Holy Writ" (vol. 2, 108). In letters to friends he explained his work on other pagan authors in similar terms:

> [...] when in my youth I embraced the finer literature of the ancients and acquired, not without much midnight labour, a reasonable knowledge of the Greek as well as the

Latin language, I did not aim at vain glory or childish self-gratification, but had long ago determined to adorn the Lord's temple, badly desecrated as it has been by the ignorance and barbarism of some, with treasures from other realms, as far as in me lay; treasures that could, moreover, inspire even men of superior intellect to love the Scriptures. (vol. 2, 53)

These comments tell us that Erasmus had a larger purpose in mind when he translated classical authors, even though the immediate purpose was mundane, that is, to elicit a monetary gift or simply to engage in useful work. The translations of classical authors were practice pieces to prepare for his *magnum opus,* the New Testament edition, and, more generally, to provide a solid foundation for his biblical studies.

Summing up the impact of travel on Erasmus's work as a translator: his motives for undertaking the versions are complex, as we have seen. The wish to practice his skills seems to have been an underlying motive in many cases; friends often provided the stimulus and gave him encouragement. Monetary considerations very frequently played a role. Erasmus seems to have used translations like American Express checks, to be cashed in whenever there was a need or an opportunity. Scholars today will most readily identify with another Erasmian motive: his eagerness to use local resources. His work on the New Testament, no doubt his most important work, was made possible or at any rate was facilitated, by his travels. They gave him access to manuscripts or led to friendships with men who later on lent him manuscripts or supplied him with variant readings. This will strike a chord with modern scholars because travel has much the same beneficent effect on research today, that is, it gives scholars access to collections of rare books and allows them to establish contact with fellow scholars in their field.

---

[1] In *Opus epistolarum* (Erasmus 1906-1958: vol. 1, 55). Unless otherwise specified, all other references to Erasmus will be from *The Correspondence* (1974-2003).

[2] Far from learning anything at Steyn, Erasmus boasts, in his *Compendium vitae,* that it was he who "inspired the whole community to study harder" (vol. 4, 407).

[3] Here I have modified the English translation.

[4] On Erasmus's translations from Euripides see Rummel (1985: 29-47).

[5] Relevant as well in this letter is his praise of other English patrons:

Lord Mountjoy, a baron of this realm, formerly my pupil, yearly gives me a pension of a hundred couronnes. The king and the bishop of Lincoln, who is all-powerful with the king at present, are showering me with splendid promises. There are two universities here, Oxford and Cambridge, and both of them are endeavouring to have me; for I taught Greek and divinity for a considerable number of months at Cambridge–always free, however, and I have made up my mind never to depart from this practice. There are colleges here in which there is so much devotion, such regularity of life, that you would reject any monastic rule in comparison, if you could see them. In London lives Dr John Colet, dean of St Paul's, a man who has married profound scholarship to exceptional devoutness, and exercises much influence in all quarters. As everyone knows, his love for me leads him to prefer nobody's company to my own. I omit countless others, in order to avoid being doubly tiresome through garrulity and boasting. (*ibid.*)

[6] See also vol. 2, 208 and 247-249.

[7] See his proposal to Fisher in (vol. 2, 172-173).

[8] On Erasmus's translations from Plutarch see Rummel (1985: 71-88).

[9] The translation, *De utilitate capienda ex inimicis*, was produced in 1512.

[10] Erasmus wrote to the king:

> I long ago translated [Plutarch] from Greek into Latin [...] Since, however, at that moment you were swept suddenly away into the storms of war [...] you had, I think, too little leisure for the products of the pen, for there was need to use the sword. And so I now submit the same work to your Highness, though already published to the world and printed a third time [...]. (vol. 5, 109 and 112)

[11] Parenthetically, it should be noted here that humanists in the sixteenth century had no reliable method of determining the age of a manuscript and Erasmus proved notoriously wrong in his assessment of manuscripts.

[12] On Erasmus's use of gospel manuscripts for the New Testament edition see Bentley (1983: 117-137) and Rummel (1986: 39-41).

[13] On Erasmus's and More's translations from Lucian see Rummel (1985: 49-70).

[14] See also vol. 9, 297 and 301; and in the *Opus epistolarum* (Erasmus 1906-1958: vol. 11, 470-472) see Epistle 3032 to John Colet.

References

Bentley, J. 1983. *Humanists and Holy Writ*. Princeton, NJ: Princeton University Press.
Erasmus, Desiderius. 1906-1958. *Opus epistolarum Des. Erasmi Roterodami* (eds P.S. Allen, H.M. Allen and H.W. Garrod). 12 vols. Oxford: Clarendon Press.
–. 1974-2003. *The Correspondence of Erasmus* (eds Wallace K. Fergusun *et al.*, tr. R.A.B. Mynors *et al.*). 12 vols. Toronto: University of Toronto Press.
Rummel, Erika. 1985. *Erasmus as a Translator of the Classics*. Toronto: University of Toronto Press.
–. 1986. *Erasmus' Annotations on the New Testament*. Toronto: University of Toronto Press.

1.3. Across the Alps–an English Poet Addresses an Italian in Latin: John Milton in Naples

Stella P. Revard

The Latin poem, "Mansus", composed by John Milton in reply to an epigram written by the elderly Giovanni Battista Manso, offers thanks to Manso for the hospitality he extended during Milton's visit to Naples. The poem, however, also gives Milton the opportunity to comment on the meeting of English, Italian, and classical cultures that his travels to Italy in 1638 and 1639 made possible. It is a poem that involves travel through time as well as space; in "Mansus" one can see Milton, the aspiring epic poet, forecasting for himself a future poetic career that will put him in conjunction not only with poets of the English past, such as Chaucer and Spenser, and with Italian poets such as Torquato Tasso, whose patron Manso was, but also with the great poets of the classical epic tradition, Homer and Vergil. In "Mansus", moreover, one can see Milton deeply involved in questions about language and translation, in particular about the vernacular and its use with regard to literary art.

Keywords: Italy, Latin, Manso, Milton, translation, travel, vernacular.

In 1638 and 1639 the young English poet John Milton traveled to Italy, visiting among many notable Italians the elderly Marquis of Villa, Giovanni Battista Manso, erstwhile friend to Tasso and Marino and a minor poet in his own right. The poetry that resulted from their meeting in Naples records the journey of the young Englishman from England and his experiences in the foreign but congenial culture of seventeenth-century Italy. Both Manso's epigram to Milton and Milton's longer poem "Mansus"–the reply to the brief epigram–were written in Latin. Though Milton was fluent in Italian and had composed Italian sonnets and Manso usually wrote poems in his native language, the two chose to correspond in Latin as the literary language of travelers. The reflections of Manso on Milton's "English" heritage and Milton's corresponding thoughts on bringing his English culture to Italy are filtered through a third language, thus presenting us with a kind of translation from English and Italian into Latin.

On one level the two poems are merely a polite exchange of host and guest. Manso compliments his English visitor and conversely Milton expresses gratitude for hospitality extended to a foreign traveler. Neither of the poems would have had a longer life if Milton had not chosen to print both in his first collection of poetry, the double book that appeared in 1645/6, the first part of which comprises English poetry, the second poetry in the learned languages Latin and Greek. Moreover, prefatory to the poetry of the second part are the verses that Italians whom Milton met during his voyage to Italy wrote in commendation of the English visitor, most of these poems, like the exchange between Milton and Manso, written in Latin. Like the poem which is the focus of this paper, the commendatory verses that these Italian poets wrote to Milton negotiate between England and Italy, translating the interaction between the two cultures into a third dimension–the ancient world. Two of the Italian poets who address epigrams to the young English poet look upon him as a future Homer or Vergil or Tasso and suggest that the Thames–rather than the Meles or the Mincius or the Sebethus, rivers associated with Homer, Vergil, and Tasso–has given birth to a true poet. Manso simply compliments Milton on his fair good looks and pleasant disposition, drawing upon the famous wordplay that Pope Gregory first made on Angles and angels:

> Ut mens, forma, decor, facies, mos, pietas sic,
> Non Anglus, verùm herclè Angelus ipse fores.[1]

> [If your piety were equal to your mind, beauty, fame, face, and manners,
> you would be, by Hercules, in truth not an Angle, but an Angel.]

Significantly, it is as a representative of the northern nation, as an Englishman–Joannes Miltonus, Anglus–that all of the poets (including Manso) address Milton. The geographical distance that separates them defines the relationship between the men of Italy and this traveling Englishman and makes Milton as a representative of England unusual and noteworthy. Milton also, after he has opened his poem with the appropriate compliments to Manso, focuses on the question of his nationality.

The headnote, which Milton included in the 1645 printing of "Mansus", advertises the poem as no more than a thank-you note to Manso, who had shown the young Englishman great kindness and offices of goodwill, that is, *humanitas*, during his visit in Naples. Milton informs us that he sent the poem to Manso before leaving Naples in order not to appear ungrateful. However, at one hundred hexameter lines, "Mansus" must be considered more than a simple expression of thanks; rather, it is a poem that attempts to bridge the distance between England and Italy. The poem begins, in fact, at the very point at which Milton is beginning his return journey and sums up not only Milton's experiences in Naples, but also those experiences he had during his sojourn in Italy. Travel always involves the penetration of one culture into another and with that interpenetration the translation of the values and views of the first culture into that of the second. Travel builds bridges between countries and their inhabitants and also builds special relationships, linking men of different nationalities but of like interests. To indicate the relationship that he has with Manso and with other literary men he met in Italy, Milton uses the word *humanitas*, a word with a distinctive resonance for Renaissance men of humanity–that is humanists, who so often dwelled far apart from one another but whose like interests and pursuits joined them into a single inter-European community. Moreover, to facilitate communication, humanists of the inter-European community used Latin as a medium by which to express their common goodwill or *humanitas*.

The humanist interplay in the poem is suggested, first of all, by the range of *personae* with which Milton associates Manso–from Maecenas, the Roman patron of Horace and Vergil, to the mythic figure, the centaur Chiron. By alluding to Maecenas, Milton characterizes Manso as the associate of poets rather than as a poet in his own right, in spite of the fact that Manso had been celebrated by his own countrymen as a poet and that in bestowing on Milton as parting gifts two books of his own Italian verse he clearly thought of himself as a poet[2]. Throughout "Mansus", however, Milton looks on Manso as a patron, a man who befriends poets, characterizing himself as the most recent poet who has attached himself to the elderly Marquis of Villa. Manso had been both patron and biographer of Tasso and Marino, having written, as Milton notes, lives for both of them[3]. Milton pays particular attention to Manso's role as a biographer, exalting his status as the biographer of Tasso and Marino by comparing him to Herodotus, that "man born in lofty Mycale", who had recounted the life of Aeolian Homer[4]. Most Renaissance editions of Homer contain a biography of Homer attributed to Herodotus by ancient and Renaissance critics, but now deemed spurious. The biographer had an honored place in the Renaissance, for it was he who preserved the mortal reputation of the poet, and the biographies of poets were printed in the sixteenth and seventeenth centuries in their poetic works as prefaces to the works themselves. Milton in "Mansus" is much concerned, as we shall see, with the after-life with which the biographer endues the poet, allowing the poet to live with his poetry.

Thus the reference to Herodotus and to the *Life of Homer* attributed to him is particularly significant, for by it Milton expands the geographical and historical dimensions of his poem in rather interesting ways. Herodotus is best known as a writer of history, and as such Milton later alludes to him (indirectly) when he draws from his histories information about visitors to Apollo's temple at Delphi. Herodotus himself had a reputation as a traveler, a man who journeyed far and wide, recording facts and legends of ancient times and places. We might now dub him a cultural historian, for he undertook comparative study of the places he visited. The pseudo-Herodotean life of Homer is both a biography and a travel book, and it is probably for this reason that it was attributed to Herodotus. In the *Life* the biographer looks at Homer as a traveler, whose poetry owes a great deal to his voyages throughout the ancient world. This characterization of Homer as a traveler is not without significance to Milton, whose fame as a poet is now being spread throughout Italy as he is compared as an epic poet to Homer. The pseudo-Herodotean biography recounts Homer's conception, birth, and legendary voyaging. His mother conceived him in Cyme and traveled to give birth to him in Smyrna, where he acquired the name Melesigenes from his birth on the banks of the river Meles. During his long life, before and after his blindness, Homer traversed the ancient world. To his biographer he was the real traveler who had told of the mythic tales of his hero Odysseus. In linking Manso as a biographer to Homer's alleged biographer, Milton, the much-traveled young English poet, was perhaps also suggesting his own connection with the epic poet Homer. Already in those epigrams addressed to him by the Italians he met during his sojourn in Italy, Milton was lauded as a future epic poet and compared to Homer[5]. Indeed, in later years Milton would himself adopt in Book III of *Paradise Lost* Homer for one of his own epic *personae*[6].

Milton's first reference to himself in "Mansus" is as a traveler–a young pilgrim sent from the Hyperborean clime to wish Manso in the names of Phoebus Apollo and the muse Clio health and long life. The coupling of a reference to England as the fabled land of the Hyperboreans with an invocation to his host Manso in the name of Apollo and the muse of history, Clio, is particularly significant. In antiquity the land of the Hyperboreans was a fabled place–alluded to by Herodotus, Pindar, and other ancient writers–as both remote and favored by the gods, particularly the god of poetry, Apollo. In connecting Britain with this special place, Milton refers not only to Britain's geographical situation in the north, but also, as we shall see later, to Britain's favor to its poets. Hyperborean means literally the place beyond–*hyper*–the north wind–*Boreas*. Taking this etymology into account, Milton contrasts the English cities of the frozen north ("gelida [...] sub Arcto") with the cities of Italy through which he has made his flight, voyaging like a Mercurial emissary from a distant world[7]. Though removed from each other geographically, Milton notes, England and Italy have long been joined to each other by their poets. He names, first of all, another poetic visitor from England who came to Italy, namely Chaucer, to whom he gives the name Tityrus. The name Tityrus is taken, of course, from Vergil's *Eclogues*, but it was also the name attributed to Chaucer by Spenser in his own eclogues, *The Shepheardes Calender*. So by using Spenser's name for Chaucer, Milton has indirectly alluded to both of his famous English predecessors–Chaucer and Spenser–and in the same breath connected them to the Latin poet, Vergil, to whom he himself was being compared. Milton also connects antiquity's poetic birds–the swans–to England's famous swans, for in English as in classical literature poets such as Pindar and Shakespeare had been traditionally dubbed swans. Therefore, when he says that he has heard the swans singing on the Thames, we know that he is proclaiming the musicality of England's swan poets–Shakespeare and Spenser. To Manso, the man closely connected with the most famous poets of Italy's recent past, Tasso and Marino, Milton takes pains to establish his credentials as a poet with national ties to poets of England's recent past–Spenser and Shakespeare–poets contemporary with Tasso and Marino. In so doing Milton becomes a propagandist for English poets, whom he subtly suggests are comparable with their Italian predecessors and contemporaries. Further, as a poet Milton also bridges the two cultures with his visit to Italy, linking the countries by travel (as Chaucer had) and by a poetic sympathy that runs still deeper.

With the next reference to travel and to poetry, Milton suggests a connection between the ancient poets of Britain–the Druids–and the ancient shrine to Apollo, poetry's god–Delos. Borrowing from and reshaping passages from two classical writers–Herodotus and Callimachus–who refer to the land of the Hyperboreans, Milton connects the Mediterranean world to Britain. In the north as in the south, Herodotus and Callimachus recount, there were cults to Phoebus Apollo–and these cults communicated with one another by travel. According to Milton, the ancient Druids, whom he styles Britain's first poets, sent offerings to Delos in homage to Phoebus. The accounts he borrows from Herodotus and Callimachus might not at first seem to concern either the Druids or Britain. For classical writers the land of Hyperboreans was merely a fabulous ancient culture located far in the north and remote from the Mediterranean civilization. According to Diodorus Siculus (II.47.2-3), Apollo's mother Leto was bred in the Hyperborean regions. In *Olympian* 3 and *Pythian* 10 the poet Pindar describes voyages to the land of the Hyperboreans undertaken by the mythic heroes Heracles and Perseus, and he recounts that the Hyperboreans had special reverence for the god Apollo and for music and poetry[8]. Whereas both of Pindar's odes describe voyages *to* the land of the Hyperboreans, Herodotus and Callimachus describe voyages *from* the remote northern land to the civilized world. In the fourth book of the histories (IV.33-35) Herodotus tells that Hyperboreans traveled from their land, sending maidens with offerings to Apollo's shrine in Delos. Two girls–Arge and Opis–first visited Delos, and later two other maidens–Hyperoche and Laodice–escorted by five men, came to Delos with offerings and died there. The Delians buried them in a tomb near the temple of Artemis, and in their honor Delian maidens continued to bring offerings and to recite songs. In his *Hymn to Delos* (283-299) Callimachus also refers to the Hyperborean maidens, who bring corn sheaves and corn-ears to Delos in honor of Artemis and Apollo. He names them Upis, Loxo, and Hecaërge, probably drawing the name Upis from Herodotus. Taking the names from Callimachus rather than Herodotus, Milton conflates the two stories, making the Hyperboreans into the British bards–the Druids–who sent ears of corn, baskets of apples, and crocuses. He also refers to the rites that Herodotus said the Delians continued to perform in memory of the visit of the Hyperborean maidens. They circled the altars at Delos near their burial places and commemorated the three maidens with songs. Milton adds several details about the fabled maidens that even more closely connect them to Britain. He makes Loxo the daughter of Corineus, one of the founders of Britain; he endues Upis with the prophetic powers of the Druids; and he describes the maiden Hecaërge as golden-haired, just like the ancient Britons. Noting how the culture of Britain and its prophetic poet-priests was brought into coordination with a similar culture of priests and gods, Milton connects the rites performed at the shrines of the Druids with those performed at Delos's ancient temple. These two different cultures, Milton affirms, though distant from each other but inspired by mutual love for poetry, were joined by travel. Now, he too, in a similar manner, a pilgrim visitor from a Hyperborean realm, has come bearing poetic offerings comparable to the offerings for Delos first brought by the Hyperborean maidens. By modifying this ancient tale, told by Herodotus and Callimachus, Milton pays tribute to the connection between Britain and the ancient world, a connection fostered by mutual devotion to Apollo and the poetic art.

Having recounted a story about Apollo's oracle at Delos, Milton now tells a tale about the god of poetry, one which provides still another link between Italy and England and between the Italian Manso and the English Milton. Manso is a fortunate old man, "Fortunate senex!" (49), beloved by the gods, equally favored by Jupiter, Mercury, and Apollo, who, as it were, baptized him in gentle light. Drawing the appellation, "Fortunate senex", from Vergil's eclogues (I, 46), Milton defines that special blessing conferred on Manso by the gods, concluding that Apollo's gift to Manso was not the poetic faculty itself, but the genius of favoring and having been favored by great poets–Tasso and Marino. Manso's own fame is so bound up with theirs that his reputation will be preserved and will mount to heaven with that of his poet-friends. To illustrate this connection, Milton recounts the tale of another traveler–a visitor from a still more skyey clime, Apollo himself, who, exiled from Olympus, came for a while to dwell with King Admetus in Thessaly. It becomes clear, as he recounts this fable, that our northern visitor–Milton–has taken on the *persona* of the god of poets. As he tells how Apollo withdrew from the court of Admetus to sing his songs in the countryside to the accompaniment of the lyre, we sense that Milton himself is speaking about how his own poetic composition has taken on new flowering in the foreign land to which he has come and also in the antique language that is associated with that land.

Although accomplished as a Latin poet while he was at Cambridge, Milton had written very little in Latin since leaving the university. He had devoted his poetic efforts to composing in his own native language and had compiled by the time of his departure for Italy a mask and a number of short lyrical compositions–the Nativity ode, "L'Allegro", "Il Penseroso", and "Lycidas", none but the mask and "Lycidas" having yet been published. However, at the academies in Florence, Rome, and Naples it was the Latin poems, composed while at university or shortly thereafter, that he read. Moreover, during the Italian journey–perhaps spurred on by the very experience of traveling–he turned once more to the Latin versifying of his youth, which now becomes the preferred medium of poetic communication with his friends in Italy. Before composing this ambitious poem to Manso–to be printed in 1645 with the Latin juvenilia in his *Poemata*–Milton had written Latin verses to Salzilli and perhaps also the epigrams on the singing of Leonora Baroni in Rome. Moreover, when he describes how the exiled Apollo visits the cave of the centaur Chiron, Milton may be translating his experience of visiting Manso in Naples into a poetic fable in which he takes the part of Apollo and Manso Chiron.

Milton provides us with the clue to decipher the mythological incident by punning on the name Manso as he describes Apollo's retreat to the cave of the gentle Chiron (mansueti. . . Chironis)–"Nobile mansueti cessit Chironis in antrum" [He withdrew to the renowned cave of the gentle Chiron] (60). There Apollo entertains Chiron with his music, singing for Chiron alone (just as Milton had "sung" for Manso), while the hills and forests and cliffs are moved with his song. Milton does not tell us what Apollo sings. Perhaps he is slyly suggesting that it is these very verses he has written for Manso. Or perhaps, as I have commented elsewhere, he is reflecting on a much more ambitious composition, which he hopes will be the subject of his song–his proposed national epic (1997: 219-220). In "Mansus", and two years later in "Epitaphium Damonis", Milton describes the heroic poem that he has been projecting on the subject of King Arthur and Arthur's wars, an epic in emulation of Spenser's *Faerie Queene*, which also dealt with the deeds of Arthur. However, by implication the projected epic will also stand beside Vergil's Latin song of arms and the man and Tasso's Italian epic of Godfrey of Bulloigne's crusade to the Holy Land. Once more we are traveling through time and space to connect works representing different cultures and different languages–English and Latin and Italian. Milton does not specifically tell us in which language he intends to write his epic. Would he, like Petrarch, compose an epic in Latin in the style of Petrarch's "Africa", or would he follow the example of Tasso and Spenser and compose a chivalric work in the vernacular? However this may be, in "Mansus" he uses the Latin hexameters of Vergilian epic to describe the wars of Arthur, determining, like the epic writers of old, that he will immortalize the heroes of his own country.

> Si quando indigenas revocabo in carmina reges,
> Arturumque etiam sub terris bella moventem,
> Aut dicam invictae sociali foedere mensae
> Magnanimos Heroas, et–O modo spiritus adsit–
> Frangam Saxonicas Britonum sub Marte phalanges! (80-84)

> [If ever I shall call back the native kings into song,
> And Arthur, waging his wars beneath the earth,
> Or I shall tell of the magnanimous heroes of the table,
> Invincible through their mutual fidelity, and (if life remains for me)
> I shall shatter the Saxon phalanxes under British Mars.]

In proposing to tell of the deeds of heroes, Milton has made some interesting inter-textual connections. Earlier he has lauded his own native poets–the Druids–as being poets who celebrated the deeds of heroes:

> Gens Druides antiqua, sacris operata deorum,
> Heroum laudes imitandaque gesta canebant. (42-43)

> [The ancient race of the Druids, experienced in the rites of the gods,
> Used to sing the praises of heroes and their exemplary deeds.]

However, in referring to the deeds of gods and heroes, he is also evoking the works of Tasso and Marino, Tasso who sang of the chivalric deeds of heroes, Marino who sang of the love of the gods.

Milton's travels to Italy brought into sharp relief the three cultures that his projected epic necessarily involves–English, Italian, and Latin. As a foreign traveler, he took along with him the heritage of his own English tradition–of his native swans that he said had sung to him beside the river Thames. However, coming into contact with the complex and manifold heritage of Italy, he has had to effect a double translation, first accommodating his English vision to that of the Italian epic tradition, personified by Tasso (a tradition vividly evoked by Manso, Tasso's patron), and then to the still more ancient Roman epic tradition. And perforce, behind the Roman tradition always lurks the shadow of the Greek–just as behind Tasso's biographer Manso is Homer's biographer Herodotus. In order to write the kind of epic he proposes–the battle epic that will glorify the wars of Arthur–Milton must coordinate Aeneas's and Godfrey's wars, translating and adapting from the Latin to the Italian before he can re-formulate his epic in English. The very act of translation involves an assimilation of the past and a reassembling of its parts in the present.

Traveling has two phases–the voyage outward and the return. On the voyage outward the traveler takes with him his native experience and culture; on the return voyage, he takes back with him the experience of the second culture fused with his own. The return home always involves an assessment of the journey, and in the final section of "Mansus" Milton does exactly this. However, he assesses his visit with Manso not from the point of view of the immediate but the final return, defining travel both in the literal and the metaphorical sense. Travel involves both time and space; it can be expressed as the distance traversed between Naples and London, but also as the distance that a man travels in his lifetime. In this final section, Milton undertakes to view travel in the latter sense. It is the journey through life as well as the accomplishment of the life work–the completion of the *magnum opus*–the proposed epic. It is also the final journey–the *translatio* of the poet's soul to a classical heaven. Leaping ahead in time, the erstwhile foreign traveler envisions his last days on earth, when he will have finished the epic poem that he now hopefully plans and that his Italian friends in their complimentary verses warmly encourage. He imagines himself as an aged man–a man of his host Manso's years–though not of Manso's status. Rather he is like Manso's friend Tasso, the poet whose reputation Manso cherished and whose passage from life to death Manso supervised, as only a friend could.

The final section of "Mansus" deals with poetic reputation, here Milton's own, a reputation that he has begun to build in Italy and which he will return to England to assure. The reputation of any poet depends partly on the work he accomplishes and partly on the care of a friend or friends–the executor or biographer. The biographer, in particular, in writing the poetic life, will nurture both poet and poetry, making sure that the poet's reputation flourishes and that his poetry endures. In Italy Milton had made friends who looked upon him as a future epic poet and who had nurtured both him and his reputation. He had identified in Manso, moreover, both the kind of friend and biographer who would be most valuable to a future poet. The headnote to the poem "Mansus" speaks of Manso as the friend to whom Tasso had dedicated his treatise on friendship[9]. Throughout the poem, moreover, Manso's role as friend, biographer, and literary executor is stressed. When Milton returns at the end of the poem to praise Manso, he does so not just to compliment his host, but to define for himself exactly what kind of friend he himself will need to assure his final success as a poet. Several biographies are alluded to in the course of the poem—Manso's biographies of Tasso and Marino, Herodotus's biography of Homer—but one yet unwritten biography is still more important—that work which Milton's literary executor and friend will compose. By placing Herodotus's biography of Homer side by side Manso's biographies of Tasso and Marino, Milton has heroized the role of the biographer. In writing of poets' lives, the biographer also heroizes the great poet, making him into an icon such as Homer had become. As the biographer assures the poet's translation to the heaven of literary fame, the poet takes the biographer along with him, assuring the biographer's renown. Who would remember Manso, if he had not written Tasso's biography—or if Milton had not extolled Manso's work as biographer in this Latin poem.

The biographer-friend has a dual role. As biographer, he immortalizes the human reputation of the poet; as friend he treasures the mortal remains of the man, ensuring that his body is properly interred and his monument built. At the beginning of the poem Milton had praised Manso's funerary tributes to his dead friends Tasso and Marino; now he wishes that a like friend might also memorialize him. At the end of a long and productive life he hopes to entrust body and "soul" to such a friend as Manso himself.

> Tandem ubi non tacitae permensus tempora vitae,
> Annorumque satur, cineri sua iura relinquam,
> Ille mihi lecto madidis astaret ocellis,
> Astanti sat erit si dicam, 'Sim tibi curae.' (85-88)

> [At last, after the span of no silent lifetime,
> When, full of years, I shall pay the ashes their due,
> He [my friend] shall stand by my bed with tears in his eyes,
> Then, it will be enough, if I shall say to him standing there, "Take me to your care".]

Milton even describes his future funeral—the depositing of his ashes in a little urn and the construction of a tomb in which his effigy might be carved in marble with fronds of laurel and myrtle adorning his head in tribute to his vocation as a poet. Such monuments Manso had constructed for his poet-friends. He even envisions the final journey of his soul to the heavenly regions—the translation to a kind of poetic Elysium, where virtue and virtuous deeds are rewarded. From this vantage he proposes to look down on earth, smiling, with his face suffused with rosy light, and applaud his own achievement from lofty Olympus. In an astonishing way, Milton's poem looks forward to his own poetic end–traversing the continent of years from the beginning of his career until its end.

In speaking of death-bed scenes, of urns and ashes, of funeral processions, and of the construction of marble monuments, Milton is not morbidly dwelling on death. Rather he is taking the concern for poetic reputation with which he has been occupied throughout the poem to its logical end–only after death is a poet's legacy secure. He had traveled to Italy in search of that which had so far eluded him in England–the assurance of lasting poetic fame. In England he was not yet widely celebrated as a poet, for his publications were few: he had printed a sonnet in the second Shakespeare folio; he had written the words for two aristocratic entertainments–*Arcades* and the *Mask at Ludlow*–and had contributed an elegiac ode–"Lycidas"–to a volume commemorating the death of his Cambridge school fellow, Edward King. In England he was not a future Tasso or Marino, much less a future Homer or Vergil, yet in Italy he had been so received, on the basis of those Latin works he had shared with his hosts in Florence and in Naples. Years later, in his Latin treatise *Pro Populo Anglicano Defensio Secunda* (1654), he includes a biographical memoir in which he recalls his warm reception in Italy–his "intimacy with many persons of rank and learning" and his attendance at their "literary parties". He specifically remembers his visit to Manso,

> a nobleman of distinguished rank and authority, to whom Torquato Tasso, the illustrious poet, inscribed his book on friendship. During my stay, he gave me singular proofs of his regard: he himself conducted me round the city, and to the palace of the viceroy; and more than once paid me a visit at my lodgings. (1957: 829)

Clearly, Milton looked at the journey to Italy as affording the break-through that had not yet occurred in England; Italy was the watershed for his poetic reputation.

Hence, the poetic thank-you to the elderly marquis of Villa, the last of those Latin poems Milton composed in Italy, carries the freight of Milton's future hopes and plans. Contextualizing his own career in terms of the achievements both of the most recent epic poets of Italy and the poets of the classical world, Milton seeks to assess the importance of the poet in the post-humanist world of Italy and England. "Mansus" is a poem that brings together representatives of Italy and England and assesses their contributions to the literary life of the world from a still higher realm–that of eternal and not earthly reputation. By the time Milton published "Mansus" in the 1645 *Poemata*, Milton's poetic thank-you has traveled a long way from its initial posting to his Italian host before the young poet left the city. With the publication of the 1645 *Poems*, Milton proceeds to establish in England the poetic reputation that his Italian journey had begun to promise.

[1] See Manso's epigram in the 1645 *Poemata, Poems of Mr. John Milton, Both English and Latin, Compos'd at several times* (1970: 4). Unless otherwise specified, all quotations from Milton will be from Merritt Hughes's *Complete Poems and Major Prose*. All translations from the Latin are my own but adapted from Hughes's.

[2] The identification of the books that Manso gave to Milton has been the subject of much conjecture by scholars. In his Latin poem, "Epitaphium Damonis", Milton refers to the "books" that Manso gave him as ornate cups and alludes to their contents by describing the scenes depicted on the so-called cups. See De Filippis (1936: 745-756), Revard (1997: 230-234) and Haan (1998: 119-121).

[3] Manso's life of Marino does not survive; however, Milton and others allude to it. His life of Tasso relates many incidents about the Italian poet, some of them probably, as critics comment, commonplace anecdotes rather than accurate biography. See De Filippis (1936a: 443-501).

[4] Milton not only refers to Herodotus's *Life of Homer* in 'Mansus', he uses material from the *Life* in *Paradise Regained*, where he refers to Homer as Melesigenes. This is the name attributed to Homer by the biographer before he became blind and took on the name Homerus, a name which the biographer says the Cumians gave to blind persons ("Nam Cumani caecos δπήρουs appellant"). See Herodotus (1528: f. 6ʳ. Milton's line in *Paradise Regained* refers to both of Homer's names: "Blind *Melesigenes* thence *Homer* call'd" (IV. 259).

[5] See, for example, the epigrams that Salzilli and Selvaggi wrote to Milton, which he printed in the introduction to the *Poemata* of the 1645 *Poems*. Both allude to Homer as the first poet who will cede his fame to Milton. Salzilli: "Cede Meles, cedat depressa Mincius urna; / Sebetus Tassum desinat usque loqui; / At Thamesis victor cunctis ferat altior undas / Nam per te Milto par tribus unus erit" [Yield Meles, let the upturned urn of Mincius yield, / Let Sebetus cease to speak of Tasso continuously, / But the victor Thames will bear its waves higher than the rest, / For through you, Milton, will be the one equal to the three]. Selvaggi: "Ad Joannem Miltonum": "Graecia Maeonidem, jactet sibi Roma Maronem, / Anglia Miltonum jactat utrique parem" [Greece Homer, Rome may boast of Vergil, but England boasts of Milton, equal to both] (1970: 4).

[6] See the passage in *Paradise Lost* III in which Milton wishes himself equal in fame to the blind poets Thamyris and Homer: "Those other two equall'd with me in Fate, / So were I equall'd with them in renown, / Blind *Thamyris* and blind *Maeonides*" (33-35). Maeonides is the patronymic for Homer.

[7] See lines 24-29. Milton uses the term "Hyperborean" in several other works to refer to England: see the Latin letter to Charles Diodati (1931-1938: vol. 12, 18-22) and also his poem, "In Quintum Novembris" (95).

[8] See Pindar, *Olympian* 3 (16, 31-33) and *Pythian* 10 (29-44) for descriptions of the land of the Hyperboreans as a land favored by Apollo. There sickness is unknown, youth prolonged, and the muses especially celebrated.

[9] See Tasso (1958: vol. 2, 842-887).

References

De Filippis, Michele. 1936. 'Milton and Manso: Cups or Books' in *PMLA* 51: 745-756.

–. 1936a. 'Anecdotes in Manso's "Vita di Tasso" and their Sources' in *University of California Publications in Modern Philology* 18 (6): 443-501.

Haan, Estelle. 1998. *From Academia to Amicitia: Milton's Latin Writings and the Italian Academies*. Philadelphia, PA: American Philosophical Society.

Herodotus. 1528. *Herodoti Halicarnssei de Genere vitaque Homeri Libellus* (tr. Conrad Heresbach). Paris.

Milton, John. 1931-1938. *The Works of John Milton [Columbia Milton]* (ed. Frank Allan Patterson). 18 vols. New York, NY: Columbia University Press.

–. 1957. *Complete Poems and Major Prose* (ed. Merritt Y. Hughes). New York, NY: The Odyssey Press, Inc.

–. 1970. *Poemata, Poems of Mr. John Milton, Both English and Latin, Compos'd at several times.* London, 1645. Facsimile rpt. London: The Scolar Press Ltd.

Revard, Stella P. 1997. *Milton and the Tangles of Neaera's Hair*. Columbia, MO: University of Missouri Press.

Tasso, Torquato. 1958. 'Il Manso overo de L'Amicizia' in *Dialoghi* (ed. Ezio Raimondi). 3 vols. Florence: G. C. Sansone.

1.4. Milton Translating Petrarch: *Paradise Lost* VIII and the *Secretum*

Anthony M. Cinquemani

The dialogue between Raphael and Adam in Milton's *Paradise Lost* VIII is a translation into prelapsarian terms of the postlapsarian dialogue between Augustinus and Franciscus in Petrarch's *Secretum*. Milton saw in Petrarch an authorizer, as mediated by the *accademici* he encountered during his Italian sojourn, of a linguistic model, as well as a writer authorized by his evident proto-Protestantism. As is suggested by the conclusion, so much resembling Petrarch's, to which Milton's colloquy draws, that which is principally translated is a sort of indeterminate dialectic, a setting-aside (to use the terms of Karlheinz Stierle) of Augustinus's cultural verticality in order to favor Franciscus's humanist horizontality. While the features of the two works correspond in many ways, the most significant form of cultural translation in Milton is the accommodation of the Humanist project of remembering to prelapsarian anticipation, the horizontal Petrarchan process of thought leading, in *Paradise Lost* as in the *Secretum*, to the velleity of the conclusion. This indeterminacy may result as well from Milton's antinomianism, and even from his adoption of the rather new Petrarchan medium of thought, love.
Keywords: dialogue, Milton, *Paradise Lost*, Petrarch, *Secretum*, translation, travel.

In various ways language is constituent of travel, and travel further elaborates language, requiring interpretation or translation. Travel is analogous to translation in that the traveler, like the translator, both perceives and creates meaning, carrying to the country he visits (or the text he reads), and attending to, whatever his own culture has prepared him to see, or his intelligence allows; perceiving likeness; sometimes misapprehending cultural idiosyncrasy as familiar; at other times regarding novelty, however partially understood, as adaptable to his own purposes; and, at still other times, as needing to be adopted in untranslated form. The traveler/translator perceives and relates, not only words, but things, postures, tones, manners, structures, processes of thought. The translation takes the form of words that suggest (rather like the situation of the traveler) transposition: terms like *translate, transfer, explain, expound, explicate, interpret, construe,* and *represent* are strikingly close in etymological sense[1]. It might be added that, while travel is a text to be read and interpreted, readers visit texts as well, and the texts are themselves, often complicatedly, those of other readers of other texts[2]. Some limit themselves to texts about travel and therefore, like Robert Burton, never travel but in map or card. Others, like Milton, travel with texts in mind and return home to translate them.

Thus, when he traveled in 1638-39, Milton carried with him whatever predispositions concerning Italy he had acquired from his culture and education: years of reading in classical and Italian literature which, I would assume, included familiarity with the *Secretum*; the experience of having composed poetry in Italian; friendship with Italians resident in England; and, among other things, the Protestant resolution of a son whose father had been disinherited for violating the Roman Catholic resolution of *his* father. As an anonymous biographer put it, Milton, in traveling to Italy, evidently wanted to get beyond book, map, and card and "polish his conversation, and learn to know Men" (Milton 1957: 1039); according to his nephew Edward Phillips, Milton wanted to observe "foreign customs, manners, and institutions [with] prudence [...] his guide, and his learning his introduction and presentation to persons of most eminent quality" (*ibid.*: 1027). While he seems to concede, on later reflection, that "there is so much moral laxity" in Italy, he reveals, in the *Second Defense* (1654), that his expectation was to find in Italy "the retreat of civility and of all polite learning" (1931-1938: vol. 8, 115).

He was not disappointed, for, especially in Florence, Milton was, as he tells us, "assiduous" in frequenting the *accademie* (principally that of the Svogliati, some of whose members belonged to the Apatisti and the Crusca as well), institutions he remembers as preserving "polite letters [in no small measure by means of commentary upon Petrarch] and friendly intercourse" (1931-1938: vol. 8, 123), in his case particularly (one would think) his friendships with Dati, Buonmattei, and Coltellini[3]. Perhaps the most prominent motif in his translation of the Florentine experience is his emphasis upon the respect accorded him by the learned and the powerful. Corns describes Milton's stay in Italy as having "achieved an ingress that constitute[d] a rare honor for an Englishman, establishing his credentials as Italian humanist" (1991: 5-6). Of his recitations at the Svogliati, he offers, in "Epitaphium Damonis", the understated brag: "And I myself even dared to compete, and I think that I did not much displease" (1957: 136)[4]. Milton's accounts of his period of travel attest to somewhat paradoxical events and cultural translations. He first reports in a letter to Lucas Holstein (March 30, 1639), momentarily forgetting the unseemliness his English Protestantism should have prepared him to recognize in the encounter, his personal delight at having been received by Francesco Cardinal Barberini, nephew of the Pope, "with truly Roman magnificence, he himself, waiting at the doors, and seeking me out in so great a crowd, nay, almost laying hold of me by the hand" (1966: vol. 1, 409-414). Yet, recovering from the glamor of that moment, years later Milton saw to it, in *Paradise Lost* (I.768-771), that the Barberini insignia of bees should be re-translated into the swarming of the fallen angels in Pandemonium, and St. Peter's Cathedral into Pandemonium. In *Areopagitica* (1644) Milton recalls his visit, presumably at the house of Vincenzo Galileo in Costa San Giorgio (Haan 1998: 44), with an heroic Galileo senior, who is characterized, from a Protestant perspective, as "grown old, a prisner to Inquisition, for thinking in Astronomy otherwise then the Franciscan and Dominican licencers thought" (1966: vol. 1, 380). *Paradise Lost*, which itself reflects thinking in astronomy otherwise than Galileo's, on second thought likens Satan's shield to the moon as studied by Galileo (I.288-290), thus demonizing the astronomer somewhat. Still, Milton was evidently proud of the praise and respect he received, as suggested by the testimonials appended to the *Poems* of 1645, from Dati, Francini, Tasso's friend Manso, and Giovanni Selvaggi, the latter declaring him worthy of a triple poetic laurel (*triplici poeseos laureâ coronandum Græcâ nimirum, Latinâ, atque Hetruscâ*), surely a commendation, in view of Milton's Protestantism, at least potentially facetious. (Milton later alluded to the Pope, in Sonnet XVIII, as "triple tyrant".)

Indeed a second prominent motif in characterizing himself as a traveler in Italy (especially Rome) is Milton's Protestantism, of which he represents himself as fearless advocate. While he did not hesitate to visit Holstein at the Vatican Library, Cardinal Barberini at his palace, or even the Jesuit-run English College in Rome, in his accounts Milton suggests this quality several times, as he does, for example, in the *Second Defense*: "On my leaving Naples", he says that, "[Manso] gravely apologized for showing me no more attention, alleging that although it was what he wished above all things, it was not in his power in that city, because I had not thought proper to be more guarded on the point of religion" (1931-1938: vol. 8, 125). Here he also makes much of his imperturbability concerning the warning that English Jesuits were plotting against him in Rome, a narration which Diana Treviño Benet characterizes as a sort of English Protestant travelers' topos (1991: 29-49)[5]. His visit to Italy confirmed in Milton his identity as learned poet and Protestant. His identification of self does, however, ignore certain evidence to the contrary: for example, his friendship with Agostino Coltellini, a censor of the Florentine Inquisition, and with Antonio Malatesti, who dedicated indecent sonnets to him[6].

Whatever he brought to Italy was, it must be assumed, momentarily imposed upon, then checked and modified by, Italian experience. When he proceeded to translate that experience, sometimes he accommodated it to whatever his education had prepared him to expect; at other times his understanding was modified; and at still other times he adopted, or adapted to new purposes, rather new ideas. I am principally interested in these latter forms of cultural translation and consider them relevant to Milton's apprehension of Petrarch's *Secretum*, which, very likely, he read before, had occasion to discuss during, and adapted to his purposes after, his visit to Florence. Thus we are dealing with at least three stages in a process of cultural translation: Milton's reading of the *Secretum*, his visits with the Florentine *accademici* (in whose conversations Petrarch loomed large), and the writing of *Paradise Lost* VIII.

Judging by such works as the Sixth Elegy (to Diodati), "L'Allegro" and "Il Penseroso", "Ad Patrem", and "Lycidas", Milton carried to the *accademie* of Florence a personal aspiration to poetry of the highest order and a preference, in Italian literature, for "the two famous renowners", as he said in the *Apology for Smectymnuus* "of Beatrice and Laura, who never write but honor of them to whom they devote their verses, displaying sublime and pure thoughts without transgression": he clearly associated the latter ability with that preparation for poetry required of the man who would "himself [...] be a true poem" or "composition and pattern of the best and honorablest things" (1957: 693-694), a status achieved, as suggested in "Lycidas", by "strictly meditat[ing] the thankless Muse" (66). So far as Petrarch is concerned, beyond the expression of pure thoughts without transgression, or perhaps as corresponding to it, Milton cannot have failed to perceive the renowner of Laura as authorized as linguistic model (as his contacts with Benedetto Buonmattei and others involved in revision of the *Vocabolario* would have confirmed) and as proto-Protestant. The latter view of Petrarch, common among Renaissance Protestants, seems to have become more pronounced in Milton after his return from Italy, especially in his capacity as controversialist. However, his experience among the *accademici* seems, in my view, to have modified his understanding of, or offered radically new ideas concerning, a number of literary matters, among them that sort of indeterminate dialectic which is transferred from the *Secretum* of Petrarch to Book VIII of *Paradise Lost*.

The *Secretum* (or, more accurately, the *Secretum de secreto conflictu curarum mearum*) of Petrarch has the appearance of stern moral judgment and intellectual integrity, for it permits the interlocutor Augustinus to contend with, even indict, Franciscus (who seems to represent the author) for the vices, principally lust and the desire for fame, to which he acknowledges himself prone, diagnosing his illness as *accidia*, and demanding that he cure himself by an act of will. Yet the ostensible Church Father is nothing of the kind, but a sort of Petrarchan translation of Augustine, appealing, for the most part, to the authority of Cicero, not Christ; and Franciscus, while acceding, out of seeming respect for the truth, to the correctness of Augustinus's argument, ultimately (or perhaps provisionally) exempts himself from it. Though the Lady Truth is present throughout the debate, Petrarch does not represent her as blushing.

After Franciscus has confessed to her, in the Proem, that he suffers from sleeplessness and stress, Lady Truth gives Augustinus the following charge: "I know the silence of meditation delights you most, but please let him hear your voice, holy and pleasing as it is. See whether you can find a way to relieve his severe depression" (1989: 38)[7]. Three days are then devoted to long conversation consisting, for the most part, of the reproaches of Augustinus and the defensive complaints of Franciscus, a conversation Milton will carry over to *Paradise Lost* VIII. In Book I, at the very outset, Augustinus accuses Franciscus of self-deception and the characteristically mortal predisposition to indulging his own unhappiness (*ibid.*: 41). Though Augustinus argues that an unhappy man must want to be happy, and that happiness is in his power, Franciscus resists the notion that unhappiness, or happiness, is willed (*ibid.*:42-50). Augustinus makes the clarification that the desire for virtue must be specific and exclusive, that is, cannot exist "unless one puts an end to all other desires" (*ibid.*: 51). According to Augustinus, meditation upon death is the way to virtue. Life must not be wasted in "oblivious[ness] to reality [and] grow[ing] old in a world of words" (*ibid.*: 54), a telling criticism if one considers Franciscus as modeled upon Petrarch. Franciscus protests that the thought of death only fills him with fear*: mementi mori* provoke terror, not virtue. The problem, observes Augustinus, is that the soul of Franciscus is cluttered with extraneous images (soon to be identified as erotic) which "weigh down and confuse the soul" (*ibid.*: 60). "[N]othing can take root and bear fruit" in his "overcrowded mind" (*ibid.*: 62). Thus one step in the path to virtue is the elimination of distraction.

In Book II Augustinus refers the illness of Franciscus to the taxonomy of sin, first enumerating his talents, especially that of rhetoric, but then relegating them to the sphere of vanity. Without self-knowledge, knowledge of the external world is quite useless. Indeed, it crowds the mind and offers no comfort: "And yet what comfort is it to have even great knowledge, if after you have learned the dimensions of heaven and earth, the extent of the seas, the course of the stars, the properties of herbs and stones, and the mysteries of nature, you still do not have self-knowledge?" (*ibid.*: 67).[8]

Augustinus begins to interrogate Franciscus in systematic consideration of the seven deadly sins, very nearly as an examination of conscience. He begins by accusing him of taking pride in his appearance, an accusation that is indignantly denied. He refers to the alienation of Franciscus arising from "comparing [himself] to the inadequacies of someone else" as an "intolerable kind of pride" (*ibid.*: 70-71), however Franciscus might construe it as excusable. He accuses him of avarice and ambition, under which are subsumed a number of implicitly humanist activities to which he will return in Book III: "The leisure, the solitude, the elaborate indifference to human affairs, and those researches of yours lead you towards ambition, and their aim is self-glorification" (*ibid.*: 79). Augustinus reserves special emphasis for the sin of lust, which Franciscus immediately acknowledges as a problem. Petrarch has Augustinus make the ironic observation that "You have always left room for your passions to make their entry; you always pray for a slow answer to your prayers" (*ibid.*: 82). At this point, though no explicit connection is made, the serious problem of *aegritudo* or *accidia* and its possible causes is introduced, the mention of which prompts Franciscus to shudder. *Aegritudo* is set in contradistinction to other passions, which "are short and momentary". Franciscus characterizes this form of melancholy as a "disease [which] holds me so tenaciously sometimes that it ties me in knots and torments me for days on end" (*ibid.*: 84). Augustinus wonders whether the depression of Franciscus is prompted by the human condition, physical illness, injustice, self-hatred, or anger at Fortune. Whichever, he reiterates that Franciscus has "fallen into this maze of [his] own free will" (*ibid.*: 95).

In Book III Augustinus concentrates upon the "two unbreakable chains [that] hold [Franciscus] in bondage", love and glory, which Franciscus vehemently denies can, in his case, be construed as fetters. Augustinus accuses him of being deceived, concerning both vices, "by the appearance of beauty" (*ibid.*: 102). Concentrating for the moment upon love, which Augustinus declares "the ultimate form of madness", Franciscus insists upon maintaining a distinction between love "as the most vile passion or the most noble":

> If I have a passion for a low woman of ill repute, that love is sheer folly; but if I am attracted by a woman who is the image of virtue and devote myself to loving and honoring her, what do you think about that? Do you not think that some distinction applies in two such contradictory cases? Is honor not to be considered at all? I, for my part, consider the first kind of love a heavy and unfortunate burden, but there is nothing more beautiful than the second. (*ibid.*: 103)[9]

At this point, Franciscus cleverly, he thinks, appeals to the authority of Cicero (*De Senectute* 23, 85), citing his phrase, "If I am mistaken on this, I am happy to be mistaken and do not want to give up my error, as long as I live". But Augustinus checks this citation-out-of-context, or, if you will, mistranslation, by observing that "Cicero said this in discussing the most noble of beliefs, the belief in the immortality of the soul". He declares Franciscus "trapped in a most shameful and false opinion, [making] wrongful use of these same words", trivializing them in application to love. The now tense exchange becomes rather bitter, Franciscus claiming never to have loved "anything base"; Augustinus observing that "[e]ven beautiful things can be loved in a base way"; Franciscus answering that he has "not sinned either in what [he] loved or in the way [he has] loved", and adding the warning, "Do not press the matter any more" (*ibid.*: 104).

Though never naming her, Augustinus zeroes in on Laura, evoking a telling response from Franciscus:

> We are going to talk about a mortal woman whom regrettably you have wasted a great part of you[r] life in admiring and celebrating. I am shocked at such long-standing folly in somebody with talent like yours.
>
> FRANCESCO Spare me your criticism, please. Thais and Livia were mortal women. But do you know that you are speaking of a woman who knows nothing of earthly concerns and burns only with love for what is heavenly, a woman in whose face (if truth has any meaning at all) a kind of divine beauty shines forth, a woman whose character is the image of perfect honor, a woman whose whole appearance–her voice, her radiant eyes, her way of moving–is unearthly? Think on this again and again and I am sure you will choose the appropriate words[10].

Augustinus admonishes him to think of Laura's death, which will "close those eyes so dangerously pleasing to you". Franciscus exclaims, "Please God that may never be". Augustinus argues that this fear is the result of Franciscus's having subjected his soul to worldly things. Still, Franciscus insists upon the spiritual, idealizing nature of his love, which Augustinus regards as the loving of a beautiful thing in a base way:

> For I have not, as you suppose, committed my soul to anything mortal. You should know that I have loved not so much her body as her soul; her character, which transcends those of ordinary humans, is what delights me, and from her I get an idea

of how life is lived in heaven. And if you ask me what would I do if she should die first and leave me [...], I would say [with Lælius], "I loved her virtue and that did not die".
[...]
If anyone could see the image of the love that reigns in my heart, it would seem very like the face of one whom I have given much praise, but who deserves much more. I call Truth, before whom we are speaking, as witness that there never has been anything base in my love, anything shameful, or anything blameworthy, except that I did not love her enough. If you add that my love never passed beyond what is right, nothing more beautiful could be imagined. (*ibid.*: 107)[11]

Franciscus adds that "[w]hatever [he is, he] owes to her, who has "fostered [...] the feeble seeds of virtue in my heart", a woman whom no one could fault, there being nothing "reprehensible, I will not say in her conduct, but even in a word or gesture" (*ibid.*: 108). Augustinus observes that it might be better if Franciscus kept silence. He rebukes the lover, accusing him of relinquishing the gifts nature has bestowed upon him–no fault of Laura, who is innocent: "you sit at her feet, captivated by her charm alone, and have become contemptuous and scornful of everything else" (*ibid.*: 109). She will be the cause of his ruin particularly because "[s]he has distracted your mind from the love of heavenly things and has attracted it from the Creator to a desire for created things. That road, quicker than any other, leads to death" (*ibid.*: 110). Franciscus insists that his love for her "was indeed reponsible for [his] love for God"; Augustinus sternly declares that "that inverts the proper order [...] [b]ecause every creature should be loved out of love for its creator, but you have been captivated by the charms of a creature and do not love the Creator as you should". In short, his love for Laura is idolatrous. His praise of her is empty rhetoric, "mere words", and the feeling he expresses is really lust, for "it was her body that you loved" (*ibid.*: 110). This lust, Augustinus maintains, is the cause of Franciscus's unhappiness. "You may put me on the rack", the lover responds, "but I shall not admit that" (*ibid.*: 111).

Still, Franciscus concedes that "the time when I went astray coincides with my meeting her" (*ibid.*: 112). He absolves Laura from blame, emphasizing that, when he was first in love with her, "she remained untouched and resolute"; "she always remained firm in her resolve and always the same". She was a model of "womanly constancy". These remarks provoke renewed criticism from Augustinus, who accuses Franciscus, as Milton's Raphael will Adam, of a sort of misprizing of self: "Do you not see how much you condemn yourself in absolving her? You like to see her as a model of virtue, while you claim to be wicked and foolish; you like saying that she is most happy, while you are most unhappy because of your love for her" (*ibid.*: 113)[12].

Augustinus reiterates the idea that nothing "leads a man to forget or despise God so much as love of temporal things, and especially that passion which people call Love and to which people even give the name god" (*ibid.*: 114). Love is particularly dangerous because it requires that passion be reciprocal, "and so a man's heart is aroused by alternate stimuli". When Augustinus suggests cures to love, Franciscus reasserts the uniqueness of his love for Laura: "Know this, then, this one thing, that I could never love another woman. My mind has grown used to admiring her, my eyes to looking at her; whatever else they look at they consider disagreeable and dark" (*ibid.*: 118)[13].

Augustinus now cites Cicero (*Tusc.* IV.35.75) on the antidotes to love: satiety, shame, and reflection. In referring to the latter, he suggests reflection on old age. Franciscus counters with a citation from Domitian (in Suetonius, *Domitian* 18): "With a brave spirit, I endure the sight of my hair turning gray in my youth". This prompts still another rebuke, a rejection of Petrarchan exemplarity: "I do not approve of those examples which teach you to disguise the fact that gray hair indicates advancing old age". But Franciscus does not concede the point, insisting upon the efficacy of humanistic exemplarity: "it is a great consolation to be surrounded by famous comrades [whom one reads or studies]. And so I do not reject the use of such examples, as part of my mental equipment" (*ibid.*: 126). Augustinus keeps hammering him with reminders of his childishness, but the discussion of lust seems to conclude in a sort of non-committal concession on Franciscus's part: "Yes, I am filled with regret and repentance, but there is nothing more I can do" (*ibid.*: 129).

His reaction to the issue of glory is analogous. The response of Franciscus to the accusation, "You desire glory among men and a name that will never die more than you ought", is, "Yes, I admit it, but I can find no remedy to curb this passion" (*ibid.*: 131). Augustinus reductively defines glory as reputation and asks whether its worldly form merits "your ceaseless toil, your constant vigils, and obsessive application to your studies" (*ibid.*: 132)? He accuses Franciscus of pretentious rhetorical posturing, of "plucking flowery sentiments from poetry, from history, and every literary form, to delight the ears of your audience", even of culling elegant citations in attempting to impress his friends. However, it does not end there: Franciscus has soaring, "long-range ambitions and [desires] reputation with posterity". The result is a sort of humanistic *oblio*: "You spend your time writing about others and forget yourself" (*ibid.*: 133).

When Augustinus accuses him of "abandoning things that will live forever", Franciscus, anticipating the indeterminate conclusion of the *Secretum*, responds, "I would not call it 'abandoning'; 'putting off' is more like it" (*ibid.*: 135)[14]. This notion of postponement begins to evolve into a formula:

> And so I think the proper order is that mortal men should first think about mortal things and that eternal things should follow transitory things, because the most logical order is to proceed from the transitory to the eternal, whereas to go from the transitory is not possible. (*ibid.*: 137)[15]

The reaction of Augustinus to this specious argument is, "Silly little man" (*ibid.*: 137)[16]. Franciscus, whose claims for the self, putting off (but not quite rejecting) those for Augustinian authority, seem to grow as the *Secretum* draws to an end, asks whether "you [are] asking me to let all my studies go and live without glory or do you advise some compromise?" Augustinus advises that "it is impossible for virtue not to beget glory, if God shine His light" (*ibid*.: 140). At a certain point toward the end of their debate, Franciscus makes a gratuitous sort of acknowledgment: "I wish you had told me this from the beginning before I had committed myself to these pursuits" (*ibid*.: 143). He nevertheless thanks Augustinus for having "cleared my vision and dispelled the thick cloud of error which surrounds me", and begs, "please do not desert me, though we be far apart". Augustinus responds, "Consider your wish granted, if you remain true to yourself. Otherwise, you will be justly deserted by everyone". Franciscus concludes in weak but recognizably Petrarchan concession, and distraction that, given the passion of the debate, has the force of *non sequitur*:

> I shall be as true to myself as I can, collect the scattered fragments of my soul, and diligently aim at self-possession. But even as we speak, many important matters, though they are of this world, await my attention. (*ibid*.: 144)[17]

Augustinus does not carry the day. Franciscus concedes in principle, and postpones. Nothing is concluded. Curiously, this setting-aside is, to borrow the terms of Karlheinz Stierle, an instance of Augustinus's cultural verticality and of Franciscus's indeterminate horizontality; that is, for Augustinus the world's cultures and their respective languages are arranged hierarchically (or diachronically), whereas for Franciscus the plurality of voices exists, so to speak, on level ground: each voice in any given dialogue is equally legitimate (or synchronic), and it is acceptable for the dialogue to end without a resolution of differing points of view–the goal, rather, for the Renaissance humanist, is to make the voices heard, to move them across that level ground, in short, to translate them (Stierle 1996: 64-65). As we shall see, it is this horizontality that Milton appropriates.

Milton transfers a number of motifs from the *Secretum* to *Paradise Lost*. Apart from God's charge to Raphael, which is analogous to Truth's charge to Augustinus, these motifs are embodied in either the didactic figure of authority (Raphael/Augustinus) or the somewhat paradoxically receptive figure of resistance (Adam/Franciscus). Milton's interlocutors correspond to Petrarch's, though their functions in the dialogue and their relationship to one another are modified somewhat. There is a certain transference of ideas or motifs. Milton must have been attracted to the emphasis upon the freedom of the will in Petrarch's Augustinus and, perhaps, the notion of distraction as inhibiting the will. While Petrarch's *accidia* cannot precisely be translated into the language of *Paradise Lost*, it is present anachronistically in the anticipation of the tedium and melancholy with which Milton's Adam flirts in being distracted, principally by Eve, and by their reversion to sense impressions as well. Like Augustinus, Milton's Raphael admonishes Adam to eschew extraneous interests and concentrate upon whatever is relevant to his spiritual survival; acknowledge his own value (arrived at by Petrarchan interiority); exert his will (or not pervert it); and not deceive himself concerning lust or uxoriousness, which Adam insists is nothing of the kind, but decent love for a perfect woman whose very gestures are worthy of reverence. Like Franciscus, Milton's Adam feels passion as an idiosyncratic "commotion strange", but protests that his love for Eve is neither superficial attraction nor lust but exalted, honorable love for a woman in all ways superior; like Franciscus, who, in Bosco's words, "non riesce, insomma, ad annullare la sua individualità presente e prepotente nel pensiero di Dio" (1965: 71), he dreads the prospect of separation from her by death, nor thinks himself capable of loving another woman, both elements appropriations from Petrarch. Raphael's stern frown concerning Adam's leaning to uxoriousness meets with Adam's challenge to his authority, a contingent argument or, more precisely, process of thought, a rhetoric of contention with authority, and of postponement, which, again, Milton transfers from Petrarch. Adam contradicts the angel and, rather than accepting his heavenly formulation of the matter of Eve, turns the tables on him and obliges him to descend to the discussion of angelic sex. Apart from these item-by-item resemblances, the thrust of Milton's use of the *Secretum* is the accommodation of the Humanist project of remembering to prelapsarian anticipation–an instance of horizontal translation.

The genius of Milton's interpretation of Petrarch is to be seen first in the correspondences between the interlocutors in the *Secretum* and *Paradise Lost* VIII. Like the Lady Truth in the *Secretum*, Eve is a silent auditress; however, she does not represent the test of conscience or the ineluctability of transcendent reality but rather a reductive form of truth, truth rendered conversational, sensory, and pleasurable. The figures of authority, Augustinus and Raphael, are conceived of in attenuated form: Augustinus, as we have observed, as a sort of Roman moralist, not Christian theologian; and Raphael as a messenger who is, in some measure, distracted from his mission and obliged to defer to a mortal's feelings. These weakened figures of authority permit the non-concessions of Franciscus/Adam.

Ultimately the Lady Truth and Eve maintain silence as, respectively, Augustinus and Franciscus, and Raphael and Adam, engage in debate. Petrarch's Lady is a transcendent figure who nevertheless engages Franciscus in conversation; serves to identify his spiritual illness, draw his attention to the presence of Augustinus, and ask that old man in "the clothes of an African provincial" to cure him. While conversation between the Lady Truth and Franciscus is preparation for the therapy of truth, in *Paradise Lost* Eve requires a nearly tactile, derivative form of truth. She is, in some measure, the engine of Adam's curiosity but nevertheless relegates herself to the position of auditress as her husband, in conversation with Raphael, begins to "[enter] on studious thoughts abstruse" (VIII.40). She rises from her seat and withdraws to the sensuous world of "her Fruits and Flow'rs, / To visit how they prosper'd, bud and bloom, / Her Nursery" (VIII.44-46). At the same time, Milton is intent upon establishing that Eve is perfectly capable of delighting in and understanding Raphael and Adam's discourse. However, she prefers truth as intimate conversation in the Miltonic sense, truth mediated by her husband–exclusive, digressive, sensual.

> Yet went she not, as not with such discourse
> Delighted, or not capable her ear
> Of what was high: such pleasure she reserv'd,
> *Adam* relating, she sole Auditress;
> Her Husband the Relater she preferr'd
> Before the Angel, and of him to ask
> Chose rather: hee, she knew, would intermix
> Grateful digressions, and solve high dispute
> With conjugal Caresses, from his lip
> Not Words alone pleas'd her. (VIII.48-57)

Thus while Petrarch's Lady Truth is silent witness to conversation, representing by her very presence the possibility for rectification of, or discriminating judgment upon, that conversation, Milton's Eve chooses momentary silence out of the desire to hear, and feel, the truths imparted by Raphael rendered in conversational form. The intuitive rationality of Raphael must be reduced to discursive; the discursive rationality of Adam must reduce itself to sense. Milton's auditress is a radical variant upon Petrarch's, suggesting a reversion, akin to the initial stage of empirical epistemology, to sense impressions, this when rational conversation in anticipation of Satan's threat is called for.

Petrarch's Augustinus is scarcely the Augustine of the *Confessions* or the *City of God*, arguing as he does that Franciscus's disease (*accidia*) is willed, and that the cure must be willed as well. There is virtually no mention of grace in the *Secretum*, a colossal omission in an Augustinian context. Augustinus offers wisdom that is almost strictly pagan (or, at most, Christian humanist) in derivation, citing Cicero, Virgil, Seneca, *et al.*, but not scripture. He is a secularly ethical, idiosyncratic version of the Church Father. While Carozza and Shey generously regard Petrarch's invention of ostensibly Augustinian dialogue as long-range anticipation of the spirit of Vatican II, and the notions that "secularity [is] not an obstacle to sanctity", and that the layman's "secular duties [have] become the prime matter for personal sanctification" (Petrarca 1989: 4), most commentators regard Augustinus's arguments as tenuously Christian and therefore, in strategic terms, dismissible. The book concludes, in Ugo Dotti's words, in "una nuova ripetizione d'impotenza" (1983: 74)[18].

Milton's Raphael is flawed as well, not so much because he is inclined to ordinary secularism, but because he is distracted to some degree, as heaven's "sociable spirit", from God's instructions, compromised by another sort of secularism, conversation with Adam. God instructs Raphael to speak with Adam "as friend with friend", advising him of "his happy state", of his free will, and of the mutability of that will. He must therefore be warned against sin arising from a false sense of security. Adam is to be advised of "[his] danger, and from whom", and the form that danger will take, "deceit and lies" (V.222-243). This instruction is to prevent any claim of surprise on Adam's part, or protest at not having been warned. Adam's more general curiosity draws Raphael into conversation that sometimes veers in unexpected directions, for Adam is intent "not to let th'occasion pass / Given him by this great Conference to know / Of things above his World" (V.453-455).

Like Augustinus, Raphael must emphasize the freedom of the will. God's charge to the angel on instructing Adam in free will is so reiterative as to take the form of word play: "such discourse bring on, / As may advise him of his happy state, / Happiness in his power left free to will, / Left to his own free Will, his Will though free, / Yet mutable" (V.233-237). From the beginning of his conversation with Adam, Raphael does indeed give prominence to this idea, at first in explanation of obedience, that "our happy state / Hold[s] [...] while our obedience holds; / On other surety none; freely we serve, / Because we freely love, as in our will / To love or not" (V.536-540). However, at this point the Petrarchan application of the doctrine of free will to conflicting forms of love is not evident.

Problems arise in Book VIII when Adam begins to raise questions concerning the apparent disproportion of the cosmos, its great magnitude serving only "to officiate light / Round this opacous Earth" (VIII.22-23). Raphael responds that the universe is meant to be admired, not speculated upon, and is an expression of the "Maker's high magnificence" (VIII.101). The issue of Adam's uxoriousness or susceptibility to glamor is foreshadowed here in Raphael's assertion "that great / Or Bright infers not Excellence" (VIII.90-91). He advises Adam to "joy [...] / In what [God] gives to thee, this Paradise / And thy fair *Eve*" (VIII.170-172). This leads to a great *a proposito* that takes up the rest of the book.

Having heard Raphael's account of the revolt and warfare in heaven and of the creation, Adam now relates his own story (VIII.204 ff.), which begins in Augustinian and Petrarchan fashion with his interrogation of nature with a view to knowing "how came I thus, how here?" (VIII.277)[19], a broad hint that Milton is translating Petrarch. Petrarchan as well is the recollection of Adam, who receiving no answer from nature, observes, "Pensive I sat me down" (VIII.287)[20]. When God does appear to him, Adam complains of loneliness and observes, "with me / I see not who partakes" (VIII.363-364); but God, perhaps facetiously, challenges the notion of man's peculiar loneliness: "Seem I to thee sufficiently possest / Of happiness, or not? who am alone / From all Eternity" (VIII.404-406)? Adam dares to argue with God, who, in his perfection, needs nothing; however, "not so is Man, / But in degree, the cause of his desire / By conversation with his like to help, / Or solace his defects" (VIII.416-419). God reveals that a helpmate had always been part of his plan, and creates Eve, whose beauty, to Adam, exceeds all other beauties and who inspires him with the "spirit of love and amorous delight" (VIII.477). Recalling Franciscus's description of Laura in the *Secretum* (1955: 136), Adam remembers that "Grace was in all her steps, Heav'n in her Eye, / In every gesture dignity and love" (VIII.488-489). Adam thanks God for the gift of Eve, in whom he recognizes "Bone of my Bone, Flesh of my Flesh, my Self / Before me" (VIII.495-496). He leads her, "blushing like the Morn", to the nuptial bower (VIII.510). However, from the recollection of this experience he offers Raphael an idiosyncratic sexual conundrum, and engages in what, to the angel, constitutes erroneous, even pernicious, speculation.

Adam characterizes his love for Eve as a peculiar form of enjoyment, for all other sensory pleasures "[work] in the mind no change, / Nor vehement desire" (VIII.525-526). Eve provokes transport, passion, "commotion strange". From this fact Adam infers his own weakness, insufficiency, indeed, the failure of nature:

> Or Nature fail'd in mee, and left some part
> Not proof enough such Object to sustain,
> Or from my side subducting, took perhaps,
> More than enough; at least on her bestow'd
> Too much of Ornament [...] (VIII.534-538)

While he seems momentarily to concede the inferiority of Eve in God's disposition of things, he cannot help lapsing into a hymn of praise which very nearly confers upon Eve the status of goddess. She is absolute, perfect; her will commands speech and action which are most wise, virtuous, and discreet; she does not serve, but is served by, authority and reason:

> [...] so absolute she seems
> And in herself complete, so well to know
> Her own, that what she wills to do or say,
> Seems wisest, virtuosest, discreetest, best;
> All higher knowledge in her presence falls
> Degraded, Wisdom in discourse with her
> Loses discount'nanc'd, and like folly shows;
> Authority and reason on her wait,
> As one intended first, not after made [...] (VIII.547-555)

Raphael (like Augustinus reproving Franciscus) finds Adam's praise excessive and reminds him that nature is not to be questioned, nor true wisdom dismissed. He accuses Adam of an unseemly attachment to Eve's external beauty, which is worth "Thy cherishing, thy honoring, and thy love, / Not thy subjection" (VIII.569-570). He accuses him, as Augustinus does Franciscus, of misprizing himself: "Oft-times nothing profits more / Than self-esteem" (VIII.571-572). Further, he takes him to be overwhelmed by sex, "the sense of touch whereby mankind / Is propagated" (VIII.579-580), categorizing physical love as a subspecies of one of the five senses, and therefore trivial, a sensation which, in any event, is common "To cattle and each beast". Raphael maintains that "Love refines / The thoughts, and heart enlarges, hath his seat / In Reason, and is judicious, is the scale / By which to heav'nly Love thou may'st ascend, / Not sunk in carnal pleasure" (VIII.589-593). Milton, it will be noted, employs Augustinus's argument in criticism of Adam's uxoriousness[21]; however, the

Platonic route to the spiritual is transferred from Franciscus, who, it will be recalled, declares Laura "responsible for [his] love for God". This shift, given that Adam has actually spoken with and has easy access to God, seems to problematize Raphael's authority somewhat, and set the stage for further compromise.

As Franciscus rejects the argument of Augustinus in the *Secretum*, Adam vehemently rejects the authority of Raphael's judgment in *Paradise Lost*, denying that his love for Eve is infatuation with her beauty, or lust. He posits an experiential basis for his delight at which Raphael, though intuitive, yet engaged in human discourse, and therefore perhaps at a disadvantage, has not guessed: intimate "union of mind" (VIII.604) which derives from "Those thousand decencies that daily flow / From all her words and actions, mixed with love / And sweet compliance" (VIII.601-603)[22]. These verses restate the assertion of Franciscus to the effect that Laura "fostered [in word or gesture] the feeble seeds of virtue in my heart". In much the manner of Franciscus, who weakly accedes to Augustinus's argument, and then postpones its application, Adam repeats Raphael's earlier formulation ("To love thou blam'st me not, for Love thou say'st / Leads up to heav'n") and then distracts him with a curious question: "Bear with me then, if lawful what I ask; / Love not the heav'nly Spirits, and how thir love / Express they, by looks only, or do they mix / Irradiance, virtual or immediate touch?" (VIII.612-617). Raphael seems to blush but nevertheless responds to Adam's curiosity about angelic sex:

> [...] we enjoy
> In eminence, and obstacle find none
> Of membrane, joint, or limb, exclusive bars. (VIII.623-625)

This is perhaps more than we would wish to know; however, the distraction of both the reader and, clearly, Raphael serves to conclude, in the same indeterminate fashion, that rhetorical structure of ambivalence which Milton translates from Petrarch. It will be remembered that Franciscus is finally concerned with "many important matters" that "await my attention". So too, before finally admonishing Adam to "Be strong, live happy, and love" both God and Eve, Raphael interrupts the exigent matter at hand by excusing himself: "I can now no more; the parting Sun / Beyond the Earth's green Cape and verdant Isles / *Hesperian* sets, my Signal to depart" (VIII.630-633). Once again, particularly if we take into account God's charge to Raphael, very little has been accomplished, for though he advises Adam to "stand fast; to stand or fall / Free in thine own Arbitrement it lies" (VIII.640-641), his message has been compromised by his condescending to Adam's triviality, and the lesson concerning the danger in Adam's uxoriousness will not be learned until it is too late.

The Petrarch whom Milton reads is, I think, the sort of figure accurately drawn by Karlheinz Stierle, "the first to live in different worlds and to enjoy the complexity of this experience", adapting the *translatio* of inherited culture to *rinascita*. "The experience of the copresence of cultures", Stierle maintains, "is perhaps the most important aspect of what we call Renaissance. It is the fundamental plurality of Renaissance that is the condition of a new dimension of dialogue. With Petrarch begins the dominance of the horizontal over the vertical axis of *translatio*" (1996: 64-65).

Of the various elements which Milton carries over from the *Secretum* to *Paradise Lost*, none is so significant as the, if you will, horizontal Petrarchan process of thought that leads to the indeterminacy, velleity, and postponement of the conclusion. Milton's culture might have prepared him to attend to Franciscus's setting aside of Augustinus's imperatives for a number of reasons. He might have subjected Petrarch to an "innocent" reading, emphasizing, as a self-defensive tactic, his "displaying sublime and pure thoughts without transgression". After his return from Italy, he would clearly have renewed the conception of Petrarch as "authorized" by his proto-Protestantism. Later in his career, perhaps during the composition of the major poems, he might have apprehended the conclusion of the *Secretum* as expressing a "radical humanist" or antinomian view. That Adam proves to be wrong problematizes *Paradise Lost* as much as Franciscus's indeterminacy does the *Secretum*.

The innocent reading of Petrarch is drawn from the *Apology for Smectymnuus* (April 1642), the last of the anti-prelatical pamphlets Milton wrote on his return from Italy, when he was thirty-three. It might be argued that the praise of Dante and Petrarch for evading transgression betrays a still-youthful idealism in a man who is very nearly *nel mezzo del cammin di sua vita*, and that Milton was not yet prepared to recognize the disingenuous element in the conclusion of the *Secretum*. Thomas Corns (1991: 6) characterizes Milton as jettisoning his adopted Italian humanism "in his republican prose [which, of course, comes a bit later than 1642], where a certain triumphalism displaces [his former] cultural edginess". However, Milton assumes a defensive posture in the *Apology for Smectymnuus* and is intent upon refuting charges of immorality directed against him in *A Modest Confutation* (which he took to be the work of Joseph Hall). He is momentarily concerned with the charge that he had been "vomited out" of the University: his answer takes the form of an account of his, for the most part, literary education; the praise of the "two famous renowners of Beatrice and Laura" constitutes a part of the defense of his youth (1957: 691, 693-694). Though, as he writes, Milton is no longer especially young, in this passage he is *remembering* the *Secretum* he brought with him (but perhaps not literally) to Italy, and his reading of Petrarch is contextualized, in a manner resembling that of the Tuscan poet, by memory of what, he insists, was his virtuous youth.

Well before his departure for Italy, Milton would have been aware of the identification of Petrarch as proto-Protestant. Sixteenth-century Italian commentators on, mainly, the *Canzoniere* had prepared the way for the Protestant construction or authorization of Petrarch. As William J. Kennedy demonstrates in *Authorizing Petrarch* (1994: 72), such commentators as Fausto da Longiano, Antonio Brucioli, and Ludovico Castelvetro took Petrarch's opposition to the Avignon papacy as general criticism of Roman Catholicism, so that

> Petrarch emerges as the model for a new type of secular hero. Practical, independent, and possessed of a deep faith in the divine word and God's promise [...], Petrarch shows the way for highborn Christians of the sixteenth century to prosper in this world without sacrificing their souls to unholy error.

Antonio Brucioli regards Petrarch's Babylonian sonnets (nos. 136-138) as

> fashioned by the poet in abomination of the Roman Church, its foul and wicked customs displeasing him above all, and in sum he reproves and condemns it so forcefully and with such derogatory words, that I would not know how to add more to it. (in Kennedy *ibid*: 75)

Fausto goes so far as to represent the *Secretum* as having a surprised-by-sin structure: as Kennedy expresses the idea, Petrarch "capitalize[s] upon the courtly milieu even while [...] resist[ing] its amatory allure" (*ibid.*: 72). Milton shows himself elsewhere to be conscious of Petrarch's supposed proto-Protestantism, arguing in the *Apology for Smectymnuus* and perhaps "Lycidas" (while alluding to the Petrarchan Babylon in the sonnets), for the abolition of (Anglican) episcopacy upon the basis of Petrarch's objections to the corruption of the Church by its removal to Avignon[23]. This too is a relatively naive reading which, however, gave way, in time, to an even more pronounced ideology.

While the literary evidence suggests that Milton, at the beginning of his Italian sojourn, was a rather conventional, though somewhat antiprelatical, Anglican, he turned to support of the Presbyterian cause, with which he eventually took issue, on his return to England (when he was not quite thirty-one). In much the same manner as, in John K. Hale's words, "Milton abandon[ed] his polyglot excellence" as humanist to compose a peculiarly English idiom (1991: 555), in maturity, including the period during which *Paradise Lost* was presumably composed, he seems to have turned toward a voluntaristic Calvinist antinomianism. In Milton the "antinomian sense of God's goodness [is combined] with the Christian humanist concept of natural law as the embodiment of that goodness" (Bennett 1989: 108). He therefore brought to his reading of the *Secretum* the notion that Franciscus's evading of Augustinus's strictures is tantamount to the transcendence of law, release from religious fear, and the manifestation of moral courage. Of course, when the terms of the Petrarchan debate, especially the conclusion, are transferred to the prelapsarian situation in *Paradise Lost*, the antinomian construction would seem anachronistic, for in Book VIII Adam and Eve have not yet fallen; much less has man been subjected to law or, by God's grace, transcended it. Still, Adam's demurral, which has the effect of occasioning sin (for his uxoriousness is wrong-headed), nevertheless suggests, in humanist terms, his dignity, and disposition to good. For Eve is no goddess, but Adam is not entirely incorrect in his estimate of her. This is the reason for the typological *"Hail"* of Raphael upon meeting her, "the holy salutation us'd / Long after to blest Mary, second *Eve*" (V.385-387). Radical Humanist remembering is transferred to the sphere of anticipation.

Apart from his Protestant theological leanings, it is likely as well that Milton's contacts with the Florentine *accademici* impressed upon him the notion of Petrarch as an authoritative linguistic model (key figure in formulation of the *Vocabolario* and in the *questione della lingua*) whose language is suited to novel constructions. Petrarch might be regarded as beginning to realize that *cortesia*, or open space for conversation, which Dante, in Stierle's view (1996: 63-65), succeeded (especially in the *De Vulgari Eloquentia*) in expressing as a desideratum. Thus Milton employs, in a special sense of the term, Petrarchan neologism, an opening across rather than a derivation down.

There is nevertheless much of the vertical in both works. That Milton reads the *Secretum*, as he does, advisedly, is suggested by the fact that Renaissance editions of the work in Latin (1473, 1517, 1604, 1649) appeared under the title *De Contemptu Mundi*[24], a theme associated with meditation or consolation. Carozza and Shey (Petrarca 1989: 9) identify the *Secretum* as a *consolatio*, a form of literature whose occasion is loss, usually loss caused by death; more generally, the consoler, addressing himself to a friend, may offer "advice to one who is generally depressed, or is unhappy over a specific circumstance", in Franciscus's case the circumstance of *accidia*. This condition is rather remote, and a far cry, from the mourning which Christian *consolatio* (such as Cyprian's *De Mortalitate* or Paulinus of Nola's *Carm. 31*) addressed, especially since *accidia* was associated with the lethargy of a scholar[25]. Nevertheless, while Augustinus offers *consolatio*, Franciscus engages in *confessio*: the assumption is that the former will resolve the issues of the latter. However, in Petrarch confession becomes assertion and ignores the imperatives of the consolatory argument. Significantly, Milton chooses the contingent argument as well, though he may still have the subgeneric classification of the *Secretum* in mind in Raphael's charge (V.229-245), in the persona he adopts, that of "sociable spirit" (V.219-21), and in the admonitions in Book VIII of *Paradise Lost,* which might constitute proleptic consolation.

Indeed, Milton translates the indeterminate conclusion of the *Secretum* in such a way as to accommodate the Humanist project of remembering to anticipation. Just as the *Secretum* "might be seen as Augustinus's attempt to get Franciscus to remember himself (his sins and the possibility of salvation) and to forget others (Laura and the reading public)" (Kahn 1985: 158), so might *Paradise Lost* V-VIII be considered Raphael's attempt to get Adam to remember himself (his disposition and the possibility of ruin) and set aside both speculation concerning the universe, and uxoriousness. The latter instruction is, however, not strictly tied to remembering but refers to the present and anticipates crisis (the fall). The transpositional terms of Milton's translation are not strictly spatial but temporal. Moreover, Adam's "reading" of Raphael's discourse is blocked, as Kahn (*ibid.*: 163) comments concerning the conclusion of the *Secretum*, "the moment of conversion [...] deferred by the act of writing itself", that is, Adam's "writing" of Eve.

Quillen's reading of the "irresolute conclusion of the *Secretum* simply as an expression of Petrarch's ambivalence about the kind of [exemplary] reading demanded by Augustinus" is useful as well in commenting upon Milton's reading of Petrarch. For Augustinus's and Raphael's instructions are forms of exemplarity that seem inefficacious when one considers that "the *Secretum* graphically constructs a space in which the 'best minds,' the *auctores*, can transcend historical circumstances to converse in a language that is also timeless", that it "assumes a humanist tradition defined by perennial questions about the human condition and comprised of authoritative writings on these questions, writings whose authority derives from their ability to speak across time and space", and yet that the

> *Secretum* resists implication in the very tradition it authorizes, by figuring writing, the medium of that tradition, as a costly activity, [severing] an author from historical circumstances [and] from himself. In other words, the cost of engaging the humanist tradition is a kind of perpetual self-alienation that persists even as it is refigured, within the terms of humanist discourse, as transcendence and self-fulfillment. (1998: 208-209)

The terms of this argument in Milton involve a more transcendent exemplarity, and the division occasioned by Adam's writing of Eve is more serious. In postponing the taking-to-heart of Augustinus's wisdom, derived from the *auctores*, Franciscus turns to his writing, which will (as Augustinus claims it has done in the past) continue to alienate him from himself and from authority. Milton's version of Petrarch's formulation has Adam momentarily rejecting Raphael's authority: this results in his being alienated, in undervaluing his sufficiency, from himself, and from his feminine "self", Eve. Before that happens, he seems, in Book VIII, to emerge from his debate with Raphael in a spirit of "transcendence and self-fulfillment". Shortly thereafter he falls[26].

Though Franciscus's demurral at the end of the *Secretum* may seem an almost comic *non sequitur*, it is still possible to argue, as Mazzotta does, that Petrarch intends resolution by a new medium of thought, the imagination (necessarily material in orientation), and that, after all, Franciscus carries the day:

> By interlocking love and thinking as complementary terms, Petrarch puts into relief the force of thought. Thought as an event, necessarily figured by material facts, is not a substance or an accident or a process, but it occurs in the imaginary. To say it differently, it is poetry, which for Petrarch can only be poetry of love, that makes thinking once again possible: love does violence to the mind and forces the lover to reflection; poetry's obliqueness submits the clarity of the philosophical discourse to the interrogation by the shadows of the imagination. (1993: 57)

There is something intellectually efficacious, then, in what might otherwise be considered poetic distraction. This notion might even be considered as tangentially related to the moral judgment expressed by Milton in *Areopagitica* whereby virtue is embodied in literature rather than philosophy:

> That virtue therefore which is but a youngling in the contemplation of evil, and knows not the utmost that vice promises to her followers, and rejects it, is but a blank virtue, not a pure; her whiteness is but an excremental whiteness; which was the reason why our sage and serious poet Spenser, whom I dare be known to think a better teacher than a Scotus or Aquinas, describing true temperance under the person of Guyon, brings him in with his palmer through the cave of Mammon and the bower of earthly bliss, that he might see and know, and yet abstain. (1957: 728-729)

The first and the last of the humanists would seem, as expected, to assert the notion that rhetoric has supplanted philosophy and indeed constitutes a better medium of thought. While Milton, in the act of writing the poem, transfers this idea to *Paradise Lost*, its bearing upon Adam's contention with Raphael in Book VIII is dubious. For Adam's poetic-love judgment of Eve, in its contingency borrowed from the horizontality of Petrarch's *rinascita*, is ultimately fallacious when it encounters sin, a vertical *translatio* initiated by the Fall[27].

---

[1] The Latinate sense of *translate* is "carried across"; of *transfer* is "carry across"; of *explain* is something like "draw out flat"; of *explicate* is "unfold"; of *construe* is "pile up together"; of *represent* is "bring back before one". One of the Indo-European roots of *interpret* (*per*) has the sense "hand over".

[2] Kennedy has the following:

> A hundred years after Petrarch's death his *Rime sparse* emerged in early printed editions accompanied by sometimes elaborate commentaries, annotations, and glosses on the text that modified their reception throughout the sixteenth century. These commentaries play an important role in bringing to Europe a succession of variously localized, highly particularized versions of Petrarchan poetry. As the commentators represent the *Rime sparse* in the image of their own regional or ideological identities, they construct a series of different Petrarchs that challenge the notion of universal model. Each of these versions of Petrarch dramatizes a conflict between large social issues and narrow homegrown claims, and such conflicts come to define specific sites of Petrarchism throughout Europe. Not the least of them concerns the poet's choice of language. Petrarch's odd vernacular is a wholly artificial composite of Old Tuscan, literary Sicilian, some Provençalisms, and classical Latinisms–a language that was spoken nowhere in Italy but that came to be imitated everywhere in Italy and in poetic styles of Spanish, Portuguese, French, English, high and low German, and every vernacular that attempted its own form of national Petrarchism. These very styles, replete with echoes of earlier native poetry, indigenous cultural forms, local accents, historical allusions, topographical references, and other situational specifics, rub against Petrarch's composite model. The resulting friction affords a palimpsest of social change, cultural adjustment, and political development, with attendant conflicts and tensions and outright contradictions enacted in them. (2001: 2-3)

[3] Milton might actually have been admitted to the Svogliati. See Haan (1998: 12-22). Haan shows that Milton had visited the Apatisti as well and might even have adopted, as was their custom, an anagrammatic name (*ibid.*: 35-37). (Perhaps *Invito Longanime?*) Rovai's lectures on Petrarch at the Svogliati were particularly acclaimed; however, Malatesti had read a lecture on Petrarch, and Dati corresponded with Milton on Petrarch in connection with Chiabrera (*ibid.*: 1-72). Contact with members of the Accademia della Crusca, of whom Buonmattei was most prominent among Milton's acquaintances, would most likely lead to discussion of Petrarch, given the importance of his language to the establishment of the linguistic standard of the *Vocabolario*.

[4] "Ipse etiam tentare ausus sum, nec puto multum / Displicui" (1957: 136). Unless otherwise specified, all quotations from Milton will be from the Hughes edition.

[5] See Haan's comments upon Manso's implied criticism of Milton's religious shortcomings (1998: 130-136).

[6] Concerning Coltellini as censor, see my *Glad to Go for a Feast* (1998: 44-49). For Malatesti's sonnets see del Romano's edition (1946); Donald Sears's translation and notes (1979: 275-317) are helpful.

[7] Quod cum ita sit, passionum expertarum curator optime, tametsi rerum omnium iocundissima sit taciturna meditatio, silentium tamen istud, ut sacra et michi singulariter accepta voce discutias oro, tentans si qua ope languores tam graves emollire queas (1955: 24, 26).

[8] Quanquam vel multa nosse quid relevat si, cum celi terreque ambitum, si, cum maris spatium et astrorum cursus herbarumque virtutes ac lapidum et nature secreta didiceritis, vobis estis incogniti? (1955: 72). The argument of Augustinus resembles that of the dramatic conclusion of the letter popularly known as "The Ascent of Mont Ventoux".

[9] Se infamem turpemque mulierem ardeo, insanissimus ardor est; si rarum aliquod specimen virtutis allicit inque illud amandum venerandumque multus sum, quid putas? Nullum ne tam diversis in rebus statuis discrimen? Adeo ne pudor omnis evanuit? Ego vero, ut ex me aliquid loquar, sicut primum grave et infaustum animi pondus extimo, sic secundo vix quicquam reor esse felicius. (1955: 132, 134)

[10] De muliere mortali sermo nobis instituitur, in qua admiranda colendaque te magnam etatis partem consumpsisse doleo; et in tali ingenio tantam et tam longevam insaniam vehementer admiror.

Fr. Parce convitiis, precor; mulier mortalis erat et Thais et Livia. Ceterum scis ne de ea muliere mentionem tibi exortam, cuius mens terrenarum nescia curarum celestibus desideriis ardet; in cuius aspectu, siquid usquam veri est, divini specimen decoris effulget; cuius mores consumate honestatis exemplar sunt; cuius nec vox nec oculorum vigor mortale aliquid nec incessus hominem representat? Hoc, queso, iterum atque iterum cogita: credo quibus verbis utendum sit intelliges. (1955: 136)

[11] [...] neque enim, ut tu putas, mortali rei animum addixi; nec me tam corpus noveris amasse quam animam, moribus humana transcendentibus delectatum, quorum exemplo qualiter inter celicolas vivatur, admoneor. Itaque si–quod solo torquet auditu–me prior moriens illa desereret, quid agerem interrogas? Cum Lelio, romanorum sapientissimo, proprias miserias consolarer: Virtutem illius amavi, que extincta non est [...]
Si enim amoris in me regnantis facies cerni posset, eius vultui, quam licet multum tamen debito parcius laudavi, non absimilis videretur. Hec michi, coram qua loquimur, testis est, quod in amore meo nichil unquam turpe, nichil obscenum fuerit, nichil denique, preter magnitudinem, culpabile. Adice modum; nichil pulcirius excogitari queat. (1955: 140, 142)

[12] Tu vero qui tantum dilecte tribuis, non advertis, illam absolvendo, quantum te ipse condemnes? Illam fateri libet fuisse sanctissimam, dum te insanum scelestumque fateare; illam quoque felicissimam, dum te eius amore miserrimum (1955: 154).

[13] Hoc igitur unum scito, me aliud amare non posse. Assuevit animus illam admirari; assueverunt oculi illam intueri, et quicquid non illa est, imanenum et tenebrosum ducunt (1955: 162).

[14] Haud equidem destituo; sed fortasse differo (1955: 196).

[15] Itaque istum esse ordinem, ut mortalium rerum inter mortales prima sit cura; transitoriis eterna succedant, quod ex his ad illa sit ordinatissimus progressus. Inde autem pregressus ad ista non pateat (1955: 198).

[16] Stultissime homuncio! (1955: 200).

[17] Adero michi ipse quantum potero, et sparsa anime fragmenta recolligam, moraborque mecum sedulo. Sane nunc, dum loquimur, multa me magnaque, quamvis adhuc mortalia, negotia expectant (1955: 214). There is an interesting interplay, upon the literal and nearly homonymic levels, among *Paradise Lost* VIII, Genesis 2.24, and the *Secretum*. Milton's Adam, deliriously happy at God's having created Eve before the eyes of his imagination, cannot suppress this speech:

> This turn hath made amends; thou hast fulfull'd
> Thy words, Creator bounteous and benign,
> Giver of all things fair, but fairest this
> Of all thy gifts, nor enviest. I now see
> Bone of my Bone, Flesh of my Flesh, my Self
> Before me; Woman is her Name, of Man
> Extracted; for this cause he shall forgo
> Father and Mother, and to his Wife adhere;
> And they shall be one Flesh, one Heart, one Soul. (491-499)

In Milton's version of this text from Genesis 2.24 ("Therefore shall a man leave his father and his mother, and shall cleave unto his wife: and they shall be one flesh"), the Hebraic term דבק, or *davaq*, usually translated as "join" or "cleave", is rendered, as in the Vulgate, *quam ob rem relinquet homo patrem suum et matrem et adherebit uxori suae et erunt duo in carne una*, as "to his wife *adhere*". Milton adds the significant notion, especially in a Petrarchan context, of Eve perceived as "my self / Before me". The suggestion that Milton may be translating Genesis through Petrarch might be sought in Franciscus's assertion, toward the end of the *Secretum*, that he intends to serve both Augustinus and Lady Truth: "But now, since you two dwell in heaven and I must abide on earth and, as you see, am upset not knowing for how long, please do not desert me, though we be far apart. Without you, best of fathers, my life would be dreary; without her there would be no life at all" (1989: 144). Augustinus admonishes Franciscus to be true to himself: "Otherwise you will be justly deserted by everyone". Then comes this ostensible expression of resolve (*Adero michi*, etc.) which is the capping, problematic velleity in Franciscus's argument, for while it promises integrity it morphs into distraction and therefore has the effect of dismissing Augustinus's admonitions by means of postponement. Carozza and Shey translate *Adero michi ipse quantum potero* as "I shall be true to myself as I can". (Enrico Carrara translates the same clause, "Sarò presente a me stesso quanto potrò".) The literal sense of the Latin cognate *fragmenta recolligam* is that of the reconnecting or recollecting of the fragmented self in an effort at integrity. A semantic relation between the two notions might be suggested, apart from the common concern in the Petrarchan and Miltonic texts with integrity, by the nearly homonymic resemblance *Adero michi/adherebit uxori suae*. Indeed the notion *adero michi*, which is more literally translated by the Italian "Sarò presente a me stesso" (literally, "I shall be present to myself", or in more idiomatic French, "J'aurai l'esprit lucide") is closely related to one of the secondary meanings of *davaq*, "to set in order". Thus Petrarch is translated in more than one sense: as Franciscus had sought to recollect the *sparsa anime fragmenta* of the self, so the principal task of Adam is, in a word translated from the Vulgate, to *adhere* to his cloven self. The reintegration of Franciscus's self involves, in part, adherence to the feminine figure of Truth, "without [whom] there would be no life at all". Milton's Eve corresponds to Petrarch's silent auditress Truth; however, her silence is predicated upon her preference for Adam's intimate translation of Raphael, so that the adherence to the truth represented by Eve is a cleaving to a now-divided fragment of the self. While Petrarch's Franciscus, observed by the Lady Truth, postpones his return to Augustinus and the Lady until he has, presumably, personally exhausted the possibilities of love and glory, Milton's Adam realizes truth by translating Raphael's data into intimate conversation with Eve, which has the effect of obfuscating a larger truth. Though Milton's Adam's identification with Eve, in the imagery drawn from Genesis, seems almost literally physical (bone, flesh, heart), he feels the need, as (literal) embodiment of their one soul, to adhere to his wife. In the emphasis upon wife as self, and the use of the term *adhere*, the passage may be an adaptation of both Genesis to Petrarch, and Petrarch to Milton.

[18] Here is a more ample representation of Dotti's observation:

> Scrivendo il *Secretum* Petrarca sa [...] che il libro dovrà chiudersi con una nuova ripetizione d'impotenza [...]. Ma qui nel *Secretum*, proprio rispetto ai modelli, una novità c'è, notevolissima: la mancanza di una conclusione, l'assenza di una risoluzione e la reale accettazione di uno stato di profonda incertezza e fluttuazione come condizione dell'uomo e come reale effettiva esperienza, anche storica. (Dotti 1983: 74)

Baron's final judgment is that "the *Secretum* is more fruitfully read not primarily as a piece of literary art but as a book of intimate confessions, in which humanism not only fuses but disaccords with Petrarch's medieval legacy" (1985: 248).

[19] See *Confessions* X.9: "And what is this? I asked the earth, and it answered me, 'I am not He'", etc. See also Petrarch's Canzone 126: "Qui come venn'io, o quando?" (62).

[20] See Petrarch's Sonnet 35: "Solo et pensoso I piú deserti campi". Canzone 129, "Di pensier in pensier", might be relevant, as well as Canzone 264, "I' vo pensando". Milton's attraction to the Petrarchan element *pensive* is suggested early on in his coinage *penseroso*.

[21] Augustinus's reproof is echoed in Petrarch's *De remediis utriusque fortune* in I.66 and II.18. See "A Beautiful Wife" and "Loss of a Wife" (1991: vol. 1, 192-194 and vol. 3, 62-64).

[22] This line very likely derives in part from Benedetto Buonmattei's discussion of gestural language, or *segni particolari*, in *Della Lingua Toscana*. See Cinquemani (1998: 92).

[23] Castelvetro's attention to biblical subtexts in Petrarch may suggest his proto-Protestantism as well. For example, in glossing Petrarch's famous canzone 126 ("Chiare fresche & dolci acque"), he relates the verse "Allhor pien di spauento" to the fear a man feels "quando [...] vede cosa diuina", and sees a parallel "Nell'euangelio [dove] dice Pietro [,] spauentato, *Exi à me [quia homo peccator sum] Domine*. Luc. 5.8". He is preoccupied with bad priests as well, evidently not limiting himself to those who occupied synagogues: "Vero è, che Christo disse queste parole d'vn altra maniera di ladroni, cioè, de sacerdoti, che sotto spetie di religione tendeuano insidie nelle loro sinagoghe e semplici per rubargli" (Commentary on Matt. 21.13 and "Il successor di Carlo", 114). See also Cinquemani (1991: 67-77).

[24] *Secretum de contemptu mundi* (Strasbourg: Rusch, <1473); *Francisci Petrarce De conte[m]ptu mu[n]di, q[uo]d Secretum inscribitur* (Siena: Simeone di Niccolo, 1517); *De contemptu mundi, colloquiorum liber, quem Secretum suum inscripsit* (Bernae: Ionnes le Preux, 1604); *Francisci Petrarchae Poëtae Oratorisque clarissimi, De remediis utriusque Fortunae, libri duo: ejusdem De contemptu mundi colloquiorum liber, quem secretum suum inscripsit* (Roterodami: Arnoldi Leers, 1649).

[25] "Originally *acedia* was the monk's inability to make spiritual progress, but Petrarch has in mind the disorders of the layman", observes Charles Trinkaus (1979: 65). See also Gregg:

> We might isolate [...] the persistent attention to man as one at the mercy of event–he is the one buffeted by fate. Here several kinds of motifs come into play. Man experiences τὰ ἀνδρόπινα as cruel frustrations–all that fills existence from birth to death is disappointed hope, and the inevitable movement towards decay and extinction. (1975: 46)

On the more general character of Latin consolation, see Favez:

> [...] la consolation est, sans doute, pour les auteurs chrétiens comme pour leurs prédécesseurs païens, un moyen d'apporter du réconfort à des coeurs qui souffrent. Mais ce n'est pas là le seul but qu'ils lui assignent: il saisissent, toutes les fois qu'ils le

peuvent, les occasions qu'elle leur offre de glorifier Dieu, de développer chez leurs lecteurs la vie chrétienne et de les instruire des vérités bibliques. Eloge des vertus évangéliques, exhortation, exégèse, enseignement théologique: voilà ce que devient très souvent chez eux la consolation. (1937: 89)

For Cyprian and Paulinus's Christian consolations, see Quacquarelli (1992: 191-192). Haan reads one of Dati's letters to Milton as *consolatio* regarding, among other things, his domestic troubles (1998: 75-79).

[26] The argument of Paul Allen Miller concerning the *Secretum* is equally applicable to *Paradise Lost*:

> Petrarch responds that, while what Augustinus says may be true in principle–that he loved Laura first for her body, and that in doing so he has perverted the divine semiotic order by placing the signifier before the signified, and the creature before the creator–all the same, Petrarch argues, human beings achieve knowledge through the senses and so must rise from the material to the spiritual. [...]
> This argument is analogous to the whole humanist problematic. The meaning of the text can only be established through an understanding of its historical and material specificity, through the evidence gathered by our perceptions. This is what makes the recovery of antiquity possible. But, to base our readings on our perceptions of the text's historical determinations is ultimately to deny the presence of a divine logos, in the Platonic sense, that anchors and guarantees all meaning. (1997: 148, 149)

[27] I do not mean to express the exaggerated view of Ilona Bell (1992: 91-120) that Petrarchism is identifiable with satanism in *Paradise Lost*. She maintains, agreeing with her feminist colleague Lynn Enterline, that the issue in Book VIII is that Adam is "in great danger of becoming a Petrarchan lover". "In exalting Eve's beauty and virtue", writes Bell, "Adam devalues himself–thus laying the foundation for the posture of the abject, embittered Petrarchan lover that he will assume temporarily after the Fall". Adam and Eve finally avoid the deleterious effects of Petrarchism through conversation–Protestant conversation, as opposed to Catholic imagery–Milton (Bell argues) *preferring sound to light*!

References

Baron, Hans. 1985. *Petrarch's Secretum: Its Making and Its Meaning*. Cambridge, MA: Medieval Academy of America.
Bell, Ilona. 1992. 'Milton's Dialogue with Petrarch' in *Milton Studies*. 28 (1992): 91-120.
Benet, Diana Treviño. 1991. 'The Escape from Rome: Milton's Second Defense and a Renaissance Genre' in Mario A. Di Cesare (ed.) *Milton in Italy: Contexts, Images, Contradictions*. Binghamton, NY: Medieval and Renaissance Texts and Studies. 29-49.
Bennett, Joan. 1989. *Reviving Liberty: Radical Christian Humanism in Milton's Great Poems*. Cambridge, MA: Harvard University Press.
Bosco, Umberto. 1965. *Francesco Petrarca*. Bari: Laterza.
Cinquemani, Anthony M. 1998. *Glad to Go for a Feast: Milton, Buonmattei, and the Florentine Accademici*. New York, NY: Peter Lang.
–. 1991. 'Papal Burgundy, Petrarchan Invective, and Milton's *Apology for Smectymnuus*' in Antonio Toscano (ed.) *Interpreting the Italian Renaissance: Literary Perspectives*. Stonybrook, NY: Forum Italicum. 67-77.
Corns, Thomas N. 1991. 'John Milton: Italianate Humanist, Northern European Protestant, Englishman' in Mario A. Di Cesare (ed.) *Milton in Italy: Contexts, Images, Contradictions*. Binghamton, NY: Medieval and Renaissance Texts and Studies. 1-7.
Dotti, Ugo. 1983. 'Miti e forme dell' 'io' nella cultura di Francesco Petrarca: dal *Secretum* all'epistolario e alle *Rime* in *Revue des Etudes Italiennes* 29 (1-3): 74-85.

Anthony M. Cinquemani

Favez, Charles. 1937. *La Consolation Latine Chrétienne*. Paris: Vrin.

Gregg, Robert C. 1975. *Consolation Philosophy: Greek and Christian Paideia in Basil and the Two Gregories*. Philadelphia, PA: Patristic Foundation.

Haan, Estelle. 1998. *From Academia to Amicitia: Milton's Latin Writings and the Italian Academies*. Philadelphia, PA: American Philosophical Society.

Hale, John K. 1991. 'The Multilingual Milton and the Italian Journey' in Mario A. Di Cesare (ed.) *Milton in Italy: Contexts, Images, Contradictions*. Binghamton, NY: Medieval and Renaissance Texts and Studies. 549-572.

Kahn, Victoria. 1985. 'The Figure of the Reader in Petrarch's *Secretum*' in *PMLA* 100 (2): 154-166.

Kennedy, William J. 1994. *Authorizing Petrarch*. Ithaca, NY: Cornell University Press.

–. 2001. *Totems for Defence and Illustration of Taboo: Sites of Petrarchism in Renaissance Europe*. Binghamton, NY: Center for Medieval & Renaissance Studies.

Malatesti, Antonio. 1946. *La Tina equivoci rusticali: in cinquanta sonetti*. Londra: Luigi del Romano.

Mazzotta, Giuseppe. 1993. *The Worlds of Petrarch*. Durham, NC: Duke University Press.

Miller, Paul Allen. 1997. 'Laurel as the Sign of Sin: Laura's Textual Body in Petrarch's *Secretum*' in Barbara K. Gold *et al.* (eds) *Sex and Gender in Medieval and Renaissance Texts*. Abany, NY: State University of New York Press. 139-163.

Milton, John. 1957. *Complete Poems and Major Prose* (ed. Merritt Y. Hughes). New York, NY: The Odyssey Press, Inc.

–. 1931-1938. *The Works of John Milton [Columbia Milton]* (ed. Frank Allan Patterson). 18 vols. New York, NY: Columbia University Press.

–. 1966. *The Life Records of John Milton* (ed. J. Milton French). 5 vols. New York, NY: Gordian Press.

Petrarca, Francesco. 1532. *Il Petrarcha* (ed. Fausto da Longiano). Vinegia: Pasini.

–. 1548. *Sonetti, Canzoni, et Trionfi di M. Francesco Petrarca* (ed. Antonio Brucioli). Venezia.

–. 1582. *Le rime del Petrarca* (ed. Ludovico Castelvetro). Basilea: Sedabonis.

–. 1955. *Prose* (eds. Guido Martellotti, Pier Giorgio Ricci, Enrico Carrara, and Enrico Bianchi). Milano and Napoli: Ricciardi.

–. 1981. *Il mio segreto* (ed. Ugo Dotti). Milano: Rizzoli.

–. 1989. *Petrarch's Secretum with Introduction, Notes, and Critical Anthology* (tr. Davy A. Carozza and H. James Shey). New York, NY: Lang.

–. 1991. *Remedies for Fortune Fair and Foul*. (tr. Conrad H. Rawski). 5 vols. Bloomington, IN: Indiana University Press.

Quacquarelli, A. 1992. 'Consolatio' in *Encyclopedia of the Early Church*. Vol. I. New York, NY: Oxford University Press. 191-192.

Quillen, Carol E. 1998. *Rereading the Renaissance: Petrarch, Augustine, and the Language of Humanism*. Ann Arbor, MI: University of Michigan Press.

Sears, Donald. 1979. '*La Tina*: The Country Sonnets of Antonio Malatesti as Dedicated to Mr. John Milton, English Gentleman' in *Milton Studies* 13: 275-317.

Stierle, Karlheinz. 1996. 'Translatio Studii and Renaissance: From Vertical to Horizontal Translation' in Stanford Budick and Wolfgang Iser (eds) *The Translatability of Cultures: Figurations of the Space Between*. Stanford, CA: Stanford University Press. 55-67.

Trinkaus, Charles. 1979. *The Poet as Philosopher: Petrarch and the Formation of Renaissance Consciousness*. New Haven, CT: Yale University Press.

Section II

The English in Italy and Spain

2.1. Writing and Lying: William Thomas and the Politics of Translation

Joseph Khoury

Translation is an art whose purpose is often abused, made to suit the political self-interests of the translator. One of the first English Italophiles was Edward VI's tutor, William Thomas, who surmised that Italian political thought, especially as he had learned it from Machiavelli's writings, might be helpful for bringing about political change in England. In the discourses he wrote for Edward, Thomas actually translated Machiavelli in such a manner as to transfer the Italian's precepts to an English ethos, but in the transpositions he made, Thomas eliminated the theological references from his original. Thomas was the first Englishman to translate the Florentine, and was also the first Englishman to argue that English, not Latin, ought to be the language of education in England, another lesson, arguably, that he learned from Machiavelli.
Keywords: Edward VI, Italy, lying, Machiavelli, translation, travel, William Thomas.

Gaveston:	What art thou?
Second Poor Man:	A traveller.
Gaveston:	Let me see; thou wouldst do well

To wait at my trencher and tell me lies at dinnertime,
And as I like your discoursing, I'll have you. (*Edward II* 1.1.29-32)

2.1.1. Introduction: *Traduttore, traditore*

As an art, translation is often shunned, relegated to the *grey* corners of scholarship. It is an art whose purpose, we are often told, is to allow us to understand but a part–perhaps only the surface meaning–of the source text. Ironically, we know what we know largely through translations, whether from the source language into the target language, or from the source's antiquated language into a modern form of the same language. We often forget that even modernized punctuation is in fact an alteration of the "original" text. In fact, one must finally admit that there is only translation or, to use Roman Jakobson's language, that translation can exist only as "creative transposition" (1987: 434). It is this "creative transposition" that finished off the French humanist Etienne Dolet (1509-1546), who in 1540 wrote a seminal pamphlet on the principles of translation entitled *La manière de bien traduire d'une langue en aultre*, and was tried and executed for heresy after mistranslating one of Plato's dialogues: the translation had implied–or so it was argued–that immortality was a myth. Translation, especially of controversial works, exists only as a tug of war between two opposing views of the source text because while the translator is esteeming his source, he is also betraying it. This betrayal, however, goes beyond language, and reaches the level of both covert and overt betrayal of ideas. One's level of covertness depends on the material one is translating and on the circumstances in which the translator finds himself. True translation is a betrayal of "the letter in order to be loyal to the meaning art, and spirit of the source text" (Barnstone 1993: 260), but politically motivated translation, what we might call lying, is sometimes a betrayal of the letter *and* spirit of the text, a betrayal, however, which nevertheless captures the essential meaning, albeit in a conveniently selective way. For the politically motivated translation must often suppress part of the source text, at times even the very presence of it, in order to achieve the desired political end. William Thomas (1507-1554), King Edward VI's tutor, provides us with an illustrative example.

2.1.2. Traveler, Translator, Tutor

Only a few modern scholars remember William Thomas. He was a Welshman, probably Oxford educated, who became clerk of the peace in several Welsh counties, and then, after the dissolution of the monastic orders in England, received some grants of monastic property[1]. In 1545, he fled to Venice with money he had embezzled from his Catholic patron, Sir Anthony Browne. Under orders from the Privy Council, Thomas was arrested upon his arrival in Venice, imprisoned, and ordered to repay the money. His penitence earned him an official pardon, but the gambler-cum-traveler decided to remain in Italy for three more years, studying its language and literature.

After Browne's death in 1548, Thomas returned to England, where he clearly had some admirers. His studies led to the publication in 1549 of the first English book on Italy, *The Historie of Italy* (probably written in 1548), which he dedicated to the Earl of Warwick, and in 1550 he published the *Principal Rules of the Italian Grammar*, the first Italian grammar for Englishmen. His panegyric for Henry VIII, *The Pilgrim*, was written in 1546, and translated into Italian in 1552 as *Il pellegrino Inglese*. Thomas was then made Clerk of the Privy Council in 1550 and became rather friendly with the young King Edward VI. Secretly, Thomas wrote discourses for the monarch in which he purported to tell him all he knew about the political arts. Unfortunately for Thomas, Edward died in mid-1553, and the newly ascended Queen Mary proceeded to execute Thomas's new patron, the Duke of Northumberland. The following year, Thomas was accused of conspiring in Wyatt's rebellion against the Spanish marriage, and even of planning to assassinate Mary. His stance against the marriage was genuine, but the evidence supporting his involvement in the murder plot is disputable. In any case, Thomas was charged with treason, and, on May 18, after an unsuccessful attempt at suicide, he was hanged and quartered, and the following day his head was set on London Bridge. In 1563, Elizabeth restored his blood line, but not his land.

This man of literary firsts is important for several reasons. He was a fervent Protestant, maniacally opposed to the Papacy, and yet enamored of Italy. He was impressed not only by Italy's political realities, such as the proverbial liberty of Venice, but also by the pageantry of the papal procession. As a Protestant, Thomas was able to appreciate Italy because, as Kenneth Bartlett says, he held ancient Rome in higher esteem than Christian Rome: his perspective was had through his acceptance of secular history (1998: 247). Thomas was a "social observer", as Parks calls him (1963: xxv), but of a practical kind: his main interest was in learning from Italy whatever he might use in his attempt to bring about a change in his own homeland.

That Thomas in his *Historie* does not talk much of the Italian scenery nor of its art, famous as it was, is not surprising because he was interested very largely in politics, for the political concerns of travelers at the time were almost universal (Parks 1951: 265). Adair astutely observes that Thomas "was really an early apologist for the Tudor ideals of government"; in order to formulate these, Thomas and other contemporary theorists had used Machiavellian thinking (1924: 155). In his *Historie*, Thomas declares his use of Machiavelli openly:

> Conferring the discourse of divers authors together touching the Florentine histories and finding the effects of them all gathered in one by Niccolo Machiavelli, a notable learned man and secretary of late days to the commonwealth there, I determined to take him for mine only author in that behalf. (1963: 98)

More important for our purposes are Thomas's secret *Discourses* to Edward, which the young king desired and commanded Thomas to write, one a week. Thomas happily complied, adding that Edward "may utter these matters as of your own study; wherby it shal have the greater credit with your council" (1822: vol. 2, 389-390). The king had not sought Thomas out; it was Thomas, rather, who had sent the king a letter in which he proposed himself as political tutor, well-versed in the most important matters of state. Thomas seemed to accept wholeheartedly the foundation that Machiavelli had established for his political philosophy, that is, that the primary business of the prince was to *maintain* his state. To the king, Thomas wrote that

> since your Highness is by the providence of God already grown to the administration of that great and famous charge, that hath been left unto you by your most noble progenitors; there is no earthly thing more necessary than the knowledge of such examples, as in this and other regiments heretofore have happened: methinks, of my bounden duty, I could no less do, than present unto your Majesty the notes of those discourses, that are now my principal study, which I have gathered out of divers authors. . . [whose main purpose] concerneth the chief maintenance of your high estate, and preservation of your commonwealth. (1822: vol. 2, 157)

The letter is nearly a word-for-word translation of Machiavelli's dedicatory letter to *Il Principe*, written to Lorenzo de Medici. The eighty-five headings attached to the letter are actually taken from Machiavelli's own *Discorsi*. Thomas of course did not want to admit to the single author he had in mind–the Secretary–and so pluralized his "source", making it "divers authors". A study of the headings reveals the specific Machiavellian borrowings Thomas made, but this is not my concern here[2].

What I should like to comment upon, rather, is how Thomas translated Machiavelli's political philosophy, how he transferred the Italian precepts to an English ethos–the first Englishman to do so[3]. Raab sees Thomas's political thinking as dichotomous. The Englishman, he argues, "was still involved in the more orthodox concept of an Augustinian universe, with its theoretical unity of politics and theology" and did not attempt to separate the two realms, but "the surprising element in his thought", says Raab, "is precisely the element of dichotomy–the degree to which he managed to keep the two apart" (1964: 48). And keep them apart he did; for like Machiavelli (*Discorsi* 1.11-15), he saw that the one required the use of the other, that is, that religion may be functional and therefore interpreted as political necessity dictates. This seems to be Thomas's keenest understanding of Machiavelli, the core of his adaptation of the Italian's philosophy to English politics. The only difference between the two men's understanding of kingship is that Thomas still accepted as a matter of fact God's place in politics, whereas Machiavelli did not. In *The Vanitee* and in the dedicatory letter, Thomas is clear that some people are divinely ordained to rule, and that it is their duty to fulfill this ordination. Machiavelli, on the other hand, replaced the concept of divine ordination with personal charisma, cunning, and deception[4]. If Thomas and Machiavelli disagreed on the question of *how* one is selected to climb the ladder to power, they nevertheless did seem to agree on the mode of using and maintaining that power, even regarding the use of religion to that end. Here, on this subject, is Thomas himself:

> For *religion*, it is necessary the princes that will observe amity be of one opinion: otherwise it is impossible the amity should longer continue than necessity compelleth th'one or th'other to maintain it. For where are contrary opinions of religion, there can be no long agreement. And there is no prince nor private man so simple, as, if it lay in his power, would not compel the whole world to believe as he doth. (1822: vol. 2, 381)

Thomas was actually speaking about the appearance of being religious, as Machiavelli does in the infamous eighteenth chapter of *Il Principe*. Closer to this theme, however, is a statement from Book I.12 of Machiavelli's *Discorsi*:

> The rulers of a republic or of a kingdom, therefore, should uphold the basic principles of the religion which they practise in, and, if this be done, it will be easy for them to keep their commonwealth religious, and, in consequence, good and united. They should also foster and encourage everything likely to be of help to this end, even though they be convinced that it is quite fallacious. And the more should they do this the greater their prudence and the more they know of natural laws. It was owing to wise men having taken due note of this that belief in miracles arose and that miracles are held in high esteem even by religions that are false; for to whatever they owed their origin, sensible men made much of them, and their authority caused everybody to believe in them. (1970: 143)

In Book III.5 of the *Istorie Fiorentine*, Machiavelli repeats his argument, from which we can extrapolate an important political lesson:

> And because religion and fear of God have been eliminated in all, an oath and faith given last only as long as they are useful; so men make use of them not to observe them but to serve as a means of being able to deceive more easily. And the more easily and surely the deception succeeds, the more glory and praise is acquired from it; by this, harmful men are praised as industrious and good men are blamed as fools. (1988: 110)

Machiavelli's lesson is that deception, which necessarily exists, must be monopolized by the state in order to ensure unity and security, for widespread deception creates disharmony in the people, eventually creating factions. In the following passages, Thomas approvingly discusses the Sultan's pragmatic approach to religion in his empire *and* the significant bearing a monarch's religion has on political affairs:

> Indeed the Turk within his dominions compelleth no man to alter his religion: by reason wherof he is the more able peaceably to enjoy so large an empire. But if he thought he might bring al men to Mahomets law, (as he seeth the contrary,) he would use that rigor in religion that he doth in other things. (1822: vol. 2, 381)

Thomas continues with the observation that when perspectives between states are so opposed it is not possible to have amity between them:

> And there was never greater folly imagined, than the French Kings device of amity with the Turk. For if the Turk observe not faith to the princes of his own religion, but destroyeth as many as come once under his power, what faith or amity can he bear to a Christian prince? So that if by the Turks means the French King might have extirpated the Emperor, (which was the end of his desired amity,) his own destruction must have followed. For with the Turk, *nulla sancta societas, nec fides regni est*. (1822: vol. 2, 381)

That is: "For with the Turk, no alliance is inviolable, nor is the faith of a realm sacrosanct". Thomas's point here leads him to his most interesting "fourth discourse to the King; touching his Majesty's outward affairs", in which he argues that there is no way for friendship to be had with England's neighboring countries "without either our extreme disadvantage, or the denying of our faith: neither of which is tolerable", adding that

> it is impossible we should have any perfect amity with any foreign prince that dissenteth from us in religion; so because we have no neighbour of uniform religion, I determine we can find no friend whose amity is to be trusted.
>
> Wherfore we must of force turn us unto *tyme*, to se how much we may win therof, and what we may win withal. And because neither is our force so ordered, that we may trust therby to win our tyme, nor our treasure such as may purchase; therfore our extremest shift is to work by policy. (1822: vol. 2, 384)

Thomas thus proceeds to argue that Edward ought to play the French King and the Emperor against each other, a perfectly Machiavellian technique that Thomas feels he must first justify philosophically and morally:

> And albeit that our quarrel is in God, and God our quarrel, who never faileth them that trust in him; yet forasmuch as wickednes reigneth in the midst of us, like as we should not mistrust the goodnes of God, so ought we neither to neglect that policy that may help us to advoid the like captivity that for wickednes happened to the elect people of Israel. (1822: vol. 2, 384)

This statement seems lifted from chapter twenty-six of *Il Principe* in which Lorenzo is metaphorised into Moses and Florence into Italy, except that here Moses is young Edward and Israel is England. Thomas is using Machiavelli for English purposes, attempting to inspire the young Edward so that his throne might remain secure, for Thomas was well aware of the rival factions surrounding the young king, and he also understood that Henry VIII had reaffirmed the English monarchy as a manifestation of God's rule in the English dominions. Edward had been raised a Protestant and continued his father's reforms with zeal.

The boy-king had been explicit with Thomas about his desire to keep their relationship of student and tutor secret. They had a trusting intermediary, Mr. Throgmerton, deliver the lessons "as it were a thing from the Council" (1822: vol. 2, 389). Tutoring a king, however, and secretly, had its difficulties, one of which involved ensuring that the king did not disagree too much with the tutor over certain socio-political questions. And Thomas was intelligent enough to recognize that one encounters difficulties when introducing new ideas to one's society, as he tells Edward in one of the *Discourses* (1822: vol. 2, 390). Thomas understood that there were differences between cultures, as he reminded his readers both in the *The Hystorie* and *The Pilgrim*, where he noted even the differences in eating habits and social mores between the English and the Italians[5]. Thomas thus rewrote Machiavelli so as to make the Florentine a more palatable dish for the English. Thomas was aware, it seems, of what Sapir, four hundred years later, would reflect upon:

> No two languages are ever sufficiently similar to be considered as representing the same social reality. The worlds in which different societies live are distinct worlds, not merely the same world with different labels attached. (1956: 69)

Thomas, in the language of translation theory, was attempting to ensure that Machiavelli's writings would be able to signify and function in the target–English–culture. His publication, in 1551, of *An Argument, wherin the apparaile of Women is both reproued and defended*, does the same for Livy's Fourth Decade of *Ab Urbe Condita Libri*, and actually furtively urges the surrender of the old debased coins for the new, 1551 issue (Carlson 1993: 553). In Raab's words, Thomas was "applying a Machiavellian critique to the English political scene–not as a set of rigid formulae, but as an organic concept" (1964: 48), which is exactly what Machiavelli taught, that is, that one must vary one's actions to conform to the circumstances at hand. For example, Thomas's insistence that it is best for a prince to ally himself with princes of like religion was of immediate concern to the English king–having adopted a new form of Christianity–whereas the uniform Catholicism of the princes of the various Italian city-states, and of the French and Spanish kings, merited no attention from Machiavelli.

Without doubt, the Henrician Church, now adopted by the young Edward, had to contend with the dilemma that Italy was still the center of great thought and civilization but also still the center of the Holy See. How could the English at once deny and desire Italy? Henry had maintained both cultural and mercantile contacts with Italy, but there was no question that to the English Italy was now a dangerous "other", a place about which one must be cautious. The caution that Thomas and other Englishmen would take was to make use of Italians such as Machiavelli, who had rebelled against the Papacy but not against the ideals of monarchy. To the English, Machiavelli–especially in *The Prince*–comes off as a supporter of a king with an iron hand, and as one who unconditionally opposes the Holy See.

Equally, Thomas was aware that speech is necessarily tied to its location, that it is dangerous to say certain things in certain places, and wise therefore to say other things in other places. The traveler must be a liar, especially because he is a pilgrim in a strange land, often bearing strange news. Ironically, as a translator in his own country, Thomas also had to be a lying pilgrim, especially with regard to his "news" from abroad which was "other" to the English[6]. Having traveled, and having become a translator, he was compelled to remain a traveler in his own culture, as he sought to make tolerable dangerous truths or doctrines from abroad. In *The Pilgrim*, upon hearing them tarnishing Henry VIII's image, he tells his interlocutors,

> you charge my patience, and the answer of so outrageous a report requireth more force than reason or writing. But, because the place alloweth me not to speak, much less to fight, I therefore will forbear. (1861: 9)

A few pages later, he reiterates that he held back his tongue and rage

> partly also for fear of the place wherein I found myself. For Bonomy (though well with wrong) is of the Pope's territory, and he that speaketh there against the Pope incurreth no less danger than he that in England would offend the King's Majesty. (1861: 13-14)

This observation reveals Thomas's awareness that, at the wrong place or wrong time, direct translation of strange or polemical ideas can be dangerous. Direct translation, if it is to do its duty and teach well, cannot interpret the ideas of the source text properly, for it dispenses with the *spatial language* of the text, that is, with the cultural realities that produced the text. We can translate such phenomena in two ways, either by altering the text in such a manner as to

English it, as Thomas did, or, as in our scholarly editions, by providing explanatory notes or glosses to the text. Either way, we are translating beyond the mere words of the text.

2.1.3. English Machiavellian

How much does Thomas rely on his Italian predecessor? Chaney calls Thomas's *Discourses* "intelligently translated paraphrases of Machiavelli's *Discorsi* and *The Prince*" (2000: 75). This analysis is not surprising to us for, as we have seen, Thomas seems to have believed that Machiavelli was correct in his views. Where there is disagreement over Thomas's borrowing is in whether he relied more on *Il Principe* or the *Discorsi*, or on Machiavelli's other writings. Weissberger is correct to note that Thomas drew more on the *Discorsi* than on *Il Principe*, but he is wrong to suggest that "Thomas was not even acquainted with the *Prince*" (1927: 593)[7]. In fact, Thomas successfully combines the premises of both of these works (Donaldson 1988: 42; Chaney 2000: 74-75). On the one hand, he diverges from the Secretary on the question of whether it is preferable for a state to be ruled by "the nobility or the commonalty". Thomas rails against the latter, concluding that "it is impossible any estate should long prosper, where the power is in the commonalty" (1822: vol. 2, 375). He does, however, grant Machiavelli his argument in favor of the power of the people, stating that it is necessary for the multitude, in extreme cases, to check the power of the nobility:

> Wherfore Macchiavegli, in his discourses of the liberty of a commonwealth, determineth that in cases of extremity, where the magistrats or nobility use this tyranny, the commotions of the people are necessary, to mitigate the excess of the great mens ambitions. (1822: vol. 2, 376)

Thomas seems here to be "saving" Machiavelli, for the Englishman was aware of how the Florentine was perceived: Cardinal Pole had attacked him as recently as 1539. Nevertheless, Thomas betrays Machiavelli to English cultural ends while also stealthily corrupting English culture by remaining faithful to the Italian's basic fundamental cynicism. Thomas's tripartite argument is similar to Machiavelli's tripartite taxonomy, which is modelled on the Trinity but substitutes God, Jesus, and the Holy Spirit with the prince, the city, and war, all for the end of achieving rebirth in the new kingdom–the city reborn without the sins that enslave it to barbarians. Here is Thomas's argument:

> In the monarchy or estate of a prince, if the prince be good, like as he keepeth his commons void of power, even so he preserveth them from the tyranny of the nobility; for he is the same bridle in power over his nobility, that the nobility is over the commons, and tendeth as wel to the rule of the one, as to the preservation of the other. (1822: vol. 2, 376)

Thomas proceeds to reason that the tyrant's power is more tolerable than the tyranny of the few nobility, which in turn is more tolerable than the tyranny of the multitude. In this, his argument is more akin to Plato and Aristotle than to Machiavelli[8]. Nevertheless, Thomas reverts to Machiavelli:

> Neither do I mean, that for the dangers rehearsed, the commons should be so kept down, as the wretched commons of some other countries be. But I would their discipline and education should be such, that the only name of their prince should make them to tremble. (1822: vol. 2, 377)

He takes this argument from *Il Principe*, and for good reason–he is writing to educate Edward VI. In the final paragraph of this discourse, Thomas bypasses the nobility to discuss the relationship of the prince to the multitude, for it is the multitude, without whose consent the prince cannot rule, that must be satisfied. Thomas ends the discourse on this note:

> For if they [the multitude] have but so much liberty as to talk of the princes causes, and of the reason of laws, at once they shew their desire not to be ruled: wherof groweth contempt, and consequently disobedience, the mother of al errors. (1822: vol. 2, 377)

Thomas Englished Machiavelli further by eliminating references to theology in his transpositions of the Italian's writings. As we saw earlier, the disagreements between Thomas and Machiavelli are not over the use of religion but, it seems, over personal beliefs. Thomas is not troubled by this difference, his only concern being the application of a political thinker's concepts in a successful manner. He would have been aware of the anti-Machiavellian sentiments regarding the Secretary's irreligiosity, and in order not to distress the king, he passed silently over that matter. Edward, after all, was continuing his father's Protestant reforms with fervor, destroying shrines and pictures of saints, reducing ceremonies, banning processions, and issuing the first English Prayer Book in 1548 (Guy 1988: 203-211). However, as I hope to show, to conclude that the Clerk borrowed from the Secretary is not to conclude that the Englishman did not have ideas of his own.

2.1.4. *Englishing* Machiavelli

Why did Thomas feel that he must translate–even surreptitiously–an Italian writer into English, not Latin? Why, in other words, did the vernacular turn take a hold at mid-sixteenth century? The answer seems to be that the break with the Catholic Church needed to be solidified, as did the language of the new English Church. Ironically, England still needed the modern philosophical world of Italy, but England borrowed–*adopted* and *adapted*–writings that seemed to advocate anti-Papal sentiments, such as those of Machiavelli. Hence, the English could still have the best of both worlds, specifically, *English-*Italians. This is exactly why, as a fervent Protestant, Thomas could write an appeal–the first of its kind–for the teaching of English, not Latin. And, of course, the fact that Italy had also been a strong advocate of the vernacular gave Thomas a stronger impulse to proceed with his view (Chaney 2000: 72). Although his translation of Sacrobosco's treatise *De Sphaera*, made for the Duke of Suffolk's son Harry, was not published, it nonetheless conveyed sentiments that became common during the mid-sixteenth century:

> [...] it is almost harde to finde any goode aucthor in our owne mother tongue [...]. Helas, is it possible to builde well w'oute foundation, or to reape wheat where hath been sowen no corne. Can the scholer write w'out matier wherof. Or thinke we w' the onelie studie of the latine tongue, to atteigne the well vnderstanding of Virgill, Aristotle or any other such. No, surelie no, that is not the right waie. [...] And albeit I might be answered that bicause we lacke Aucthours in our owne tongue to direct the scholmaisters vnto this trade of teaching, yet w' more reason can I replie, that if the Scholemaister teache the latine tongue he ought to know the sciences, and knowing them in latine, it shulde seeme he shulde be sufficient to teache them in Englishe: and if he know them not, than may he chaunge his latine for pewter well enough. Wherefore if our nation desier to triumphe in Civile knoledge, as other nations do, the meane must be that eche man first covett to florishe in his owne naturall tongue: w'out the whiche he shal haue much ado to be excellent in any other tongue. (in Adair 1924: 159-160)

Thomas clearly helped to propel English nationalist fervor forward, which in turn increased the desire for the vernacular, which in turn helped to propel the art of translation forward, to the extent that translation during the Tudor period came to be regarded as a literary art in its own right (Wright 1958: 340). Clearly, however, Thomas was not an original thinker. That he synthesized others' ideas has been recognized. Most scholars agree, for instance, that his grammar and dictionary rely almost entirely on Alunno and Acarisio's *Le ricchezze della lingua volgare* (Venice 1543) and the *Vocabolario, Grammatica, et orthographia de la lingua volgare* (Cento 1543), respectively[9]. But if he was a synthesizer, he was a remarkable one, fully deserving of John Strype's observation that he was "one of the most gifted of those times" (Thomas 1822: vol. 2, 13). In any case he certainly was a good teacher to Edward, who owed his understanding of the complex matter of the debasement of the coin to Thomas, as Loach (1999: 16) and Jordan (1970: 417-418) have shown[10].

Granted, it is difficult to say with certainty what Thomas believed and what he did not believe. Much of what he wrote, as Raab points out (1964: 47), can be seen as "a polite exercise" to gain favor with the nobility–suitable work for a synthesizer. But surely Thomas did more than synthesize the ideas of others. Did he not, through his translations, help to broaden the English philosophical mind? He has been largely forgotten because scholars have thought he merely repeated the ideas of Machiavelli in a shallow form. Such scholars tend also to be the ones who will attack a translator for failing to render a text accurately. Should they not be more cautious in their attacks and ask, first of all, whether the translator was attempting to reproduce the text or rather to adapt it? In other words, critics ought honestly to declare whether they are looking for sameness between the source text and the target text. If it is sameness they are looking for, and if that was not the translator's goal, then that sameness must be sought out elsewhere; but it may not exist at all. Often, indeed perhaps always, the translator's attempt is to adapt the source text to a particular local ethos. Such was the case with Thomas's *Discourses* for Edward VI. Interestingly, the case seems to have been reveresed with regard to *The Pilgrim*, if, that is, we accept Martin's argument that the *Il Pellegrino* is an adaptation of *The Pilgrim* by an Italian. This is to say that the exercise of translating Thomas's dialogue, probably carried out by an Italian sympathetic to Protestantism, seems to have reversed the process of Thomas's adaptation of Machiavelli. This possible Italian translator, like Thomas, understood that translation is also a political art, that it cannot but be so, and that in the final accounting our question must not be whether one has translated a text accurately but, rather, what ideas has one translated, and what values has one betrayed?[11]

[1] The most thorough study of Thomas is by Adair. See also Chaney's superb chapter on Thomas (2000: 58-101).

[2] On this matter see Raab (1964: 42-45) and Donaldson (1988: 42).

[3] Sydney Anglo argues that Thomas was the first *European* "to attempt topical political analysis on the basis of Machiavelli's work" (1984: 43).

[4] The relevant sections of *The Vanitee* are quoted in Raab 46 and 48.

[5] See especially *The Pilgrim* (1861: 6-8).

[6] I am using the three categories concerning travel as a genre advanced by Peter Womack: "bearer of strange news; liar; pilgrim" (2001: 149).

[7] This conclusion rests on the assumption that Machiavelli had little to offer that would have interested English political leaders of the Early Modern period. Raab's book offered a much needed corrective. Gasquet's study of Machiavelli's concentrated reception in Elizabethan England, however, is by far the best available, though it seems to be little read in the English speaking world.

[8] See the *Republic* (8 and 9) and the *Politics* (5).

[9] Martin's excellent article provides a summary of the scholarship on Thomas's sources (1997: 636-637).

[10] While admitting that Thomas "may for a short season have influenced the King at a moment when important decisions were in process being made", Jordan maintains that "Thomas was not a considerable thinker" (1970: 419).

[11] Here I have revised Jakobson's question (1987: 435).

References

Adair, E. R. 1924. 'William Thomas: A Forgotten Clerk of the Privy Council' in R. W. Seton-Watson (ed.) *Tudor Studies*. London: Longman, 1924. 133-160.

Anglo, Sydney. 1984. ' "Our Extremest Shift is to Work by Policy": William Thomas and Early Tudor Machiavellism' in *The Transactions of the Honourable Society of Cymmrodorion* (1984): 31-50.

Barnstone, Willis. 1993. *The Poetics of Translation: History, Theory, Practice*. New Haven, CT: Yale University Press.

Joseph Khoury

Bartlett, Kenneth R. 1998. 'The Reception of Italian Renaissance Models in England in the Mid-Sixteenth Century' in Donald Beecher (ed.) *Critical Approaches to English Prose Fiction: 1520-1640*. Ottawa: Dovehouse Editions. 241-256.

Carlson, A. J. 1993. '*Mundus Muliebris*: The World of Women Reviled and Defended ca. 195 B.C. and 1551 A.D. And Other Things' in *Sixteenth Century Journal* 24(3): 541-560.

Chaney, Edward. 2000. *The Evolution of the Grand Tour: Anglo-Italian Cultural Relations since the Renaissance*. London and Portland, OR: Frank Cass.

Donaldson, Peter S. 1988. *Machiavelli and Mystery of State*. Cambridge: Cambridge University Press.

Gasquet, Emile. 1970. *Le Courant Machiavelien dans la pensée et la littérature anglaises du CVIe siècle*. Montréal, Paris, et Bruxelles: Didier.

Guy, John. 1988. *Tudor England*. Oxford: Oxford University Press.

Jakobson, Roman. 1987. 'On Linguistic Aspects of Translation' in Krystyna Pomorska and Stephen Rudy (eds) *Language in Literature*. Cambridge: Belknap. 428-435.

Jordan, W. K. 1970. *Edward VI: The Threshold of Power*. London: Goerge Allen & Unwin.

Loach, Jennifer. 1999. *Edward VI*. New Haven, CT: Yale University Press.

Machiavelli, Niccolò. 1970. *The Discourses* (ed. Bernard Crick and tr. Leslie J. Walker). Harmondsworth: Penguin Books.

–. 1988. *Florentine Histories* (trs. Laura F. Banfield and Harvey C. Mansfield, Jr.). Princeton, NJ: Princeton University Press.

Marlowe, Christopher. 1969. *Christopher Marlowe: The Complete Plays* (ed. J. B. Steane). Harmondsworth: Penguin.

Martin, Ian. 1997. 'The Manuscript and Editorial Traditions of William Thomas's *The Pilgrim*' in *Bibliothèque d'Humanisme et Renaissance* 59: 621-641.

Parks, George B. 1951. 'Travel as Education' in Richard Foster Jones (ed.) *The Seventeenth Century: Studies in the History of English Thought and Literature from Bacon to Pope*. Stanford, CA: Stanford University Press. 264-290.

Raab, Felix. 1964. *The English Face of Machiavelli: A Changing Interpretation, 1500-1700*. Toronto: University of Toronto Press.

Sapir, Edward. 1956. *Culture, Language and Personality*. Berkeley, CA: University of California Press.

Thomas, William. 1550. *Principal Rules of the Italian Grammar, with a Dictionarie for the better understandyng of Boccace, Petrarcha, and Dante, gathered into this tongue by William Thomas*. London: Thomas Berthelet.

–. 1822. 'Discourses' in John Strype (ed.) *Ecclesiastical Memorials, Relating Chiefly to Religion, and the Reformation of it, and the Emergencies of the Church of England, Under King Henry VIII, King Edward VI, and Queen Mary 1*. 3 vols. Oxford: Clarendon Press.

–. 1861. *The Pilgrim: A Dialogue on the Life and Actions of King Henry the Eighth* (ed. J. A. Froude). London: Parker, Son, and Bourn.

–. 1963. *The History of Italy* (ed. George B. Parks). Ithaca, NY: Cornell University Press.

Weissberger, Arnold L. 1927. 'Machiavelli and Tudor England' in *Political Science Quarterly* 42: 589-607.

Womack, Peter. 2001. 'The Writing of Travel' in Michael Hattaway (ed.) *A Companion to English Renaissance Literature and Culture*. Oxford: Blackwell. 148-161.

Wright, Louis B. 1958. *Middle-Class Culture in Elizabethan England*. Ithaca, NY: Cornell University Press.

2.2. John Frampton of Bristol, Trader and Translator

Donald Beecher

John Frampton of Bristol mastered Spanish in the course of his career as a merchant in the Seville trade, a career that exposed him to the changing fortunes of Anglo-Hispanic relations. In due course, he would be arrested by the Inquisition, tortured, tried, and compelled to endure the confiscation of his ship and goods. Forbidden to return to England, he nevertheless made his escape. From merchant he turned translator, and produced for English readers six distinguished works ranging from Monardes's study of the herbs and medical simples brought back from the New World to the Travels of Marco Polo. He was the Elizabethan traveler-translator par excellence. Many of the most incisive insights into his adventures survive in the records of the Admiralty Court to which he made application for damages in his later years.
Keywords: Bristol, John Frampton, Inquisition, medicine, Spain, translation, travel.

By any standards, John Frampton had a remarkable career, first as a merchant venturer in the Seville-to-Bristol trade, and then as a translator who, within a four-year period from 1577 to 1581, produced six timely and demanding works from the Spanish–a language he had clearly mastered during his six (according to some up to fifteen) years abroad. We can piece together only a sketch of his stay in Cadiz or on the Guadalquivir and his subsequent life in London, wedged between two certain dates, his apprehension by the Spanish Inquisition in 1561, and his appeal, late in 1572, to the English High Admiralty Court for compensation for his many losses. Letters demonstrate that he was still in Seville in 1567 and in some degree of financial difficulty. He might well have spent the rest of his life there under the kind of house arrest imposed by the Spanish Inquisition upon those who had passed before the tribunal, had he not been able to arrange for an escape[1]. Trade with Spain in those same years came under considerable pressure. The arrival of The Duke of Alba in Flanders (1567), followed by the treacherous attack against Sir John Hawkins in San Juan de Ulloa (1568), and ultimately the English capture of the Spanish payships destined for Flanders brought relations to the breaking point. Yet even during the five-year embargo imposed upon English merchants by Philip II, which began in 1568, some trade continued, although residence in Spain became impossible for all but the most "Hispanized" of the English traders. For that reason, other traders besides Frampton found themselves back in London by 1571[2]. That he would ever return to the south, even after the lifting of the embargo in 1573, seems most unlikely under the circumstances, although Frampton talks about daily trade out of Spain in 1577, leading N.M. Penzer to think that he had remained there until 1576, and only then returned to England with personal copies of the works he would undertake to translate, including those of Monardes published in Seville in 1574[3].

A remarkable fact of Frampton's career is his reticence to write about his experiences in Spain, at least in conjunction with his literary translations, for in none of his prefaces or dedications–despite the implicit patriotic and promotional spirit of his endeavors as a translator–does he tell us about his encounter with the Inquisition or his efforts to recover his losses. Thus the mood and motives behind his literary endeavors can only be guessed at. In his biographical reticence he is not alone. An even more extraordinary case in point is the silence of Thomas Lodge regarding the privateering venture to the Azores with Captain Clarke during which he wrote his pastoral romance *Rosalind*, and his months aboard the *Leicester* with Cavendish on a second attempt to pass the Straits of Magellan. He tells us merely that he found the source of his *Margarite of America* in a Brazilian monastery in Santos, thereby inviting us to imagine him translating this bizarre tale amidst the utmost peril and privation, including near mutinies, the loss of two ships, and the death of 250 mariners and venturers, including Cavendish himself, without a single hint from his pen (Lodge 261-262). Frampton's reticence is nearly as striking in light of the very poignant account of his tribulations presented to the High Court of the Admiralty some time earlier. Had the intervening years mellowed his feelings of revenge, or had they been displaced by a new enthusiasm for the Iberian trade which, by 1577, was two years into a golden decade that would last until 1585 when Philip II would again retaliate against the English merchants?

Frampton, in the dedication to Sir Edward Dyer of his *Most Noble and Famous Travels of Marco Polo* (1579), reports only that the Spanish edition was lying by him in his chambers, that the merchants, pilots, and mariners who dropped in for visits took great delight in it and urged him to translate it, and that he dallied in hopes that a more qualified author would take the task off his hands. At least this bit of modesty might have provided an insight into the man, were it not taken from the words of Rodrigo Fernández Santella y Córdoba, the Spanish translator of the work some three-quarters of a century earlier. It was false modesty, in any case, because Frampton did not begin his career as a translator in this seemingly accidental way, performing by default what others had not done. His *Marco Polo*, published in 1579, was his fourth project, all of them of some magnitude[4]. This book was a plain and accurate translation of Santella's rendition of the famous Italian's travels to China along the great silk road, through which–and this is the only sign of intent Frampton offers for his pains–he hopes to provide "great light to our seamen, if ever this nation chanced to find a passage out of the frozen zone to the south seas, and otherwise delight many home dwellers, furtherers of travellers." In short, Frampton vacillates in his intent between furnishing useful knowledge about the Far East to actual mariners (once England had solved the matter of sea routes to China), and entertaining the at-home consumer of books who was, at best, a potential arm-chair backer of expansionist policy and trade. Frampton's incentive as a translator may well have been to maintain these exotic places and the prospects for trade in the forefront of the collective English imagination, which, arguably, was lagging behind in matters of exploration, territorial claims, aggressive trade, colonization, and the creation of foreign markets for domestic goods such as coarse woolens. But his finer motives are never clear, whether he preferred to rival Spain in the foreign markets, or to encourage the conditions propitious to direct trade with Spain. In pragmatic terms, the two positions were mutually exclusive and the cause of some contention, but Frampton, in his choice of texts, may, nevertheless, have represented both lines of thinking.

Frampton was not only a patriot and propagandist, but a man with reasons of his own for willing the humiliation of Spain, which could be accomplished only at the hands of a new generation of corsairs, navy men, explorers, traders and settlers. Whether the thrust of his "program" is essentially to enhance trade directly with Spain, or to assault her trade on the high seas, or to rival her in foreign markets, remains a point for debate, but the six works together do constitute a kind of "School for English Seamen and Traders" by furnishing them with a treasury of Spanish knowledge concerning geography, navigation, and *materia medica* from her colonies. At the same time, through the budding book trade, Frampton furnished fresh news for English "common readers" to employ as they might in seeking England's place in an expanding mercantile world. It has been thought that his books constitute a kind of revenge for all that he had endured at the hands of the Inquisition–a point to which we shall return–but he may also have remained an optimistic Bristol trader at heart, still open to "legitimate" commerce.

The first title in that "program" was a remarkable choice, for it was no less than an English translation of the botanical treatises of Nicholas Monardes of Seville, published in London in 1577 by William Norton under the enthusiastic title: *Joyfull Newes out of the Newe Founde Worlde wherein is declared the rare and singular vertues of diverse and sundrie hearbes, trees, oyles, plants and stones, with their applications, as well for phisicke as chirurgerie*. The work represents not only a full cabinet of medicinal curiosities from Spanish America, from Florida to Peru, but a reminder to all diseased and dying Englishmen that Spain had a monopoly on half the world's pharmacopoeia, such as it had been provided by the Almighty for human health. Frampton, of course, never says as much, but there could be no "joyful news" unless such simples came into the possession of practitioners to the benefit of their patients. Monardes, the author of these treatises, had been a life-long collector who had incorporated his New World imports into a lucrative practice[5]. Publication in English could only suggest utility and need, and raise the troubling question of supply once a sense of demand had been raised in the reader's mind. But the most likely means for establishing that supply were quite out of keeping with any thoughts of revenge; Spain was still open for legitimate trade, and would remain so until 1585.

In the very year Frampton's *Joyfull Newes* was published, merchants from London and the outports had succeeded, against great opposition, in founding The Spanish Company with its 373 inaugural members, 76 of whom were from Bristol. The trade deficits with Spain in England's favor were then being balanced through the illegal exportation of silver. Pharmaceuticals, through increased demand, might therefore play a significant commercial role. The north coast of Spain was far safer for trade than the Mediterranean ports, but the risks were taken in seeking the Andalusian ports because the products shipped from Seville, San Lucar, Malaga and Cadiz were more varied and the profits were greater (Haynes 1992: 84). To be sure, by 1581 Don Bernardino de Mendoza was warning Philip II to keep a close watch over the Englishmen trading in Spain because they were sending reports on Spanish naval activities back to Sir Francis Walsingham. Such suspicion in the period leading up to the armada would result in the embargo of 1585 that was to last into the seventeenth century. Yet trade continued, whether by disguising the identity of the ships or by unloading and reloading into French ships in the south of France[6]. Even in times of war, Spain remained dependent upon English goods and staples, and Spanish merchants, at their own peril, were willing to circumvent the embargo in order to maintain an active import-export trade (Croft 1989: 281)[7]. Frampton's *Joyfull Newes* may have been his bid to introduce new pharmaceuticals obtainable through the Andalusian trade, and an implicit solicitation of support, through his dedication to Sir Edward Dyer, for the new Spanish Company. This was a potentially polemical matter, however, insofar as Dyer and his circle may have been altogether more interested in harrying the King of Spain by going directly to Spanish America, through piracy or settlement, to obtain the desired commodities.

Frampton's disingenuous dedication of his *Joyfull Newes* contains only the slightest hints at his motivating agenda. He tells us that he is no longer "pressed with the former toils" of his old trade and hence has turned to translating merely to avoid idleness and to do something of benefit for his country. His purpose is, he says, to bring new cures to the profit of the "country folks of England", while at the same time dedicating his labors to "some rare lover of knowledge for the worthiness of the work" (1925: vol. 1, 3-4). That "rare lover" was Edward Dyer, the Earl of Leicester's secretary and member of a circle of scholars that included the likes of John Florio, Thomas North, and Philip Sidney–men who were, for the most part, politically Protestant, bent upon expanding England's foreign holdings and trade through the containment of Spain, and through the discovery of a passage to China, whether by the northeast or the northwest. Frampton's book could also be enlisted in their cause.

But the passage that most fixes the reader's attention is the following: "and since the aforesaid medicines mentioned in the same work of Doctor Monardes are now by merchants and others brought out of the West Indias into Spain, and from Spain hither into England by such as doth daily traffic thither" and are known to the English to be precious remedies for all manner of illnesses incurable by "the old order and manner of physic, as also proven by their use in Spain and other countries [...]" (1925: vol. 1, 4). Was there, indeed, a regular trade between Seville and Bristol in *materia medica* accounting for Frampton's enthusiasm for the pharmaceuticals of Florida, Mexico and Peru? Frampton states as much, endorsing as he goes, the legitimate trading of these products through Spanish ports. And yet John Gerard, in his herbal of 1596, nearly two decades later, mentions a mere handful of New World plants, which is scant evidence that anything like a representative selection of Monardes' herbs had become actual and familiar remedies in the English dispensary[8]. Still, merchants from the West country, in significant numbers, continued to trade with Spain until Philip's patience ran out with English intelligencing by mid decade[9]. Perhaps the best we can conclude is that if Frampton was living in the past, his motives might have ranged from disinterested leisure to a perceived need to divulge anything Spanish that might hurt their monopoly in New World commodities, while if he was living in the present, his interests may have been purely commercial in whetting English cravings for Spanish commodities apt for importation. Sassafras, in particular, was making its debut as a catholicon or general healer and as the cure of choice for syphilis. Monardes's description of the plant helped to establish that primacy. Thus, in subsequent years, the need to secure the supply was put forward as one of the leading reasons for colonizing Florida and regions to the north[10]. Frampton's mind in the matter of modes of supply may simply remain beyond recovery, though such questions would have been in the thoughts of all his contemporary readers.

Whatever Frampton's intentions of a political or mercantile nature, one fact remains incontestable, namely that his efforts were a contribution to the expansion of European pharmacology. Compounds were giving way to pharmaceutical treatments based on simples, one ingredient per condition. Moreover, pharmacology had been under stress, not only because of its spectacular failures in the face of such diseases as syphilis and the plague, but because of the hundreds of new plants appearing in Europe threatening or promising to modify or replace old remedies. Many were accompanied by lore concerning their indigenous uses, especially in the treatment of tropical diseases by then afflicting European travelers to foreign parts. Nicholas Monardes was a giant in the pan-European effort to integrate these drugs–a phenomenon in which the English, apart from Frampton, had virtually no part[11]. Frampton's innovative translation had been anticipated by a year in the Italian version of Annibale Briganti, with a French translation soon to follow. Meanwhile, the great Charles l'Ecluse of Leiden had incorporated all of Monardes into his botanical writings in Latin.

As a physician, botanist, researcher and entrepreneur, Monardes had collected all that he could from the docks of Seville, commissioning travelers and writing letters to Mexico and Peru in his search for new medicinal plants. Many of those he received he replanted in gardens established in Seville, cataloguing and harvesting them for clinical use. Speculation is, of course, free with regard to what Frampton may have known first hand of Monardes's gardens and dispensaries. It is paradoxical, in light of the highly specialized nature of this scientific treatise, that among all of Frampton's works, the *Joyfull Newes* was to enjoy the greatest success commercially and the greatest *succes d'estime*, followed by his *Marco Polo*[12].

The exceeding rarity of the remaining four titles is a fact difficult to interpret: only one was reprinted, to be sure, but are the few copies extant today due to the fact that all the others were read into oblivion, or discarded because they fell from favor and interest? A few bibliographical facts can be teased out of the archives, but for our purposes, a citation of their typically long descriptive titles will suffice to round out our sense of Frampton's translating "program", for they tell us much at a glance about his personal interests, his assessment of the English book market, and the implicit value of his work for strategic, patriotic, and mercantile reasons.

If the translation of Monardes points to legitimate trade with Spain, and the Marco Polo enhances English interest in finding a passage to China, the second title runs a counter course. The work was inscribed in the Stationers' Register by Henry Bynneman in March, 1578, as *A brief Declaracon of all the portes, creekes, baies, and havens conteyned in the West India, the originall whereof was Dedicated to the mightie Kinge, Charles the V Kinge of Castile*. No copy survives of this single edition, according to Penzer, but it was copied by Ames and Herbert for the second volume of their *Typographical Antiquities*. What might appear at first glance as a mere travelogue could also serve as a corsair's manual[13]. It is no mere literary pastime if only because it singles out the Caribbean topography from a larger work. As a promoter of the Iberian trade, Frampton, in a sense, could not allow himself to think that the English had any place in western waters. This was a theater of operations only for corsairs and privateers whose booty was generally repaid to the Spanish crown through confiscations of English goods and ships ventured in the "legitimate" Spanish trade. That very issue was at an apex when the book appeared. Reports had come back of Drake's activities in the Pacific, particularly concerning the ballasting of his ship with silver from the *Cacafuego*. The diplomatic exchanges were in full course throughout 1579, long before Drake's return in 1580. The Spanish demanded reparations, and Mendoza made use of the political leverage of The Spanish Company members, who vigorously protested Drake's exploits and called for his condemnation. This ostensible sympathy for the Spanish cause was simple self-interest, for Philip II had declared his intentions of repaying himself through the confiscation of English goods in Spain (Croft 1973: xxiii). Could the Frampton who supported legitimate trade with Spain in his first book suddenly employ his talents in translating a work that could only be of practical use to pirates and corsairs? Can his motives have been to abet Drake and pure opportunist retaliation?

Bernardino de Escalante published his *Discurso* in Seville in 1577. This was to become Frampton's third production. He came by it quickly, for he had finished his translation by October, 1578, and had it published under the title: *A Discourse of the Navigation which the Portugales doe make to the Realmes and Provinces of the Eest partes of the worlde, and of the Knowledge that growes by them of the great things, which are in the Dominions of China.* Escalante, a one-time missionary to the Orient, and later one of the most zealous of the inquisitors, collected the materials for the *Discurso* from the works of others; his purpose was to incite the Spanish to compete against the Portuguese in the Pacific for trade and colonies. Frampton, in translating the work, could only intend a similar message to the English, namely that they race the Spanish for control of the Cathay trade. This and *The Travels of Marco Polo* were the best of the descriptive "geographies" available to Frampton concerning the Orient. Making them available in English was the most that he could do, as a retired merchant, to abet the English mercantile cause[14].

The third of his books on China, this one following the publication of his *Marco Polo*, appeared in 1579 under the title *A Discoverie of the countries of Tartaria, Scithia, & Cataya, by he North-East: With the manners, fashions, and orders which are used in these countries*, as printed by Thomas Dawson. This book is likewise rare, with perhaps only one surviving copy. Circumstantially, it would seem a timely production relating to England's quest for a passage to China or India, more valuable in that regard than for its contents, for it is a mere digest of observations drawn from the writings of Marco Polo and Nicolò de' Conti as they were assembled by Francisco Thamara of Cadiz, active in that city as a scholar at mid-century. Frampton merely culled out the parts of interest to him[15], and dedicated his production to Sir Rowland Howard and the governors of the Company of Merchant Venturers for the Discovery of New Trades, to whom he "wisheth all happy success in all their attempts." This modest hint further aligns Frampton's fixation upon China with England's current prospects for opening trade to the East. The timing of its publication coincides with the intended departure of Pet and Jackman in one last try for a Northeast Passage, for which the book may have been intended as a manual. According to Wroth, Frampton gave the leaders of the expedition copies in manuscript (1954: 312).

Frampton's last work appeared in 1581–another important choice even though its materials were dating rapidly–this one also dedicated to Sir Edward Dyer. It was republished in 1595. The Huntington Library has a copy of the second edition, but both are rare. Pedro de Medina's *Arte de navegar* was issued in Valladolid as early as 1545. The book had been enormously successful in its time, not only in Spanish, but in its Dutch, six French, six German, and two Italian editions: hence Frampton's assurance that it held an on-going importance for the training of English seaman. He called it *The Arte of Navigation, wherein is contained all the rules, declarations, secrets & advises, which for good Navigation are necessarie & ought to be knowen &*

practised. This was to be Frampton's alternative to the book of navigation by Martin Cortés translated by Richard Eden. These two foreign imports on the navigational arts would not be superseded before the publication, in 1599, of Edward Wright's *Certain Errors in Navigation Detected and Corrected*.

These often misguided guides to foreign places and customs were the best available, even for those who were to attempt navigation to these parts in English boats. Frampton's contributions to the knowledge of men and manners were based on the translations of travelers whose impressions barely amount to a nascent form of anthropology, but they observed what they could, and of these things Frampton was a loyal disseminator[16]. These books found their way into the print culture as a combination of marketable research and scientific entertainment, making their bid for the attention of both the "rare lovers of knowledge" and the book-buyers among the shop-keepers and the gentry for perusal during their leisure hours. Frampton was working for English printers keen to cultivate markets wherever they could be found. Given England's tortured and vacillating relations with Spain throughout the 1560s and 1570s, such translations by one of England's partially Hispanized seamen were certain to arouse interest. In the first instance, then, Frampton may have been a translator by opportunity, for he needed publishers convinced of the commercial viability of his books. So viewed, Frampton's selections may have been as much calibrated in relation to his perception of the book market as to his views of the changing tides in Anglo-Hispanic relations involving mercantile interests.

That publishing niche was actually larger than Frampton's six titles would suggest, for he was not the only English merchant out of Spain who later turned translator. That career pattern seems to have been at the foundation of a small industry, the products of which surrounded and extended Frampton's "program." Not only do they share in his market, but in his political and mercantile motivations, and in the personal vendetta that he may have felt toward the Spanish for the abuses of the Inquisition. In the first instance, the act of revealing to one's own nation the private cache of knowledge of an enemy nation makes translating an act of strategic intelligencing bent upon injuring those by whom one has been injured. That fundamental idea of the translator as revenger, if only by enhancing the competitive advantages of one's own nation, is a notion not easily laid to rest.

But first a word about the Hispanized Englishmen of the 1550s and 1560s who traded and lived in Spain, who sometimes married Spanish wives and often sailed for the King of Spain even while spying for the English, yet who lived as Catholics and attempted to dodge the Inquisition[17]. These are the men whose respective experiences parallel John Frampton's career. Consider the case of Captain Roger Bodenham, a Hereford man who settled in Spain in the 1550s to join in the Barbary trade. When this became impracticable he turned, in 1563, to shipping cargo to the West Indies for Spain. John Hawkins, knighted by King Philip of Spain for services rendered during the Marian period, thought his credit sufficiently high during this later period that he might conduct his own Caribbean trade. Bodenham offered to accompany Hawkins on his second slaving voyage, but Sir Thomas Challoner, then Ambassador in Madrid, made choice of another. Nevertheless, Bodenham enjoyed a confidence that Hawkins did not, for in 1565 he shipped again to the West Indies in the convoy of galleons under Pedro Menendes de Avila, even though he was, all along, acting as an English spy, and was back in London in 1566 in that capacity. Still confident of his place in Spain, he set out with English goods destined for Seville in 1567, only to have them seized by Turkish pirates. Following his escape, he was made leader of a Spanish expedition to the Philippines. When he is next heard of, he is again in London, in the same year that found Frampton before the Admiralty Court, writing a pamphlet to William Cecil, Lord Burghley, on the importance of foreign trade. Bodenham's story gives plausibility to the view that Frampton too may have returned for another five years, for Bodenham is living in Seville a full decade later, and still sending regular communications to Walsingham about Spanish naval activities (Croft 1973: xxi)[18].

Or consider Frampton's friend Henry Hawks, who assumed a Spanish name, married a Spanish wife, lived in Grand Malaga in 1552, traveled to Mexico in 1567 on business, the very year of the San Juan de Ulloa incident, and who, for that reason, was detained by the Mexican Inquisition–the first to be convened–but who escaped to Spain and then to England in that same critical year, 1571. Hawks managed to send out of Mexico, before his arraignment, a wonderful report on the ports and cities, the culture, the fauna and flora of the land, celebrating New Spain as a garden of paradise, mythologizing as he might in order to arouse admiration and stimulate trade. Remarkably, in fact, English coarse woolens continued to be sent to Mexico until 1572. Hawks would turn up at the Admiralty Court hearings as a witness to Frampton's treatment at the hands of the Inquisition. Richard Hakluyt probably first met him there while rendering that very service. The common subject matter linking Hawks and Frampton as translators speaks for itself.

Or consider the story of Richard Eden whose mentor was Sebastian Cabot in his later years. Eden participated in the capture of Le Havre in 1562 in aid of the Huguenots, and gave to Humphrey Gilbert, on that occasion, the idea of raiding the Spanish West (Williamson 1965: 40). Eden had been active as a translator in providing the English with treatises on navigation and travel, beginning in 1561 with the *Breve Compendio de la Spera y de la Arte de Navegar* (1551) of Martin Cortés. This was his contribution to the program for training English seamen. In 1553 Eden had brought out his *Treatyes of the New India* based on Münster's *Cosmographia*, and two years later his *Decades of the Newe Worlde*, of which a second and expanded posthumous edition appeared in 1577, the same year that saw the first edition of Frampton's *Newes*. Here was an Englishman who, twenty years ahead of Frampton, recognized the importance of translating navigational guides from the Spanish.

Or consider the case of Thomas Nicholas who, in 1578, produced a translation of Lopez de Gomara's *Historia de las Indias y conquista de Mexico*, originally published in Zaragoza in 1552. Following Frampton and the current mode, he entitled his book *Newes lately come from the great Kingdom of Chine; The Pleasant history of the Conquest of the West Indies, now called New Spain; The Discovery and Conquest of Peru*, hinting both at the novelty of his subject and the spirit of intelligencing in retailing "news" till then known only to Spanish readers. In this single title he confirms the call for knowledge relating to both the Indies, much as Frampton does through his collective publications. Revealing too is his second title, *A Pleasant Description of the Fortunate Islanas called the Islands of Canaria*. In the year of Frampton's last publication, Eden released his *History of the Discoverie and Conquest of Peru* from the *Historia del discubrimiento y conquista del Perú* of Augustino de Zarate, first published in Antwerp in 1555 and again in Seville in 1577. Nicholas, too, had spent many years in Spanish territory as the English factor in Tenerife where he had been arrested by the Inquisition in 1560, a year earlier than Frampton. He too was held in prison for months and had all his goods confiscated. He may, in fact, be the English merchant in the Canaries mentioned by Froude who was shackled and kept in a dark cell for twenty months throughout 1561 (1896: 33).

During that year, Frampton had been in Lisbon and Cadiz, and from there went overland to Malaga to buy wines. During his absence, officials sent out by the Inquisition searched his ship, and according to Williamson found an "innocuous pre-Reformation book in English" (1965: 45), which was pretext enough to accuse him of heresy. That book, as Frampton reports to the Admiralty Courts in his "Querela", was the *Disticha de Moribus* of Cato, presumably in the edition published by Caxton in 1493[19]. Such were the reasons for his trip on mule-back from Malaga to the Castle of Triana in Seville where he was questioned and found to be in contravention of the rules imposed upon him as a resident in Spain. Frampton provided many details to the Admiralty Court of self-evident interest to scholars in several disciplines. He had sailed from Bristol in the *Jesus*, with cloth destined for Lisbon. There he received bills of exchange on Seville for 2100 ducats. He sailed on to Cadiz where he left his ship, making his way to Hugh Tipton's house in Seville to deposit the bills. From there he went overland to Malaga in search of wines for export, where he was arrested and bound with heavy chains to make the 100 mile trip back to Seville to the castle of the Inquisition. Henry Hawks, as E.G.R. Taylor says (Hakluyt 1967: vol. 1, 10), was milling in the crowds when he witnessed Frampton's "ignominious entry into Seville with his feet tied underneath a mule's belly"[20]. The trial lasted sixteen months and consisted of short interrogations and solitary confinement. He was accused by "unnamed" individuals, and tortured by racking on three separate occasions to force a confession. According to regulations, only one session of torture was permitted, but that session could be interrupted and then resumed as often as the inquisitors desired. At some point he must have broken down. Frampton was then forced to participate in an *auto de fé* in the Plaza of San Francisco where he recanted and was released to secular authorities for a further fourteen months of imprisonment. He would have been placed among the prisoners on a scaffold to hear their sentences read out, the mildest first, the burnings retained till last. Confiscation was the main motive behind the activity, but life itself was in the balance for some, for in 1562 alone, 26 Englishmen were burned at the stake in different parts of Spain (Froude 1896: 33). Lesser punishments consisted of fines, whippings, forced service in the monasteries, or rowing in the galleys. Frampton was ultimately released under a pledge of secrecy concerning all that he had endured. He was to wear the San Benito thereafter, and to remain always in Spain, or, in his words, "at the Inquisitors' pleasure" (Williamson 1930: 554)[21]. Escape was dangerous; to be caught was death at the stake. He then returned to Cadiz where he lived for three years, talking to many English merchants who called in there and who later witnessed on his behalf in the Admiralty Court. He spent his time collecting books and learning Spanish, perhaps half reconciled to his exile, given that all his goods in Bristol had been confiscated by the cloth owners in lieu of their 2,100 ducats, for as a matter of course at the time of his arrest, his ship and cargo had been confiscated, along with the bills of exchange already deposited with Tipton, in a manner amounting to legalized piracy. Both Nicholas and Frampton escaped, and upon their returns to England, began intense publishing careers in overlapping years, translating from the Spanish (exclusively in Frampton's case) works that would expose to the English imagination impressions of the rich lands monopolized by Spain and Portugal[22]. The absence of complaint in these publications shows the remarkable resiliency of these pioneering merchants, perhaps to be explained by the enthusiasm both continued to hold for the future of the Spanish trade[23].

In effect, both Nicholas and Frampton were literary participants in an unofficial trade war, one that was based on religious hatred and intolerance on both sides. Both countries throughout the 1560s sought to maintain normal relations in order to stand united against France. During that decade, however, the Channel filled with privateers based on a *de facto* league between Huguenot corsairs and West Country mariners–activities toward which the Queen turned a blind eye or shared surreptitiously in the profits. In 1563 alone they numbered 400 ships and carried out over 700 attacks on "Catholic" shipping, whether French or Spanish, including those carrying provisions to the Spanish troops in Flanders (Froude 1896: 39). Through this "Machiavellian" arrangement, Cecil's hard line taken against Spain was literally paying off. In Wernham's words, "[t]he Spanish and Netherlands ships and goods seized by the English were worth far more than the English ships and goods seized in Spain and the Netherlands" (1966: 302), which is tantamount to saying that those attacked in Spain and the confiscations they endured were the price to be paid for the successes of Thomas Cobham, Martin Frobisher and the Cornish rovers in the

Channel[24]. The cycle was, of course, incremental, for the sufferings by English seamen at the hands of the Inquisition became blatant justification for revenge against Spanish shipping on the high seas, making raiding as far as the Caribbean a significant unofficial component of Elizabethan maritime policy and practice. J.A. Froude understood matters in precisely these terms; for the seamen it was a question of revenge. With minor exceptions, Spain had closed the Indies to all foreign shipping by 1565. That a few Englishmen managed to stay active in those waters until the early 1570s, still presuming upon old privileges, as Hawkins had attempted to do, was decidedly the exception–and only at the cost of accommodating themselves completely to the Catholic practices demanded of them.

There are, of course, more gentle constructions to be placed upon Frampton's activities. Upon his return, Frampton found himself part of a culture, as it were, that was actively championing exploration and trade relating to England's bid, as an emerging mercantile state, to claim her share of overseas trade. Frampton's activities in the late 1570s chimed perfectly with the efforts of George Best, Richard Hakluyt, John Florio, Nicholas Lichefield and others who were promoting through publication these exploration initiatives[25].

Frampton, like his contemporaries, was caught up with trade routes rather than with colonization. He would extend equal advocacy for China as for America. To the English mind of that moment, America remained something of an accident of geography that stood in the way to reaching the true East. Frobisher had set out with three small ships in 1576 to find the Northwest Passage, which he reattempted under the Queen's patronage in 1577. If China was his goal, any enterprise for arousing interest in that part of the world would serve as propaganda for the cause. This misguided preoccupation would continue to dominate the English imagination for another twenty years. It was a long span of time, beginning in the 1550s, during which the English hurled themselves at the impossible, only to discover that Vasco de Gama had solved the problem as well as it could be solved. Sebastian Cabot and John Dee, with the means provided by John Dudley, Duke of Northumberland, had to be proven wrong the hard way. Who can say what impetus Frampton's *Marco Polo* or *A Discoverie of the countries of Tartaria, Scithia, & Cataya, by he North-East* may have had in launching or guiding the last fateful try by Pet and Jackmann to pass the Kara Sea where once again ice and the advanced season would drive them back. Frampton's *Newes* of 1577 also corresponded with the appearance of a document signed by Humphrey Gilbert called "How Her Majesty may Annoy the King of Spain", at a time when Dyer was simultaneously promoting schemes of overseas development. It was the year in which Barker in the *Speedwell*, in alliance with Blondel, the Huguenot corsair, embarked from Bristol on their pirating excursion to the Caribbean. It was in these years that Hakluyt was campaigning for a more systematic training of seamen in imitation of Seville's Casa de Contratacion, for a more rapid colonizing of North America, and even for opening overland trade routes through India to China, for which reason he too included large sections of the travels of Marco Polo in *The Principal Navigations*.

Who can say what motives prompted Frampton as he passed from translation to translation, turning linguistic skills that he had acquired at considerable risk to the benefit of his nation. His cataloguing and inventorying of plants, bays and harbors, stretching out to the geography of Asia were investments in the expansion of the English imagination that served as prelude to a variety of actions not entirely consistent among themselves. His retirement from Spain turned him into a man of the print-shops as his way of informing the new men of action, trade, travel, cartography and the gathering of news–an exercise paralleling the humanist recovery of the ancient world through travel to Italy and the translation of treatises. Yet how different these enterprises were in spirit and purpose. Frampton had gone as far as Seville and the southern ports to do business, not to collect lore. Yet he, too, brought home a language whereby, in due course, he was able to collect for the English what the Spanish had collected in the fields or through their own translators. Frampton intended his works not only for armchair travelers, but for the men of wind and waves. They were the productions of a unique historical configuration of events and circumstances, and the work of a traveler who through his translations would incite new travelers to the benefit of his country. In his old age, Frampton, in effect, remained a traveler through his translations, which he pursued with the particular vision of his age and with true Elizabethan flair.

---

[1] Frampton's circumstances were alluded to in a letter from Henry Chillon in Cadiz to Henry Hawks, Frampton's friend. Frampton was in trouble with his debtors and had only three years and three months to pay (Hakluyt 1967: vol. 1, 74).

[2] One of the most indicative incidents of this kind was the expulsion of John Man, the English ambassador, from the Court in 1668, "most discourteously dealt withall" considering his high position, and despite his indiscretion in speaking badly of the pope. In typical Spanish fashion, he was banished to a small village, and he and his servants were compelled to attend mass, all of which Elizabeth took "in ill part" (Camden 1970: 86).

[3] The size of the English community in the south of Spain after 1570 remains something of an historical tease. Both Richard Hakluyts were in constant contact with the English merchants there who, according to E.G.R. Taylor (Hakluyt 1967: vol. 1, 8), formed, as late as 1570, "the most numerous and influential group of Englishmen abroad". Principally they were in San Lucar and Seville where Hugh Tipton had a house that provided a point of social assembly. Richard Hakluyt, the London lawyer, was involved in receiving and passing on to Cecil news from Spain concerning the build-up of Spanish forces, and it is unimaginable that Frampton was not canvassed for all he knew upon his return, for he was in England in 1571-1572, at least for a time if not permanently. More to the point, however, is that by 1577 there was a pressing need for the formation of a Merchant Company uniquely concerned with the Spanish trade. When the organization came together, some 200 London merchant venturers signed on, together with another 173 from the outports, including 76 from Bristol. That is a substantial number by any count, giving clear evidence for a continuing trade with Spain in a variety of commodities from nearly all the ports of England from Chester around to Yarmouth and King's Lynn (McGrath 1975: 13). The *Patent Rolls*, 19 Eliz. pt. 8 states the number of members to have been 389.

[4] The origins and transmission of the materials relating to Marco Polo's travels are of such complexity as to require a monograph-length treatment to do the matter justice. But for our purposes, Frampton worked from the translation by Santella made in 1493 and published frequently in the sixteenth century: Seville in 1503; Toledo in 1507; and Seville again in 1518 and 1520. The copy used by Frampton may well have been the one from Loganaño published in 1529 (Frampton 1937: xvii).

[5] The life of Monardes is a by-way to our purposes, but it is a most fascinating one. He had been trained in Madrid, and had shown an interest in medical simples from early in his career. He lived in Seville until his death in 1588 where he practiced medicine, invested in trade ventures to the New World involving such commodities as slaves, leather and pork, and established a grand botanical garden where he raised plants sent to him from the Americas. His grand prosperity received a set-back in 1563 when Monardes fled to a monastery to escape his creditors (Wroth 1954: 306). His final years were devoted to his practice and to restoring his fortune, although speculation holds that he, like others, may have joined the priesthood in his last years. Monardes' writings on the botanical simples of the New World were revolutionary in nature, doing much to arouse interest in their commercial and pharmaceutical potential. In a sense, both he and Frampton labored in the same rhetorical vein to increase the profits of traders by raising the popular demand for new commodities through the press in books that appealed variously as medical manuals, herbals, and *cabinets de curiosité* containing the descriptions and histories of exotica.

[6] Significantly, Richard Hakluyt, an avowed propagandist for foreign expansion and colonization, raises the topic of medications in chapter 3 of his 1584 *Discourse of Western Planting* (1967: vol. 2, 222-223). There he prioritizes the exotic and medicinal flora of the New World, its "commodities" and wonder plants, as a reason for colonization. Although second to gold and precious minerals, the pharmacopoeia of the Americas was gaining in importance as a motive for exploration and settlement. In that regard, Frampton's *Joyfull Newes* enjoys an inaugural place. Without doubt, Hakluyt had been reading Frampton, for he cites his passage on sassafras and its wondrous properties, generalizing from there to include the many trees not found in Europe with their "drugs and spicerye" (*ibid.*: 225). The Spanish quest for spices and medications, in addition to their thirst for gold, is a topic of emerging interest; Philip II had sent Francisco Fernandes to Mexico as early as 1558 to investigate the medicinal plants and the pharmacopoeia of the natives. For an outline of that history see Beecher (1997: 1-13).

[7] The ups-and-downs of the Spanish trade from 1560 to 1581, covering the years when Frampton was active as a merchant and as a translator back in London, constitute a continuously evolving state of current affairs to be calibrated in terms of diplomacy, trade charters and companies, trade volume and trade deficits, the supply and demand of specific commodities, and the confiscations and imprisonments of factors and traders. Beliefs were volatile concerning these events, with feelings ranging from hatred and a desire for revenge to enthusiasm for the prospects of increased trade, and a relish for the political roles to be played by the merchants in securing their interests in relation to the duplicity of Elizabeth, the Spanish mission in London and the feuding Spanish emissaries, not to mention the revolving threats and remissions on the part of Philip II concerning trade, particularly to the Andalusian ports. Singular among these events were the embargo of 1568 lasting until April, 1573, following the confiscation of the Duke of Alba's payships in 1568, and the threatened embargos and confiscations following Drake's capture of silver during his Pacific coast raids. For further information on the commercial and diplomatic preludes to the 1585 closure of Spanish ports to all English shipping see Croft (1989: 281-302), and for a larger account of the negotiations and threats during the Drake affair from 1578 to 1580 (precisely the years of Frampton's activities as a translator) see *Calendar of State Papers* 94 (1), 230-231, and Croft (1973: xxiv). The point in question, where Frampton is concerned, is the degree to which his translations as political gestures should be read against this background of events, and the degree to which we can presume political positions on his part through his choices of subject matter.

[8] By actual count, of the dozens of plants collected and described by Monardes, only six are mentioned in the most complete and definitive list of *materia medica* in use in England, the *Pharmacopoeia Londinensis*, compiled by the royal physician, Theodore Turguet de Mayerne in

1618; among them, the best known are the Michoacan root, sassafras, guaiacum wood and nicotiana.

[9] The story of John Donne (not the poet) trading out of La Coruña is a revealing case in point. He had been delivering valuable information to Walsingham (as Roger Bodenham continued to do from Seville) about the build-up of the Spanish fleet, and was betrayed to the Spanish by a fellow Englishman, a factor in San Sebastian. By 1585 he managed to regain his freedom and return to England where he wrote a full report on Spanish shipping out of the northern ports (Haynes 1992: 85).

[10] The sassafras tree was represented pictorially on the Ferrar map of Virginia. Hakluyt included this plant in his *Discourse of Western Planting*, quoting from Frampton (Hakluyt 1967: vol. 2, 224). Raleigh requested Amadas and Barlowe to be on the look-out for it during their North American explorations. When Mace returned from Virginia without the lost members of the Roanoke colony, he brought sassafras in their place (Wroth 1954: 308). The plant commanded very high prices in England.

[11] The English remained largely uninvolved in the development of western pharmacology before the seventeenth century. They had no extensive botanical gardens nor did they contribute treatises on the medical classifications of plants. Hence, by pure default, Frampton's translation became the most important publication on medical simples in England between the herbal of William Turner, published in 1551, and Gerard's herbal of 1596. The great work of Cesalpino, L'Ecluse and Dodoëns, among many, would remain unknown in England before the seventeenth century.

[12] These two alone enjoy twentieth-century editions (see list of references), both in facsimile formats with scholarly introductions, both now rare collectibles in their own rights. The *Joyfull Newes* has eleven North American listings in the *National Union Catalogue*, while the *Travels* has only three.

[13] The original of this work was written by Martín Fernández de Enciso, who went to Santo Domingo as an adventurer as early as 1508, returning to Spain a decade later with a manuscript ready for publication that appeared in Seville in 1519 as the *Suma de geographia*. It was a book about navigation, and the earliest book on North American travel. The work purports to be a guide to world navigation. Much of it was presumably based on Enciso's personal experiences. This work was republished in Spanish in 1530 and 1546, and remained in circulation until it was called in by the King in 1558 because it contained too much specific information about the colonies that could fall into the wrong hands. This is a tell-tale fact. Frampton was not the first to translate it; Roger Barlowe did portions of it in 1541, while Jean Alfonce turned it into French in 1544. It may be no accident that Frampton dedicated his rendition to Sir Humphrey Gilbert who in those very years was planning a voyage to Spanish America. Who among his successors, including Francis Drake, may have used the book in making raids in the West Indies is open to speculation. If the book was intended for such use, Frampton's agenda again becomes transparent and in potential conflict with the Spanish merchants' desire to bring piracy to an end.

[14] This is the second book on China to appear in English. It missed being the first by only a year–anticipated by the translation made by Samuel Purchas of Da Cruz's *Tractado das cousas da China e de Ormuz*, published in Evora in 1569-1570. In its own right, it was borrowed from Galeotto Pereira, who had been a prisoner in China. Purchas published it in Willes's *Historye of Travaile*, London, 1577. Frampton's Escalante also incorporated information from Da Cruz and Joano de Barros, who started his great history of Portuguese explorations, the *Decades*, in 1540. Frampton's work on China would not be superseded until the publication of Robert Parke's 1588 translation of *Historia de las cosas mas notables, ritos y costumbres del gran Reyno de la China* of Juan Gonzales de Mendoza, first published in Rome in 1585.

[15] Thamara's book was published in Antwerp in 1556, bearing the title *Il libro de las Costumbres de todas las Gentes del mundo, y de las Indias*. It was based on the *Omnium gentium mores* of Johannes Boemus, a work already known to the English in the translation of William Waterman entitled *The Fardle of Facions*, published in London in 1555.

[16] The whole question of the biases of European investigators of foreign cultures, the prevalence of myth interfused with appraisals and misappraisals of aboriginal rites and mores cannot become

a part of the present study, although inevitably Frampton, as translator, becomes a retailer of all such matters invested in the perspectives of the original travelers. For information on this challenging *topos* see Margaret Hodgen's study.

[17] The Inquisition in Spain, even by popular reputation, is well-known for its "new dimensions of bigotry, nastiness, and terror" (Baigent and Leigh 2000: 62). It was under the direction of a secular government free to use the institution to its own political ends. There had been complaints of abuse from the outset against the autocratic Torquemada, who was not the only Inquisitor to send loyal Christians to execution on the testimony of rivals, enemies, and slaves. Moreover, the search for material wealth through confiscations had been an incentive to corruption from the outset.

[18] Bodenham turns out to be a rather ambiguous individual. He was not at all liked by the other members of the English community. He had a cousin in the service of the English-born Countess of Feria and was himself related to Sir James Croft, who was stoutly pro-Spanish and one of Leicester's enemies. Burghley seems to have refused his services as a spy, but Walsingham put him on the payroll. His fellow merchants may have distrusted him because he was too close to the Spanish, and perhaps acting as a double agent. The Spanish were, in fact, very well informed about Elizabeth's naval forces throughout the build-up of the Armada, undoubtedly encouraged by the fact that she was doing very little to repair deficiencies. That he was appointed the consul in San Lucar of the new Spanish Company had much to do with its failure (Croft 1973: xiii).

[19] Williamson examined these records carefully concerning Frampton's case, that is, both the *Libels* and the *Examinations* of the High Court of Admiralty. The *Libels* are records in Latin, on vellum, grimed, stained and chewed by rats, whereas the *Examinations* are on paper, in English, clean, and well-preserved (Williamson 1930: 546). The party made his case to the court as recorded in the *Libels*. Witnesses were then called, and the court prepared a series of questions which were then put to all witnesses and to the accused. Their answers appeared in the *Examinations*. Then the judge made a decision. In Frampton's case, there were no defendants present insofar as he was pursuing the King of Spain for the restitution of goods seized. His "Querela" was presented on December 21 and 30, 1572, and January 5 and 8, 1573. The exact details of his experiences with the Inquisition of Seville are derived from these accounts.

[20] Lawrence Wroth elaborates upon many of the details contained in the Admiralty Court proceedings. His account was presented at the Huntington Library in 1954 and published in the *Quarterly*, although regrettably without his references and documentation. Some of the details are presented rather novelistically: that Frampton was, at the time he allegedly walked from Lisbon to Seville in October, 1559,

> twenty-five, decently dressed, mounted upon a mule, wearing a sword, and carrying fixed to his belt something he called a 'bowgett' [or budget], that is, a leathern pouch or wallet in which he carried his cash, his book of accounts, and small articles of daily necessity. I [Wroth] know from documentary evidence that his clothes were decent, that he was armed and accoutered as I have said, and that he was riding a well-caparisoned mule of considerable cost. I know that but for the danger of robbery he might also have been wearing his two gold rings, one set with a diamond, the other with a ruby. (1954: 302).

Wroth relates Frampton's *faux pas* before the tribunal, which was his ignorance of the line "Sancta Maria, Mater Dei, ora pro nobis peccatoribus" in the "Ave Maria" which he could otherwise cite in the "English" fashion. Allegedly this was the reason for his torture. Frampton tells us in his own words that he was taken prisoner "to the house of torment, where he [the jailer] left me standing, God knows, in a place of great sorrow. And forthwith came in to me two men covered with white canvass coats, from their heads to their feet, and every of them a vizard upon their faces; and they said never a word to me, standing by me" (*ibid*.: 303). A description of the strappado follows. Wroth attributes Frampton's motives as a translator entirely to revenge, citing the article of 1930 by J.A. Williamson in which it is stated that Frampton and Nicholas, as victims of the Inquisition, "were 'responsible for much of the propaganda of Elizabethan imperialism' which 'was a more effective revenge than they could have taken by fitting out privateers and adding wrong to wrong at sea'" (*ibid*.: 305).

[21] During Frampton's ordeal there would have been a notary and a secretary present, together with the Inquisitors, a representative of the local bishop, a doctor and one or more torturers. Torture was used in accord with "the conscience and will of the appointed judges following law, reason and good conscience. Inquisitors should take great care that the sentence of torture is justified and follows precedence" (Kamen 1977: 188). Frampton was subjected to the "potro" or rack three times by resuming the first session after interruptions. Clearly the charges had been trumped up during his absence in order to confiscate his goods and make an example of him to the English community. Even common seamen before the mast were apprehended, to the great outcry of English diplomats, but to little avail (Tenison 1933: vol. 2, 120). The local tribunal, by vote of its members, decided upon the need for torture, and announced its vote to the victim. Frampton seems to have renounced his chance to confess, either because he had nothing to offer, or was not allowed to do so, and thus had the sentence read out to him. The only rule was that no blood could be drawn, and thus the "potro" along with the "garrucha" or pulley (strappado) and the "toca" or water torture by enforced drinking were employed. Once the Jews and Muslims were banished, Protestants became the favored target. The most outstanding case of English complaint where common seamen were concerned was put forward on behalf of her husband by Dorothy Seely. Her protest reached Philip II himself through diplomatic channels. Meanwhile her husband, Thomas, had paid three years of his life for striking a Spaniard in the process of defending his Queen's reputation abroad.

[22] Williamson (1930: 555) places his escape in 1567, and relates from the Admiralty Court records how Frampton left his San Benito behind, which the Inquisition recovered and burned in the next *auto de fé*. That was a significant gesture because Frampton was thereby turned into a non-entity, no longer having a "being" upon which he could claim restitution of his losses. Frampton, nevertheless, hired Spanish lawyers to initiate a procedure on his behalf, the first of the several forms of justice he would have to pursue before the Queen would agree to pay his losses by "letters of reprisal." Even the appearance before the Admiralty Court was merely a prelude to that final recourse, which was his only hope, given that the capture of the payships in 1568 had brought all legal relations between the two countries to an end.

[23] There is more work to be done in tracing the diverse roles played by the community of English merchants in Spain during these years. A few contributed writings to the anthologies on exploration and foreign trade compiled by the Hakluyts, in addition to Henry Hawks and Roger Bodenham. Further names meriting investigation, besides the Thornes and Barlowes (among the earliest out from Bristol), include John Chilton, Robert Tomson (also Bristol bred), Robert Sweeting, son of John Sweeting by his Spanish wife, and Sweeting's brother-in-law Leonard Chilton. Edward Hawks also shipped out of San Lucar de Barrameda, along with Thomas Wall. We can only have some idea of how Hispanized they must have become as a precondition to maintaining residence. Hakluyt (1967: vol. 2, 221) describes how Spanish officials would harass them, subjecting them to searches, often by priests of the Inquisition looking for signs of heresy, and who then demanded provisions and solemn secrecy concerning their activities at the same time. For English Protestants, it was an act of perjury in swearing to be Catholics, attending masses, and relinquishing all forbidden books–best defined as containing any language other than Spanish.

[24] Cecil's part in this moment of history was an important one. When the Spanish banned all foreign shipping in their colonial waters–territory defined as extending well beyond areas they had settled–Cecil declared to de Quadra, the Spanish ambassador, that England could not accept the Spanish-Portuguese monopoly on New World trade, or that their unsettled regions were not open to claim and settlement. The English protest was based on a pact of open trade declared by Charles V in the time of Henry VIII, permitting the English, by law, to participate in the Caribbean trade. Hawkins, from that perspective, had been seeking to do no more than exercise his rights, and acted surprised to have had his goods from the Guinea trade confiscated in Seville, despite the fact that he had returned them to Spain rather than to England in open belief that they were legitimately acquired (Black 1969: 123-124).

Donald Beecher

[25] George Best published in 1578 his *A True Discourse of the Late Voyages of Discoverie for the Finding of a Passage to Cathaya*. In 1582, there appeared Richard Hakluyt's *Divers Voyages Touching the Discoverye of America*. John Florio, after coaxing, had undertaken to translate Jacques Cartier's *The Two Navigations and Discoveries*. This work, more than any other, alarmed the English, given the inroads of the French into the northern part of the new land mass in the settlement of which the English were beginning to imagine themselves opposing the pretensions of Spain in Florida. Then Nicholas Lichefield undertook the translation of Lope de Castanheda's *Historie of the Discoverie and Conquest of the East Indias*, which appeared in 1582. Just such works as these provided the context in which Frampton's efforts were created, generating among them a common mythos in their collective preoccupation with the expansion of trade both to the east and to the west.

References

Acosta, Christoval. 1578. *Tractado de las drogas y medicinas de las Indies*. Burgos.
Baigent, Michael and Richard Leigh. 2000. *The Inquisition*. London: Penguin.
Beecher, Donald. 1997. 'The Book of Wonders of Nicholas Monardes of Seville' in *Cahiers Elisabéthains* 51: 1-13.
Black, J.B. 1969. *The Reign of Elizabeth 1558-1603*. Oxford: Clarendon Press.
Braudel, Fernand. 1966. *La Méditerranée et le monde méditerranéen à l'époque de Philippe II*. Paris: Seuil.
Calendar of State Papers Spanish, Elizabeth (ed. M.A.S. Hume). 1892-1899. 4 vols. London.
Camden, William. 1970. *The History of the Most Renowned and Victorious Princess Elizabeth Late Queen of England* (ed. Wallace MacCaffrey). Chicago: University of Chicago Press.
Carrington, C.E. 1968. *The British Overseas: The Exploits of a Nation of Shopkeepers*. Cambridge: Cambridge University Press.
Cartier, Jacques. 1580. *The Two Navigations and Discoveries* (tr. John Florio). London.
Carus, Wilson E. 1933. 'The Overseas Trade of Bristol' in Eileen Power and M.M. Postan (eds) *Studies in English Trade in the Fifteenth Century*. London: George Routledge & Sons.
Croft, Pauline. 1973. *The Spanish Company*. London: London Record Society.
–. 1989. 'Trading with the Enemy, 1558-1604' in *Historical Journal* 32(2): 281-302.
Fernándes de Enciso, Martin. 1519. *Suma de Geographia* (tr. Roger Barlowe). Seville.
Frampton, John (tr.). 1925. *Joyfull Newes out of the Newe Founde Worlde* by Nicholas Monardes (ed. Stephen Gaselee). 2 vols. London: Constable; New York, NY: Knopf.
– (tr.). 1937. *The Most Noble and Famous Travels of Marco Polo With the Travels of Nicolò de' Conti* (ed. N.M. Penzer). London: Adam and Charles Black.
Froude, James A. 1896. *English Seamen in the Sixteenth Century*. London: Longman's.
Gerard, John. 1596. *Herball or generall Historie of Plantes*. London.
Hakluyt, Richard and Richard Hakluyt. 1967. *The Original Writings & Correspondence of the Two Richard Hakluyts* (ed. E.G.R. Taylor). 2 vols. Nendeln, Liechtenstein: Kraus Reprint Ltd.
Hawkins, Sir John. 1569. *The Troublesome Voyage*. London.
Haynes, Alan. 1992. *Invisible Power: The Elizabethan Secret Services 1570-1603*. Wolfeboro Falls, NH: Alan Sutton.
Hodgen, Margaret. 1971. *Early Anthropology in the Sixteenth and Seventeenth Centuries*. Philadelphia, PA: University of Pennsylvania Press.
Kamen, Henry. 1977. *The Spanish Inquisition*. London: White Lion.
Loades, David. 1992. *The Tudor Navy: An administrative, political and military history*. Aldershot: Scholar Press.
MacCaffrey, Wallace T. 1981. *Queen Elizabeth and the Making of Policy 1578-88*. Princeton, NJ: Princeton University Press.

Maltby, William S. 1983. *Alba: A Biography of Fernando Alvarez de Toledo, Third Duke of Alba, 1507-1582*. Berkeley, CA: University of California Press.

McGrath, Patrick. 1975. *The Merchant Venturers of Bristol: A History of the Society of Merchant Venturers of the City of Bristol from its origin to the present day*. Bristol: The Society of Merchant Venturers.

Monardes, Nicholas. See John Frampton (1925).

Oviedo y Valdez, Fernandes de. 1526. *La natural historia de las Indias*. Toledo.

Penrose, Boies. 1967. *Travel and Discovery in the Renaissance 1420-1620*. Cambridge, MA: Harvard University Press.

Polo, Marco. See John Frampton (1937).

Pyenson, Lewis and Susan Sheets Pyenson. 1999. *Servants of Nature: A History of Scientific Institutions, Enterprises and Sensibilities*. New York, NY: Norton.

Ribaut, Jean. 1563. *The Whole and True Discoverye of Terra Florida* (tr. Thomas Hackett). London.

Rowse, A.L. 1955. *The Expansion of Elizabethan England*. New York, NY: Harper and Row.

Tenison, E.M. 1933. *Elizabethan England, Being the History of this Country in Relation to All Foreign Princes*. 13 vols. Royal Leamington Spa.

Tudor Royal Proclamations (eds P.L. Hughes and J.F. Larkin). 1964-1969. 3 vols. New Haven, CT: Yale University Press.

Vanes, Jean. 1975. *The Overseas Trade of Bristol in the Sixteenth Century*. Doctoral Dissertation: University of London.

Wernham, R.B. 1966. *Before the Armada: The Growth of English Foreign Policy 1485-1588*. London: Jonathan Cape.

Williamson, James A. 1930. 'Piracy and Honest Trade: An Elizabethan Contrast' in *Blackwood's Magazine* 227(1374): 546-556.

–. 1965. *The Age of Drake*. London: Adam and Charles Black.

Wroth, Lawrence C. 1954. 'An Elizabethan Merchant and Man of Letters' in *The Huntington Quarterly* 4: 299-314.

2.3. Thomas Hoby, Translator, Traveler

Kenneth R. Bartlett

Thomas Hoby's travels exerted a profound influence on his work as a translator. His use of classical authors almost as guides, and his close reading of Leandro Alberti's *Descrittione di tutta Italia* (1550), which became such a basic source of material in his journal that sections of it are direct translations from the Italian text, as well as his association with other foreign travelers and translators, such as William Barker, make Hoby's role in integrating the experience of travel and translation unique. Hoby's autograph journal, *The Travaile and Lief of Me, Thomas Hoby*, provides a highly detailed a running commentary on his Italian travels, undertaken in two separate visits in 1549-1551 and 1554-1556. An examination of this journal reveals an extremely rare insight into the thoughts and actions of a mid-sixteenth century author while travelling abroad, and as such illuminates the practice and purpose of translation.
Keywords: Italy, Leandro Alberti, Thomas Hoby, William Barker (Bercher), translation, travel.

As a translator, Thomas Hoby is best known for his version of *Il libro del cortegiano*, or *The Courtyer of Count Baldesar Castilio*. The influence of this text upon the intellectual and cultural imagination of the English Renaissance was enormous, and the function of its experimental use of the English language for translation seminal. Even during his own lifetime, Hoby's skills as a translator and his views on the role of undefiled, pure English and the avoidance of inkhorn terms were celebrated. No less a scholar than Sir John Cheke–tutor to prince, later King, Edward VI, secretary of state under Jane Grey, and luminary of classical scholarship at Cambridge where he held the first regius professorship in Greek–wrote a congratulatory letter to Hoby, printed at the end of the *Book of the Courtier*, in which he praises his former pupil at St. John's for his judicious use of pure English[1], an obsession with Cheke, whose own experiment with "pure" English for translation is represented in his partial rendering of the Gospel of St. Matthew crafted to avoid words without English roots.

Similarly, Hoby's profound experience with and knowledge of Italian culture is well reflected in his translation. The first edition of *The Book of the Courtier* contains as well an introductory sonnet by Thomas Sackville, another English traveler to Italy, who was not only to know adventure and incarceration in the peninsula but also to fulfill his literary promise under Elizabeth[2]. Furthermore, Hoby's more senior colleague at St.John's, another celebrated student of Cheke, Roger Ascham, witnessed for Hoby's ability as a translator both of Italian literature and Italian Renaissance culture when he recommended in *The Scolemaster* (1863: 82) that young Englishmen should avoid travel to the peninsula because of the moral and religious contagion everywhere to be found, and instead read Hoby's excellent English version of Castiglione at home in England where these promising youths might remain safely out of temptation's way. There can be no doubt, then, but that Hoby was recognized as that perfect union of reformed religion, high moral principle and deep knowledge of Italy: an ideal vehicle for the transmission of contemporary Renaissance Italian culture to the still rather rude England of mid century.

It is consequently of great importance to determine exactly how the creation of this paragon occurred: how did this young Englishman, furnished with a good but not extraordinary education, possessed of sufficient wealth and influence to travel freely, manage to become the model translator of mid sixteenth-century England? A youth who began his travels at seventeen and who was dead at age thirty-six somehow succeeded in developing a set of skills which quickly established him as the premier translator from the Italian for a receptive, but still insular and wary, English educated audience. The purpose of this paper is to explicate this mystery and trace the sources of Hoby's genius as translator, reflected in his education, his experience on the continent, his contacts and associations and his reading. What will emerge is a remarkable young man whose interest in translation began almost immediately after his first departure from England when he was still in his teens, continued through his travels in Europe and reached maturity in his version of Castiglione. He, moreover, had access to the best minds of Europe through his brother's connections, and to the university environment of Padua, which was then at the height of its acclaim as a humanist academy, located in one of the most liberal intellectual environments in Italy. Finally, Hoby's knowledge of Italian permitted him to take advantage of recent Italian language materials unavailable to those who could not read the vernacular. It is this element, Hoby's use of Italian sources, that will be the focus of my investigation.

We are fortunate to know more about Thomas Hoby than about most other contemporary Tudor translators[3]. First, he was the scion of a powerful family at court whose connections were wide, largely through the court and diplomatic career of his much older half brother, Sir Philip Hoby, and through his own rapid rise in Elizabeth's service as an ambassador. Also, these cultivated colleagues often shared Hoby's own education and intellectual ambitions, resulting in a certain amount of commentary about his life and his personality. But, finally, and most significantly, Hoby left an autograph travel journal, a kind of autobiography which traces his life from his teens until his last years, with most of the detail concentrated on the years of travel and education abroad, the seed ground of his success as a translator. This manuscript[4], *The Travaile and Lief of Me, Thomas Hoby*, is the key to his development as a traveler and translator; it also unlocks his profound dependence on Italian sources, illustrating how Hoby was in many ways a very ambiguously self-fashioned Tudor gentleman, with much of the material of his experience not really firsthand at all but dependent upon and often conditioned by what he read. In particular, Hoby's heavy reliance upon Leandro Alberti's *Descrittione di tutta Italia* (1550) gives rise to the serious question of whether Hoby's travel journal is the result of personal experience or of his reading of

Alberti. Was Thomas Hoby, then, the model integration of traveler and translator or was he instead more a translator of another's knowledge and experience? Where does Hoby the traveler end and Hoby the translator begin? Did he also translate his experience and make it his own without acknowledgement; and to what extent was his travel journal filtered through the lens of Leandro Alberti's *Descrittione*?[5]

First, it should be noted that Hoby was already a practiced translator before he began his work on Castiglione. I suspect that his interest in interpreting the thought and culture of the continent resulted from his humanist education and his remarkable set of intellectual mentors. Hence, some basic biography is in order.

Thomas Hoby, the son of William Hoby of Leominster, Hertfordshire, by his second wife, was half brother of the fiercely Protestant diplomat and courtier, Sir Philip Hoby. Thomas matriculated at St.John's College, Cambridge, in 1545, where he had studied with the Cheke-Ascham circle of humanists and where he had already exhibited his great facility in languages. By 1547 he was on the continent resident in Strasbourg with Martin Bucer with whom he studied divinity. He also enjoyed the tuition of Peter Martyr Vermigli in theology, Johan Sturm in humanities and Paul Fagius in Hebrew. Moreover, Hoby made repeated contacts with educated Englishmen returning from Italy, stopping in Strasbourg *en route* home. It was thus that he met William Thomas, the author of the first Italian grammar in English (1550) and of the *History of Italy* (1549), which is really more of a guide to the peninsula. Sir Thomas Wyatt the Elder, the popularizer of Petrarchan poetry at the court of Henry VIII and the translator of the first original translation from the Italian since Chaucer to see print in England (Aretino's *Penitential Psalms*), was another visitor who was introduced to the young man; Wyatt was passing through the city, bound for Italy. Bucer's household was, therefore, a dynamic intellectual environment and one in which Hoby clearly developed his native gifts as a translator and an interpreter of Italian Renaissance culture.

It was in Strasbourg that Hoby prepared his first translation, which would become his first published work: *The Gratulation of the Most Famous Clerk, Master Martin Bucer*, a version in English of Bucer's response to Stephen Gardiner's, Bishop of Winchester's, book on clerical marriage. The text is on the one hand easily explained as the work of Hoby's teacher and host, Bucer, on an English subject and translated from Latin rather than a vernacular language. It can be seen as the recognition of a master's preparation of a pupil for further studies and a work clearly associated with the religious and intellectual circle at St. John's as much as Strasbourg. Nevertheless, the point should not be lost that it is a work of translation. Of the many possible genres or instruments that could have been employed to honor his mentor, Hoby chose translation. Thus, the pattern of his literary career was already fixed.

After leaving Strasbourg in August 1548, Hoby set out for Italy by way of Venice before settling into studies at the University of Padua. There, as in Bucer's house, he made the most of a wonderful opportunity, although it is interesting that he did not appear to have registered as a formal student. He followed the lectures of Lazaro Bonamico (Niccolo Leonico's successor) in humanities, particularly in classical languages; he read civil law with Mantuanus, Turnellus and Caniolus, logic with Bernardino Tomitano and Italian literature with Claudio Tolomei: a galaxy of Padua's stars. Regardless of this rich curriculum, his education was designed to be practical as well as academic, so Hoby set out in June 1549 for a grand tour of Italy, visiting Ferrara, Bologna, Florence and Siena (all university cities) before departing for Rome in order to see the ancient monuments. There followed a very unusual journey through Naples to the south and to the island of Sicily. Hoby explains this unusual voyage for an English traveler at mid century as an opportunity "to absent my self for a while owt of Englishe mennes companie for the tunges sake" (Egerton 2148: 60r)[6]. Indeed, the tongues he must have heard in these often very remote regions of the Italian *mezzogiorno* were dialects, far distant from the literary Tuscan of Tolomei's lectures. Moreover, his experiences are extremely broad, another unusual element for his period. Not only does he discuss topography, history, political structures, curiosities, cities and natural phenomena, he also mentions folklore, such as the popular beliefs surrounding Mount Aetna–or Mongibello–and contemporary monuments: for example the fountain sculptures in Messina carved by Giovan Angelo Montorsoli, a follower of Michelangelo: "There I saw a fountain of verie white marble graven with the storie of Acteon and such other, by one Giovan Angelo a florentine, which to my eyes is one of the fairest peece of worke that ever I sawe" (*ibid.*: 69v-71v).

Hoby returned to Siena by way of Rome, reaching the Tuscan city on 9 May 1550. This second period in Siena is extremely important in Hoby's development as a translator as well. It is known that he sought formal studies of some kind at the university, as he notes that he settled himself "sumwhat to [his] booke" (*ibid*: 91v, 92r); but he also frequented the company of other English residents in the city, at least two of whom had some connection with the translation of Renaissance Italian literature: Henry Parker and, most significantly, William Barker (sometimes Bercher).

Parker was almost certainly the son of Henry Parker, Lord Morley. The commitment to Rome and the Catholic cause would result in the younger Parker spending most of his life on the continent, ending his days as a pensioner of Philip II of Spain[7]. Parker's father, Lord Morley, had exhibited a strong interest in contemporary Italian culture during the reign of Henry VIII, not only translating Petrarch's *Trionfi* but also introducing Thomas Cromwell to the historical works of Machiavelli (Bartlett 2000: 77-85 and Appendix 2, 230-231). Morley's son, therefore, was preconditioned to appreciate the Italian world, even if he himself seems not have written anything himself. And, of course, the example of the elder Parker as a translator would have been present in the son.

Barker, however, is far more interesting and important[8]. What Barker was doing on the peninsula is far from certain, although it is likely that he served as an intelligencer for the English court. He, too, had been a student at St.John's, despite his humble birth. Through the patronage of Anne Boleyn, Barker had gone up to Cambridge, a particularly ironic connection, given Barker's insistent Roman Catholicism and his own subsequent role in sending Queen Anne's enemy, the Duke of Norfolk, to the block in 1570. Also, the association with Parker then becomes interesting, as Parker's sister was married to Anne's brother, Lord Rochfort, who went to the scaffold with Queen Anne after a trial in which his own father-in-law, Lord Morley, was a commissioner, in another example of Henry VIII's signal cruelty and Cromwell's viciousness. Nevertheless, Barker seemed to have enjoyed access to the best society of Siena, staying at the villa at Petriolo of the Contessa d'Elci, which would thereafter serve as the frame for his translation of Lodovico Domenichi's dialogue, *La nobiltà delle donne*: *A Dyssputacion off the Nobylytye off Wymen*[9]. Indeed, Barker knew Domenichi quite well, having met Duke Cosimo's librarian in Florence when Barker was there as a student of the "popular" university surrounding the poligrafici Anton Francesco Doni and Giovanbattista Gelli. Barker knew this salty world of dialect vernacular and sharp observation sufficiently well that he would become the translator of one of its most celebrated works, Gelli's *I capricci del bottaio* (1549) or *The fearefull fansies of the Florentine cooper* (1568).

Hoby shared another passion with Barker, which must have not only linked them intellectually but also animated their travels together: collecting funerary epitaphs, both classical and modern. Hoby's journal is widely adorned with these inscriptions, copied from tombs throughout Italy. It is interesting how Hoby changes his orthography and hand in reporting these epitaphs, switching from his highly legible English secretary to a very refined italic[10]. The degree to which Hoby shared his transcriptions of epitaphs with Barker is clear, inasmuch as Barker returned to England to have printed in 1554, that is almost immediately after his travels with Hoby, his *Epitaphia et inscriptiones lugubres* reflecting his investigation of the entire peninsula; or, as might well be possible, borrowing from Hoby those epitaphs he did not personally transcribe, using instead his fellow traveler's work as his own in the recording of ancient and royal tomb incriptions[11].

What an environment for Hoby to encounter in Siena: the aristocratic but Catholic Henry Parker, son of one of the first major translators of Italian material at the English court, and the base born but brilliant and ambitious, and also steadfastly Catholic, William Barker, translator of the piquant wit of the best of the poligrafici! There must have been discussion of translation and contemporary Italian literature in this company, adorned as it was as well by the celebrated, if perhaps over-rated Domenichi, with his access to the Grand Ducal Library, and the elegant gentlemen and ladies of the Sienese nobility, bearing names such as Borghese and Elci. Also, it should be noted that, although Barker did not attempt to use a "pure"English in his translations, he did recognize that he was doing more than rendering the words of his original, given his fundamental changes to Domenichi's text and his addition of uniquely English material, such as the praise of learned Englishwomen. Again, Hoby's travels and his experiences abroad paid dividends to his work as a translator, as he absorbed knowledge, insight, techniques and indirect lessons. Consequently, despite the evident fact that Hoby was interested in and inclined to translation from the moment he set out from England, as witnessed by his version of Bucer's Latin tract on clerical marriage, his facility in translation from the vernacular was polished by his time abroad in Italy which provided both experience of the culture he would interpret in *The Book of the Courtier* and practical advice on how to go about transmitting a complex text, deeply embedded in one place and time, to another. Given the intensity of Hoby's Italian experience and its duration, it can be reasonably said that he would come to know contemporary Italy as well as his native England, making him the ideal vehicle for their mutual revelation.

Hoby was summoned from Siena by his brother, Sir Philip, and required to attend upon him at the imperial court then at Augsburg. Thomas dutifully obeyed and left for Germany, abandoning his informal studies (no record of him remains in Siena, not even a licence to bear arms). His time there was short, as he is recorded in London in December of 1550; but it was extremely productive, again in the genre of translation, but this time of a very recent and controversial Italian vernacular text. Although he might have begun his version of Francesco Negri Bassanese's *Tragedia di F.N.B. intitolata, Libero Arbitrio* (printed 1546) here, it was in Augsburg that he completed it. The text is a morality play with powerfully Protestant, hence in Italy heretical, elements. This is Hoby's first completed translation from the Italian, as he records in his journal: "I translated into Englishe the Tragedie of ffree will, which afterward I dedicated to my Lord Marquess of Northamptone" (Egerton 2148: 94v). It was, however, not sent to the press and consequently does not survive. Still, the example is instructive, for we have Hoby, resident at the imperial court with his hot gospeller half brother, the ambassador, just fresh from his sojourn in Siena where he had lodged with the Catholics Parker and Barker, producing an Italian *spirituale* text which clearly reflects his own religious perspective and challenges that of his compatriots and their Italian colleagues in Italy.

It is also possible that the text might actually survive under another name. A translation of Negri Bassanese's work was printed under the name of Sir John Cheke's son, Henry (in 1589?), as *A Certain Tragedy Written First in Italian by F.N.B. Entitled Freewill*[12]. Perhaps this is only a remarkable coincidence; but Sir John Cheke was well known to Hoby from his time at St. John's, and they would be intimate once more during the reign of Mary when both were in Italy as religious and political exiles, studying in Padua and sharing the fruits of their scholarship. Perhaps this translation was produced as a result of Hoby's early death and Henry Cheke's possession of his father's papers. However, in the absence of concrete evidence, this can only remain conjecture.

Hoby's return to England and his entry into the service of the Marquis of Northampton was the occasion for his beginning the translation of Castiglione's *Cortegiano*. In his journal he writes that after an illness he repaired to France to study; and "after I had convayed my stuff to Paris and settled my self there, the first thing I did was to translate into Englishe the third Booke of the Cowrtisane, which my ladie marquess had oftene willed me to do and for lacke of time ever differred it" (Egerton 2148: 114r). Hoby's own account, then, seems to indicate that he only began his famous translation in 1552 and, strangely, in France, and as the result of a request from his patron's wife, who had a particular interest in Book Three, which deals with the ideal court lady. Again, could his knowledge of Barker's interest in the equally feminine content of Domenichi's *La nobilità delle donne* have had some influence? Could Hoby have hoped to pre-empt Barker's text, which was first presented in manuscript and not printed until much later, even though internal evidence indicates that it was written while Barker was in Siena during the reign of Edward VI? Again, it is impossible to say, but once more the experience of Hoby in Italy might well have had an influence on his work as a translator.

There were other fruits from Hoby's Italian experience and cultural knowledge made manifest at the court of Edward VI. In his journal Hoby records how another important courtier, Sir Henry Sidney, father of Sir Philip Sidney who would himself be a traveler to Italy, requested him to write for his own use an epitome of the Italian language (*ibid*.: 114r). Unfortunately, the work does not survive, so it is impossible to say how thorough a guide it was. Hoby notes that he did as he was asked but does not reflect its contents: was it merely a synopsis of William Thomas' *Italian Grammar*, printed just a few years before? This seems unlikely, given that Thomas' book must have been still available, and indeed Thomas himself was a favored companion of the young king and was actively engaged in his education, teaching him politics from the writings of Machiavelli[13]. It is probable, then, that Hoby's work was much shorter and simpler and directed exactly to Sidney's needs, whatever those might have been. Still, it is instructive to note that Hoby's reputation as a master of the Italian language and a devotee of Italian culture was such that he would have been requested by someone of Sidney's stature to introduce him to Italian.

Hoby completed his translation of Castiglione in Italy during his second residence, most likely in early 1555. He, together with his brother, left England in May 1554 to escape Mary's restoration of Catholicism and to protect themselves from Sir Philip's involvement in conspiracies against the new reign and restored religion. This period of enforced leisure was not dissimilar from Hoby's earlier sojourn in the peninsula, except that his maturity and his powerful friends disassociated him to some extent from the lives of students and even Italians more so than before. Also, Sir Philip's poor health, and his own, required visits to baths, trips he describes with some measure of detail, including the insertion of material collected at the spas themselves attesting to their efficacy and often written by celebrated physicians (*ibid.*: 161v-169v). He continued to travel, usually in the company of former high office holders or courtiers from the time of Edward VI who had sought refuge in Italy after the failure of Northumberland's attempted coup. Men such as Sir John Cheke, Sir Thomas Wrothe, Sir Henry Neville and Hoby's brother, Sir Philip, now constituted his companions. They lived together in Padua, where Cheke read Greek with Thomas Wilson, future author of *The Art of Rhetoric*[14], and informally studied Italian and civil law; they traveled to Mantua together and eventually out of Italy where Sir Philip Hoby and Cheke would become leaders in the continental conspiracies against Philip and Mary (until Cheke's kidnapping, that is) while Thomas Hoby continued on to England, recording his repatriation in January of 1556.

The *Travaile and Lief of Me, Thomas Hoby* becomes extremely sketchy after his return to England where he took up residence on his brother's estate of Bisham Abbey, lands he would inherit on Sir Philip's death. He notes important moments, but in small detail, including his marriage in 1557 to Elizabeth, learned daughter of the courtier Sir Anthony Cooke and sister to the remarkable, educated wives of Sir William Cecil (whose first wife had been Cheke's sister), Sir Henry Killigrew (Hoby's fellow traveler in Italy), and Sir Nicholas Bacon. Upon inheriting Bisham Abbey he translated other, more concrete Italian ideas into England. At great expense he had built an Italianate fountain, now lost, which reflected his love of Italian gardens and perhaps his respect for the Renaissance sculpture he admired enough to describe in his journal, such as the Montorsoli Acteon fountain in Messina. Subsequently, after the accession of Elizabeth, Hoby was quickly preferred at court, rising eventually to a knighthood and an appointment as ambassador to France in 1566. Tragically, Hoby died almost immediately after assuming his place at the French court and was buried, together with his brother Sir Philip, in a splendid Renaissance tomb in Bisham church.

The period of quiet repose in Italy between January 1556 and his return to court under Elizabeth almost four years later is, I think, the critical moment for the creation of his journal and the most vivid evidence of his self-definition as a translator, because, I suggest, it is the time when he translated himself, fashioning his experience on the continent, especially in Italy, into the detailed, coherent experience which emerges from the autograph manuscript of the journal. I am proposing that the journal was not composed while Hoby was abroad but was the result of his emotion recollected in tranquility, a conscious self-fashioning of his experience, and not altogether his own. Although there is no doubt but that Hoby did traverse the Italian peninsula, his memory was clearly reinforced through his close reading of Leandro Alberti's

Descrittione di tutta Italia, a book he could not have used as his guide since it was first printed in 1550 and thus was available only for Hoby's second voyage to Italy, whereas much of the description comes from the earlier period. Hoby, then, embellished both his experience and his journal by using a printed Italian text to structure his experience. His real role as traveler was supplemented by his subsequent knowledge of armchair travel. This, then, poses the question of whether Hoby really did see and do all he describes in the journal; or, did he mix the vicarious knowledge available from Alberti with real experience? A close reading of Hoby's journal against Alberti's text in the 1550 edition can provide evidence concerning Hoby's actual experience abroad and his unacknowledged debt to one of the most popular guides to Italy written during the early modern period.

First, it is important to know Leandro Alberti and his extremely successful text. Alberti (1479-c.1552) was a Dominican trained in both *litterae humaniores* and theology[15]. He traveled widely throughout Italy, especially in 1525 when he accompanied the general of his order through southern Italy and Sicily. Subsequently, he was very active in the Dominican house in his native Bologna; and in 1536 he was named vicar of Santa Sabina in Rome. Although he had written numerous works on the history of his order, his first secular study was a history of Bologna (*Historie di Bologna*) to which he added material throughout his life, and which was printed in a much enlarged posthumous edition.

The first printing of his immensely popular *Descrittione* appeared in 1550 in Bologna. Between 1551 and 1631, ten more editions followed, eight of them appearing in Italy and two (1566 and 1567) in Cologne. The text is heavily indebted to the pioneering work of Flavio Biondo, particularly his *Italia illustrata*; however, Alberti adds much material, such as economic and demographic observations. His own description of his book was *geografico, topografico e historico insieme*. The last years of his life saw him at work with the Inquisition while preparing his last work, *Tavola delle principali famiglie Bolognesi, et delle piu notabili cose raccolte in tutti i libri cronicali di Bologna*, which was not printed until 1592, some 40 years after the death of the Dominican.

It is clear that the organization, structure, varied content and encyclopedic character of Alberti's popular guide to Italy reflected Hoby's own interests and his needs. Also, the nature of Hoby's other reading becomes clear in those passages where he does not rely either on his own experience or on Alberti. For example, Hoby's excellent classical education at St. John's emerges as he notes places significant in the ancient world by quoting or paraphrasing Livy in particular but also Pliny, Virgil and other authors. Livy, indeed, serves as a kind of secondary guide for Hoby as he passes by and through sites described by the ancient authors. His references to the poets are clearly often from memory, inasmuch as he commits minor errors in his quotations (Bartlett 1993: 155-156); consequently, there can be little doubt but that these associations are immediate and personal and not dependent upon any singular source. The same can be said of Hoby's interest in folklore and society gossip, and of his record of his personal social connections, whether repeating details of a famous murder in Venice, discussing advice offered by peasants as he traveled through Calabria or describing his reception in Siena by the Spanish governor, Don Diego de Mendoza, or the Piccolomini-Aragona prince, the Marquis of Capistrano, son of the Duke of Amalfi, or the circumstances in the Roman conclave to which he repaired quickly by joining the entourage of Cardinal Salviati as it made its way to Rome in expectation of the election of Reginald Pole as pope. The very current observations on famous events or buildings, such as his comments on the still incomplete Villa Giulia, which he encountered as he entered Rome through the Porta Flaminia, equally seem immediate and personal. And, these examples in particular make Hoby stand out for his tolerance and understanding, something quite absent in the contemporary observer of Italy, William Thomas. Nowhere does Hoby take the opportunity to repeat the scurrilous gossip about the builder of the villa he describes, Julius III, who, when raised to the see of Peter, elevated his boy monkey keeper, well known to be his catamite, to the sacred college. Nor is there any Protestant invective against the papacy, cardinals or the Roman clergy, something Thomas execrates so viscerally. Thus, there can be no doubt but that many of Hoby's descriptions, observations and experiences are his own and reflect his educated, tolerant and enquiring nature.

The same cannot be said, however, about Hoby's use of Alberti. In fact, Hoby's complete reliance on the *Descrittione* tells much about his work as both traveler and translator, because it can be shown that significant passages of Hoby's journal do not represent the individual experience of the traveler recording his personal observations and reflections but rather of an armchair traveler sitting comfortably in his library at Bisham Abbey in Berkshire reconstructing his travels in Italy and embellishing his experience through the work of others. Alberti, then, was not necessarily Hoby's guide through Italy on his first voyage but rather an ex post facto mnemonic, a store of details to add to his recollections and a structure which might have greatly influenced his own. And, since Alberti's book was written in Italian, and Hoby wrote his journal in English, this unacknowledged derivation of important passages constitutes in its own way a translation, both in word and in deed: Hoby made Alberti's eyes and words his own.

It should be noted immediately that Hoby was not unique in his use of secondary sources for his original travel material. His contemporary and acquaintance, William Thomas, did it as well. The most telling passage comes from Thomas's discussion of Rome where he notes two distinct full size equestrian bronzes of *il gran villano*, the other of an ancient emperor, Marcus Aurelius or Lucius Verus: one he describes as in front of San Giovanni in Laterano; the other on the Campidoglio. Of course, they refer to the same statue of Marcus Aurelius. Thomas could not possibly have seen the bronze by San

Giovanni, since it had been moved by Michelangelo a decade before as part of the redesign of the Capitoline for Paul III: as Parks points out, then, Thomas must have taken this information from an older source unacknowledged (Thomas 1963: 42-43). So, the question remains whether Thomas saw San Giovanni at all, because he should have known that the horse and rider were no longer there.

Hoby's reliance on Alberti, however, is profound, and today would certainly constitute an act of plagiarism. This debt to Alberti was first described in a *tesi di laurea* by Maria Grazia Padovan at the University of Pisa in 1981. Padovan compares passages of Hoby's journal with Alberti's text, in the 1551 edition. The conclusions are startling. Just one of Padovan's six selected parallel passages should indicate how much of the descriptive material in Alberti is nothing short of an almost verbatim translation in the Englishman's journal. This is the description of the *terra di lavoro*, outside of Naples, as it appears in Hoby's manuscript:

> Departing therfor owt of the noble Citie of Naples there appearethe Before owr eyes this pleasant and sweet Cou*n*treye which bringeth furthe suche necessarie matters for the use of man*n* and Beast. And there is gathered great abundance of Wheate, Barlie and other graine, with sundrie sortes of good wines, so abunantlie that a man*n* would think it a straunge thing and almost incredible how it were possible to gather owt of on*e* self feelde so great abundance of Corne and Wyne. Ffor so many vines are upon*n* a verie highe tree and Brances of them*e* so dispersed abowt the boowes of the tree, that som*e* times of on*e* of them*e* they make two hoggesheades of wine, as I was informed by thinhabitant*es* of the Countrey, and indeede a man*n* may iudge no lesse (albeit it appeare a straung matter at first) yf he behold it well. And of this dothe plinie make mention*e* in the 14 Booke, 2. chapter. declaring it as a wondrous matter. (Egerton 2148: 52r)

This passage should be compared with Alberti's description:

> Vscendo poi fuori della molto magnifica Citta di Napoli (uolendo ritornare alla descrittione principiata) apare l'ameno & diletteuole paese, & grandemente produceuole non solamente delle cose necessarie per uso degli huomini & degli animali, ma altresi per le delitie & piaceri sensuali. Et prima se ne trahe da esso grand'abondanza di grano, orzo, & d'altre biade, con molte generationi di buoni Vini, & tanto copiosamente che parera a chi non hauera ueduto, cosa quasi incredibile, come sia possibile che d'un medesimo campo si caua tanta abondanza di Frumento & di uino. Conciosia cosa che si uedeno tante uiti sopra d'un altissimo albero, & tanto alargate sopra li rami di essi, che alcuna uolta da uno di quelli se ne cauano due dogli di uino o siano dodici barili, & altresi sedici come a me diceuano gli habitatori de'l paese, & etiandio Facilmente si po giudicare da chi le vede benche prima a me paresse cosa difficile da credere, auanti gli hauesse ueduto. Et di cio ne fa memoria Plinio nel quarto decimo libro nel capo secondo, narrandolo come cosa marauigliosa. (1550: 167b)

The resemblance is more than reliance on shared experience: Hoby's text is a translation of Alberti's. This example is one of the most egregious in Padovan's analysis. She notes other characteristics of the translator, such as the collation of two passages in the original into a single description in the Hoby manuscript

(1980-1981: 215). She observes, as well, that Hoby did interpret the original in some instances, rendering the Italian into extremely clear and evocative English, a facility that reflected Hoby's profound understanding of the nuances of Italian and that permitted him to translate the difficult text of Castiglione (*ibid.*: 219-220). Moreover, Hoby's careful rehearsal of Alberti's classical allusions (as in the Pliny entry above) indicates clearly that Hoby saw the value of the original ancient text and copied the precise reference drawn in the *Descrittione*; this characteristic of the careful translator should be seen as an additional indication of Hoby's classical education and his concern for the most effective application of the information in his own journal. Nevertheless, Hoby's use of Alberti is seldom extremely literal in many of the passages studied by Padovan. As she says: "raramente Hoby ricorre ad una traduzione strettamente letterale. In genere, preferisce compiere una rielaborazione, più o meno sintetica, del testo originale, forse per maggiore chiarezza o, forse, per evitare gli scogli di certe frasi troppo ornate dell'Alberti" (*ibid.*: 220). Here Padovan recognizes Hoby's intent to use clear and simple English in his journal, as was his ambition in *The Courtier*. And Cheke's recognition of Hoby's desire to avoid inkhorn terms or euphuistic, heavily italianate language is thus prefigured in this personal journal, written in Hoby's own hand.

Padovan compared only those passages in Alberti and Hoby that described southern Italy: as a *tesi di laurea*, however, her work was of necessity limited in scope. It is important therefore to replicate her conclusions elsewhere in the two texts. Let Hoby's description of Tuscany stand alongside Alberti's. Tuscany is an instructive area for such a comparison. First, Hoby knew the region very well personally, having spent much time in Siena, and having traveled through it on several occasions while visiting the south and Rome. It was also where he shared the company of other Englishmen, especially William Barker, whose own experience could have served as an independent source for Hoby's memory of the Tuscan landscape and major cities. In short, unlike southern Italy, which Hoby passed through but once and was the first recorded Englishman to do so extensively (Chaney 1984: 139), Tuscany was very familiar territory which did not require a measure of secondary research to record or reveal. Nevertheless, Alberti figures here as well. Compare Hoby's discussion of Florence with Alberti's:

> Within fflorence is the faire churche called Santa Maria del fiore all of marble, in the top of yt is the marvelous peece of worke called la Cupula, worthie to bee seene of all travellars. Withowt this Churche there is a rounde temple dedicated to Saint Ihon*e* Baptist, which in times past was the temple of Mars, with gat*es* of Brasse, within the *whi*che is a faire vessell made of riche stohnes, where childr*ene* are christened. Abowt this vale yet was *that* Hannibal lost on*e* of his eyes riding throwghe the marishes, as lyvie maketh menti*one*. (Egerton 2148: 24r)

> Et prima uedesi quel maraueglioso Tempio di S. Maria de'l Fiore tutto di marmo crustato, oue e quella stupenda cupola tanto arteficiosamente fatta da Filippo Brunelesco Fiorentino eccelente archittetore [...]. Et poi poco si dimostra l'antiquissimo

Tempio di Marte, fatto a forma ritonda, con grand'ingegno, hora dedicato a S. Giovanni Battista, oue e il soperbo vaso de'l quale si bateggiano li fanciulli, Le cui Porte sono di metallo con tanto arteficio condotte [...]

Et quiui al presente si uedono tutti cultiuati, & lauorati che paiono uaghi giardini, che sono nomati Valle di Arno. Ne fa memoria di questa diletteuole Valle Liuio, descriuendo il uiaggio fatto da Annibale per questi luoghi, dimostrando come era paludosa in quelli tempi, & come ui perse un'occhio per la fredda stagione [...]. (1550: 41b, 46a)

Here Hoby has clearly taken passages separated widely in Alberti and collated them in order to achieve a briefer, more focused description. His interest in classical authors required him to include the observations from Livy on Hannibal's loss of his eye; but much else that Hoby might have included has been edited out. His intent, therefore, was not to produce a translation of large selections from Alberti but rather to use Alberti's information as needed to enliven or elaborate his own narrative.

Compare these short passages as well:

Bolsena: This [Bolsena] is an antient towne and in times past on of the xii of Tuscane called urbs vulsinentium. These were the xii: Gianiculum, Arinianum, Fesuli, Aringianum, fregenie, Volce, Volaterra, Carriara, Oggiano, Arezzo, Roselle, Volsinio. By this towne there is a faire lague, so called. (Egerton 2148: 28v)

Vi e sopra questo Lago, Bolsena assai honoreuole Castello, & ben pieno di popolo, edificato sopra le ruine dell'antica Città, nominata Vrbs Vulsinensium dagli antichi, annouerrata fra le prime dodici Città d'Hetruria [...]. (1550: 63b)

Significantly in these selections Hoby has added substantially to the text of Alberti, once more as a result of his classical education and interest in the ancient world. Naming the twelve towns of the Etruscans as opposed to merely noting that Bolsena was among them provides useful information of a kind to which Hoby would have had direct access from his knowledge of Livy. Rather than merely depend on Alberti for his material, then, Hoby uses the text of the *Descrittione* as a platform on which to construct a more complex analysis of the places described in his journal.

There appears soon after the above passage Hoby's discussion of Montefiascone:

This towne was wont to be named Mons Phiscon and Arx Iti. Betwext Bolsena and this we ride throwghe the woode of Tuscane called in the olde time Lucus Vulsinentium or lucus Hetruriae. Abowte this towne there growe verie good and plesant wines, as malueseye and suche other [...]. (Egerton 2148: 29r)

[...] & entrando nella Via che conduce da Bolsena a Viterbo, & caminando per essa arriuasi al Bosco di Monte Fiascone, dagli antichi Lucus Vulsinensium nomato, & da Plinio Lucus Hetruriae.
Fu altresi dimandata questa Città, Mons Phiscon, & Arx Iti come dinota Catone [...]. (1550: 64b-65a)

What is interesting in this pair of passages is that Hoby suppresses Alberti's use of classical sources, Cato and Pliny in this instance. Why did the Englishman, so familiar with ancient literature not do what he had done so often before, either repeat or elaborate on Roman material? It is impossible to say. It is obvious from many other examples that he knew Pliny extremely well; it is likely he also knew the text of Cato as well. The only reasonable conclusion is that Hoby felt it unnecessary, as it appears in a section of the journal describing his journey from Siena to Rome. He does, though, choose to comment on the wine of Montefiascone!

The relationship of Hoby's journal to the printed version of William Barker's *Epitaphia et inscriptiones lugubres, a Gulielmo Berchero, cum in Italia, animi causa, peregrinetur collecta* is equally ambiguous. A collation of the long sections of epitaphs included in Hoby's work and in the printed text by Barker reveals a great many parallels. The possibilities are these: Hoby and Barker traveled together and obviously both enjoyed transcribing Latin inscriptions; so, they might have each independently recorded the most important examples of Latin epigraphy in the cities they visited. Equally, Barker might have taken advantage of Hoby's material and copied the epitaphs recorded during Hoby's first journey through Italy, the occasion when most of the inscriptions were to be found. Or, finally, back in England, at Bisham, while completing his fair copy of the journal, he had beside him Barker's phantom 1554 edition and transcribed the epitaphs he found in his former friend's text. (He could not have used the 1566 printing, since that is the year of Hoby's death and he was at court and in France at the time of its appearance.)

It is possible, then, that Hoby borrowed not only from Leandro Alberti in the preparation of his journal but also from his traveling companion, William Barker, whose transcription of epitaphs was used to augment the experience of his own travels. It should be noted, however, that the text printed by Barker is quite different from Hoby's: Barker includes inscriptions from many cities that Hoby does not record. Certain important centers, such as Naples, appear very much as they do in Barker, but such instances might be coincidental or evidence of shared experience and mutual interest on the part of the two Englishmen.

This, then leads to the question of why Hoby wrote his journal at all and why he included the material he did. Why was there the imperative for Thomas Hoby to recreate his journey on the continent in the form of what can be seen as the first record of what would become the grand tour? Several conclusions are possible, but all revolve around my contention that Hoby wrote the journal in England, after 1556, that is, after his repatriation following his second voyage to the continent. The evidence in the manuscript is suggestive and might indeed reveal his motives and explain why Hoby helped invent the genre of the autobiographical travel account.

There can be no doubt but that the MS is a fair copy. It has very few corrections and is in a clear, elegant, coherent English secretary script. The Latin and Italian passages, significantly, are in a practiced italic and reflect the italianate nature of their subject. The structure of the text is also one on which very complex principles of edition have been imposed. For example, in noting the distances traveled from day to day he carefully places his material in an easily searched, indented format. He also imposes rather mysterious symbols associated with particular places: some of these are quite easily broken, such as the orb for an imperial city; but others are very obscure, especially since two references to the same city can contain two different symbols. It is likely that these symbols mean more than the size or allegiance of a town: they likely refer to Hoby's method of travel to it and some other personal assessment. It is very likely that this unique, in fact eccentric and obscure, system of notation developed as Hoby traveled on the continent and constituted a means of recording his experience. Once back in England he retained it. Also, he is careful to note distances, something he likely had to verify, given his means of transport. And, the interpenetration of Alberti's text, the epitaphs and elements of local and international news reflect the hybrid quality of the work. Hoby was clearly receiving information from various sources: some of this was necessarily local, such as gossip, folklore and regional history; some was derived from his powerful contacts in Italy: Diego de Mendoza, Cardinal Salviati, the Marchese di Capistrano, for instance. This material is obviously unique and immediate, indicating that he collected it while abroad and merely transcribed it in England. This is illustrated in his detailed descriptions of the rooms he and his English companion, Henry Whitehorn, the musician, occupied in the castle at Amalfi as guests of the Duchess and her son, the Marchese di Capistrano, or of the elegant entertainments offered to him in Siena by Mendoza, the Spanish governor (Egerton 2148: 82r-v, 25r). Despite the fair copy script and the integration of such material into the narrative, there can be no doubt but that these elements are Hoby's alone, and dependent upon no other source.

Hoby's journal is, therefore, a complex weaving of secondary and primary knowledge, carefully fashioned into a singular narrative reflecting the experience of the translator-traveler abroad. He constructed a coherent piece of autobiographical writing which described both the nature of his travels and the contours of his life until his return to England in 1555, after which the entries become few and brief, noting only the most significant events–such as illnesses, deaths, his marriage, the birth of children, his work on the fabric of Bisham, and some pointed observations about the political and religious events of his time. These, however, are almost in chronicle format, listed succinctly and without any attempt at narrative structure. It is obvious, then, that Hoby either lacked the opportunity to sustain his journal when at Bisham or no longer felt it necessary. He must have been extremely occupied during his last years; and his efforts on his travel journal were perhaps limited to the recreation of his time abroad in the fair autograph copy which survives, embellished with material from Alberti and Barker. Furthermore, he was also probably polishing his translation of Castiglione's *Cortegiano*, since his English version did not see print until 1561, some years after he likely completed it. What is extremely interesting is that there is no mention of its printing in Hoby's journal.

The manuscript offers some additional clues to Hoby's intention in preparing the fair copy that now survives as BL Egerton 2148. There are marginal notations in a second hand, that of his son, either Edward or Thomas Posthumous. These marginal comments provide a kind of digest of the material in the narrative and occasionally add more detailed identifications of individuals. Also, appended to the end of the manuscript is an index, again prepared by one of Sir Thomas's sons. It can be suggested, then, that Hoby, who was very often ill in the last years of his life, prepared the finished, polished version of his journal for the edification of his son, in case he did not live to see the boy reach maturity. Hoby would certainly have been familiar with the Italian tradition of the *ricordanze* and this might have provided the motivation for his most unusual autobiographical travel account. In many ways it parallels those of Florentine patricians, such as the diary of Buonaccorso Pitti[16].

Therefore, once more, it can be argued that Hoby's experience in Italy defined his culture: his journal is a translation of an indigenous Italian genre into an English text, largely without parallel or earlier examples in the 1550s and 60s. Hoby was in every way, then, a translator, applying his Italian models to his English experience. It is not only the splendid monument of his translation of Castiglione's *Cortegiano* that witnesses for his role as one of the first translators of Italian contemporary literature and culture into English; it is also his life itself which served as an instrument of cultural mediation. He was the first Englishman to travel extensively through southern Italy and Sicily and to record his experiences for others; he was also one of only a small group of mid century English traveler-translators who approached the civilization of cinquecento Italy as a subject worthy of interpretation and understanding in its own right, with no overt, compelling religious bias but with a deep appreciation and knowledge born of familiarity with the language and the context of contemporary Italian culture. Hoby was, therefore, not just a traveler and translator, he was in some ways the instrument through which Elizabethan England would ultimately connect with Italy. There was no Venetian ambassador in England under Elizabeth and the issue of religion isolated that kingdom to some degree both from the ancient tradition of the Roman *respublica christiana* and from the modern fascination with things Italian that the previous generation of English Protestant writers had scorned, as witnessed in the text of Hoby's teachers–Ascham in his *Scolemaster* and Cheke in his letters to his wife from Italy, and in Archbishop Parker's identification of Cardinal Pole with evil, the consequence of his residence in the peninsula[17].

Hoby was thus an instrument in reconnecting the educated, cultured English mind to the traditions of Italy. The ancient world continued to offer wisdom and *exempla*; Hoby proved that contemporary Italy could equally dispense riches for the mind and spirit, despite its popery and the seductions of its Circe-like beauty. Sir Thomas Hoby can be consequently seen as a true translator, both of literary texts and of a civilization. This remarkable achievement could only have been possible for a traveler whose experience was personal and direct and sufficiently powerful to require him to record it in the manuscript which would eventually become his travel journal.

[1] This letter is reprinted in Hebel and Hudson (1953: 680-681).

[2] For Sackville, see Bartlett (1991: 27).

[3] For Hoby's biography, see Bartlett (1991: 208-209; 1993a: 187-191).

[4] Bodelan Library: Egerton 2148. Powell's edition of 1902 is partial. I am now editing a complete edition.

[5] Hoby's reliance on Alberti was first noticed by Chaney (1988: 5). See also Padovan's dissertation, which was directed by Chaney.

[6] See also Bartlett 1993: 151-159).

[7] See Loomis (1963: 95). Lord Morley received a pension from Philip II of 80 fl. a year in 1573.

[8] For Barker, see Parks (1957: 126-140) and Bartlett (1989: 209-217; 1993a: 48-52).

[9] There is an interesting parallel here as well between Hoby and Barker. Hoby notes that the Sienese have a tradition of entertaining strangers well; but he also notes their tradition of learned women and identifies by name Laudomia Forteguerra and Virginia Salvi (Egerton 2148: 24v).

[10] See, for example, Hoby's journal (Egerton 2148: 42v and the following pages).

[11] It is interesting to compare Hoby's inscriptions from Naples (Egerton 2148: 48r and the following pages) with Barker's in the *Epitaphia* (1566: Sig. D. i-ii).

[12] Printed in London by John Tysdale, but with no date. Significantly, this title was registered with the Stationers' Company on 11 May 1561, that is, the year Hoby printed *The Book of the Courtier*. See Scott (1916: 202-203).

[13] See Parks's introduction to his edition of Thomas's *History of Italy* (1963: ix-xxviii).

[14] Wilson himself attests to this in his dedicatory epistle to his translation of Demosthenes's *Three Orations In Favour of the Olythians*.

[15] For Alberti, see Redigonda (1960: 699-702) and Avery (1972: 13).

[16] Compare, for example, Pitti's journal, which is in a modern edition edited by G. Brucker.

[17] Parker's description of Pole in *De antiquitate Britannicae ecclesiae* (1572) reads:

> When he had remained there [Italy] for some months in safety in the very lap and bosom of the pope himself, he emerged infatuated and changed, as if he had drunk from the cup of Circe, from an Englishman to an Italian, from a Christian to a papist [...] a great and monstrous metamorphosis contrary to both human and divine nature [...].That simplicity which I think had been in the Englishman originally proper and ingenuous now acquired in the daily contact with the people of Rome their craftiness, still retaining the exterior and feigned appearance of an honest nature, but concealing deep within the heart the cultivated vice of deceit and fraud. (Quoted in Bartlett 1980: 60)

Kenneth R. Bartlett

References

Alberti, Leandro. 1550. *Descrittione di tutta Italia*. Bologna: Anselmo Giaccarelli.
Ascham, Roger. 1863. *The Scolemaster* (ed. J. Mayor). London: Bell and Daldy.
Avery, Catherine B. ed. 1972. *The New Century Italian Renaissance Encyclopedia*. New York, NY., Appleton-Century-Crofts.
Barker, William. 1566. *Epitaphia et inscriptiones lugubres, a Guilielmo Berchero, cum in Italia, animi causa, peregrinetur, collecta*. London: John Cawood. There is a phantom 1554 edition, but no copies are extant.
–. 1568. *The fearefull fansies of the Florentine cooper. Written in Toscane, by John Baptista Gelli, one of the Free Studie of Florence, and for recreation translated into English by W. Barker, pensoso d'altrui*. London: Henry Bynneman.
–. 1904. *The Nobility of Women by William Bercher, 1599* (ed. R. Warwick Bond). London: Roxburghe Club.
Bartlett, Kenneth R. 1980. 'The Strangeness of Strangers: English Impressions of Italy in the Sixteenth Century' in *Quaderni d'italianistica* 1: 46-63.
–. 1989. 'The Creation of an "Englishman Italified": William Barker in Italy 1551-4' in *Bollettino del C.I.R.V.I.* 20: 209-217.
–. 1991. *The English in Italy, 1525-1558: A Study in Culture and Politics*. Geneva: Slatkine.
–. 1993. 'The Journey Into Sicily of Thomas Hoby, 1550' in E. Kanceff and R. Rampone (eds) *Viaggio nel sud II: Il Profondo sud: Calabria e dintorni*. Geneva: Slatkine. 151-159.
–. 1993a. 'Thomas Hoby' in D. Richardson (ed.) *The Dictionary of Literary Biography*. Vol. 132. Detroit: Bruccoli, Clarke, Layman. 187-191.
–. 1993b. 'William Barker' in D. Richardson (ed.) *Dictionary of Literary Biography*. Vol. 132. Vol. 132. Detroit: Bruccoli, Clarke, Layman. 48-52.
–. 2000. 'Morley, Machiavelli and the Pilgrimage of Grace' in M. Axton and J. Carley (eds) *The Triumph of English: Henry Parker, Lord Morley, Translator to the Tudor Court*. London: British Library. 77-85 and Appendix 2, 230-231.
Brucker, G. ed. 1991. *Two Memoirs of Renaissance Florence* (tr. J. Martines). Prospect Heights, IL: Waveland Press.
Castiglione, Baldassare. 1561. *The Courtyer of Count Baldesar Castilio* (tr. Thomas Hoby). London: William Seres.
Chaney, Edward. 1984. 'The Grand Tour and Beyond: British and American Travellers in Southern Italy, 1545-1960' in Edward Chaney and N. Ritchie (eds) *Oxford, China and Italy: Writings in Honour of Sir Harold Acton on his Eightieth Birthday*. London: Thames and Hudson.
–. 1988. 'Quo Vadis:Travel as Education and the Impact of Italy in the Sixteenth Century' in P. Cunningham and C. Brock (eds) *International Currents in Educational Ideas and Practices*. London: History and Education Society.
Cheke, Sir John. 1843. *The Gospel According to St. Mathew and Part of the First Chapter of St. Mark and VII Original Letters* (ed. J. Goodwin). London: William Pickering.
Domenichi, Lodovico. 1549. *La nobiltà delle donne*. Venice: Giolito de' Ferrari.
Hebel, J. and H. Hudson (eds). 1953. *Tudor Poetry and Prose*. New York, NY: Appleton-Century-Crofts.
Hoby, Thomas. *The Book of the Travaile and Lief of Me, Thomas Hoby*. B.L. Egerton, 2148.
–. 1549. *The Gratulation of the Most Famous Clerk, Master Martin Bucer*. London: Richard Jugge.
–. 1902. *A Booke of the Travaile and lief of me Thomas Hoby* (ed. E. Powell). *The Camden Miscellany* (vol. 10). London: Office of the Royal Historical Society.
Loomis, A.S. 1963. *The Spanish Elizabethans: The English Exiles at the Court of Spain*. New York, NY: Fordham University Press.
Padovan, Maria Grazia. 1980-1981. *Il Primo viaggio in Italia di Sir Thomas Hoby scritto da lui medesimo (1548-1550)*. Università di Pisa: dissertation (directed by Edward Chaney).
Parks, George B. 1957. 'William Barker, Tudor Translator' in *Papers of the Bibliographical Society of America* 51: 126-140.

Redigonda, A.L. 1960. 'Alberti, Leandro' in *Dizionario Biografico degli italiani* (Rome: Istituto della enciclopedia italiana). Vol. 1. 699-702.

Scott, Mary Augusta. 1916. *Elizabethan Translations From the Italian*. Boston, MA: Houghton Mifflin.

Thomas, William. 1963. *The History of Italy, 1549* (ed. George B. Parks). Ithaca, NY: Cornell University Press.

Wilson, Thomas. 1570. *Three Orations in Favour of the Olythians*. London.

2.4. "A poore preasant off Ytalyan costume": The Interplay of Travel and Translation in William Barker's *Dyssputacion off the Nobylytye off Wymen*

Brenda M. Hosington

Travel and translation are intimately linked in the person and writings of William Barker, an Englishman born in roughly 1520. This is particularly true of his translation of Lodovico Domenich's 1549 *La nobiltà delle donne*, entitled *A Dyssputacion off the Nobylytye of Wymen*. Barker's preface reads like a travelogue, with its detailed description of Petriolo, a spa-town just outside Siena, while his dedicatory letter to Queen Elizabeth, to whom he presented his translation in 1599, makes plain his belief in the importance of foreign travel. The translation itself also shares some features with a travelogue, relying on imagination and at times interweaving reality (passages indeed translated from the Italian original) and fiction (changed or invented settings and characters, passages entirely invented by Barker, and various "englishings" of the original). Thus this text, unjustly neglected, fascinatingly merges Italian and English culture and travel and translation.
Keywords: Italy, Lodovico Domenichi, William Barker (Bercher), translation, travel.

Travel and translation are intimately linked in the person and writings of William Barker, or Bercher, an Englishman born in Norfolkshire in roughly 1520. Nowhere is this seen more clearly than in his translation of Lodovico Domenichi's 1549 *La Nobiltà delle donne*, which he entitled *A Dyssputacion off the Nobylytye off Wymen*. This translation was never printed in Barker's lifetime, although six of his others were, yet its subject would surely have been very à propos in 1559 when Barker presented the manuscript to the newly crowned Queen Elizabeth. It was not printed until 1904, when it came in for some pretty harsh criticism from its editor. It has been the subject of only one article since. In the present essay, the *Dyssputacion* will be examined anew, specifically in order to discuss the ways in which Barker ties travel and translation together and to analyze some of his translating strategies within the context of modern translation theory.

Literally speaking, travel played a crucial role in the English production of Domenichi's text. Barker was one of the many English travelers who spent time in Italy in the mid-sixteenth century. Some earlier biographers and the editor of his *Dyssputacion* put the dates of his Italian sojourn as 1551-1552[1], but in fact we know from Sir Thomas Hoby's diary (1902: 19-33) that Barker was with him in Siena in September 1549, went with him to Rome on November 16th to witness the funeral of Pope Paul III and search out antiquities, just missed him in Naples in March 1550, and caught up with him again in Siena in May of that year. We cannot be certain as to when Barker left Italy but in his Preface to the translation he refers to the delight of being in a Siena that enjoyed "a majestie of State" before being afflicted with the cruelties of war, which can only refer to the years 1552 to 1554, after the end of the

Spanish occupation and before the invasion of Cosimo I. More specifically in his dedicatory letter to Queen Elizabeth, he says he returned to enter the service of "the Duke of Norfolke that nowe is", which puts the year as 1553, before Norfolk's title was restored to the Howard family[2]. Barker must, then, have spent three to four years in Italy, living for a large portion of that time in Siena.

During his sojourn there he visited many cities, as is evidenced by his *Epitaphia et inscriptiones lugubres* where he describes epitaphs from thirteen of these. In Florence he must have met Domenichi, who between 1547 and 1552 was connected to the Accademia Fiorentina and the court of Cosimo and was a friend of Gelli, whose *I capricci del bottaio* (1549) Barker translated into English[3]. While this is supposition, more certain are his discovery of contemporary Italian literature[4], his observation of various features of Italian cities, notably Siena, and his motives for traveling to Italy, all of which are demonstrated in his translation and its paratexts. It is to the latter that we shall now turn. We shall firstly discuss the elements of travel writing present in the Preface and Dedication accompanying the *Dyssputacion off the Nobylytye off Wymen*, and then describe how they also operate on an imaginative level.

In his Preface, Barker tells us that "It was my chaunce to travell a brode and see the worlde at lardge, and lyve a tyme in Ytalye a place of sutche Renowme as all men crave the sight of yt and passethe for no more" (1904: 90). He roams as if with a camera over Italy, at first using a wide-angle lens to describe all the cities in typical Renaissance travel clichés: "the walles so highe of Rome", the "plesant platt of naples", "Myllayne great & plentyfull", then "Mantua the mylde & Genua the prowde", and finally "the learned haunte of Padoa, Pysa, & Perugia, Pavia & Bononia". He then focuses on the city that he chose to stay in: Siena "the place of Curtesye", with a "majestie of State [...] exelencye of learnenge [...] aer of Purytie" and the most temperate climate in Tuscany. Finally, he further narrows the focus–on the nearby village-spa of Petriolo where the great and the good of Siena repair in summer-time[5]. His detailed account of Petriolo again reads rather like a travel book: he suggests an etymological explanation of its name ("the huge hylles and stonye rockes that thear do growe") (*ibid*.: 91) and describes the hot waters that spring forth in the nearby baths, cascading over a paved cistern before casting themselves into the River Parma ("Farma"). Petriolo itself is a "walled towne with towers and a Palace of Potestate with a common gallarye to walke, withe howsis wel buylded", but now abandoned except in May and September when people come to take the waters.

Moving from observations of Petriolo's physical features, Barker returns to praising Siena for its social and intellectual virtues. It is international because it "is not as the common sorte of Cyttis, only an inhabytacion of gentlemen, marchantes and other artyfycers: but allso a studie and a Receipt of learned men which we call an unyversytie". In no other city on earth could be found "more lyvely wyttes, more lerned men, more cortese to straingers, nor more goodly gentlewymen" (*ibid*.: 91). He asserts that few families were without somebody learned in them and Sienese scholars were called upon by princes throughout Italy. Nor is he wrong if we think of Aeneas and Alessandro Piccolomini, Bernardo Ochino and Fausto Soccini, to name but a few. The intellectual exchange that took place in Petriolo is thus not surprising, being in part attributable to the Sienese's dismissal of "wastefull surfett and banquetenge" and their preference for "some devyse wherin lernenge and vertue maye be shewed and encreased" (*ibid.*: 92). Also important were the properties of Petriolo's curative baths, especially one that was good for the head. Lastly, the Sienese elite owned vineyards near Petriolo and came there with friends and acquaintances of all nationalities.

In his dedicatory letter to "the Quenis moste excelent Majestie", Barker again alludes to travel. He tells Elizabeth that he was once one of Anne Boleyn's scholars at Cambridge and that, unlike many of the students she supported but who had left their studies, "after [her] crewell deathe [...] [I] made myne habode a good tyme travelenge in sutche maner of Stodye, as then was theare approved" (*ibid.*: 87). Barker did in fact graduate with an M.A. in 1540 from St. John's College but, as he says, "[then] colde I not have anye determynacion withe my selffe, to professe anye one thynge more then other but was content onelye to satysfye my meanenge ioyned with the memorye of hyr majestie" (*ibid.*: 88). However, he goes on, "I thought good to add an experyence of travell and knowledge off more contris then myne owne". Alas, travel in Italy only made the "formor fancye of professenge nothinge partyculary was very mutche encreased" for, he adds perhaps rather sarcastically, the Italians believe that a gentleman's studies are supposed to be in and of themselves sufficient reward, not the passport to a good job, enabling one to "becom a Servaunte to every mannis Salarye". Certainly the mid-century English saw travel to Italy as culturally and intellectually enriching–"experience added to learning that makes a perfect man", to quote the Queen's secretary, Davison who echoes Barker's sentiments in a travel book of the time[6]–but at the same time they saw it as career-advancing: travel could prepare one for high posts at court or in government circles.

Actual travel, then, is spoken of several times in Barker's paratexts and in terms found in various travel writings of the period. In the Preface, however, we find a blend of travel writing and fictional creation, which suggests that Barker was a more competent writer than he has been given credit for. Like many Renaissance prefaces but particularly, I think, like More's Letter to Peter Giles prefacing the *Utopia* and his opening paragraph of that work, it contains a mix of real and fictional elements. Barker makes use of actual facts he has observed and people he has met during his travels and weaves them into the imagined debate in Petriolo that will be the subject of his translation. Like More, who uses his own stay in Antwerp as the King's commissioner as a context for his imagined meeting with Hythloday, and who draws his friend Peter Giles into the fiction, Barker uses the experience of his stay in Siena and Petriolo as an introduction to the debate about women. They, rather than the Milan of Domenichi, will serve as the setting for his fiction.

Like More in his Letter to Peter Giles, which serves to introduce the audience to the world of Hythloday and Utopia, Barker uses several strategies in his Preface to lead the reader into the text. We have already mentioned his description of the physical features of Siena and Petriolo, based on his personal observation, and how this provides a setting for his debate. His praise of the baths of Petriolo is not limited to their physical features, however. They encourage people to set aside solemnity and enmity and be "dysspoced to the myrthe of the mynde, that the water of the bathe might the better worke in theyr bodies" (*ibid*.: 91). The idea that body *and* soul might find solace and health at the spa is repeated in the opening lines of his translation, not provided by Domenichi. There Philida, who takes her title of Countess of Elci from the nearby town of that name, expresses her gratitude to the baths for affording "remedye for my wretched bodye" and "consolacion of myne afflycted mynde [...] [that] cawseth the better workemanship of my bodyes recoverye" (*ibid*.: 93). Barker might or might not have known the countess of Elci, yet he presents her in the Preface as if he had actually met her at the baths. In the account of the debate that follows he has her play the role of president, just as Domenichi had had Violante Bentivoglia, Mutio Sforza's mother, preside over the Milan debate. Barker describes the Countess as being so weak she cannot stir hand or foot "but onlye hyr tonge", which at first sight looks like a traditional slur on women. But, Barker goes on, she used the tongue with such discretion and wisdom that everyone spoke good of her and enjoyed going to her house to sing Italian verse, play musical instruments, dance, and discuss some "reasonenge of matters bothe plesant and important" (*ibid*.: 91). All this prepares us for the opening lines of the translation, where the assembly is said to have repaired to the Countess's house, singing, dancing and finally pausing for debate (*ibid*.: 94).

Another lead that the Preface provides concerns the nature of the Sienese. In his list of Italian cities, Barker talks of the "Cortesye of Siena" and explains why, after traveling to many Italian cities, he chose Siena to stay in: it was the "place of Curtesye" (*ibid*.: 90). He then says more specifically, and on two occasions, that the city was famous throughout Italy for its courtesy to strangers (*ibid*.: 90, 91). He ends the Preface by saying that Petriolo was full of gentlemen from all over Italy, from France and Germany, and even from England. Two Englishmen were invited by a gentleman of the country and thus even more courteously received. And indeed they appear in his translation, taking part in the debate. Again, they are a creation of Barker's, not Domenichi's. The gentleman Barker claims in the Preface took him to Petriolo was "a gentleman of the howse off borghese". The illustrious Borghese family were indeed still in Siena when Barker was there, not moving to Rome before Camillo, later Pope Paul V, became cardinal. The reference again leads us into the translation, for there a fictional character who supplies the comic elements in the debate is one John Borghese.

Last but by no means least is the lead provided in the Preface by comments on women. Praising the intellectual tradition of Sienese scholars, Barker says that "the Gentlewymen allso were geven to knowledge in sutche sorte as theyr was no matter propoundid but they colde reason probablye in yt" (*ibid.*: 92). Here he is drawing on a tradition that praised Sienese women not only for their grace but also their intelligence and learning, but he is also establishing yet another link between the Preface and the account of the debate[7]. One of the subjects that the people at the baths liked to discuss, Barker says, is "the Nobylytie off wemen". He thereupon proposes that "in as trewe manner as I cann I will nowe reporte to youre most noble maiestye" (*ibid.*: 91). With this direct address to his dedicatee, Barker seeks to authenticate the dialogue that he purports to be recounting in his text. By pretending that the debate actually took place during his stay in Petriolo and that he is going to report it "in as trewe manner" as he can, Barker is playing the same game with the reader as More does when he twice tells Peter Giles in his fictive letter prefacing the *Utopia* that he has had merely to repeat Hythloday's travel tales and "write out simply" what he has heard. Barker's game with the reader is taken even further than More's, however, for nowhere does he mention that his text is a translation. Domenichi's name never graces his lips. The reader is to imagine that this is Barker's own composition, inspired by his travel experience in Italy. Before turning to that translation, it is necessary to say something about its source.

Lodovico Domenichi's *La nobiltà delle donne*, published in 1549 in Venice by Gabriele Giolito, who specialized amongst other things in publishing works about women, fits the genre of what one critic has called a "quasi-documentary dialogue", that is, a fictional dialogue with some real-life contemporary figures participating in it (Cox 2000: 385-400). In Domenichi's case, we can also add that he provides a real-life setting. He assembles some guests on the occasion of the Milan wedding of Mutio Sforza, Marquis of Caravaggio, and Faustina Sforza in October 1546. Some of them retire from the dancing to a quiet room where Violante Bentivoglia, Mutio's mother, suggests they discuss a given topic. They choose "the nobility of women", and debate it over several evenings. Drawing heavily though silently on Agrippa's 1529 *De nobilitate et praecellentia foeminei sexus* and Capella's 1525 *Della Eccellenza et dignità delle donne*, and with more than a nod at Castiglione's *Il Cortegiano* and several works on women, which to his credit he mentions in an accompanying letter to Bartolomeo Gottifredi[8], Domenichi creates a lively dialogue, divided into five books and covering 272 closely printed octavo folios. Three men lead the defence of women's learning and virtues and three lead the attack. Violante Bentivoglia rarely offers her own point of view; her role is simply to preside over the debates. The fact that she represents a real person no doubt added to the constraints of decorum that dictated that women could not be given leading roles in dialogues of mixed company[9]. The debate seems to end rather inconclusively in Book III. Books IV and V, however, in which Mutio and Faustina Sforza participate, present a very long list of learned women from the Classical world and contemporary Italy. The weight of the evidence is impressive. Thus the women's champions do seem to gain the edge in the debate. Nor is this very surprising given that Domenichi included in his 1544 *Rime*, which was dedicated to Isabella Sforza, several poems to and by women.

In discussing the Preface to the *Dyssputacion* we emphasized its mix of actual facts, observed by Barker in his travels, and fictitious elements, events and people he invented. He appears there as both traveler and writer, both dispenser of information and creator of fiction, both purveyor of truth and inventor of lies. Now this is peculiarly in keeping with the very nature of translation and, furthermore, links the roles of traveler and translator in ways that have been exploited over the years, beginning with St. Jerome, patron saint of translators. In his preface to his translation of Eusebius's *Chronicle*, he says the search for equivalents in source and target languages forces the translator to "make a long detour" and to "cover the distance of a long path to what in reality is but a short way" ["dum quaero implere sententiam longo ambitu, vix brevis viae spatia consummo"] (1845: 372). In later prefaces, too, including several in the Renaissance, the metaphors of the journey and traveler are used in similar fashion while the translator-traveler analogy is sometimes made more specific by calling the translator a discoverer returning from distant shores, arms full of "rich treasures". A notable example of this is Ben Jonson's description (1947: vol. 8, 388-389) of Chapman as a discoverer of the passage to "the Greeke coast" and his translation of Hesiod as a "treasure". The appropriateness of the metaphors speaks for itself. For what, after all, is translation but traveling towards a foreign language and culture, covering the distance between source and target texts, and bringing home the newly-found composition?

There is another way, too, in which the analogy between travel and translation holds true. Both traveler and translator may feel constraints to "tell the truth", the former by recounting accurately what he or she has seen and experienced, the latter by searching out the greatest possible equivalences–a word fraught of course with ambiguity, as is its companion notion, "fidelity". However, both traveler and translator also employ imagination in their tasks. They can, and often do, tailor their accounts and translations to suit their audience. It is the imagination that transforms travel experience into travel account, original text into translation. And there's the rub. The problem of verisimilitude threatens both productions, and traveler and translator alike have been accused of altering, deforming and manipulating their sources. This is why Barker's translation and paratexts are of such interest. The Preface, as we have seen, interweaves the reality and fiction of travel. The translation maintains this hybrid form, but adds a further fiction. Barker has us believe that the *Dyssputacion* is of his own creation. He never once mentions his original. In so doing, he reverses the "invisible translator" paradigm that Lawrence Venuti says characterizes Anglo-American translators from the Renaissance on. Here it is not the translator who is invisible but the author. The lie that all translations embody–namely that the translated text "reads like the original", that when we are reading translations of the *Illiad* we are reading Homer–is given a further dimension when the translator himself purposely supplants the author. Barker's only nod to Domenichi consists of four passing references in his text to the discussion at Milan (1904: 94, 95, 112 and 150). However, if one did not know the *Nobiltà delle donne* firsthand, these would be passed over. Never, it seems, would the old Italian tag *traduttore, traditore* be more applicable, although the betrayal here connotes something a little different.

Barker not only fools his audience by removing explicit references to the original author's name and text, but he also manipulates his source in several ways to ensure its autonomy. Firstly, in presenting his work to his dedicatee, he calls it "a poore preasent off Ytalyan costume", suggesting not that it is of Italian origin but that it deals with a custom then prevalent in Italy, namely the conducting of a learned debate on a specific topic in pleasant surroundings (*ibid.*: 88). Secondly, as we have already said, he changes the setting from Milan to Siena, to a place with which he himself is familiar. Thirdly, he changes the characters. Unlike Domenichi's participants in the debate, who represent a mix of real and fictional characters, Barker's are creatures of his imagination, although some are said to be members of real Italian families like the Elci and Borghesi. Only the ladies' chief opponent, Camillo, shares a name with someone in the *Nobiltà*, Camillo Lampugnano. Barker creates one comic character by taking some elements of Domenichi's humorous Pier Francesco and, perhaps, Castiglione's Morella da Ortona, the only old courtier in the *Cortegiano*, whose rather irritable character might have inspired Barker's John Borghese, who we are to presume is a relative of the Borghese family mentioned in the Preface. He offers caustic comments on women that are often refuted and deplored by the Countess Elci. A character in his own right, he is blustering and impatient, interrupting the discussion, and adding a dimension to the passages of banter that Barker found in his source. Domenichi has no equivalent character.

Another strategy Barker employs to hide the fact that his *Dyssputacion* is a translation concerns the structure of the work. Instead of spreading the debate over successive evenings as Domenichi does, he compresses it into one evening. He often rearraanges the materials he borrows, bobbing backwards and forwards in the Italian text and reassembling passages from sentences borrowed here and there. He also often switches speeches, putting the words of one character into another's mouth. One of his biggest changes concerns Domenichi's Books IV and V, which praise lesser known Classical and contemporary Italian women. By omitting them completely, Barker shifts the reader's attention from a specific list of unfamiliar women to a catalogue of traditional female figures which he found in Domenichi's first three books but which are not exclusive to him; they could be found in virtually any contemporary writings on women. Barker's handling of this particular list demonstrates clearly how he worked. He translates word for word a brief passage in Book III where examples are called upon as proof of women's learning (1549: 139) but then leaves Domenichi aside, as Bond points out (Barker 1904: 194), to follow Plutarch's exordium to his *De Mulierum Virtutibus*. He also puts the examples, not in the mouth of the chief defender of women, but in that of the minor character, Flaminio, and at the very end of the work, where he uses the occasion to hint at his source text. Flaminio bolsters his case by saying that at "this dyssputacion at Millayne, that after reasons had bynn made suffitient, the mater was concludid with examples" (*ibid.*: 150).

Flaminio and his catalogue also serve another purpose not found in Domenichi. It has to do with what we might call the "englishifying" of the text, a strategy that is a little different from the "englishing" technique used by Florio and some other Renaissance translators in order to make foreign works more accessible to an English audience. Barker does not "english" his setting but he does add elements to his source which make the translation more oriented towards an English audience, seem to make his account more authentic, and at a stroke of the quill pen flatter both his dedicatee and his employer, the Duke of Norfolk. In short, he "domesticates" Domenichi's text, or to use modern translation terminology, he produces an ethno-centric translation, geared towards the target text and audience. The source text has thus been made invisible by the many changes the translator has made, but also by his addition of specific allusions and references to the target, not the source, culture.

One of these ethno-centric strategies is the reappearance of the fictional Englishmen that Barker introduced in his preface. These reappear twice in his translation. In Book II of the *Nobiltà*, Domenichi has one of the defenders of women ask whether no one has heard of Thomas More's three learned daughters who know Latin, Greek and Hebrew. Barker translates this word for word, putting the question into the mouth of Flaminio[10], but then uses it to add a whole section on the Englishmen's contribution to the discussion. The addition turns out to constitute the concluding summary of all that has been said in favor of women and is therefore crucial in tipping the balance of the argument more firmly towards them than in the source text. Let us examine the scene in some detail. Flaminio turns to the Englishmen for confirmation about the More girls and tells the Countess they would be glad to talk about their gentlewomen. She invites them to do so because it would praise their country and, Barker has her say in a deft compliment to the English, because they have so far "accompanyed vs in our other talke and have well spoken in the same" (*ibid.*: 151). One of the Englishmen politely demurs, but not before saying that the example of the More daughters is "testymonye suffitient that wymen be worthy the prayse that have hear ben geven them" and adds "modestly", again a nice touch on Barker's part, that "our lyttle Countreye have regarde and desyer of the same". Encouraged to continue, he states that he is bound to find in favor of women, whom he believes "equall or superior" to men despite the fact they have been "restrayned from the course of vertues race by the order of men" (*ibid.*: 152). He pursues his argument, translated in large part and often word for word from Domenichi, for another thirty lines before returning to his subject, his learned countrywomen.

Domenichi's list starts with Margaret Roper (1549: 88) but Barker adds to it her three daughters whom she has tutored in learning and vertue (1904: 153)[11]. Next come Mary and Elizabeth who, the Englishman says, in words echoing the opening lines of the dedication, inspire in him duty-bound honor and patriotic love. Described as princesses and the sisters of Edward VI because Barker is supposed to be recounting an event that happened much earlier, Mary is renowned for her "learnenge and langwage", Elizabeth for her "towardnes of awntyent vertue", notable learning and other qualities (*ibid.*: 154). Both had already appeared in the *Dyssputacion*. Barker added them to Francesco Grasso's list of accomplished women (Domenichi 1549: 34), straight after Queen Mary of Hungary and Queen Isabella of Spain and in place of Pope Joan, another learned if controversial Englishwoman who appears elsewhere in Barker's text. Mary, Orlando says, "hathe shewed marvelous examples off wysdeome and constantnes and by her godlye and Syncere lyffe hathe put to sylence all her enemyes and adversaris" (1904: 100). Elizabeth, still young, "have shewede sutche great and wonderfull proffe of Royall harte in troubles that she of late have had as all men do honor hyr vertues and thynke she shalbe a moste Noble Prynces" (*ibid.*: 101)[12]. Barker then has Orlando say, in a strategy designed to authenticate the discourse, that he learned all this while ambassador to the Emperor in Flanders. Moreover, the Englishmen present will later add to what he has to say about the princesses' "Syngler vertues" (*ibid.*: 101). The stage, then, is set for their intervention at the end of the work.

After speaking of Mary and Elizabeth, one of the Englishmen lists the three Howard daughters, amongst whom Jane is given special praise; the Seymour sisters, particularly Jane; Jane Grey and her sisters; Jane and Mary, daughters of the Earl of Arundel; and the daughters of Sir Anthony Cooke. All are commended for that inevitable tandem, learning and virtue, but some are mentioned specifically for their linguistic skills, particularly in Greek and Latin, and verse composition. It is striking that the girls given the most praise, and who immediately follow the princesses Mary and Elizabeth, are the sisters of Thomas Howard, 4th Duke of Norfolk, Barker's employer. Next in terms of the length of the praise are the daughters of the Earl of Arundel, one of whom, Mary Fitzalan, married the Duke in 1556 (Wharton 1996: 53-69). The mention of these women, moreover, allows Barker to deplore the long imprisonment of the 3rd Duke of Norfolk, Thomas Howard's grandfather, and the execution of his father, Henry, Earl of Surrey, in 1547.

Furthermore, in another authenticating strategy, Barker has Flaminio interrupt by saying he is happy to hear about Mary Fitzalan because when in Rome he heard so much about the Howards from Paolo Giovio, who had "muche lamented the harde happ" that the family had suffered (1904: 154). Thus Barker is able to remind his English audience of a recent fact of English history, flatter his dedicatee and, hopefully, catch the eye of his employer. His "englishifying" of Domenichi's text, then, was certainly no innocent gesture.

Bond, in his 1904 edition of the *Dyssputacion*, says rather condescendingly that Barker's obligations to Domenichi's *Nobiltà* "almost reduce his achievement to mere translation". A few lines further on, after pointing out the original parts of the *Dyssputacion*, which make up roughly one-fifth of the whole, he says Barker's "task lay in simply translating, plus the selection, and generally the abbreviation, of the portions translated" (*ibid.*: 44). We no longer have such a negative attitude towards translating, which today–as in the Renaissance–is perceived as a difficult and demanding exercise, while translators generally are viewed in a more favorable light than in Bond's day. Indeed, especially since critics such as Walter Benjamin (1969: 69-82) and, later, Derrida (1985: 165-207), the translator's real "task", to use Benjamin's word, has been elevated to that of transmitter of cultural values and guarantor of a work's *nachleben*, or afterlife, embracing the other and transferring it *in toto* to the target culture. Barker of course does not fall into this category. On the contrary, as we have said, he is what some other translation theorists, following Benjamin's lead, have called an ethno-centric translator, one who translates for the target language and culture[13]. Worse yet, they would think, he translates purely for his own material benefit; his comments on the Howards and his dedication to Queen Elizabeth make that quite clear. The fact that he mentions neither source nor original author does not help his cause, although this was common practice in the sixteenth century and although, by a stroke of irony, Domenichi did the same thing in his *Nobiltà*, where whole passages are silently lifted word for word from Agrippa and others. A case, then, of *voleur volé* for the man whom a previous friend, Anton Francesco Doni, called an "abominable plagiarist"[14]. Yet this does not rob Barker's translation of all merit. As I hope I have demonstrated, his selecting, rearranging and rewording, like his creation of characters and his introduction of English features, are done cleverly. His Preface and Dedication form an integral part of the literary production that is the *Dyssputacion* by the use of strategies found in other authors of the time. The dialogue between his participants is lively, courtly, and at times more emotional than in Domenichi's *Nobiltà*, perhaps stylistically closer in some ways to Castiglione's *Cortegiano*, which he must have known. Parks has said (1957: 131) that Barker should be credited, along with Hoby, with transferring the sophistication and faint pathos of the Italian courtesy-book to England. As Kenneth Bartlett has pointed out (1985: 249-258), the frame of reference of the *Cortegiano* was not alien in England even before Hoby's translation of 1561. In short, then, the "italyanified Englishman", as the Duke of Norfolk bitterly called Barker in 1572 after the latter's testimony helped send him to the scaffold[15], was able successfully to merge in one short text Italian and English culture, travel and translation.

[1] These early authors, like Bond, did not have access to Hoby's Diary. Basing their opinion on Barker's comment in his preface to his translation of the six books of the *Cyropaedia*, which they said predated his Italian tour, and on the publication of his *Epitaphia* in England in 1554, they surmised that the tour took place between 1551 and 1553.

[2] The young Duke of Norfolk, Thomas Howard, acceded to the dukedom on 23 August 1554, but his family's fortunes had already improved with the accession of Mary to the throne in 1553. A William Barker signed the oath to Mary on 26 July 1553, but whether this is our translator remains a moot point. Bond (1905: 7) believes that it is, because another member of Norfolk's household, Henry Cantrell, signed the oath one day later. Parks (1957: 126-140) points out, however, that two William Barkers signed the same oath to Elizabeth in 1559. Given the profusion of men by this name in the period (there were no fewer than five at Cambridge), the question must remain open.

[3] For Domenichi's years in Florence (1547-52) see D'Alessandro (1978: 171-200). For a list of Barker's translations see Parks (1957: 126-140), which, although containing a few errors, is still useful.

[4] While Barker takes the example of Vittoria Colonna, Marchesa di Pescara, directly from Domenichi (1549: 88v), he adds confirmation, as Bond says (Barker 1904: 195), of Colonna's poetic abilities by comparing her favourably with Molza, a contemporary of great literary repute.

[5] Petriolo was famous for its curative baths as early as the thirteenth century. For its history, see Redon (1994: 106 and onwards).

[6] See Devereux *et al.*

[7] Piero Misciatelli (1931: 5) quotes Enea Silvio Piccolomini, Pope Pius II, as saying in his *Storia di Federigo III* a century earlier that Sienese women were known throughout Italy for their beauty, exceptional courtesy, and learning, being able to discourse in Latin and compose verses. Misciatelli provides the names of a dozen Sienese women renowned for their learning, amongst whom one Cintia dei conti d'Elci, perhaps an inspiration for Barker's Philida, and he also quotes (*ibid.*: 369) a fifteenth-century visitor to Siena, Antonio Cammelli, who asserts that "la bellezza delle donne senesi è proverbiale".

[8] In 'Al suo molto honorando M. Bartolomeo Gottifredi', dated September 16, 1548, Domenichi (1549: MMv) says he has brought together what was dispersed throughout other writings on the topic of women and he mentions specifically Plutarch, Agrippa, Capella, Martelli, Maggio, Castiglione and Speroni.

[9] Cox says that women speakers are included in about forty Cinquecento dialogues but in the majority of cases their role is reduced to commenting on the opinions of the male interlocutors (2000: 387-91).

[10] Domenichi's original–"Non hauete voi inteso che Thomaso More Inglese hebbe tre figliuole le quali & bene & ornatemente fauellauano Latino, Greco, & Hebraico?" (1549: 88)–is translated by Barker thus: "I thynke you have herd of Thomas Moore a knight of Englond who had thre daughters that speake well lattyn, greke and hebrewe" (1904: 151).

[11] Domenichi also alludes twice to More in the passage containing the reference to Roper. He combines two of his epigrams on the jealous astrologer to prove that men are not as clever as they think (*Aliud in astrologum uxoris impudicae marium* and *Aliud in astrologum*) (1549: 89v) and mentions the *Utopia* (*ibid.*: 90). For a discussion of More and Domenichi see Meijer (1973: 37-45).

[12] Bond believes the remarks about Mary prove that Barker was a Catholic (Barker 1904: 169). They might, of course, simply be traditional words of flattery. They say no more nor less than compliments paid the young princess by other writers whose credentials are most definitely Protestant. That said, Barker was nevertheless counted a Catholic when the members of Norfolk's household were assessed as to their religious views. Similarly, Bond believes that the difficulties Elizabeth had borne so patiently refer to her imprisonment in 1554. If Barker did the translation

Brenda M. Hosington

in Italy he must have added this later but I see no reason why we should believe that he did not compose the translation in 1559, the date of the dedication.
[13] See in particular Berman (1982: 35-91) and Meschonnic (1984: 192-222).
[14] For an account of the quarrel between Doni and Domenichi see Tiraboschi (1805-1813: vol. 7, 1033-1038).
[15] Barker was arrested along with the Duke of Norfolk in 1569, was released, then re-arrested in 1571 with regard to the Ridolfi plot to put Mary, Queen of Scots, on the English throne. Threatened with torture, Barker confessed and betrayed Norfolk. Both men were condemned to death but Barker, after two years in the Tower, was pardoned. For a full account of his trial, see Murdin (1759: vol. 2, 87-129).

References

Barker, William. 1566. *Epitaphia et inscriptiones lugubres, a Guilielmo Berchero, cum in Italia, animi causa, peregrinetur, collecta*. London: John Cawood. There is a phantom 1554 edition, but no copies are extant.
–. 1568. *The fearefull fansies of the Florentine cooper. Written in Toscane, by John Baptista Gelli, one of the Free Studie of Florence, and for recreation translated into English by W. Barker, pensoso d'altrui*. London: Henry Bynneman.
–. 1904. *The Nobility of Women by William Bercher, 1599* (ed. R. Warwick Bond). London: Roxburghe Club.
Bartlett, Kenneth R. 1985. 'The Courtyer of Count Baldasser Castilio: Italian Manners and the English Court in the Sixteenth Century' in Quaderni d'italianistica 6(2): 249-258.
Benjamin, Walter. 1969. 'The Task of the Translator' in *Illuminations* (ed. Hannah Arendt and tr. Harry Zohn). New York, NY: Schocken Books. 69-82.
Berman, Antoine. 1982. 'La traduction et la lettre-ou l'auberge du lointain' in *Les Tours de Babel: Essais sur la traduction*. Paris: TER Éditions. 35-91.
Bond, R. Warwick. 1905. *Addenda, Glossary and Index to William Barker's Nobility of Women*. London: Roxburghe Club.
Cox, Virginia. 2000. 'Seen but not heard: the role of women speakers in Cinquecento literary dialogue' in Letizia Panizza (ed.) *Women in Italian Renaissance Culture and Society*. Oxford: European Humanities Research Centre. 385-400.
D'Alessandro, Alessandro. 1978. 'Prime ricerche su Lodovico Domenichi' in Marzio A. Romani (ed.) *Le corti farnesiane di Parma e Piacenza, 1545-1622*. Vol. 2. Rome: Bulzoni. 171-200.
Derrida, Jacques. 1985. 'Des Tours de Babel' in Joseph F. Graham (ed. and tr.) *Difference in Translation*. Ithaca, NY: Cornell University Press. 165-207.
Devereux, Robert, *et al*. 1633. *Profitable Instructions; describing what speciall observations are to be taken by travellers in all nations. By the three much admired, Robert, late Earle of Essex. Sir Philip Sydney. And, secretary Davison*. London: [J. Beale?] for Benjamin Fisher.
Domenichi, Lodovico. 1549. *La nobiltà delle donne*. Venice: Gabriele Giolito de' Ferrari.
Gelli, Giovanbattista. 1549. *I capricci del bottaio*. Florence.
Hoby, Thomas. *The Book of the Travaile and Lief of Me, Thomas Hoby*. B.L. Egerton, 2148.
–. 1902. *A Booke of the Travaile and Lief of Me, Thomas Hoby* (ed. E. Powell). *The Camden Miscellany* (vol. 10). London: Office of the Royal Historical Society.
Jerome, St. 1845. 'De optimo genere interpretandi' in *Patrologiae Cursus Completus* (ed. Jacques-Paul Migne). Vol. 22. Paris: Migne. 372.
Jonson, Ben. 1947. 'To my worthy and honour'd Friend, Mr. George Chapman, on his Translation of Hesiod's Works, & Days' in C.H. Herford and Percy and Evelyn Simpson (eds) *Ben Jonson*. 10 vols. Oxford: Clarendon Press.
Meijer, Marianne S. 1973. 'Thomas More, Lodovico Domenichi et "L'Honneur du sexe féminin"' in *Moreana* 10(38): 37-45.
Meschonnic, Henri. 1984. *Poésie sans réponse (Pour la poétique V)*. Paris: Gallimard.

Misciatelli, Piero. 1931. *Studi Senesi*. Siena: La Diana.

Murdin, William. 1759. *A Collection of State Papers [...] left by William Cecil, Lord Burghley*. 2 vols. London.

Parks, George B. 1957. 'William Barker, Tudor Translator' in *Papers of the Bibliographical Society of America* 51: 126-40.

Redon, Odile. 1994. *L'Espace d'une cité. Sienne et le pays siennois*. Rome: École française de Rome.

Tiraboschi, Girolamo. 1805-1813. *Storia della letteratura italiana. Nuova edizione*. 9 vols. Firenze: Molini, Landi e Co.

Venuti, Lawrence. 1985. *The Translator's Invisibility: A History of Translation*. London and New York, NY: Routledge.

Wharton, Janet. 1996. 'William Bercher's *Dyssputac[i]on off Wymen*: Text and Transmission' in Sabine Coelsch-Foisner *et al.* (eds) *Trends in English and American Studies: Literature and the Imagination. Essays in Honor of James Lester Hogg*. Lewiston, NY: Edwin Mellen Press. 53-69.

Section III

The European as Other and the Other in Europe

3.1. The Pilgrimage of Konrad Grünemberg to the Holy Land in 1486

Kristiaan Aercke

In 1486, the German knight Konrad Grünemberg undertook a pilgrimage to Jerusalem. He followed the usual itinerary via Venice, stayed an exceptional twenty days in the Holy Land, and returned after thirty-one (or thirty-three) weeks to chronicle his experiences. His narrative emphasizes language and translation and even contains an Arabic glossary for future pilgrims. Being monolingual in the linguistically very diverse Eastern Mediterranean increased his awareness of alterity. Indeed, the constant intervention of translators and interpreters reduced him and his fellows to a state of infantilized helplessness in the hostile territory of the Holy Land, where Saracens, in the spirit of *jihad*, systematically treated the pilgrims with aggressive contempt. These late-medieval Christian visitors would not recognize themselves in the Western orientalists of Edward Said's famous 1978 book. But the humiliations Grünemberg suffered, and the spiritual gains he made, allowed him to transform himself from a proud, self-conscious German knight into a humble, communal figure, and to metaphorize, or translate, his painful pilgrimage, his own *via dolorosa*, into an *imitatio Christi*.
Keywords: Arabic, Germany, Holy Land, Konrad Grünemberg, pilgrimage, translation, travel.

[…] Archites of Tarentum left us a testimony in which he argues the following. When man, whom God endowed with the power to contemplate nature and the entire creation, first saw the beauty of the starry sky, *he felt no pleasure in this miraculous spectacle until he could communicate it to someone else.* Likewise I, Sir Konrad Grünemberg, have written down as faithfully and as diligently as I could for my beloved patrons and friends, all the special, interesting and curious things that I have seen during my pilgrimage to the Holy Sepulcher [...] My purpose was to give my friends and good patrons at least an idea, *as a shadow of the reality,* of the trip and journey to the land where our Lord Jesus Christ assumed His human form [...][1]

Konrad Grünemberg's narrative presents itself in the opening statement as a translation and a gift. Although only "a shadow of the reality", it is designed to offer the same benefits to the recipient as the traveler-observer has received. It is not just a first-person journal kept by a traveler or an itinerary for pilgrims. Medieval travelers were expected to report to the home community, and many accounts of travel to the Holy Land have survived[2]. Such texts were among the first to be printed, and they have often been treated as historical sources. Was this due to a scarcity of Western scholars with mastery of the languages of the Middle East? Or was it part of a textually-based European plan "to render [the Orient] completely open, to make it totally accessible to European scrutiny [...]" (Said 1979: 83, 91-2)?[3] Many of these narratives, but not Grünemberg's, were translated into English during the heyday of Orientalism in the nineteenth century[4].

Grünemberg set out from Constance on 22 April 1486, and within a few days he had entered the dialectic of the alien and the familiar. He took a servant and three horses. We do not know if he left behind a family, who his patrons and friends were, why he undertook the pilgrimage, his age, what happened to him after his return, or even when he wrote the text. By his own admission, he was, in the tradition of travel writers, "an insatiable learner of foreign cultures and all new things", "not someone who takes hearsay seriously" (1947: 27, 16)[5]. He confidently represents himself as a knight with a servant and a third horse, a gentleman who is received by important people: "I, Sir Konrad Grünemberg" (*ibid.*: 11). All goes well as long as he is traveling through German-speaking lands. In Venice, he joins a polyglossic group of pilgrims, a "temporary community traveling towards the sacred" (Dahlberg 1991: 37), who are held up for seven weeks before their *padrone* can be persuaded or forced by the Senate to sail. Our novice pilgrim is still extremely impressed with the evidence of a decadent, ostentatious Western Christianity that, unaware of the approaching Reformation, flaunts its wealth:

> I saw golden robes with two or three layers of color and others interwoven entirely with gold. Also many crimson ones dyed with murex from Tyre and Astrum, with a motif of flowers against gold. There was multi-colored velvet [...] many vestments had buckles and hems all stitched and clasped in gold and ornamented with precious stones and gorgeous pearls. Upon these [participants in the procession] followed large groups bearing torches, and then came the Holy Sacrament, to the sound of trumpets and many other instruments [...] (1947: 19-20)

The painted ladies, the same ones whom other pilgrim-writers considered vulgar for their false hair and gaudy jewelry, greatly appealed to him. After a long description of these women, fairly useless because full of extravagant clichés from romance literature, he writes, surprisingly coarsely, "it would not be at all amazing if these women made the men and their husbands continuously tremble with desire, worse than bucks in heat", but he abruptly censors himself: "I have been writing too much about this subject" (*ibid.*: 21).

Their galley finally sailed on June 2 for a nine-week sea voyage. His comments offer a glimpse of his personality. His "classical" background is limited (he sails past Ithaca without referring to Odysseus, and he thinks that "Theodora" is a Latin name and "Sorora" a Greek one). He is interested in architecture, matters of chivalry, military details and in all sorts of minute information without distinguishing between the objective and the subjective: on the one hand, nautical charts, mileage and exchange rates, on the other, lists of (dubious) relics. In Rhodes, he is awed by "a large piece of the True Cross, [...] the skull [of...] one of the 11,000 virgins, [...] a hand of St. Anne [...] and the finger of St. John the Baptist with which he pointed out our Lord Jesus Christ [...]" (*ibid.*: 39). On occasion, he reminds us of some of Chaucer's pilgrims. He likes good wine and points out pretty women, and he cares enough about people to write about the wretched condition of the *galiots*[6]. In general, he calls a spade a spade, especially when writing about bodily functions. He is fond, in medieval fashion, of rhetorical devices such as hyperbole and the "outdoing topos".

Already in Venice, a problem emerges: Grünemberg only speaks his own language. From now on, he cannot take much initiative and much of the experience is lived second-hand. He does not speak but is spoken to by translators and interpreters. The infantilization and dependency (Cronin 2000: 43) that characterize his evolution as a pilgrim begin right here, and he seems to resent it, as he admires a gentleman from Zara who speaks four languages and can act like a grown-up, independent man. He does not say how he communicates with locals in the ports of call, and he describes what he sees rather than what he understands. When attending a Greek-Catholic service he focuses on the body-language of the officiating clergy, reducing and translating the spirituality of the ritual to its mere physical expression: "Four more Greeks with long beards were standing by [...] and they sang during the service and they gesticulated in such a manner that the Duke and I could not pray for laughing" (1947: 37). This is what Freud refers to as "projection": "what we most despise in ourselves we repress and then magically 'rediscover' in someone else" (Robinson 1997: 122). Grünemberg translates his unstated frustration at his infantile inability to speak or understand into the allegedly childish and uncontrolled gesticulation of the bearded (and therefore adult) men. The same happens later in a bathhouse in Jerusalem, where the monolingual pilgrims do not get the sense of what the bathhouse attendants are doing or saying to them[7]: "[...] they made such funny gestures and such a fuss in general, that my lord and I were frequently provoked to laughter" (1947: 84). The most practical *lingua franca* remains money. Coins need no translation and facilitate "exchanges" between people who do not share a common language: "Get enough *zechine*–those are the new ducats–as well as new *marcelins* and *marchetti*. Greeks and Orientals accept these coins readily" (*ibid.*: 14). Money is more eloquent than language and more powerful than even the barriers of religion. He writes about the wife of his donkey-driver: "[she] was holding a baby on each arm and she showed them to me. This Infidel woman was not veiled; she was extraordinarily pretty, with a sweet face. I gave her two *marcelins*" (*ibid.*: 55).

The presence of untranslated foreign words is fairly typical of travel narrative, and Grünemberg's text is no exception. What I take to be a dialect of Italian (it is not Venetian), probably blended with the dialects of the Adriatic, abounds in certain parts of the text, especially with reference to the equipment of the galley and to navigation[8]: "dritsa galeen!" ("Bring the galley up straight!") (*ibid.*: 23). Some Turkish and German words, which refer to military matters and dress, are left untranslated, a fact which emphasizes the writer's awareness that the Eastern Mediterranean world is becoming increasingly unfamiliar, that other rules apply. Foreign words also authenticate the narrative by translating the reader into a foreign climate and by suggesting the traveler's cultural knowledge if not assimilation. Words are souvenirs brought home for others to ponder (Cronin 2000: 13, 40).

The sea journey was dangerous and uncomfortable, but Grünemberg rarely complains. Indeed, from a spiritual point of view, "arduous travel" is a "devotional necessity" and "a form of penance [...] to make the invocation of divine power effective" (Eade 1991: 12). And from a traveler's point of view, a journey without obstacles is not worth writing about. Especially the sixteen days spent riding at anchor in the stinking galley, with the two towers of Jaffa and the shoreline of the Holy Land in sight, must have been a sore penance for the pilgrims. But once they had received their *billets,* or passports, Grünemberg's party was rewarded with an unusually lengthy tour (twenty days) of the holy places[9].

That foreign words demonstrate "how fraught the process of translation is in the first place" (Cronin 2000: 40-41) becomes very clear when Grünemberg is ejected from the womb-like pilgrims' galley and is reborn, i.e., forced to confront hostile rather than friendly forms of alterity in the Holy Land. His linguistic helplessness turns against him in what must have been a prank on the part of the Muslim immigration officer. Our pilgrim is very proud of the *billet* that the emir's secretary gives him at Jaffa, and he reproduces the calligraphy in his narrative, thinking that the words refer to his servant and to himself. But in fact the *billet* reads "Abdur Rab–Friend of God–and Mohammed Gausz Hindi"[10]–hardly appropriate names for Christian pilgrims! The *billet* reminds us that lack of translation highlights cultural difference and that words signal the untranslatable–in this case, the idiosyncratic sense of humor of the immigration officer.

On a couple of rare occasions, Grünemberg quotes–or *thinks* he is quoting–Arabic. What he thinks to be phonetic Arabic really isn't. In the Jerusalem bathhouse, he quotes the angry "Infidels" as saying "in an ugly tone", "undar, undar, marsus roch roch", which he translates (according to de Vrankrijker) as "you greatest villains and most evil people in the world, get out of here or something nasty will happen to you!" (1947: 84). "*Okhroj*" does mean "get out!" but the phrase as a whole is incomprehensible to native speakers of Arabic. Two "Infidels" reportedly use the same phrase to chase him from a mosque, and others scream "schubuppup, schubuppup" at the pilgrims–which is not Arabic but gibberish. Note that the only phrases that Grünemberg passes off for Arabic express anger, aggression and contempt. Arabic is an extremely difficult language to write down phonetically. Whereas Grünemberg inserts many Italian terms, he tries only twice or thrice to write down Arabic and in each case fails to render it correctly. The language resists being "trans-lated" onto paper and therefore–unlike the Italian one–it becomes suspect and threatening. Its speakers, who cannot be translated, become even more sinister. The relationship between "host" and "visitor" is easily spoiled by the language barrier alone (Cronin 2000: 14).

The heart of Grünemberg's narrative, however, is his description of the extended visit. Once in the Holy Land, the pilgrims waste no time valorizing the metaphorical *via dolorosa* of their journey, their road of sorrows;

in fact, they barely have time to sleep. They immediately retrace Christ's life–noting every indulgence earned in the process–as the Franciscan Guardians of the Holy Places take them on a thorough tour of sites where specific events mentioned in Scripture had, supposedly, taken place[11]. The Franciscans' role in the pilgrims' experience was a vital one, since, in concert with the Saracen authority, they controlled the "organization of space and time in relation to shrine activities" (Eade 1991: 11), they imposed conformity on the rituals, and they acted as translator-interpreters, literally, like "fathers"[12]. They exacerbated the pilgrims' infantilization because they exercised a moral and spiritual authority that the pilgrims quickly interiorized, rather than the mere physical or legal authority of the Venetian Senate or the *padrone*. To the repressive authority exercised by the "Infidel" officials (head-counts, passport checks, extraction of money) is now added the subtler control of the Franciscans, whose language skills the pilgrims realize to be vital for the success of their enterprise:

> [...] a Friar announced loudly in Latin the name of the place and what had happened there. Another Franciscan repeated the information in French and in Italian, and another one in German, which was necessary to the pilgrims because we spoke at least ten different languages among us. (1947: 58)

Travel and translation, says Cronin (2000: 72), are "explicitly bound up".

"Holy" sites on the itinerary include the school of the Virgin Mary, the Golden Gate to the valley of Jehoshaphat, the place where Christ first fell under the Cross, St. Veronica's doorway, the spot where Lazarus was begging for the crumbs from the rich man's table, Adam's grave, and so forth. At each spot, a dry note: "indulgence +" (plenary) or "indulgence T"(partial)–except at King Herod's palace: "it is a big house, and its front must once have been painted. No indulgence there" (*ibid.*: 60)–maybe because at that time the palace housed the harem of the Governor of Jerusalem [...] (Prescott 1954: 129). Following the conventions of Roman Catholic pilgrimage, texts were read by the group leader at specific sites, following an itinerary designed to authenticate the assumed biography of Christ. As the tour progresses, the actual city is dismembered, as the Franciscans reduce her to a checklist of sites, marginalizing the places where real people live and work. The *bazaar*, probably the principal site in the daily lives of the fixed residents, is hastily dismissed as uninteresting and worthless (1947: 87). But this is typical of major holy places.

To some readers of the narrative, the visit to the holy places may seem rather a disappointment. As compared to the colorful episodes in Venice, at sea or in the ports of call, the account of the twenty days in the Holy Land is rather dry and only intermittently revived by scuffles with Infidels. It lacks the immediacy and the variety of experience that relates other parts of this narrative to the early adventure novel. But I suggest it would be wrong to take Grünemberg to task for this development in tone and style, for the same reason that it would be unfair (or "Romantic") to criticize Milton for making God a plain-speaker in *Paradise Lost* and giving all the great speeches to Satan. The accountant's record of sites and indulgences does become annoying but it is for the sites and indulgences that the pilgrims were risking their lives. This record may well be the part of the text that his audience was most interested in. There is no reason to think that Grünemberg is disingenuous when he writes, after the visit to the Basilica of the Nativity: "At dawn [...] the pilgrims prayed devoutly and kept saying that never before in their lives had they experienced such joy as in that holy church and that they thought themselves amply recompensed for all their trouble and misery" (*ibid.*: 81). This shift towards a more sober, more controlled, tone and style is echoed by, or maybe caused by, a gradual change in the personality of the writer. Maybe it would not be amiss to refer to Grünemberg's narrative as a metaphorical *imitatio Christi* through suffering.

And there was a lot of suffering. The Jerusalem pilgrimage differed vastly from the other two great pilgrimages in the Middle Ages–those to the tombs of SS. Peter and Paul in Rome and to that of St. James the Greater in Compostella–in that, unlike the *romeos* or the *jacquaires*, the Jerusalem pilgrims or *palm-bearers*[13] could not enter into linguistic or cultural dialogue with those who held the holy place. In order to do so, they needed to go through translators: Franciscans, local Christians or Jews[14]. Relevant here is the appended glossary. Unlike the few "Arabic" phrases quoted in the main text, the glossary's 224 items are phonetically quite accurate. They are mostly nouns useful in daily situations, although some items make no sense to native speakers[15]. Edward Said interprets such inclusion of lexicographic material–especially in such an ideologically motivated genre as travel literature–as part of the Orientalist plot to acquire power over the helpless, stable "other" through one-way scrutiny and acquisition of knowledge (Said 1979: 32, 283-4)[16]. Significantly, the items we expect most—hello, please, thank you, goodbye–are absent, which suggests that genuine contact through language was not the major concern of the compiler. Maybe it is an example of Orientalism, after all. It is ironic that a glossary should symbolize the failed encounter between the Europeans and their Arabic-speaking hosts[17].

Indeed, the pilgrims moved within hostile territory, and "old acquaintances" had long become "intimate enemies" (Lewis 1993: 17). The Jerusalem pilgrimage necessitated an encounter (but without dialogue) with *absolute* otherness as the pilgrims moved out of the Christian brotherhood altogether into a world where only a handful of Franciscan friars provided *caritas* and relative protection for the stranger. The *romeos* and the *jacquaires*, too, were strangers to the local communities through which they moved, but, encountering only *relative* otherness, they cannot have known the cultural isolation, or the outright danger, that the Jerusalem pilgrims faced.

Even the other Christians they encountered, the non-Latins, were aliens. The Church of the Holy Sepulcher is read like a natural museum of Christianity, with live display, full of bizarre situations:

> [...] the din in the Church was so curiously loud, what with all these people shouting, that it was fit to wake the seven sleepers. The priests and clerics of these sects had wives and children living with them in the church. I even pushed some straw mats and curtains aside and I saw them sitting or lying about. (1947: 72)

Alterity within Christianity is announced somewhat sarcastically: "here follows an account of all peoples who also think they are Christians" (*ibid*.: 72). The account deals only with difference (the number of lamps that each group tends in the Church is crucial) and it is confusing because the situation is confusing and because the observer's notions of geography and political and church history are not very sound. There is no trace of personal interaction between the Latin pilgrims and any other groups. *En route* to the Holy Land, Grünemberg describes the Greek-Orthodox: he does not like them–he ridicules their liturgy–but he is offended that Orthodox priests ritually purify an altar after a Latin priest has officiated at it (*ibid*.: 74)[18]. The other groups include the Suriani (or "Assyrians") and the Jacobites, both members of the Monophysite Syrian Orthodox Church; the Nestorians, the Armenians, the Georgians from the region of the Caspian Sea, and the Abyssians (or "Indians", as he also calls them)[19]. Yet, in spite of his aloofness, he never suggests that these "sects" are blasphemous or irreverent, that they should reconvert, or that they should team up with all other Christians to combat Islam. He spends many words on the Church of the Holy Sepulcher because that site had the most intrinsic religious significance for his creed, and also because of its universalist character, which allowed for a multiplicity of religious discourses[20]. Grünemberg did not believe in a new crusade.

Multiplicity, however, did not imply dialogue. The encounter between pilgrims and Infidel hosts is marked not only by the language barrier but indeed by the hosts' provocative and gratuitous aggression, which starts even before the pilgrims are given their *billets*. During a risky food-shopping expedition on the beach at Jaffa, some pilgrims complain that the pancakes for sale are only half-baked, upon which an Infidel immediately runs a monk through, three times, with a long sword. The authorities mockingly make up for the murder by presenting the *padrone* with a ... turtle. Every non-Christian is always armed to the teeth, with sharp sticks and swords, lances and bows. By contrast, the pilgrim had no right to carry arms both by the laws of Islam and those of the Christian pilgrimage.

Their arrival in Raman (Ramleh, Ramallah) is traumatic. Raman was the most important place between Jaffa and Jerusalem, and the population was notoriously hostile to Christians:

> [...] the Infidels would not let us ride any further and we walked to the town, and when we entered the town and walked in the narrow alleys, the Saracens gathered to gawk at us. Many carried short, pointed sticks with which they stabbed us poor pilgrims in the sides, and they pulled our beards so that many of us cried out. And we arrived at the hospice that was founded by a Duke of Burgundy, and one after the other we skulked through two narrow, little gates, and in between these stood two Infidel scoundrels with

their asses bared, to deride us. Once safely inside the hospice, four comrades collapsed on the floor, and we lit candles for them [...]. (*ibid.*: 52)

Two of the four, German nobles both, died that same night. The other two, a French abbot and a monk, were able to continue the journey to Jerusalem on horse-stretchers, "at very considerable expense", "where they both died among the Friars of Mount Sion" (*ibid.*: 52).

Communication with the Saracen authorities went by means of an official interpreter or translator who, according to Grünemberg, was one of the six most powerful men in the Holy Land. Which languages he worked with is not mentioned. Communication with private Muslim individuals often involved Jews as intermediaries and "fixers". When Grünemberg and Count Sigmund of Lupsen decide to take a bath in the *hammam* of Jerusalem (needed because "our shirts [...] were so filthy and so full of vermin that it was bothersome" (*ibid.*: 84)), they take "for [their] only escort [...] a young Jew [...] who spoke both German and the Infidel language" (*ibid.*: 83). When their peaceful presence is discovered, they are violently evicted, as if their delight in cleanliness (unusual in Christians?) pollutes the magnificent building and the religion it serves: "The walls were covered with many Infidel inscriptions, and when I asked the Jew about their meaning, he answered that they were sayings in praise of God" (*ibid.*: 83). Half-washed and in wet shirts, the two German noblemen are chased like street-dogs: "We hastily went back to the house where our fellows were staying. Infidel guttersnipes ran behind and threw stones at us" (*ibid.*: 85).

This experience, and others like it, confirms the suggestion that the Islamic world in the Middle Ages and the Renaissance looked upon Christian Europe in the same way that Victorian Europeans looked upon Black Africa (Lewis 1993: 13-14). Europe could be simplified and represented as a lower level of civilization, stubbornly clinging to superseded rituals, cackling away in a chaos of primitive unimportant languages, hopelessly divided, and characterized by a marked lack of hygiene. Christianity was a contemptible retrograde religion, established 600 years before Islam and since then superseded. To the Europeans, Islam had come to "symbolize terror, devastation, the demonic hordes of hated barbarians" (Said 1979: 59). In order to visit the holiest of sites, the pilgrims had, indeed, to make themselves ideal targets for the *jihad*.

Jihad is usually, but badly, translated as "holy war", whereas it really means "striving", especially *fi sabil Allah*, "in the path of God", although the military sense was often confused with the spiritual one (Lewis 1993: 9). The purpose of the *jihad* is to strive until the "submission" (Islam) of the "other", and to wage *jihad* was seen as an obligation especially on the frontiers of Islam or when in contact with the most fervent zealots among the unbelievers–such as our pilgrims. In a way, all of Islam is fundamentalist (Lewis 1993: 14; Mansfield 1991: 13) since Muslims should fight *all* men until they say "there is no God but God" (Hourani 1991: 19)[21]. Grünemberg defines *jihad* as the duty "to practice eternal and deadly enmity towards all other religions and to kill without hesitation anyone who praises another religion than theirs" (1947: 90). This situation of conflict between the infantilized pilgrims and their aggressive hosts contradicts the basic scenario of Orientalism as popularized by Said[22].

In fact, Grünemberg accords the fifteenth-century Europeans the status that nineteenth-century Europeans would accord the "oriental" in much of their literature, politics and art: "a [...] powerful difference posited by the Orientalist as against the Oriental is that [...] for the latter, passivity is the presumed role; for the former, the power to observe, study, and so forth" (Said 1979: 308). The nineteenth-century Orientalist portrays the European as strong and active, rational and aggressive, in control, "male" and "subject". The "oriental" is weak and passive, irrational, subdued and helpless, "female" and "object". Grünemberg's fifteenth-century scenario of the power play is exactly the opposite. His "Infidel/oriental" (whether Mamluke, Arab or Turk) is "male". He is armed and rides horses, exercises power and aggression, and rationalizes his contempt for the superseded faith of the pilgrims. The pilgrim is "female". He is infantilized and speechless, he rides a donkey and begs permission, he is the victim of exploitation and physical violence, only very rarely does he put up a feeble resistance, and he tries hard to respect the Islamic sensibilities of which the Franciscans have made him aware (no stepping on graves). We have come a long way from those militant pilgrims of the eleventh century, the crusaders (Johns 1990: 172). Furthermore, Grünemberg shows a relative respect for the cultural, linguistic, historical and social heterogeneity among the host population of the Holy Land (Turks, Egyptians and Arabs), unlike Said's nineteenth-century Orientalist for whom "orientals" means a homogeneous race of "others". In Grünemberg's narrative, it is not the European pilgrims who are indifferent racists but rather the "Infidel" hosts whose position of power and whose religious mission allow them to discard alterity among their "guests", lump them together as khafir, and generally harbor an opinion of Christian Europe that is "monolithic, scornful of ordinary human experience, gross, reductive, unchanging"–to redirect Said's words (1979: 299)[23].

Grünemberg's narrative does, however, anticipate some standard features of nineteenth-century Orientalism as described in Said's controversial study. For example, the "Infidels" are said to be notoriously cruel to animals (Said 1979: 38): "When we wanted to get going, the donkeys began to kick and skip, and I believe the Infidels were pricking them with something [...]" (1947: 51). They are shown as given to "'fulsome flattery, intrigue, cunning" (Said 1979: 38). They often shout for no reason, and when among themselves, they are irrationally quarrelsome and hopelessly inefficient[24]:

> And after we had stood there for almost an hour, and when the Infidels and Mamlukes were more or less complete in number, the Infidels suddenly started a quarrel, and they drew their swords and sabers, and they cut, hewed and sliced with their weapons with all their might [...]. The Infidel emirs rode back and forth, restored order [...] and yet

another scuffle followed; ere this had been resolved, another two hours of daylight were lost. (1947: 55-56)

However, the feature that most blatantly anticipates nineteenth-century Orientalism is the association of Islam with lechery[25]: "Saracens, Turks and Infidels practice indecent relations with animals and each other" (*ibid.*: 90). The reader almost gets the impression that Grünemberg would not mind converting to Islam, so long does he dwell on the physical delights of Paradise: "[here] too, does one satisfy all the voluptuousness that one can desire, and everybody is handsomely built and mature; there is desire and voluptuousness, and there are partners who are willing" (*ibid.*: 91). But immediately afterwards he turns precisely to the subject of the renegade Christians, "these traitors to the true God" (*ibid.*: 92).

At the end of his account, Grünemberg writes that, in all, he has been away for thirty-three weeks. However, the chronological record of saints' feasts, weekdays and dates that he intermittently provides proves that he would have been absent for only thirty-one weeks, give or take a day. Why does he insist on making it thirty-three? As a reference to the life span of Christ? He left home, he falsely claims, on a Friday for a journey of hardship whose ultimate purpose was spiritual re-birth and rejuvenation and the sharing of these experiences with his neighbors[26]. Grünemberg translates, or metaphorizes, his personal pilgrim's experience as an *imitatio Christi* in the context of the *via dolorosa*. He emphasizes increasing physical suffering as the goal draws nearer, as well as increasing emotional suffering brought on by the constant humiliations and the debilitating dependency of imposed passivity. But more than that: by Grünemberg's account, the pilgrim becomes a "trans-lation" himself–literally, an object that is carried or ferried across, whether across the Eastern Mediterranean by a Venetian galley or across the bad roads of Palestine by a donkey. In the host environments, the pilgrim has no intrinsic value–not to the Christians in Venice nor to the Muslims in Palestine–except for the economic advantage of his passage. He is rendered helpless and is exploited by Venetian shopkeepers and by his *padrone*; mocked by vulgar Venetian women; humiliated by an uncaring immigration service; quarantined in stinking caves; harassed by constant passport checks and head-counts; threatened by officials; ridiculed by quarrelsome drivers and impudent street-boys; robbed by thugs, thieves and ambulant merchants[27]. Much like a written text, which in the process of being translated is also estranged from itself, or betrayed, or at least transformed into something new, so this forcedly passive, translated body–the pilgrim–is "translated" and thus, in a sense, made new.

Once "trans-lated" onto the filthy pilgrims' galley, Grünemberg–far removed from the glittering ostentation of St. Mark's and surrounded by total alterity in language and religion–begins to change. Riding a donkey or walking, eating bad food, sleeping in unfurnished rooms or outside on the rocky ground, he enters the humbler beginnings of his own religion. His self-conscious "I"–remember, "I Sir Konrad Grünemberg"–fades into the shadows of the Holy

Places and is replaced by the frequently repeated third-person appellation, "the group of pilgrims", of which he is only a member. His individual experience becomes communal. Since the encounter with alterity is a painful experience for the weaker party, that "group defines itself in relation to the perceived threat of otherness, [which] can lead to the assertiveness of nationalistic, religious, or ethnic fundamentalism" (Coulson 1997: 2). This certainly applies to "the group of pilgrims". That Grünemberg should concentrate on what unites them (religious experience, hostile environment, dependence on translation) rather than on individual personalities or cultural differences, is only human.

The "translation" that Grünemberg undergoes, which amounts to a renunciation of the self, begins to resemble a penance, a "means of participating in the Passion of Christ" (Dahlberg 1991: 38)[28]. Maybe it is in this experience, and not in the accountant's listing of indulgences earned, that the real value of the pilgrimage rests. This experience finds its richest expression in the three wakes at the Holy Sepulcher:

> You should see these good, pious Christians at prayer on their knees, arms spread wide like a cross; you should see how the pilgrims weep, how their tears moisten the floor. And every single one of them [including, of course, himself] said that never in his life had a night passed so swiftly as during this vigil in the Church. (1947: 71)

So it was worth it, after all!

But was it, really? And did the journey even take place at all? At this point, I must confess that I have harbored some suspicion ever since I started working on Grünemberg. Did he really go to Jerusalem, in 1486 or at any other time? Was he a real traveler or is his narrative a fake? Hilda Prescott did not include him in *Jerusalem Pilgrimage* (1954), although she did include many other German pilgrims; again, Grünemberg's text would have been available in the 1880 German edition and in the Dutch edition of 1947. There is no proof that the illustrations were drawn on location. Many bits of information and several specific incidents can be found almost *verbatim* in other pilgrims' accounts[29]. It is of course well known that these authors read one another's books (Felix Fabri's two-volume *Evagatorium* was a famous example) and that copying took place[30]. He does claim that he has been reading up on Islam in order to write about it (without being more specific), but that hardly counts as evidence either for or against the authenticity of his account. If he made it all up, he was certainly not the first or the last one to do so, the number of travel books proven to be fictitious, or partly fictitious, being enormous–and that includes accounts by Jerusalem pilgrims[31]. It is precisely with such liars that Langland, in the Prologue to *Piers Plowman*, is concerned:

> Pilgrims and palmers plighted hem togidere
> To seke Seint James and seintes in Rome;
> They went forth in here wey with many wise tales,
> And hadden leve to lie al here lif after. (ll. 46-49)

It is probably also this feature of travel writing–the endless possibilities for lying–that links it most to the development of, and to early theories of, the novel. The only way to authenticate Grünemberg's account would be to investigate the records of the Franciscans in Jerusalem, if they ever kept or preserved such records.

[1] From the opening paragraphs of Konrad Grünemberg's account of his journey to the Holy Land, in A.C.J. de Vrankreijker's Dutch translation (1947: 11). The emphasis is mine. All English translations from this text are my own and based on this Dutch edition.

[2] Perhaps the most influential pilgrim accounts were those of William Wey from Eton, who went twice (1458 and 1462); Felix Fabri, German Dominican monk (1480 and 1483; and Bernard Breytenbach, canon of Mainz (1483). Like Grünemberg's, the latter's account is very richly illustrated.

[3] "As propaganda for international trade and for colonization, travel accounts had no equal" (Adams 1983: 77).

[4] For example, in the fourteen volumes of the *Library of the Palestine Pilgrims' Text Society* (1887-1897). This is not the place to discuss the interesting relationship between travel literature and the development of the novel, but I should like to mention here that, in several ways, Grünemberg's text deviates from the standard pilgrimage account and anticipates the budding romance, or early novelistic, literature.

[5] The text is preserved in two manuscripts in a dialect of late Middle-High German. Although the technology was available, Grünemberg's story was not printed in his own time. Ms. "C" was found in Karlsruhe and is the shorter and less detailed. Ms. "G", which was found in the Ducal Library of Gotha, is longer, more literary and very beautifully illustrated (given the fact that Grünemberg also produced a well-known armorial, the illustrations are probably by his own hand). The "G" ms. was exhibited in the Badischen Landesbibliothek in the summer of 2000. The text was briefly summarized in *Deutschen Pilgerreisen nach dem Heilige Lande* by Reinhold Röhricht and Heinrich Meiszner (1880), who also reprinted a few excerpts in the original language. Twenty years later, Röhricht referred to it again in another study with the same title (Innsbruck: 1900). Walther Fränzel's annotated translation, into modern German, appeared in 1912. Fränzel worked from the Gotha manuscript, referring to the Karlsruhe text when in doubt. He claims to have modernized the punctuation but to have respected the syntax as well as the late-medieval spelling of place names. De Vrankrijker made his Dutch translation from Fränzel's modern German and published it with black-and-white reproductions of some illustrations as well as an Arabic-Dutch glossary of 224 items under the heading: "Here follow many frequently used words from the Saracen language as well as some of their numbers" (1947: 95). De Vrankrijker does not give any information about the authenticity of the glossary or about its maker. I act on the assumption that Grünemberg is the compiler.

[6] *Galiots* are essentially rowers. The term is often translated as "galley slaves" but this is misleading since in Grünemberg's time most of them were paid professionals, free men from Venice and her dependencies. Slaves were used only later, mainly because of recruitment problems. In Crete, for instance, men went to extremes–including self-mutilation–to avoid being drafted for galley-service (Greene 2000: 59).

[7] It is not clear which of the several bathhouses in Jerusalem Grünemberg visited. For a description of the Jerusalem bathhouses (Boas 2001: 161-63).

[8] This was probably the "Italian known as the lingua franca that some Muslims (merchants, sailors) also used" (Lewis 1993: 34). In the fifteenth and sixteenth centuries, the usual language of interaction with the "Orient" was Italian (Hauser s.d.: viii).

[9] Normally, pilgrims considered themselves lucky if they got two weeks; Felix Fabri's group only had nine days, after six weeks at sea.

[10] Note in the Dutch (and German?) text (1947: 100). The *billet* as reproduced by Grünemberg (*ibid.*: 50), probably from memory, would be illegible even to an Arab linguist.

[11] The canons of the Holy Sepulcher and other important institutions had adopted the Franciscan canon only since the early fifteenth century. Previously, Augustinian, and somewhat less importantly, Benedictine rule was followed.

[12] See Cronin:

> The fear of ridicule, vulnerability and helplessness that comes from the inability to express oneself in another language is a key element in the language infrastructure of the tourist industry. Ferried from coach to museum to hotel, the tourist is insulated from the shock of language contact by the omnipresent guide/interpreter. (2000: 43)

The "parental function" of tour guides and interpreters, he adds (*ibid*.: 43), is "a logical consequence of the tourist fear of being suddenly orphaned in a strange house of language where the parents are not around to hear the cries for help".

[13] Pilgrims would buy palm branches in the Ruga Palmariorum, or Palm Street, to carry during processions and to take back home.

[14] There are no anti-Semitic strains in Grünemberg's narrative. He emphasizes the role of Jews as multi-lingual mediators and able "fixers". Jews were mostly Arabic speaking, although they had their own slang of Arabic; Hebrew was still used for the liturgy (Hourani 1991: 97). Only six years after Grünemberg's journey, in 1492, the Jews would be expelled from Spain.

[15] My colleague Dr. Tarif Bazzi, and my former research assistant Zeina Arakji. Dr. Bazzi, a linguist, was struck by the highly unusual, inexplicable haphazard mix of registers (standard-classical-formal and colloquial-informal). The entries in Grünemberg's glossary that were not recognized by my native speakers of Arabic might either be simply inexactly rendered or else forms of an old Palestinian-Arabic dialect. Grünemberg's fellow pilgrim/authors often produced similar glossaries. According to Dannenfeldt (1955: 100), a "very inexact Arabic alphabet appeared in the *Peregrinatio in terram sanctam* of Bernhard von Breytenbach in 1486", whereas "Arnold von Harff included a glossary in Palestinian Arabic of over one hundred words, the numerals up to 30 [...]. Gabriel von Rattenberg included a vocabulary of about 200 Arabic words".

[16] "And of course", says Said (1979: 93), "many writers of travel books or guidebooks compose them in order to say that a country *is* like this, or better, that it *is* colorful [...]. The idea [...] is that people, places, and experiences can always be described by a book, so much so that the book (or text) acquires a greater authority, and use, even than the actuality it describes".

[17] If the author had made the same journey some 30 years later, he would not have compiled an Arabic but rather a Turkish glossary.

[18] Grünemberg's notes reflect the tension between Latin and Eastern Christians. The Ottoman capture of Constantinople in 1453 had positive consequences for the Orthodox Christians but resulted in tense relations with Latin Christianity. Later, when the Ottomans conquered Crete and reinstated an Orthodox hierarchy on the island, they extinguished the last important state in the Eastern Mediterranean that owed its origins to the Crusades (Greene 2000: 5).

[19] See Boas (2001: 38 and onwards) for a summary of the principal Eastern Churches. With regard to the Abyssians, he mentions the inevitable Prester John, but he does not repeat the conventional idea that the empire of this alleged Christian leader might serve to attack Islam from the South or the East. A glaring omission in the survey are the Copts (also known as the Nubians) because they, too, had a chapel in the Church of the Holy Sepulcher. In the fifteenth century, they were still an important part of the Egyptian population although their numbers were shrinking because of conversion (Hourani 1991: 96).

[20] It provides, as Eade says,

> [...] a ritual space for the expression of a diversity of perceptions and meanings which the pilgrims themselves bring to the shrine and impose upon it. As a result, the cult [contains] within itself a plethora of religious discourses [...] an arena for the interplay of a variety of imported perceptions and understandings, in some cases finely differentiated from one another [as among the various Christian groups], in others radically polarized [Christian versus Muslim]. (1991: 10-14)

[21] A powerful weapon in the service of *jihad* and of Islam in general, was the standard or classical Arabic language. Muslims believe that God communicated Himself by His word in Arabic; the Qu'ran was the first book written in Arabic: "writing [in Arabic] is used to proclaim the glory and eternity of God" (Hourani 1991: 56-7). Standard Arabic, the language of the Qu'ran, has been from the beginning the unifying language of many millions of people, and in Grünemberg's time Christian Europe had little to offer in competition. In spite of the Humanists' work the classical Western languages, Greek and Latin, were either dead or artificially maintained, at any rate closed to development. The modern "national" languages were not yet fixed, and each of these was spoken only by a small number of people.

[22] And since then thoroughly criticized by Lewis (1993: 107-118) and by Lisa Lowe (1991).

[23] The cultivated Arab world knew better; witness the European and Asian maps and travel accounts of the great twelfth-century traveler Idrisi.

[24] In 1972 still, a retired member of the U.S. Department of State wrote that "while the Arab value system demands absolute solidarity within the group, it at the same time encourages among its members a kind of rivalry that is destructive of that very solidarity" (in Said 1979: 48).

[25] "[T]he Arab", says Said (1979: 286), "is associated either with lechery or bloodthirsty dishonesty".

[26] In 1486, Easter (Sunday) fell on March 26. Therefore it is easy to calculate that April 22 was a Saturday, not a Friday.

[27] The constant tipping and paying of entrance fees everywhere was a real problem. A famous piece of advice to pilgrims was: "bring three bags: one with food, one with patience, and one with money, and let the last one be the largest". The practice did not start, however, until the beginning of Grünemberg's own century. It was abolished in the nineteenth (Moore 1961: 71).

[28] "The pilgrims to [...] Jerusalem", says Cronin (2000: 64-65), "are the expression of an ancient link between travel and transcendence. Spiritual quest like the metamorphosis of the hero is the pilgrim's progress from the familiar to the promised land of redemption, illumination, rebirth".

[29] Examples of such information and incidents include the description of palaces and churches in Venice, with their mosaics; a parade; a detailed shopping list, and mileages; the silver dishes of the *padrone*; admiration for the design of the galley and the lightning speed of work on board; the salt lake at Larnaca, and the Cyprus carob beans; a tempest at sea; wine so strong that you cannot drink it without water; advice on taking food (including biscuits, fruit syrup, a cage for fowl); fish playing around the ship at Jaffa; being thrown off a donkey (Prescott 1954: *passim*).

[30] On the other hand, Grünemberg contradicts many other narratives in significant details. He writes very positively about the *padrone* Agostino de Contarini and about the Venetian ladies. His berth is much wider than in any other narrative; he says nothing about the use of the oars, what pilgrims do on board, the prevalence of theft, or the permanent noise below decks even at night. He does not seem to know that the ladders of the hatchways were removed at night and he insists that people used them day and night. He does not describe exotic animals such as buffaloes and camels (Prescott 1954: *passim*).

[31] Adams has also studied realistic and believable travel fabrication. See his chapter, "The Truth-Lie Dichotomy" (1962: 81-102).

References

Adams, Percy G. 1962. *Travelers and Travel Liars, 1660-1800.* Berkeley, CA: University of California Press.

–. 1983. *Travel Literature and the Evolution of the Novel.* Lexington, KY: The University Press of Kentucky.

Boas, Adrian J. 2001. *Jerusalem in the Time of the Crusades: Society, landscape and art in the Holy City under Frankish rule.* London and New York, NY: Routledge.

Chafic Hout, Syrine. 1997. *Viewing Europe from the Outside. Cultural Encounters and Critiques in the Eighteenth-Century Pseudo-Oriental Travelogue and the Nineteenth-Century "Voyage en Orient". The Age of Revolution and Romanticism* Vol. 18. New York, NY: Peter Lang.

Cheyfitz, Eric. 1991. *The Poetics of Imperialism: Translation and Colonization from* The Tempest *to* Tarzan. New York, NY and Oxford: Oxford University Press.

Coulson, Anthony (ed.). 1997. *Exiles and Migrants: Crossing Thresholds in European Culture and Society*. Brighton: Sussex Academic Press.

Cronin, Michael. 2000. *Across the Lines: Language, Travel, Translation*. Cork: Cork University Press.

Dahlberg, Andrea. 1991. 'The Body as a Principle of Holism: Three Pilgrimages to Lourdes' in John Eade and Michael J. Sallnow (eds) *Contesting the Sacred: The Anthropology of Christian Pilgrimage*. London and New York, NY: Routledge. 30-50.

Dannenfeldt, Karl. 1955. 'The Renaissance Humanists and the Knowledge of Arabic' in *Studies in the Renaissance* 2: 96-117.

Eade, John, and Michael J. Sallnow (eds). 1991. *Contesting the Sacred: The Anthropology of Christian Pilgrimage*. London and New York, NY: Routledge.

Greene, Molly. 2000. *A Shared World: Christians and Muslims in the Early Modern Mediterranean*. Princeton, NJ: Princeton University Press.

Grünemberg, Konrad. 1912. *Ritter Grünemberg's Pilgerfahrt ins Heilige Lande, 1486* (tr. Walther Fränzel, intr. Johann Goldfriedrich). Leipzig.

–. 1947. *De Pelgrimstocht van Ridder Gruenemberg* [sic] *naar het Heilige in 1486* (tr. A.C.J. de Vrankrijker). Amsterdam.

Hauser, M.H. (tr.) and Philippe du Fresne-Canaye (ed.). s.d. *Le Voyage du Levant [...] 1573*. [Paris]: Ed. de Poliphile/PUF.

Hourani, Albert. 1991. *A History of the Arab Peoples*. Cambridge, MA: Harvard University Press.

Johns, Jeremy. 1990. 'Christianity and Islam' in John McManners (ed.) *The Oxford Illustrated History of Christianity*. Oxford: Oxford University Press. 164-95.

Kamps, Ivo and Jyotsna G. Singh (eds). 2001. *Travel Knowledge: European "Discoveries" in the Early Modern Period*. New York, NY: Palgrave.

Kardawi, Cheikh Youssef El-. 1997. *Le Licite et l'Illicite en Islam* (tr. Marwan Jardaly) 2 vols. Beirut: Dar Ibn Hazm.

Lewis, Bernard. 1993. *Islam and the West*. New York, NY and Oxford: Oxford University Press.

–. 1994. *The Shaping of the Modern Middle East*. New York, NY and Oxford: Oxford University Press.

Library of the Palestine Pilgrims' Text Society. 1887-1897. 14 vols. London.

Lowe, Lisa. 1991. *Critical Terrains: French and British Orientalisms*. Ithaca, NY: Cornell University Press.

Mansfield, Peter. 1991. *A History of the Middle East*. Harmondsworth: Penguin.

Mitchell, R.J. 1964. *The Spring Voyage: The Jerusalem Pilgrimage in 1458*. London: J. Murray.

Moore, Elinor. 1961. *The Ancient Churches of Jerusalem: The Evidence of the Pilgrims*. Beirut: Khayats.

Parise, Frank (ed.). 1982. *The Book of Calendars*. New York, NY: Facts on File.

Prescott, H.F.M. 1954. *Jerusalem Journey: Pilgrimage to the Holy Land in the Fifteenth Century*. London: Eyre & Spottiswoode.

Robinson, Douglas. 1997. *Translation and Empire: Postcolonial Theories Explained. Translation Theories Explained*. Manchester: St. Jerome Publishing.

Röhricht, Reinhold and Heinrich Meiszner. 1880. *Deutschen Pilgerreisen nach dem Heilige Lande*. Berlin: Weidmann.

Said, Edward. 1979. *Orientalism*. New York, NY: Vintage.

Shaw, Ezel Kural & C.J. Heywood. 1972. *English and Continental Views of the Ottoman Empire, 1500-1800*. Los Angeles, CA: William Andrews Clark Memorial Library UCLA.

Taylor, Joan E. 1993. *Christians and the Holy Places: The Myth of Jewish-Christian Origins*. Oxford: Clarendon Press.

3.2. Leo Africanus and the Limits of Translation

Oumelbanine Zhiri

Leo Africanus's celebrated *Descrittione dell'Affrica* is not *stricto sensu* a translation; however, it is an attempt by an Arab-speaking author to describe the geography, the culture, the customs of North and West Africa, in a language, Italian, that he did not master, for readers who presumably knew next to nothing about the subject. His work is thus a linguistic, but also a cultural, translation. Its important impact on European culture shows that this translation basically succeeded. However, sometimes his text reaches the limits of the powers of translation, especially because it was written at a time when its potential Italian and other European readers had very few other books to refer to in order to complete and contextualize Leo's; nor did the Italian language always offer Leo the words he needed in order to express foreign concepts. His use of numerous Arabic and Berber (Amazigh) words is one manifestation of the difficulties he encountered.
Keywords: Arabic, exile, Islam, Italy, Leo Africanus, translation, travel.

The task of a translator entails more than to make readable in a given idiom a text conceived and written in another language, and its difficulties and challenges go well beyond the purely grammatical and lexical ones, as important as those may be. The limits of translation can be felt most acutely in more than the conveying of the text, its words, its sentences, or even its topics; they are reached when the translation attempts to express the various subtexts, and sometimes fails to do so. The case of Leo Africanus allows an approach to these problems. Though his work is not, as we shall see, strictly speaking a translation, it cannot be properly understood without taking into account the challenges of transcribing meanings in another language. The particular circumstances of his writing, its context, offer a striking magnification of the powers and limits of translation–the powers to open new routes for readers to approach what was previously beyond their knowledge or imagination, and the limits reached by a translator as he struggles with his task, with his own ignorance, but also with his own knowledge, too vast to be conveyed in an adequate form.

Through his work and his biography, Leo Africanus is emblematic of the cultural and political relations between Europe and North Africa in the Early Modern period, and, far from being forgotten, is attracting more and more attention. Most importantly, he helped to transform in a profound way the European vision of North Africa. The story of his life reads not only as a travel account, but also as an adventure novel. Born Hasan al-Wazzan around 1490 in Granada, he left with his family for Morocco after the 1492 Spanish conquest of this last Muslim Kingdom of the Iberian Peninsula. He was schooled in grammar and law in Fez, the capital city; his family was close to the Wattasid dynasty that ruled a part of Morocco at that time, and at a young age he became a high ranking official; he traveled extensively for the service of the dynasty, and also in a personal capacity, in North and West Africa, Egypt, and parts of the Middle East. He was returning from an embassy to Istanbul when, in 1518, the ship he was traveling on was seized by Italian pirates. When Hasan was recognized as an ambassador and a scholar, he was sent as a captive to the learned Pope Leo X, known for his interest in Oriental languages and cultures. After one year of captivity, during which he received instruction in Christian doctrine, and presumably in Italian and Latin, he converted to Christianity, and received in baptism the names of the pope, Johannes Leo de Medici. He is thought to have spent about 10 years in Italy, and to have left for North Africa in 1528, presumably converting back to Islam.

During his sojourn in Italy, Leo Africanus, as tradition has elected to call him, wrote a number of texts, in Italian and Latin, of which only some still exist, at least to our knowledge. One of those works however was published several times during the Early Modern period, and exerted a profound and long-lasting influence on European representations of Africa. Entitled by its first editor *Della Descrittione dell'Affrica*, or "Description of Africa", it is designated in the only known manuscript as the *Libro della Cosmografia dell'Affrica*, the title I will be using here. The text itself is a geographical description of North and West Africa, centered mainly on the part that Leo knew best, the Maghrib. Completed in March 1526, it was first published in 1550 in a very large and influential collection of travel accounts assembled by Gian Battista Ramusio and entitled *Delle Navigazioni e Viaggi* (1978: 19-460). This groundbreaking collection was reprinted several times during the sixteenth and seventeenth centuries, and partially translated into French, by Jean Temporal, in 1556. Among the texts of this collection, Leo Africanus's was arguably the one that attracted the most attention and had the most impact on the culture. Its success was such that, during the sixteenth and seventeenth centuries, it was published separately in French, in Latin, in English, and in Dutch. During the few decades following its first publication, it came to constitute the foundation of the knowledge of a great part of Africa in the Early Modern period, and beyond[1]. Geographers and historians used it to renew their descriptions of a continent still basically unknown to Europeans, to such an extent that some texts seem to be basically rewritings of the *Cosmografia dell'Affrica*. One can find Leo's historical accounts and his descriptions of customs and institutions quoted by a large number of historians and geographers; they are also present in the works of philosophers and writers, including the likes of Montaigne's *Essais*, Jean Bodin's *Methodus ad Facilem Historiarum Cognitionem* and *Les Six livres de la Republique*, Robert Burton's *Anatomy of Melancholy*, Gibbon's *Decline and Fall of the Roman Empire*, among many others; the African toponyms it revealed to Europe were still used in maps drawn in the second half of the nineteenth century. Besides the published texts, editions and translations, a 900-page manuscript, certainly close to the one used by the first editor, was acquired in 1931 by the Biblioteca Nazionale in Rome[2]; it is the only manuscript that we know of, and it is the text on which my study is based, since it is the closest text to the one written by Leo Africanus. It presents a large number of differences from the text edited by Ramusio, differences of content as well as of style.

One of the fascinating aspects of Leo's work is that it was written in Europe, in a European language, by an Arab author, an occurrence that was exceedingly rare in the Early Modern period. We do not know with any certainty the reasons why Leo took on the project to describe Africa and thus to transmit to Europe a good deal of the Arabic knowledge on the subject. We may surmise that he had been at least encouraged to do so, and in particular to transmit the Arabic knowledge on a region that was highly strategic in the politics of the time. Africa had been recently circumnavigated by the Portuguese, who were establishing a series of fortresses and strongholds on several islands and on the Atlantic coast of Africa, in order to control the Straits of Gibraltar and the Atlantic route to India. Moreover, North Africa was one region where the two superpowers of the time, the Spanish Hapsburg Empire and the Ottoman Empire, were fighting for control, either directly or through satellite powers. These circumstances greatly heightened the interest in the region.

Before Leo Africanus, there was very little to help scholars and readers to satisfy their curiosity. In fact, modern Africa was almost unknown to the potential readers. The European texts describing this continent in the first half of the sixteenth century. were still often based on classical sources, such as Strabo, Pliny or Ptolemy[3], with little new information brought by the Portuguese navigations and the European interventions on the coast of Africa. And this new information usually concerned some toponyms and names of people and brought little knowledge of the society or the customs. In the preface of the first edition of the *Navigazioni e Viaggi*, Ramusio himself stresses the exceptional quality of the first text in his collection, which would greatly benefit both prince and scholar; according to Ramusio, the information about North Africa they can find here is of such abundance and precision that all other sources will seem almost worthless[4]. There had been some speculation as to the language in which this new groundbreaking information was conveyed. For a long time, it was assumed that the text was originally written in Arabic, even before Leo's capture. This view was offered by Ramusio in the same preface, according to which Pope Leo X asked his scholar captive to translate into Italian this already written text, and his version of events had been widely accepted for centuries. It actually does not seem likely, as the study of the text shows. Although it is probable that Leo had written at least notes in Arabic, either before or after his capture, he had obviously written and composed the text with potential foreign readers in mind. Thus, as far we know, the *Cosmografia dell'Affrica* is not a simple translation of one text from one language to another; nevertheless, as suggested earlier, it belongs fully in the field of translation studies. It attempts, indeed, to translate a whole culture, a society, a civilization, a history, to another one. Leo's task was not only to collect his memory of his travels and his readings, and then write them down. He faced a much bigger challenge: how to talk about customs, social rules, a judicial system, a political system, a history, that were very different from those of his readers, and were unknown to them, and, most importantly, about which almost no one had told them before. As mentioned earlier, the massive fact about this translation is its remarkable success, evidenced by the depth and the extension of its impact. Nevertheless, here we are going to focus on the difficulties encountered by Leo as author/translator.

The first challenge concerns the content of the text, and the potential reader's lack of familiarity with this content. Leo had to "construe the strange" for his readers, to use Clifford Geertz's expression (1983: 48), and to make it understandable to them. He had to bring the realities he describes to an audience who knew close to nothing about them. He was relying in part on a bibliography that was unknown to them, that could not evoke anything to them (and that furthermore was for the most part unavailable to him while he was writing). But if his task was to bring a region to life through language and to evoke its realities as accurately as possible, he certainly could not ignore the ways in which his culture had devised to talk about itself; at the same time, he had to be aware that those ways were not necessarily evocative for his potential readers. Thus, content was only part of the problem. Leo represents a long tradition of Arabic writing, and his works show that he was, if not a true erudite, at least familiar with a great number of famous texts and authors, in the diverse fields of literature, poetry, geography, history, philosophy, and medicine. This familiarity appears in his quotations of such texts and authors in the *Cosmografia dell'Affrica*, and in a less well-known but still influential collection of biographies of famous men that he penned in Latin, the *Libellus de Viris Quibusdam Illustribus Apud Arabes*[5]. He thus had assimilated a whole practice of writing, with its rhetoric, its commonplaces, its formulas, that he had in mind while writing in Italy. In other words, in his case, writing is wholly confused with translating, which is what gives it its specificity and makes it an acute experience of the limits of translation. In fact, to translate this text into Arabic[6] is to attempt to reconstruct the text that Leo would have written had he composed his work in North Africa rather than in Europe, or rather, to attempt to reconstruct the text that Leo had in mind when he was conceiving this work.

Another of the specific aspects of Leo Africanus's work resides in the fact that, rather than bringing things closer to himself, he had to push them away, and to go from what he knew toward what he did not know. He had to bring the African world and culture to readers belonging to a culture that he himself did not fully know or understand. This makes his case all the more interesting in trying to understand "how the massive fact of cultural and historical particularity comports with the equally massive fact of cross-cultural and cross-historical accessibility" (Geertz 1983: 48). Linguistically, this enterprise of crossing the boundaries between cultures is made obvious first by the use of Italian to write down what was thought and maybe even noted in

Arabic. This is one of the unusual aspects of the case of Leo: he translates his own language into the other language, while it usually is the other way around. To write in Italian rather than in Latin as is the case in the other texts that Leo had written while in Italy[7] probably tells us that he, or whoever asked him to write the *Libro*, was willing to reach readers beyond the scholarly circles–as Ramusio would say, people interested in politics, and maybe more precisely people involved in politics. Italian is a language that Leo had learned, but certainly not mastered. The study of the manuscript shows that it was written in such a faulty Italian that Ramusio had to edit it and correct the innumerable grammar and spelling mistakes it contained. In fact, the Italian editor went quite further than that, and did not hesitate to intervene heavily in the text, cutting off passages or even adding interpolations[8]. This is the reason why it is crucial here to study the manuscript rather than the printed text.

Translation is the effort of making something–information, content of any kind–understandable in another language. But texts, of course, have subtexts, to which belong all the common ground, the unspoken things that do not have to be spoken in any text written by an author who addresses readers belonging to the same cultural area, and sharing, at least potentially, the same knowledge and assumptions. Here, Leo knew that his readers did not share the subtext of his culture, and he himself had only superficially assimilated the subtext of the European culture in which he was now operating. One consequence of this unusual situation of writing was that he had, as much as was possible, to give textuality to the subtext of his own culture, to spell out what would normally have gone without saying, and, in doing so, to guess sometimes at the subtext of the European culture in which he now lived. This difficulty is tremendously compounded by the historical and cultural circumstances of his writing. Another was that, in the early sixteenth century, so little had been written in European languages about modern Africa, or even about Islam, that there was almost no vocabulary, no conventions, already available to convey particular meanings. In fact, Leo Africanus found himself, willingly or not, in the role of pioneer in his field, and thus had to invent the vocabulary with which to talk about the religious, political, and social realities of Africa. He had to make a constant effort to reach out to European readers, by writing in a European language, by trying to find equivalences between the words and realities he described in his text and what he had learned of Italy and Europe, and by making explicit what could have been implicit if addressed to a reader of the same culture; at the same time Leo was using the devices already in place in the Arabic tradition of geographical writing and attempting to adapt them to a different readership. This is how Leo, being in a limit situation for a translator who cannot rely on much common ground with his readers, traveled the distance that separated him from his readers, and this effort can be partially retraced in the text. Translation itself can here be considered as metaphorical travel from one point to another: not only from one language to another, bringing to readers information that is presently unavailable to them because they do not know a certain language; but also from one set of assumptions or kind of knowledge to another, making comprehensible to readers a world that otherwise would remain unknown to them or culturally alien. Not a translation *stricto sensu*, the *Cosmografia dell'Affrica* reaches the limits of translation.

Obviously, this study can only scratch the surface of the problem, but it is necessary to keep this frame in mind in order to understand Leo's work, especially his work on the language itself, the Italian language. To approach this vast subject, I would like here to discuss the inscription of foreign words, belonging to African languages, in the Italian text. The question of language obviously was paramount in the mind of Leo, not only as a translator, but also as a transmitter of the language itself, especially the Arabic language, his mother language. Among the other texts that he wrote and, in part, have been conserved, two are concerned with teaching the Arabic language to Europeans. One is the Arabic/Hebrew/Latin glossary, written for a Jewish physician friend, Jacob Mantino, according to an Arabic dedication on the manuscript. Another is the Arabic grammar book, written in Latin. Interest in Arabic was high in some intellectual circles at the time, especially among people who were interested in the study of the Kabbalah and of Hebrew, and who considered the study of Arabic an important adjunct to these studies. Among them was Cardinal Egidio da Viterbo, a crucial figure in those circles and one of the Roman protectors of Leo Africanus, who taught him Arabic[9]. So, the matter of giving some knowledge of the Arabic language to his readers was obviously important to Leo. It can partially explain the use of foreign words in the text. But at a deeper level, this use attracts attention to the limits of translation, and points to moments when Leo's task seems impossible.

In the *Cosmografia dell'Affrica*, the question of language is so important that the first sentence of the text contains an Arabic word and its translation. In fact, in a rather strange way, the most important word in the text, Africa, and the first to appear in the manuscript, is one that should constantly remind the readers of the difficulties of Leo's enterprise of cultural translation: "Africa in Arabic is called Ifriqiya, from the verb faraqa which means to separate"[10]. Beyond the obvious etymological error, this example is emblematic of the traps that Leo could meet in his task. There is a word *Ifriqya* in Arabic, which comes from the Latin word, but which did not designate the whole continent, as was already the usage in Europe. In the sixteenth century, *Ifriqya* in Arabic texts still designated only the region that the Romans used to call *Africa Proconsularis*, roughly modern Tunisia. And in the same page, Leo proceeds to explain that the two words do not mean the same thing: "The Arabs call Africa only the region of Carthage, and all of Africa they call the Western region"[11]. Obviously, Leo wants to use the European name, the one familiar to his readers, but in the very first page of his text, he has to amend the meaning, since it is not adequate to the Arabic word. He will later frequently use "Africa" and its derivatives in a sense that is not consistent with European usage. In particular, *Affricani*, the Africans, is most often used to designate the Berbers, the native inhabitants of North Africa, rather than all inhabitants of the continent. In the same way, Leo tried to find some common ground with his readers by using names belonging to the European tradition, such as Numidia or Libya. Here too, the attempt was not altogether successful. His familiarity with the conventions of European geography was so limited that he in fact used those toponyms erroneously (for him, Libya is the equivalent of the Sahara, which is obviously wrong), which would lead to a number of misconceptions and mistakes on the part of authors who would later quote his text; thus, his attempt to bridge the gap between himself and his readers would fail in part.

Beginning then with the first sentence of the text, there are, inscribed in the Italian text, quite a number of words belonging to the languages used in Africa, mainly Arabic, but also Berber and a few words borrowed from sub-Saharan languages–about 150 words in all, some used several times. These always appear in transcription, not in the Arabic script. They can be classified according to the semantic field to which they belong. A number of words designate animals and plants, for which Leo gives a description, replacing the often absent translation. For example, he says that one calls in Arabic *Dabuh* or in Berber *Jesef* an animal that he describes without naming it in Italian. The naturalists who would use his work would in fact not have much trouble in identifying it with the hyena, a word that Leo obviously did not know. These cases can be compared to a small number of blanks left in the manuscript, for a word that Leo could not find. Here, the blank is filled by the foreign word. In other instances, there is simply no word in Italian or Latin that corresponds exactly, and Leo gives the only name that exists, the Arabic or Berber name. Such is the case for items of clothing or food. Sometimes, the description is fleshed out by a comparison with European usage: *el chise*, for instance, is a coat that looks like the one used by physicians in Italy. But in general, the text gives only a minute description of the thing. For food, such as *cuscus*, Leo talks of the ingredients it involves, of the way it is prepared, of the meals in which it is taken.

Some toponyms can be put in the category of foreign names because they are accompanied by a translation, and thus attract the reader's attention by their foreignness. In Arabic, *Mersalcabir* means "the big port", *al-Jazair* (Algiers) means "the islands", and *Culeihat elmuridin* means "the Castle of the disciples"; in Berber, *Tetteguin* means "eye".

Other words belong to the field of culture, mainly high culture. Leo Africanus was probably the first author to ever mention to European readers the word sufi, or *essofia*[12], as well as a number of other words belonging to the fields of mysticism and occultism. In the long chapter devoted to Fez *intra muros*[13], after the evocation of monuments, mosques, craftsmen and shops, Leo describes the educational and cultural institutions, from children's schools to poetic contests, as well as the mystical brotherhoods and the different sorts of divination, scholarly or popular. A number of Arabic words are used there, such as *elcothb*, which designates the "pole" or central figure in the mystical hierarchy. Many Arabic titles of books also appear in these pages, with their translations, such as "Sensus Meharif, that is the Sun of Sciences" by al-Buni[14].

Finally, a number of foreign words designate institutions, names of high-ranking officials or soldiers in some governments; they are especially numerous in the case of the Mamluk dynasty who ruled Egypt until the Ottoman conquest of 1517. The foreign words appear, with a description of the function: the *Chazendare* is "the office of treasury that keeps count of the revenue of the kingdom"[15]; sometimes, Leo finds an approximation with a European equivalent: the *amirals* are comparable to the European colonels[16]. Also to be noted, in the same semantic field, is a word that is widely used throughout the text: *Chalifa*, or Caliph, sometimes in conjunction with the translation offered by Leo, pontiff (*pontife*), sometimes on its own. At other times, only the word pontiff appears. In fact, Leo, having once translated the term, uses the Arabic word and its translation indifferently. Of course, this indifferent use is somewhat misleading, since it implies a highly debatable identification between the institutions of the caliphate and the papacy.

Studying the distribution of the words belonging to African languages in the text helps to better understand their function. The part that contains the fewest of those is the one that deals with the country most foreign to Leo, West Africa. It is true that a number of its inhabitants were Muslims, some educated in the Arabic language (some of whom have left literary and historical texts). But on the whole, the languages used in the region were the native languages. One might expect that most foreign words would appear in this part of the text. The opposite is true; there are not more than four words in these pages: *Songai*, *Guber* (these are names of West African languages), *Guighimo* (the "lord of the sky", in one pagan religion), *gano* (a fruit). So in fact, the foreign words of the text belong mainly to the two languages with which Leo was most familiar, Berber, and for the most part Arabic. It seems that, the more he knows about the subject, the more tempted he is to use foreign words in the Italian text. In the part dealing with West Africa, a region in which he had only traveled, Leo is close to an anthropologist describing a foreign culture, the usual situation of anthropology. In this situation, he does not appear to be at a loss for Italian words. On the other hand, when dealing with parts of Africa that were the closest to his experience or to his culture, his uneasiness with the approximations entailed by any translation becomes sometimes quite apparent, leading him to use the word that in his mind, culture, and language, was the only right word.

As far as the rest of the text is concerned, the translated toponyms are evenly distributed in the pages that describe North Africa and Egypt. On the other hand, most of the foreign words belonging to the two last categories previously mentioned (culture and institutions) appear respectively in specific parts of the text. Among the words that designate political institutions and positions, most can be found in the description of Egypt, where there is a complete description of the main positions in the government and the army. It contains 25 names, followed by the descriptions of the official's duties, as well as a translation at times or a comparison with a similar function in European courts. Interestingly, at the time that Leo was finished writing the *Cosmografia dell'Affrica*, he knew that it had been almost ten years since the Mamluk government had been overthrown by the Ottomans; Leo was actually in Egypt when the Sultan Salim entered Cairo as a conqueror. So, the minute description of a government that did not exist anymore can be considered as a true historical work, describing something that then already belonged to the past.

Furthermore, these are not the only Arabic words that appear in the description of Egypt; many others are present, especially in the chapters about Cairo. There, Leo gives us what he does not do in any systematic way for other cities, such as Fez or Tunis: the names of Cairo's monuments, such as its mosques, and of the different neighborhoods and the gates of the city. To explain the names, Leo often has to evoke famous events and characters in Arabic history, as in the chapter entitled "Of the old city, called Misr al-'Atiq": "This was the first city built in Egypt after the Muslim conquest, by 'Amr capitan of 'Omar the second caliph"[17]. Egypt of course was important as a center of Arab culture, and the site of the siege of an illustrious dynasty. It was a venerable place for educated Maghrebi people, who would travel there in order to visit prestigious shrines and study with famous professors. One can get a sense of that veneration by reading the awed description of Cairo by Ibn Khaldun, another Maghrebi author, in his autobiography. In Leo's text, the foreign words seem to aim at making palpable the greatness of the city and of its history, and not only at conveying information.

We can push this analysis a bit further by studying the ones that concern the culture. Many of those appear in the description of the Moroccan city of Fez, a city Leo knew very well, in which he had been raised and schooled, and which he evokes in almost incredible detail. As was noted above, in this part of the text appear a number of foreign words, designating cultural and religious institutions and functions, and book titles. Elsewhere in the text, Leo quotes a number of authors to support his numerous historical accounts of different places. Obviously, he cannot refer to these writers in order to bolster his own authority as a historian in a very significant way, since they were unknown to his readers, who would not necessarily be impressed by his knowledge of authors whose stature they could not appreciate. His readers certainly could not go back to the texts themselves and verify the accuracy of the quotations or further their information on the subject. The mention of these authors has to be understood in a different way, as a strategy that aimed to make Leo's readers aware of the existence of the body of knowledge on which he was drawing in order to write his description of Africa. In this way, their presence in the text could only remind his readers of what they did not know, of what they could not catch. These references provided indeed information, but this was information that was not likely to be used in any meaningful way, especially by the non-scholarly readers for whom this Italian text was destined.

The foreign words and the unavailable books, then, seem to produce the same effects: they signal the limits of the powers of the translator, and of the possibility of translation. It is obvious when foreign words are used because an adequate corresponding word was lacking, or because knowledge of the object or concept in question was lacking. But the other cases also attract attention, albeit differently, to the difficulty of the text. On a more subtle level, the translation of toponyms exemplifies how the subtext needs to be textualized, or spelled out; exemplifies how the translation reaches out to the readers–without necessarily reaching them. Other types of inscription of foreign words are moments in which the act of translation stops short of its aim. When Leo uses the Arabic names of the famous monuments of Cairo, he may add as much explanation and as many comparisons as he wants, but he still cannot recreate the evocative power that those names would have for a reader familiar with the history of Africa and its literature–at a time, it bears to be said again, when there were few writings that could provide Europeans with greater information and allow them to put Leo's description in a context. Thus, these elements of the text are similar to the mention of famous authors, who were not famous to Leo's readers and therefore could not tell them how educated or thorough he was.

One passage seems to present in condensed form all the difficulties met by Leo in his translation, all the ways in which he tried to solve them, all the elements that I have mentioned: use of foreign words, quotations from authorities, and comparisons. It is a case where the translator tries as much as he can to push the limits of his power to translate, but nevertheless reaches that limit, expressing almost explicitly his frustration at not being able to go beyond it. He is not helped by the mysterious nature of the subject. In the pages in which Leo presents a summary of the Arabic literature of mysticism and occultism, he mentions one divinatory art called the *zayraja*, a word he then attempts to translate and explain: it is, he says, a word "which means Kabbalah, but not the Kabbalah that is based on Scripture, for the zayraja is considered to be a natural thing"[18]. It is a fitting example of the way he deals with his task as a translator, trying first to find a word that would have the same meaning as the Arabic one he has in mind, or a comparison that would make this meaning closer, but then having to amend the definition because the translation he offers is only an approximation. The use of the word "kabbalah" certainly suggests the influence of the intellectual circles around Egidio da Viterbo. Leo then proceeds to describe the practice of this art, explaining that it takes one whole day to reach the answer to the question concerning the future, and recounting the two times that he had seen it performed. He ends by saying that there are two descriptions or analyses of the *zayraja*, one figuring in the work of the illustrious historian Ibn Khaldun[19], mentioned above, and another in the work of a less famous Tunisian author, al-Marjani. Then he adds: "If one of the lords and readers wants to witness this art and read the commentaries, it would cost him less than 50 ducats since this book can be found in Tunis which is close to Italy"[20]. Having exhausted all his tools as a translator, Leo seems to renounce, and sends his readers to another text, but that's a remedy that they would be unlikely to take. He seems here to be almost yearning for his readers to have, or hoping that they would get, all the background that they do not share with him, all the subtext that he now feels he simply cannot make manifest, despite all his efforts as a translator.

[1] On the influence of Leo Africanus in European literature, see Zhiri (1991 and 1996).

[2] All of my references to the *Cosmografia dell'Affrica* will be to this manuscript.

[3] Good examples of this continuing hold of the ancient authors can be found in influential texts such as Joannes Boemus's *De Omniium Gentium* (1520) Sebastian Münster's *Cosmographia* (1544).

[4] Ramusio's enthusiatic recommendation is as follows:

> Perché, ancora che ne possino esser informati e instrutti da altri che abbino quei paesi trascorsi, gli scritti e ragionamenti de' quali essi leggendo e udendo hanno già fatto giudicio esser molto copiosi, son cerstissimo che, leggendo questo libro e considerando le cose in esso comprese e dichiarate, conosceranno quelle lor narrazioni a comparazione di questa esser brievi, manche e di poco momento, tanto sarà il frutto ch'a piena satisfazione d'ogni lor desiderio ne trarranno i lettori. (1978: 5)

> [For although they may have been informed and instructed by others who have traveled through those countries, and whose writings and arguments have been read and heard and already been deemed quite thorough, I am utterly certain that, in reading this book and considering what is contained and said therein, they will find those other narratives, in comparison with this one, brief, defective and of little importance–such will be the fruit that the readers, to the complete satisfaction of their every desire, will get from it.]

[5] The manuscript is conserved in the Biblioteca Laurenziana in Florence. It has been published twice, by Johan Heinrich Hottinger in 1664 and by Johan Albert Fabricius in 1726.

[6] Hajji and al-Akhdar, in *Wasf Ifriqiya*, have done just that.

[7] In addition to the *Libellus de Viris Quibusdam Illustribus apud Arabes* previously mentioned, there is a grammar of the Arabic language of which only the part on poetic meter still exists (see Codazzi), and also an Arabic-Hebrew-Latin glossary, which can be found in the Escurial Library of Madrid.

[8] For an overview of the differences between the manuscript and the Ramusio edition, see Zhiri (2001: 161-174).

[9] On these matters, see Secret (1963: 107).

[10] "Affrica in lingua Arabica e/ chiamata Ifrichia dicta da faracha verbo el quale significa separavit" (f. 1a).

[11] "Li Arabi non tengono per Affrica se non la Regione di Cartagine e tutta Affrica la chiamano la parte occidentale" (*ibid.*). "La parte occidentale" is a translation of the word "Maghrib".

[12] The word itself is omitted in the version of the text published by Ramusio. It reappeared only in the modern French translation by Epaulard, who partially corrected the text by consulting the manuscript.

[13] This long chapter was divided by Ramusio in numerous shorter ones, to which he gave titles. This division is present in all published editions and translations of Leo's text.

[14] "Sensus Meharif cio e el sol de le scientie" (f. 184b).

[15] "[...] el officio del thesaurero el quale tene el cuncto de le intrate de lo Regno" (f. 423a).

[16] "[...] sonno como li colonelli in la Europa" (*ibid.*).

[17] "De la cipta vecchia chiamata Misrulhetich": "Questa e / la prima cipta che fu edificata in Egipto nel tempo de li Mucamettani da Hamre capitano di Homar Chalifa secundo" (f. 410b).

[18] "[...] zairagia che vol dire la caballa / non caballa che sia cosa de le scripture, ma la dicta zairagia e/ tenuta per una cosa naturale" (f. 177a).

[19] See *The Muqqaidmah, an Introduction to History.*

[20] "[...] voi altri signori e lettori a quillo / che li piace vedere la dicta regula con li comenti li constaria la manco ducati / 50 / per che el dicto libro se trova in Tunis che e / vicino de Italia" (f. 178b).

References

Africanus, Leo. s.d. *Libro della Cosmografia dell'Affrica.* Ms. VE 953. Biblioteca Nazionale di Roma.

–. 1664. *Libellus de viris quibusdam illustribus apud Arabes* (ed. Johan Heinrich Hottinger) in *Bibliothecarius Quadripartitus.* Zurich: Tiguir.

–. 1726. *Libellus de viris quibusdam illustribus apud Arabes* (ed. Johan Albert Fabricius in *Bibliotheca Græca* Hambuurg.

–. 1896. *The history and description of Africa and of the notable things therein contained written by al-Hassan ibn Mohammed al-Wezaz al-Fasi, a Moor, baptised as Giovanni Leone, but better known as Leo Africanus; done into English in the year 1600 by John Pory* (ed. Robert Brown). London: Hakluyt Society (nos. 92-94).

–. 1956 and 1980. *Description de l'Afrique* (tr. A. Epaulard). 2 vols. Paris: Adrien-Maisonneuve.

–. 1978. *La descrizione dell'Africa e delle cose notabili che quivi sono per Giovan Lioni Africano* in Giovanni Battista Ramusio *Navigazioni e viaggi* (ed. Marica Milanesi). Vol. 1. Turin: Einaudi, 1978. 19-460.

–. 1983. *Wasf Ifriqiya* (trs Muhammad Hajji and Muhammad al-Akhdar [Rabat]). Beirut.

Codazzi, Angela. 1956. 'Il trattato dell'arte metrica di Giovanni Leone Africano' in *Studi orientalistici in onore di Giorgio Levi della Vida.* Vol. 1. Rome. 180-198.

Geertz, Clifford. 1983. 'Found in Translation: On the Social History of the Moral Imagination' in *Local Knowledge, Further Essays in Interpretive Anthropology.* New York, NY: Basic Books. 36-54.

Khaldun, Ibn. 1951. *Ta'rif Ibn Khaldun wa Rihlatuhu gharban wa Sharqan.* Cairo.

–. 1958. *The Muqqaidmah, an Introduction to History* (tr. F. Rosenthal). New York, NY: Pantheon Books.

–. 1980. *Le Voyage d'Occident et d'Orient* (tr. A. Cheddadi). Paris: Sindbad.

Secret, François. 1963. *Les Kabbalistes chrétiens de la Renaissance.* Paris: Dunod.

Temporal, Jean. 1556. *Historiale Description de l'Afrique.* Lyon.

Zhiri, Oumelbanine. 1991. *L'Afrique au miroir de l'Europe, Fortunes de Jean Léon l'Africain à la Renaissance.* Geneva: Droz.

–. 1996. *Les Sillages de Jean Léon l'Africain du XVI' au XX' siècle.* Casablanca: Wallada.

–. 2001. 'Leo Africanus Translated and Betrayed' in Daniel Russell and Renate Blumenfeld-Kosinski (eds) *The Politics of Translation During the Middle Ages and the Renaissance.* Ottawa: University of Ottawa Press. 161-174.

3.3. From Incan Realm to Italian Renaissance: Garcilaso el Inca and his Translation of Leone Ebreo's *Dialoghi d'Amore*

James Nelson Novoa

The salient moments of Garcilaso el Inca's life suggest what compelled him to translate Leone Ebreo's *Dialoghi d'Amore*. The biographical affinities between these two writers may have been Garcilaso's greatest motive. Both of them were transplanted from one culture into another, in their case the common culture of the Renaissance, in which they found themselves after having abandoned their respective native lands and original cultures and even their original names. In addition, both were literary translators, expressing themselves in languages that were not their own, or that they had, forcibly, to make their own. Garcilaso's translation of the *Dialoghi d'Amore* is thus a rendering into Spanish of a work that Leone Ebreo conceived in a language, Italian, that was not his own. In both cases translation becomes an act of appropriation, of forging the cultural identity of each writer's choice.
Keywords: exile, Garcilaso de la Vega, identity, Leone Ebreo (Hebreo), translation, travel.

When Garcilaso de la Vega el Inca (1539-1616) left his native Peru in 1560 little did he suspect that he would be leaving his South American homeland for good and that his paternal homeland of Spain would be the stage for his meeting with one of the most ambiguous works of Renaissance thought. His translation of Leone Ebreo's *Dialoghi d'Amore* was a unique production of sixteenth-century literature and for two principle reasons: it was the first work published by an American author in the Iberian Peninsula and it was a translation by an author for whom Spanish was not his native tongue.

In several respects both Garcilaso de la Vega and Leone Ebreo led very similar lives: both participated in the culture of the Renaissance, whether consciously or not, despite their origins in at least partly alien cultures, both left their homelands at an early age, and both wrote in languages that were not native but acquired. Literary history has accorded both of them a respectable place in the canon; their books are regarded today as standard Renaissance masterworks. Garcilaso's work is looked upon as a pivotal point in Classical Golden Age Spanish prose, for, as Marcelino Menéndez Pelayo has said (1974: 490), it was the most correct rendering in that language of a work which, already a popular bestseller at the time, would become a classic representative of Renaissance Neoplatonism.

3.3.1 Garcilaso de la Vega: a Man Between Two Worlds

Garcilaso de la Vega el Inca was born on April 12, 1539 in Cuzco, the capital of the waning Incan empire, eleven years after the Spanish conquerors arrived and forever devastated the ancient realm[1]. His father was a Spanish captain,

Sebastián Garcilaso de la Vega, of Castilian aristocratic origins, and his mother was Isabel Chimpu Ocllo, the niece of Huayna Cápac, the last ruler of Peru, whom Garcilaso's father never married. At birth he was baptized with the name Gómez Suárez de Figueroa after the names of the oldest of his uncles and other relatives who belonged to the noble house of Feria. Though from his father's side he boasted Castilian credentials, he was brought up in his mother's household along with the children of the emperor, listening to fables and accounts of his Incan ancestors in his maternal language, Quechwa, accounts which later on would serve him as an inspiration for this composition of the *Comentarios Reales*. This Incan upbringing was further strengthened when his father left Garcilaso's mother to marry a Spanish woman, Luisa Marten de los Rios, under pressure of the Imperial crown. Garcilaso was ten years old.

In 1554 his father's fortunes changed considerably as he was named Governor of Cuzco, a position he held until his death in 1559. He bequeathed to Garcilaso land in the Paucartambo region along with four thousand pesos in gold and silver, which would enable him to pursue studies in Spain. Although officially a bastard because he was the fruit of an unrecognized union, his father evidently always cared for him and there is no reason to believe that he was resentful. On the contrary, Garcilaso always admired his father and went to lengths to defend his good name and reputation. In his youth and throughout his life he lived the contradiction of the *mestizo*. Spanish and American by birth, he could not feel fully accepted at either hearth, and disparate origins contended for supremacy in his cultural commitments in successive years.

In January 1560, Garcilaso undertook a harrowing voyage which saw him traveling through Lima, then to *Ciudad de los Reyes*, Cartagena, Havana, the Azores, Lisbon and Extremadura where he had relatives. He finally settled in Montilla, a small Andalucian town where his uncle, Alonso de Vargas, lived. The following year he attempted to receive honors and privileges on his father's behalf from the *Consejo de Indias* in Madrid, but this failed as his father was accused of having aided Gonzalo Pizarro (1506-1548), brother of Francisco Pizarro (1476-1541). In his frustration he contemplated the possibility of returning to Peru in 1563 but entered the Spanish army instead, fighting under Don Juan de Austria (1545-1578), King Philip II's brother, against the *moriscos*, rebels of North African descent dwelling in the Alpujarras. In the same year he registered his name as Garcilaso de la Vega, thereby reclaiming his paternal name, perhaps cognizant that such a name chimed with that of the famous Spanish poet (1503-1536). Following his uncle's death in 1571, he was allotted some goods which permitted him to live a quiet and comfortable life of literary retreat in Montilla until his death on April 23, 1616.

3.3.2 Leone Ebreo's Ambiguous Position in the Renaissance

Leone Ebreo is the name by which western literary posterity has come to know Judah Abravanel (1460?-1530), son of the last great Sephardic exegete, Isaac Abravanel (1436-1508), whose views on ritual and legal matters remain authoritative even today in Rabbinical Judaism. Born in Lisbon, he was schooled in medicine and Jewish, Christian and Muslim philosophy. The Portuguese capital boasted both an important Jewish community and the Christian court of Alfonso V for whom Leone's father was the minister of finance[2]. Abravanel was reared in the Iberian Judaic tradition, which, unlike the Central European Askenazic one, boasted a longstanding respect for philosophical and classical thought, largely due to its links to Arabic philosophy which had developed side by side with Jewish thought during *Sepharad*. Hebrew was the language in which he received his education and religious training for it was in Hebrew that the Jewish community of Lisbon conducted its cultural life (Netanyahu 1998: 14). His father wrote in no other language, and, as Manuel Augusto Rodrigues has shown (1981: 527-595), Leone Ebreo's extant Hebrew poems display his command of the tongue.

Following an accusation and a death warrant issued by Alfonso V's successor, Joao II, Isaac moved his family to Spain in 1484 and quickly gained favor there as a financial adviser to the Catholic rulers, Ferdinand and Isabella. Even his father's intercessions, however, could not convince the Spanish monarchs to revoke the order of expulsion imposed upon the Jews of Spain in 1492. Once again the family followed the route of exile, this time to the capital of the Aragonese Kingdom of Naples. It was in Italy that Judah, now in his early thirties, took up the name Leone Ebreo, a name shared by many Jews in Italy during the century. There his father was accepted by the local monarch, Ferrante, permitting Leone to lead a life of relative ease, it seems, until the French invasion of the kingdom in 1494, when he was forced to flee to the relatively safer haven of Genoa. What followed was a life of wandering which took him to places as far afield as Barletta, Naples, Venice, Ferrara, Pesaro and possibly Rome in his later years. Though we do not know for certain when he died, in his dedication of the work to the Sienese noblewoman, Aurelia Petrucci, the editor of the first edition of his *Dialoghi d'Amore,* Mariano Lenzi (Ebreo 1983:2), mentions the fact that Leone was no longer among the living at the time of publication in 1535.

The work itself is like its author: a meeting of apparently disparate traditions, in which age old philosophical controversies which had dogged Jewish, Islamic and Christian thought, such as the eternity of the world and the question of creation, are addressed. The views of Maimonides (*il nostro rabi Moisé* throughout the text), Avicenna, Averroes, Samuel Ibn Gabirol (*Il nostro Albenzubron*), Algazel, Alfarabi, Aristotle and Plato converged with whole portions of Boccaccio's *De Genealogia Deorum*. Leone's two interlocutors, Filone and Sofia, begin with the dichotomy of lover and the beloved, of desire and its satiety, but move on to a multitude of speculative philosophical issues. In many respects the treatise was a first, in that it incorporated elements which were alien to the Sephardic philosophical tradition; it was also a last in that it was the note on which, in many senses, that very tradition ended (Pines 1983: 365-398).

To this day the original language in which the work was composed continues to divide Leone Ebreo scholars. Research in the last fifty years has demonstrated that behind the text of the first edition (1535) there were constant revisions of the work. This points to two possibilities: either the work was composed by Ebreo in the South of Italy and then it was progressively Tuscanized to make it fit for publication or it was written in a language other Italian, perhaps Hebrew, Spanish or Latin[3]. In any case, Tuscan Italian was not Ebreo's native language, but rather, at least his fourth, thus even if he were to have composed the work in Italian he would have surely conceived of it in another, making even the earliest redactions tantamount to a translation.

Understandably, the fact of the *Dialoghi's* Jewish provenance was all but lost upon its first Italian readers, who saw in the text the elucidation of Renaissance Neoplatonism of the Ficino variety, and therefore granted to it a privileged place among the *trattati d'amore*, which included Tullia d'Aragona's *Della infinità di Amore* (1547), Baldassare Castiglione's *Il cortegiano* (1528), Mario Equicola's *De Natura Amore* (Latin version 1495 and Italian 1525) and Pietro Bembo's *Gli Asolani* (1505), works which populated the literary landscape of Italy and Europe in the sixteenth century. More than one critic has pointed out that the strength of the text and what sets it apart from the other *trattati* is the fact that substance takes precedence over style and is treated in a graver, more original and more rigorous fashion[4].

These works served to disseminate the Neoplatonic ideals outside of the confines of the university where philosophy was traditionally taught. The *trattati* in which conversation, its rules and procedures, was so important in the developing Renaissance court culture of Central and Northern Italy, were bestsellers, turning Petrarchism and Neoplatonism, dormant for some time, into dominant literary and philosophical currents in Italy towards the beginning of the sixteenth century. Ebreo's book was classed alongside these love treatises, wrongly so according to Carlo Dionisotti (1959: 420-422), for the Jewish author was far more profound than his Christian literary peers. Although its author's Judaism might have posed problems, it seems to have been overlooked by Renaissance syncretists who valued the work's fundamental truths above other considerations. A Christian reading was also made easier by the announcement, in two editions, of Leone's conversion, together with an almost certainly spurious allusion to Saint John the Evangelist, contained in all Italian editions as well as in published translations[5].

3.3.3. Spanish Translations of the Work

By the time Garcilaso de la Vega petitioned for permission to print his rendering of the work in 1588, the Italian text had already gone through twelve printings by printers as prestigious as Aldo Manuzio and sons, Domenico Giglio, Giorgio de Cavalli, and Nicolò Bevilacqua. Previous to the publication of Garcilaso's translation, there had been two Spanish editions[6]. The first of these two was published in 1568 (and later in 1598) in Venice and was attributed to a certain Guedeliah Yahia. This would seem to have been a Thesalonikan-based Sephardic Jewish author, a descendent of a prestigious Portuguese family who was also a known translator of works from Latin into Hebrew. The work was dedicated to Philip II and it is curious that it is the only edition to mention Leone Ebreo's real last name, Abravanel (Abarbanel in the author's rendering) instead of simply Leone Ebreo. In his dedication, the translator stresses the Catholic nature of the work, the fact that the author was Spanish himself, as well as the work's benefit to the Spanish nation. He also claims to have translated it in his spare time. Written in a decidedly archaic Spanish for a late sixteenth century work, this translation must have seemed awkward to Peninsular readers at the time[7]. In spite of its dedication, this version did not seem to have fared particularly well in Spain; as Marquez points out (1984: 237), it is only mentioned in a requisition of Italian books by the Inquisition in Murcia in 1604 and in Zapata's *Index* of 1634. At the end of the text there is a small treatise on the soul, *Opiniones sacadas de los más autenticos y antigos philosofos que sobre la alma escrivieron y sus definiciones*, attributed to *el piritissimo doctor Aron Afia, Philosofo y Metafisico excelentissimo* who, we know, was an important cultural figure in the Jewish community of Thesalonika, in particular as a translator and friend of Amatus Lusitanus during his stay in the city (1565-1568). This translator's work corresponds almost perfectly to the text of the manuscript in the British Library (ms. Or. Gaster 10688), which, very likely of Ottoman provenance, is written in Spanish but in Hebrew characters. We can assume fairly safely, then, that the translator was eyeing both a Sephardic Jewish public who maintained the Spanish language even after the expulsion and who would have read the work in Hebrew characters, as well as a Christian readership who naturally would have read it in Latin ones.

The second translation, published for the first time in Zaragoza in 1582, bore the title *Philographia universal de todo el mundo*[8]. This was the work of Carlos Montesa, the son of Hernando de Montesa, who was part of the staff of the embassy in Rome, Don Diego de Mendoza (1502-1575) at the time of Pope Julius III (1550-1555). Montesa claims to have translated the work from Latin into Spanish, motivated by his desire to share the contents of the book and to continue the work of his father, who had begun the translation before him (1582: 2r-v). In his work, dedicated to the Inquisitor of Aragon, Don Francisco Gasca Salazar, Montesa claims to have safeguarded the sense of the original, hence justifying himself for having taken certain liberties in his translation, avoiding matter that would only have obscured the meaning of the text: "Creo haver guardado la propiedad, que es lo principal que en las traductiones se requiere aunque he añadido y quitando en partes, algunas cosas que escurecían la materia, para facilitarla, la qual en muchas estava escura y difficultosa" (*ibid.*: 2v). Montesa's dedication, which also serves as prologue, is long and decidedly pedantic, cluttered with allusions to classical authors and subjects, and thus puts the translator's learning on display. Indeed, before the translation proper, there is a composition of Montesa's own, entitled *Apologia en alabança del amor*, which, as its name suggests, spells out the author's defense of love in Neoplatonic terms. Ficino, Saint Paul, the Gospels, the Psalms, Petronius, Cicero, Catullus, Saint Augustine and Saint Ambrose are all quoted in this rather convoluted if not confused work which provides the doctrinal basis for what is contained in Ebreo's text.

3.3.4. Garcilaso's Translation of Leone Ebreo's *Dialoghi d'Amore*

Garcilaso's translation came out in Madrid in 1590. On the title page, he identified himself as both Indian and Inca for the first time, proudly flaunting his origins: *La traduzión del Indio de los tres Dialogos de Amor de León Hebreo, hecha de Italiano en Español por Garcilaso Inga de la Vega, natural de la gran Ciudad de Cuzco cabeça de los Reynos y Provincias del Piru*. The work was dedicated to Philip II of Spain: *Dirigidos a la sacra catolica real magestad del Rey don Felipe nuestro Señor*. We do not know when exactly Garcilaso began to translate Ebreo's book or what moved him to do it. That he chose Madrid for putting the treatise through press is not as surprising at it would seem, for even though Andalucia had an active press, it was under the constant surveillance and censorship of the authorities (García Oro 1995: 88-91). Madrid, moreover, as the new capital (until 1561 the imperial court was in Valladolid), was the center in which decisions on book privileges and *impramaturs* were taken as well as the place where the most interesting commercial prospects for retailing books were to be found (*ibi*d.: 112-113). The importance of Philip II's construction of the San Lorenzo del Escorial monastery (built between 1563 and 1584) outside of Madrid partly in order to house his personal library should not be underestimated, given that many books were dedicated to monarchs in the hope that they would end up in such libraries (Chartier 1996: 193-211). In actual fact this work did enter the King's personal library though in the seventeenth century although it is possible that it had been in King Philip II's possession beforehand[9].

The King's secretary, Juan Vázquez, granted His Majesty's official approval on 7 September 1588, recognizing Garcilaso's desire to serve the Spanish nation and in particular to give an example to the New World, especially Peru, of the kinds of literary activities their people should be engaged in (Ebreo 1949: 2). According to norms of the times, any manuscript was subject to Royal scrutiny through the *Consejo Real* in order to be accorded permission to be printed (García Oro 1995: 76-77). That Garcilaso's work got through this inspection demonstrates that, for the authorities at least, this time nothing was found in it deemed injurious to Christian values and morals. It was published by Pedro Madrigal, a publisher active in Madrid from 1586 to 1594, who was known for works of historical, literary and philosophical interest and for his commercial attachment to the Jesuits of Alcalá de Henares (Delgado Casado 1996: 410-411).

Garcilaso presented the work for approval to Don Maximiliano de Austria, the King's representative in his court, on 12 March 1587. In his prefatory letter, dated 18 September 1598, to Maximiliano, Garcilaso claims that he had wanted to present the work to him earlier but that this was his third draft of the work, that there had been no one to help him with his corrections, and that when someone had offered to help the result was so disastrous that he had to intervene personally. In the typically subservient language of the era he excuses himself for any errors and offers himself in service to the sovereign. Garcilaso also claims here that while he was working on this translation he had also been writing *La Florida*, the work in which he deals with the discovery of Florida by Hernando de Soto (1500-1542), of which more than a quarter was already written by that time (Ebreo 1949: 5). Maximiliano did not receive the work until June 18 and told him that he would hold onto it until September. In his warm message of reception, he thanks Garcilaso for his gift, excusing his own lack of culture, stating that Garcilaso could send him any of his works for official approval when he wished (*ibid.*: 7). It can be safely assumed that Maximiliano's appraisal was positive.

In his dedication to King Philip II, dated 19 January 1586, Garcilaso claims that he was moved to translate the *Dialoghi* for four reasons: 1) because of the excellence of their author; 2) because such offerings to the monarch–and this would be the first by a subject of the New World–were necessary, for his subjects depended on him; 3) because in his youth Garcilaso had served Don Juan of Austria, Philip II's brother, as a captain; and 4) because Garcilaso was a descendent of the Incas and related to the last king of Peru (*ibid.*: 8-9). The king's acceptance of this offer, says Garcilaso, will show how universal and august love can be, for through such an acceptance the king will imitate God himself. In addition, betraying more than a little nostalgia and admiration for his homeland, Garcilaso expresses the hope that the work will reach Peru and most especially its capital: "Y la merced que vuestra clemencia y piedad se dignaré de hazerme en recebirlo con la benignidad y afabilidad que yo espero, es cierto que aquel amplíssimo imperio del Pirú, y aquella grande y hermosíssima ciudad su cabeça la recebirán y tendrán por summo y universal favor: porque le soy hijo, y de los que ella con más amor crió [...]" (*ibid.*: 12). Garcilaso concludes his dedication by mentioning *La Florida* which, although now languishing in the shadows, he soon hopes to offer to King Philip II in addition to a work he envisions on the conquest of Peru, a work which became his *Comentarios Reales* (*ibid.*: 13).

In his letter to Maximiliano, Garcilaso says that he had previously thought that the excuses offered by authors of translations for their works were a means of exonerating their own shortcomings–that was, he says, until he began to translate the *Dialoghi*, a task he initially undertook for himself, as the life of relative leisure he now led allowed him to do (*ibid.*: 16-17). Upon showing the work to some of his erudite friends, he says, he was encouraged to persist in his efforts, which he knew to be far from perfect: "Todos ellos me mandaron e impusieron con gran instancia que passasse adelante en esta obra, con atención y cuydado de poner en ella toda la mejor lima que pudiesse, que ellos me asseguraban que sería agradable y bien recebida. Bien entiendo que lo fuera si mis borrones no la desluzieran tanto, de que a V.S y todos lo que los vieren suplico y pido perdón que en mi caudal no hubo más" (*ibid.*: 17). The desire to perfect what had begun as a pastime led him, he says, to conceive of his translation as a real occupation and something which might go on to merit a royal dedication. To that end, therefore, he requests Maximiliano's intercession with the monarch, which he likens to that of the High Priest in the temple in Jerusalem (*ibid.*: 17-18). Garcilaso offers two warnings to the reader–to read the work carefully and as the author intended it, as an invitation to philosophize; and to be attentive to some difficult passages which he left as they were because they demonstrated that the book was not intended to be read by the masses–and stresses the difficulty he faced in correcting errors and maintaining a fidelity that would not, at the same time, obscure meaning (*ibid.*: 19-20). In another letter, this one to King Philip II, dated 7 November of the same year, he once again states that in translating the *Dialoghi d'Amore* and having it published he wishes to give an example to his people of what kind of cultural endevors an Incan subject of the Spanish crown should be engaged in: "De mi parte no hay en ella cosa digna de ser recebida en cuenta, si no fuesse el atrevimiento de un indio en tal empresa y el desseo que tuve de dar con ella exemplo a los del Pirú, donde yo nací" (*ibid.*: 22-23).

Garcilaso's translation far eclipsed the other two and went on to become the standard Spanish translation of the *Dialoghi d'Amore*. In recent times it has been edited even more often than the Italian text, enjoying a reprint as recently as 1996. Such successes, however, did not fall within Garcilaso's lifetime, during which there were no subsequent reprintings. Leone Ebreo's book had already been censured in 1581 under the Portuguese inquisitors, who ordered it expurgated for containing Jewish or Platonic fables (De Bujanda 1995: 543-544). No single edition was spelled out in this condemnation, so it comprised the Italian editions, Saraceno's Latin translation, as well as Guedeliah Yahia's Spanish one and the two French translations. Portugal adopted the Tridentine Index in 1564 and had imposed the need for books to be approved by the local bishop and inquisitor. In addition, stringent control of foreign books coming into the country was also imposed (De Bujanda 1996:

153-171). Even though there was pressure to unify the Inquisitions of both Portugal and Spain and hence their indexes, individual titles continued to receive different treatment (De Bujanda 1995: 111-119). The book was condemned to be expurgated in the 1590 Roman Index without mentioning a particular edition or translation (De Bujanda 1994: 430). Although this Index was printed, it was never promulgated or distributed in the Catholic world (*ibid.*: 280). Nonetheless, Spain closely watched Rome and this initial condemnation of the work must have been behind the decision not to allow the work to be reprinted, in spite of the author's wishes, and it was censured by the Inquisition in 1593 (Pupo-Walker 1982: 19).

Garcilaso's rendition of the work is much superior to the two previous efforts, both in faithfulness to the text and in style. The Golden Age, linguistically, was a period of transition when the norms of what has become known as classical Spanish were being established. Garcilaso's text, as Alfonso D'Agostino has shown (1992: 77), reflects these norms even using certain words in Spanish for the first time according to the existing historical dictionaries, many of them derived from the specialized lexicon of Philosophy. Certainly the text is imperfect and there are some omissions and departures from the original, but in some respects Garcilaso's rendering of Ebreo's work is even more correct; and on the level of syntax, the Inca's Spanish is, in some cases, even more correct that the Sephardic Jew's original Italian (*ibid.*: 62-64).

What then, aside from what he mentions in his dedication, could really have moved Garcilaso in his choice to translate Leone Ebreo's work? The popularity of the *Dialoghi* in sixteenth-century Europe is attested to by the number of Italian editions and translations of the work. Some of these, certainly the Italian editions, the Latin translation, as well as Montesa's 1582 translation, must have circulated in Spain. Given the Spanish possessions in Italy, the Kingdom of Naples in the south (incorporated into Spain in 1504) and Milan in the north (a Spanish possession from 1535 to the eighteenth century), contact with the Italian peninsula must have been quite common, and it was not strange that a cultured Spaniard should be able to read works in Italian; Italian, after all, enjoyed cultural preeminence at the time.

The imitation of Italian literary forms and genres, and the adoption of Italian words, was the great fashion of the day in Spain, as it was in France. The Peruvian writer's namesake had imported Italian poetic styles as well as literary themes into Spain, and the influence of Petrarch was widespread among the literary avant-garde of Spain in the sixteenth century. Also moving in this literary world was Garcilaso's great friend Juan Boscán (1495-1542) with whom he had his poetry published posthumously in 1543. Together they experimented with using the Italian eleven-syllable meter, instead of the traditional Spanish eight, and the *canzone*, the *terza rima*, the *ottava rima* and blank verse Italianate forms.

In addition Boscán translated Castiglione's *Cortegiano* (*princeps* 1528), the first edition coming out in Barcelona in 1534. This translation was vastly popular, going through eight additional editions in the sixteenth century alone[10], and testifies to the popularity of the *trattati d'amore* in Spain as well. It is not known with any certainty whether Boscán ever set foot in Italy, though he may have accompanied King Ferdinand to Naples as a member of his court. He did know Castiglione (1478-1525) personally, however, visiting him daily in Granada in 1526 while the author of *Il cortegiano* was the Papal envoy in Spain. Unlike Garcilaso, the Catalan author had enjoyed a humanistic formation thanks to his links to the Spanish court at an early age (Darst 1978: 15-17).

At the time, a familiarity with Italian culture and language was a given among cultured Spaniards. Authors of the Spanish Golden Age clearly were able to read Leone Ebreo's work in the original text. In his prologue to *Don Quijote* (1605), Miguel de Cervantes claims that anyone with a smattering of Tuscan could read the *Dialoghi d'Amore* and derive from it all that one needed to know about love: "Si tratárades de amores, con dos onzas que sepáis de lengua toscana toparéis con León Hebreo que os hincha las medidas" (1905: cxvii). In fact, as Gabriella Rosucci points out (1995: 211-220), Cervantes's first published work, *La Galatea* (1585), a pastoral novel, relied heavily on Leone Ebreo's book as a foundation for his theory of love. Another writer, the Portugese-born Jorge de Montemayor, also relied heavily on Ebreo's ideas in his pastoral novel *Los siete libros de la Diana* (1560) and most certainly would have read the work in Italian, given that the first Spanish translation did not appear until after the publication of this book[11]. Neoplatonism was both a stylistic recourse and an intellectual element in these works as in others and Leone was always a cited reference. Yet another popular work at the time, Maximiliano Calvi's *Tratado de la hermosura y del amor* (Milan), has been called, by Menéndez Pelayo (1974: 532), a "scandalous plagiarism" of Leone's text. In late sixteenth-century Spain, the impetus to disseminate the contents of the *Dialoghi d'amore* through translation is clear.

How Garcilaso went about it, what method he used, is unknown. No documented evidence shows that he ever set foot in Italy; he must have learned Italian on his own. The inventory of his library, taken in 1616, shows that he possessed several books in Italian, among them certainly an Italian edition of the *Dialoghi*, Aldo Manuzio Jr.'s *Eleganze della lingua toscana e latina*, Leone Battista Alberti's *L'architettura*, Ludovico Dolce's *Palmerino d'Oliva*, Giovanni Boccaccio's *Filocolo*, Alessandro Piccolomini's *Della instituzione morale* as well as his plays, Guicciardini's *Storia d'Italia*, Nicolo Franco's *Dialoghi piacevoli*, Anibal Caro's *Lettere familiari*, Aretino's *Ragionamenti* and Torquato Tasso's letters. In addition there were works which he may have possessed in Spanish translations or in the original Italian (this was not taken down in the inventory) by Pietro Bembo, Boccaccio, Lodovico Ariosto, Matteo Maria Boiardo, Pandolfo Collenuccio, Piccolomini and Girolamo Muzio. In all of these cases, of course, it is not certain when the books entered Garcilaso's library. His library also held Cristóbal de las Casas's *Bocabulario de las dos lenguas toscana e castellana*, first published in Seville in 1570, although we cannot know for sure if he used this either[12]. This was not the only Italian-Spanish dictionary available then; he could have consulted several which ciruculated in the sixteenth century[13]. We know that he possessed four copies of the *Dialoghi* and a French translation, so he may have compared the Italian original with the Latin or one of the two Spanish translations. His library also held copies of *Il cortegiano*: he may very well have studied Boscán's translation and used it as a model for his own. Such conclusions, however, as they are derived from the holdings in his library, are perforce speculative.

In Montilla and Cordoba, Garcilaso was in contact with a cultured circle of people, some of whom must have possessed a degree of familiarity with the language. He was, however, an essentially self-taught man, never able to dedicate himself to the studies he went to Spain to pursue in the first place. Garcilaso translated the *Dialoghi* from a language which was foreign to him, and which he probably never got to speak, into another which was also an acquired one for him. His maternal language, we must not forget, was Quechwa, although he was certainly also schooled in Castilian. In his dedication to Philip II he claimed that neither was his natural language and that his Spanish was deficient on account of his lack of schooling in Peru and the endless conflicts there, something he remedied by going to Spain: "[...] ni la lengua italiana, en que estaba, ni la española en que la he puesto, es la mía natural, ni de escuelas pude en la puericia adquirir más que un indio nacido en medio del fuego y furor de las cruelísimas guerras civiles de su patria entre arma y caballos y criado en el ejercicio de ellos porque en ella no había entonces otra cosa, hasta que pasé del Pirú a España a mejorar [...]" (Ebreo 1949: 11). In a letter of December, 1592, to his friend Juan Fernández Franco, he claims further that in childhood he had learnt grammar poorly, again on account of the wars, and that he had taken up the profession of arms, which he continued in Spain. That way of life ended due to the ingratitude of princes and the little favor of the king which "enclosed him in his corner", causing him to find solace in translating Leone Ebreo in his spare time:

> En mis niñezes que óy una poca de gramática, mal enseñada por siete preceptores que a temporadas tuvimos, y peor enseñada por siete preceptores que a temporadas tuvimos, y peor aprendida por pocos más discípulos que éramos, por la revolución de las guerras que en la patria avía, que ayudavan a la inquietud de los maestros. Quando se cansó el postrero dellos, que seríamos de treze a catorze años, nos passamos mis condiscípulos y yo al exercicio de la gineta, de cavallos y armas, hasta que vine a España, donde también ha avido el mismo exercicio, hasta que la ingratitud de algún príncipe y ninguna gratificación del Rey me encerraron en mi rincón. Y por la ociossidad que en él tenía, di en traduzir al León Hebreo, cevado de la dulçura y suavidad de su Philosophía. La qual obra, aunque yo no puse nada en ella sino muchas imperfectiones, ha causado que V.m y otros señores míos me favorescen, sin que en mí aya de escuelas más que el perpetuo desseo dellas. Por tanto suplico a V. m me trate como a soldado que, perdido por mala paga y tarde, se ha hecho estudiante. (in Asencio: 1949: 585)

In his own view, then, Garcilaso was a soldier who only late in life became a student.

3.3.5. Conclusion

The place of this translation in Garcilaso's *oeuvre* has much divided critics who have seen it as a philological exercise, a kind of training in his vocation as a writer which would pave the way to his future literary endeavors, or an indication that the Incan author identified himself squarely with the Neoplatonic and Renaissance conception of the world. At least one critic, Susana Jákfalvi-Leiva (1984: 14-15), has seen the work as a means of permeating Spanish and European culture in general with South American indigenous culture, an intent that is borne out, she says, by the dedications that Garcilaso appended to his work.

The parallels that can be drawn between Ebreo's and Garcilaso's lives invite speculation. Although officially excluded from what was considered Hispanic culture, Sephardic Judaism was a fundamental component of Iberian history and identity. Perhaps Garcilaso's translation of Ebreo's work was a means of reclaiming the Sephardic writer and including him in the Spanish fold, of extending the narrow confines of what Hispanic culture was considered to be in the emerging Golden Age, of rendering what was considered foreign and alien, and hence suspect, part of the accepted national literary tradition. Doris Sommer (has suggested that Garcilaso may have seen himself in Ebreo and thus attempted to redeem him by showing that Ebreo, the exiled Spanish Jew, also had a "cultural claim on Spain":

> El Inca Garcilaso, of the ethnically mixed name and culturally conflicted heritage, may very well have recognized the self-exiled Spaniard as a figure for himself. Abravanel had been an intimate of the Iberian kings, their compatriot of countless generations. Hebreo was a homeboy, even if he was hounded by fanatics as a foreigner. He had a cultural claim on Spain, the kind of claim that Garcilaso was making when he assigned himself the paternal name.
>   The overlapping circumstances make for an almost uncanny echo system between the "Italian" writer and his "Castilian" interpreter, as if one life simply evoked a surprising intimacy with the other. The intimacy seems metaphorical, a result of fortuitous similarities between terms that belong to different and unconnected discourses, Incan and Jewish. (1998: 116)

Both authors, Leone Ebreo and Garcilaso de la Vega, imply a first time: the first time a Jewish author became standard reading by Renaissance audiences and an Incan became a standard name and a recognized master of Castilian prose. In both cases, they also imply a last time, and the waning of their respective civilizations: Leone Ebreo belonged to the last generation of Sephardic Jews to live on Iberian soil; he was the last to be privy to a national life which, though at times difficult, had for centuries been characterized by the living side-by-side of Muslims and Christians. Similarly, Garcilaso was the last of his nationals to be reared in the lore of the Incan empire. In both cases their respective works were the result of travel and translation: Leone Ebreo through his Italian exile and his adoption of a language and a means of expression which were not his own; Garcilaso de la Vega, the Inca, through his move to Spain and his translation of Ebreo's work, which initiated his literary career in a language that, to a certain point, was foreign to him as well.

[1] For a brief biography of Garcilaso, see Enrique Pupo-Walker's study (1982: 5-25), from which the following sketch has been drawn. For the question of Garcilaso's Incan background and its influence on his aesthetic ideal, see María Antonia Garcés.

[2] For Abravanel's childhood and formation see Heinz Pflaum (1929: 55-59).

[3] The most recent summation of positions held on this subject is in Barbara Garvin (2000: 181-210).

[4] See, for instance, the Italian Historian of Philosophy, Giuseppe Saitta (1950: 109-110), who distinguishes Ebreo from Bembo, who never rises above common moralizing, saying that in *Gli Asolani* one finds a rehashing of Plato, Ficino and the Church fathers, and a demonstration of the by then banal thesis that true beauty is divine and immortal, not human.

[5] The titles of the second and third editions, published in 1541 and 1545, read *Dialoghi di Amore, composti per Leone Medico, di Natione Hebreo, et dipoi fatto Christiano.* And in all the published versions of the work, there is, in the third dialogue, the following allusion to Biblical personages who, along with Saint John the Evangelist, were spared physical death: "Enoc, et Elia, et ancor Santo Giovanni evangelista sonno immortali in corpo et anima [...]"

[6] Before these, there had also been a Latin translation (1564) by Joannes Carolo Saraceno and two French translations, one by le Seigneur du Parc Champenois (Lyon 1551 and 1559, Paris 1577 and 1580) the other by Jean de Tournes which is generally attributed to Pontus de Tyard (Lyon 1551). There are, in addition, two unpublished manuscripts: One is in the British Library (ms. Or. Gaster 10688); see Nelson Novoa (2003 and 2005)). The other is in the Biblioteca Real in Madrid (ms. 1881/1). Both are from the sixteenth century. A third unpublished manuscript, thought to be from the seventeenth century, is held in the Biblioteca Municipal of Oporto (ms. 1507); see Nelson Novoa (2004).

[7] For example, the translator uses *fallecer* for lack when *faltar* was already beginning to be used in the sixteenth century, or *dubda* for *dudar* which, by the second half of the sixteenth century, was considered an antiquated usage (see Joan Corominas's *Breve Diccionario etimológico de la lengua castellana*).

[8] Although this and the subsequent editions of the work carry different dates on the back page, there is a declaration in all of them claiming that it was printed in 1582, which shows it was printed once and then published several times: "Acabose de imprimir esta presente *Philographia universal de todo el mundo, de los Dialogos de Leon Hebreo,* traduzidos de Italiano en Español, y corregidos y añadidos, por el excellente letrado Micer Carlos Montesa ciudadano Çaragoçano. En casa de Lorenço y Diego de Robles Hermanos, Impressores, en Çaragoça, en año de la corrección a 22 días del mes de deziembre, día del solticio Hyemal de 1582".

[9] Apparently the copy possessed by the library of Escorial has the Royal crest on its inside covers although it formally became part on the library after Philip II's death. I must thank Brother José Luis del Valle Merino o.s.a of the Escorial library for this information.

[10] Toledo, 1539, Salamanca, 1540, Amberes, 1544, Zaragoza, 1553, Amberes, 1561, Valladolid, 1569, Amberes, 1574, in addition to another one published without the place or the date.

[11] See Francisco López Estrada and María Teresa López García-Berdoy's introduction to their edition of this work (1997: 9-49).

James Nelson Novoa

[12] This work was republished in Venice in 1576, 1587 and 1608, and once again in Seville in 1583. On Garcilaso's library, see José Durand (1948: 239-264).
[13] On Spanish and Italian lexicography of the time, see the study by Anna Maria Gallina.

References

Asencio, Eugenio. 1953. 'Dos cartas desconocidas del Inca Garcilaso' in *Nueva revista de filología hispánica* 7(3-4): 583-593.
Boscán, Juan and Garcilaso de la Vega. 1543. *Las obras de Boscán y algunas de Garcilaso de la Vega repartidas en quatro libros*. Barcelona: Garles Amorós.
Cervantes, Miguel de. 1905. *El ingenioso hidalgo Don Quijote de la Mancha*. Madrid: D. Juan Antonio Pellicer, Imprenta de los hijos de M.G. Hernández.
Chartier, Roger. 1996. 'Poder y escritura: El príncipe la biblioteca y la dedicatoria (Siglos XV-XVII)' in *Manuscrits* 14: 193-211.
Corominas, Joan. 1987. *Breve Diccionario etimológico de la lengua castellana*. Madrid: Gredos.
D'Agostino, Alfonso. 1992. 'El Inca Garcilaso traductor de los *Dialoghi d'amore* de León Hebreo' in *Del Tradurre*. Rome: Bulzoni Editore. 59-77.
Darst, David H. 1978. *Juan Boscán*. Boston, MA: Twayne Publishers.
De Bujanda, J.M. 1994. 'Dialoghi di Lione Hebreo, se non saranno emendati' in J.M. De Bujanda *et al.* (eds) *Index de Rome Avec étude des index de Parme 1580 et Munich 1582*. Centre d'Études de la Renaissance. Editions de l'Université de Sherbrook. Geneva: Librarie Droz.
–. 1995. *Index des livres interdits, IV, Index Portugais*, Centre D'Études de la Renaissance. Editions de l'Université de Sherbrook. Geneva: Librairie Droz.
–. 1996. 'L'exercise de la censure de l'inquisition Portugaise au XVIème siècle' in J.M de Bujanda (ed.) *Contrôle des Idées à la Renaissance. Actes du colloque de la Fisier tenu à Montréal en Septembre 1995*. Geneva: Librairie Droz. 153-171.
de la Vega, Garcilaso. See Juan Boscán and Leone Ebreo (1949).
Delgado Casado, Juan. 1996. *Diccionarios de Impresores españoles siglos XV-XVIII*. Madrid: Arco Libros.
Dionisotti, Carlo. 1959. 'Appunti su Leone Ebreo' in *Italia medioevale e umanistica*. Vol. 2. Padova: Editrice Antenore. 409-428.
Durand, José. 1948. 'La biblioteca del Inca' in *Nueva revista de filología hispánica* 2(3): 239-264.
Ebreo, Leone (Abrabanel, Jehudah). 1564. *Leonis Hebraei doctissimi, atque sapientissimi, viri De Amore Dialogi Tres, nuper a Joanne Carolo Saraceno purissima candidissimaq; Latinitate donati. Necnon ab eodem et singulis Dialogis argumenta sua praemissa, & marginales Annotationes suis quibusque locis infertae, Alphabetico & locupletissimo Indice his tandem adiuncto, fuerunt* (tr. Joanne Carolo Saraceno). Venice: Franciscum Senensem.
–. 1568. *Los Dialogos de amor de Mestre Leon Abarbanel Medico y Filosofo excelente de nuevo traduzidos en lengua castellana, y deregidos a la Maiestad del Rey Filippo. Con privilegio della Illustrissima Señoria* (tr. Guedeliah Yahia). Venice.
–. 1582. *Philographia universal de todo el mundo de los Dialogos de amor de Leon Hebreo Traduzida de Italiano, corregida y añadida por Micer Montesa, Ciudadano de la insigne ciudad de Çaragoça. Dirigida al muy Illustre Señor Francisco Gasca Salazar Inquisidor Apostolico del Reyno de Aragon y Maestre Escuelas de la Universidad de Salamanca, Es obra sutilissima y muy provechosa, assi para seculares como Religiosos Visto y examinado por orden de los señores del Consejo Real* (tr. Carlos Montesa). Zaragosa: Lorenço y Diego de Robles Hermano.
–. 1949. *Dialogos de amor traducidos por Garcilaso Inca de la Vega, edición según la de Madrid de 1590* (ed. Eduardo Juliá Martínez). Madrid: Libreria General Victoriano Suárez.
–. 1983. *Dialoghi d'Amore* (ed. Giacinto Manuppella). 2 vols. Lisboa: Instituto Nacional de investigação científica.

Gallina, Anna Maria. 1964. *Contributi alla storia della lessicografia italo-spagnola dei secoli XVI e XVII*. Firenze: Leo S. Olschki editore.

Garcés, María Antonia. 1991. 'Lecciones del Nuevo Mundo: la estética de la palabra en el Inca Garcilaso de la Vega' in *Texto y Contexto* 17: 125-150.

García Oro, José. 1995. *Los reyes y los libros. La política libraria de la corona en el Siglo de Oro (1475-1598)*. Madrid: Editorial Cisneros.

Garvin, Barbara. 2000. 'The Language of Leone Ebreo's *Dialoghi d'Amore*' in *Italia. Studi e ricerche sulla storia, la cultura e la letteratura degli ebrei d'Italia*. Vol. 17. Jerusalem: The Hebrew University Magnes Press. 181-210.

Jákfalvi-Leiva, Susana. 1984. *Traducción, escritura y violencia colonizadora: un estudio de la obra del Inca Garcilaso*. Syracuse, NY: Maxwell School of Citizenship and Public Affairs.

Marquez, Antonio. 1984. *Literatura e Inquisición en España (1478-1834)*. Madrid: Taurus.

Montemayor, Jorge. 1997. *Los Siete Libros de la Diana* (eds Francisco López Estrada and María Teresa López García-Berdoy). Madrid: Espasa Calpe.

Nelson Novoa, James. 2003. 'An *aljamiado* version of Judab Abravanel's *Dialoghi d'Amore*' in *Materia giudaica. Rivista dell'associazione italiana per lo studio del giudaismo* 8(2): 311-327.

–. 2004. 'El ms. 1057 de la Biblioteca Pública Municipal de Oporto: una traducción de los *Diálogos de amor* de León Hebreo' in *Rivista di Filologia e Letterature Ispaniche* 7: 9-42.

–. 2005. 'Consideraciones acerca de una version aljamiada de los *Diálogos de amor* de León Ebreo' in *Sefarad* 1: 103-126.

Netanyahu, Benjamin. 1998. *Don Isaac Abravanel Statesman and Philosopher*. Ithaca, NY: Cornell University Press.

Pelayo, Marcelino Menéndez. 1974. *Historia de las ideas estéticas en España*. Madrid: Consejo Superior de Investigaciones Científicas.

Pflaum, Heinz. 1929. *Die Idee der Liebe Leone Ebreo Zwei Abhandlungen zur Geschichte der Philosophie in der Renaissance*. Tübingen: J.C.B. Mohr (Paul Siebeck).

Pines, Schlomo. 1983. 'Medieval Doctrines in Renaissance Garb? Some Jewish and Arabic Sources of Leone Ebreo's Doctrines' in Bernard Dov Cooperman (ed.) *Jewish Thought in the Sixteenth Century*. Cambridge, MA: Harvard University Press. 365-398.

Pupo-Walker, Enrique. 1982. *Historia, creación y profecía en los textos del Inca Garcilaso de la Vega*. Madrid: José Porrúa Turranzas, S.A.

Rodrigues, Manuel Augusto. 1981. 'A obra poética de Leao Hebreu. Texto hebraico com versao e notas explicativas' in *Biblos, Revista da Facultade de Letras* 57: 527-595.

Rosucci, Gabriella. 1995. 'Corrientes platónicas y neoplatónicas en *La Galatea*' in Giuseppe Grilli (ed.) *Actas del II Congreso International de la Asociación de Cervantistas* [*AION-sr*, 37(2)]. Naples: Istituto Universitario Orientale. 211-220.

Saitta, Giuseppe. 1950. *Il pensiero italiano nell'umanesimo e nel Rinascimento*. Vol 2. Bologna: Cesare Zuffi.

Sommer, Doris. 1998. 'At Home Abroad: El Inca Shuttles with Hebreo' in Susan Ruben Seleiman (ed.) *Exile and Creativity. Signposts, travelers, outsiders, backward glances*. London and Durham, NC: Duke University Press. 109-142.

3.4. The Translator Translated: Inca Garcilaso and English Imperial Expansion

María Antonia Garcés

As the foremost translator of Inca culture and history for a European audience, Inca Garcilaso de la Vega was continually translated and published by English, French, and Dutch scholars and printers in early modern times. His *Royal Commentaries of Peru* not only became a best-seller in France and the Netherlands in the seventeenth and eighteenth centuries, but also in Restoration England, where another cultural translator, Sir Paul Rycaut, rendered the Peruvian's work into English. Examined for their performativity, the translations of Garcilaso's works emerge as sites for early modern mercantile expansion and for the staging of cultural difference. The literary activities of English merchants, buccaneers, and diplomats, which contributed to the commercial success of Spanish chronicles of travel and discovery in England, are of great importance, but the Continental translations are equally important. In the wake of the boom of English publications on the New World, which began in the 1650s with Cromwell's attack on Jamaica, the fortunes of the *Royal Commentaries* speak both to the ideological needs of an emerging modern world and to the transatlantic endeavors that marked English imperial expansion.
Keywords: England, France, Garcilaso de la Vega, Paul Rycaut, Peru, translation, travel.

In a renowned essay on literature and translation, Octavio Paz claimed that translation is the principal means we have of understanding the world we live in. The world, claimed Paz, is presented to us as an ever increasing heap of texts:

> Each slightly different from the one that came before it: translations of translations of translations. Each text is unique, yet at the same time it is the translation of another text. No text can be completely original because language itself, in its very essence, is already a translation–first from the nonverbal world, and then, because each sign and each phrase is a translation of another sign, another phrase[1]. (1992: 154)

In Paz's view, translation is not a marginal activity but a primary one that defines our interpretation of the world. His definition illuminates the pattern of translations that structures the work of Inca Garcilaso de la Vega, the foremost translator of Inca culture and history in early modern times, for whom translation became a search for identity tied to a defense of Amerindian cultures. A translator of cultures who lived on the edge of cultural frontiers, Inca Garcilaso did not live to see the extraordinary resonance his works would have in seventeenth- and eighteenth-century Europe. Continuously reprinted in various European languages during the age of transatlantic expansion, his oeuvre lived on in "a kind of permanent exile", as Paul de Man said (1986: 92), speaking of translation in his remarks on Walter Benjamin's "The Task of the Translator". Inca Garcilaso's works, then, circulated in early modern Europe, transformed and recycled according to the interests of English, French, and Dutch scholars, merchants, and printers. The following study explores the performativity of the translations of Inca Garcilaso's works, seen here as both the site of early modern mercantile expansion and the staging of cultural difference. Beginning with the important role of translations of Spanish works in Elizabethan England, I examine Inca Garcilaso's fortunes in the last decades of the sixteenth century, at the time of the Restoration. As it turns out, the extraordinary success of the French versions of Inca Garcilaso's works in early modern France and the Netherlands announces the reception of the *Royal Commentaries of Peru* in seventeenth-century England, when another cultural interpreter, writer, and translator, Sir Paul Rycaut, turned the Peruvian author and translator into a best-seller.

Born in Cuzco to a Spanish conquistador and Inca *palla*, or princess, Inca Garcilaso de la Vega (1538-1616) was also born to the Quechua language and culture, which compelled him to serve as translator between his parents during his childhood. Leaving for Spain in 1560 never to return again to Peru, Garcilaso settled in Montilla, near Córdoba, where he occupied his leisure studying Castilian and Italian literatures and associating with scholars, Latinists, and antiquarians. His future as one of the most translated authors of early modern Europe seems to have been foreshadowed by his own career as a translator, especially by his inaugural work, a Castilian version of Judah Abravanel's *Dialoghi d'Amore* (1590), written in Italian by the Jewish humanist known in Italy as Leone Ebreo and in Spain as León Hebreo (1460?-1530). To this exacting task, Garcilaso applied himself for several years and, in 1590, published his elegant version, *Diálogos de amor*, dedicated to Philip II. As emphasized by the translator's prefatory letter to the King, this book was the first gift presented to Europe by an American writer. Though two other versions of León Hebreo's treatise had already appeared in Spanish, Inca Garcilaso, presumably, did not know about them[2]. Literary historians have agreed that Inca Garcilaso's translation surpasses the other Spanish versions in clarity, purity, and simplicity of style; his translation thus went on to become the sanctioned Spanish translation of the *Dialoghi d'Amore*. Explaining his reasons for undertaking the translation of Hebreo's powerful work, Garcilaso states, in his prefatory letter to Maximilian of Austria, that he was attracted by "the gentleness and sweetness of his philosophy"[3]. His next words adumbrate his theory of translation:

> I can affirm that the printer's errors gave me much trouble, and even more my pretension to interpret (the work) faithfully using the same words that its author wrote in Italian, without adding other superfluous words, for it is sufficient that he be understood by the words he wanted to say and no more.

If Inca Garcilaso's version of León Hebreo reveals a sure dominion of the Italian language, it also confirms his adoption of Renaissance humanistic values. In the words of an Italian critic (Bellini 1982: 32), this translation "si configura soprattutto come il documento di una sensibilità nuova, quella con cui il Rinascimento considera la traduzione, impegno di fedeltà allo spirito del testo, tesa, cioè, a ricreare l'opera tradotta in tutta la sua vitalità originale" [it forms a record above all of a new sensibility, by which the Renaissance considers translation an undertaking of spiritual fidelity to the text, given over, that is, to reproducing the translated work in all its original vitality].

The importance of this venture for the *mestizo* translator cannot be stressed enough. As the symbol of rewriting through translation, Inca Garcilaso's appropriation of León Hebreo's work also represents the writer's transition from the maternal space, constituted by his Amerindian culture, to his inclusion in the European Renaissance milieu[4]. His elegant translation of the *Dialoghi d'Amore* prepared him for his role as translator of the history and traditions of his people for a cultured European audience. From this moment on the *mestizo* writer would begin to develop an ambitious project which entailed rescuing his Amerindian culture, recollecting the voices of the vanquished which had been drowned amid the clamor of the battles, and offering his interpretation of a new world (Hernández 1993: 128).

Garcilaso's long engagement with his first translation project, then, led him to work simultaneously in other related enterprises, such as a forthcoming account of Hernando de Soto's expedition into Florida. Moreover, in his dedication of the *Diálogos* to Philip II, the translator reported his progress on a comprehensive history of Peru replete with details of the ancient customs, rites, ceremonies, and practices of the Incas which, "as a native son, I will be able to relate better than one who is not". His letter to the king, in effect, stresses the translator's privileged function as interpreter of the history of the great Amerindian empire. A *mestizo*–or half-caste–whose figure emerges as a metaphor of the translator, as Margarita Zamora has proposed (1988: 39), Inca Garcilaso was also a mediator between two languages, two worlds, and two different cultural realities. Drawing on both his Indian and his Spanish heritage, Garcilaso composed some of the most important early modern chronicles on the New World: *La Florida del Inca*, brought out in 1605, the same year that Cervantes published the first part of *Don Quijote*; *Comentarios reales de los Incas*, published in 1609; and finally, the second part of *Comentarios reales*, entitled *Historia general del Perú*, which appeared posthumously in 1617.

Claiming that the historians who have written the histories of the New World, such as those of Mexico and Peru, have proved inadequate to the task, Inca Garcilaso states, in the preface to the reader that opens *Comentarios reales*: "My purpose is not to gainsay them but to [...] interpret many Indian expressions which they, as strangers to that tongue, have rendered inappropriately" (1960: vol. 1, 3)[5]. Yet, beyond his plea for a correct translation from his native Quechua, which would offer a truthful reinterpretation of Inca culture, Garcilaso was acutely conscious of the difficulties involved in the task of the translator. Alluding to his translation of the legendary history of the Incas, he elucidates his position as a translator:

> I have tried to translate it faithfully (this account of the origin of our kings) from my mother's tongue, that of the Inca, into a foreign speech, Castilian, though I have not written it in such majestic language as the Inca used, nor with the full significance that the words of that language have [...]. On the contrary, I have shortened it, and left out a few things that might have been odious. (*ibid.*: vol. 1, 17)[6]

Years later, in the *Historia general*, Garcilaso would argue that the tragic events of Cajamarca and the ensuing conflicts between the Spanish and Inca cultures were the result of a bad translation[7]. As Julio Ortega (2002: 32) has advanced in a brilliant reading of these events and of their representation by the *mestizo* writer, Garcilaso, more than a cultural translator, would be "a modern intellectual who produces a subtle and complex reconversion of opposite terms into the new mappings of history as translation".

At his death in Córdoba in 1616, Garcilaso was already recognized as the leading translator of the Inca civilization in Spain. The humanist Bernardo de Aldrete, Canon of the Cathedral of Córdoba, cites him in *Del origen y principio de la lengua castellana o romance* (1611). And the Jesuit Francisco de Castro, who enthusiastically approved the second part of *Comentarios reales*, dedicated his Latin *Arte rethorica*, in 1611, to "Garcia Lasso de la Vega Ynca Peruano clarissimo". In his dedication, Castro paid tribute to Garcilaso's works, notable for "their agreeable and varied arguments, full of erudition, [and their] sweet and elegant style"[8].

3.4.1. The English Connections

It is beyond Spain, however, where Inca Garcilaso's treatises were most acclaimed. The first translations of his work appeared in London in 1625, in Samuel Purchas's edition of Richard Hakluyt's unpublished papers, entitled *Hakluytus Posthumous or Purchas his Pilgrimes*, which included translations of selected chapters from *Comentarios reales*, Parts I and II. Hakluyt had been the leading historian of the English Oceanic enterprise under Elizabeth I. During her reign (1558-1603) a significant expansionist drive toward the Atlantic was developed by figures such as Francis Drake, John Hawkins, Walter Raleigh, and the young Richard Hakluyt, among others who made major contributions to overseas travel or its literature[9]. The climax of Hakluyt's output came in 1598-1600 with his second edition of the *Principal Navigations of the English Nation*, a monumental work which celebrated English navigation and promoted England's expansion overseas. Couched in economic terms, Hakluyt's work, with its focus on England's mercantile trade, would, as Richard Helgerson has said (1992: 163-168), incite and inform future enterprises and adventurers. Both the young Richard Hakluyt and his cousin, the elder Hakluyt by the same name, had connections with the merchant communities of London and Bristol, and both drew heavily on the archives of these companies in assembling their writings. In effect, as Richard Helgerson has argued, Hakluyt's Voyages represent "a fundamental new alignment of power in England, one in which merchants and mercantile activity had an ever increasing share" (*ibid.*: 181). David Armitage (1995: 59) concludes that the *Principal Navigations* would live on as the founding text of the British Empire. During Elizabeth's reign, English merchants who frequented Spanish ports during the 1560s and 1570s, until trade was cut off by a royal edict in 1585, would have a special interest and involvement in the translations of Spanish works. The dependence of Spain and her American colonies upon the North invested the English traders with great importance. Suffolk cloths, in western reds and blues, were almost exclusively consumed in Spain, as well as fine white cloths, Welsh and Manchester cottons, lead and tin. This ready market also included wheat, since Spain was forced to rely upon England for a supply of this vital staple in this period (Underhill 1899: 152)[10]. Fine silks, gold cloths, wines, and wool were exported in return from Spain.

The exigencies of this trade required the presence of large numbers of Englishmen in the Peninsula, either in the capacity of factors or as independent merchants. Living chiefly in the principal seaports–Cádiz, San Sebastian, Lisbon, Bilbao and San Lucar de Barrameda–aand in cities, such as Madrid or Valladolid, English merchants followed in some measure the customs of the country: they intermarried in their adopted homes, often became Catholic, or, if they did not, they concealed all traces of Protestantism (*ibid.*: 154)[11]. In addition, they were appointed consuls, or agents of the English ambassadors; they cultivated friendships with Spanish aristocrats and bureaucrats; and they observed affairs at court, providing valuable information on Spanish domestic policies. Moreover, in spite of the absolute trade embargo imposed by Spain on England in 1585, which remained in force until 1603, trade continued through intermediaries or as contraband, which included thousands of books prohibited by the Inquisition. The merchants who were detained abroad for comparatively short periods of time were those who engaged in the task of translating Spanish books into English.

The last decades of the sixteenth-century, then, saw a revival of English interest for Spanish books not seen since the 1550s, when Richard Eden published his *Decades of the New World* (1555), a compilation of works on America by Peter Martyr, Fernández de Oviedo, López de Gómara, and other chroniclers. Twenty years later, the real contact of refugees, travelers, ambassadors, and merchants with Spaniards in the Peninsula fostered a movement of translations from the Spanish, whose bulk and kind were unprecedented. Every species of literature from Spain, except for drama, became an object of attention. Travelers began to visit the Peninsula and to bring with them Spanish books. And in spite of the mediation of foreign countries, such as Italy and France, and that of the enemies of Philip II in London, as Underhill claimed, the Spanish influence came to be a movement among the English themselves, particularly among those who had visited the land from which these literary works had sprung (*ibid.*: 150-151).

Translations of chronicles of discovery and of treatises on medical and military topics gave expression to the inquiring spirit of the merchants, to their taste for the unknown, the marvelous and the adventurous which characterized the England of Hawkins and Drake. The chronicles of discovery not only captivated the imagination, but they also appealed to the business instinct of a rapidly developing merchant class. To know a space, in effect, was to acquire dominion over it, first in the form of a map, a description, or a list of attributes that could be transported to Europe through journals and chronicles. After spending some years in Spain, John Frampton, a merchant, translated a series of chronicles on the New World that appeared in London in 1577, such as Nicolás Monardes's *Historia medicinal de las cosas que traen de nuestras Indias Occidentales* (Parts I and II), which appeared under the title of *Joyfull News out of the newe founde worlde* (1577). Frampton's residence in Seville, when Monardes was publishing his treatises, afforded the Englishman an opportunity of getting acquainted with the writings of the physician, which enjoyed a wide vogue in Spain and the continent. Frampton followed up with his translation of Bernardino de Escalante's *Discourse of navigation which the Portugales doe make to the realmes and provinces of the east partes of the worlde* (1579), a chronicle of discovery, in turn succeeded by a treatise of another stamp, though also dealing with the sea, Pedro de Medina's popular *Arte de navegar* (1545), to name only a few works on discoveries and navigation published by this translator[12].

Among other merchants, Thomas Nicholas, who had resided in the Canary Islands during the 1550s and 1560s, dedicated himself solely to the translation of chronicles of the Indies after his return to London. In 1578, he published his English version of the second part of López de Gómara's *Historia de las Indias*, entitled the *The pleasant historie of the conquest of the West India now called New Spayne*. Both Frampton and Nicholas had been imprisoned by the Spanish Inquisition. Moreover, they had no academic pretensions, had learnt Spanish for practical (mercantile) reasons and, having lived in Spain, were well aware of the wealth of the Indies. In his translation of López de Gómara's *History of the West Indies*, Nicholas wrote that his work was "but a poore gift, the which I have translated out of the Spanish tongue, not decked with gallant colours, nor yet siled with pleasant phrase of Rhetorike, for these things are not for poore Merchant travelers, but are reserved to learned Writers"[13]. In addition, Nicholas translated Augustín de Zárate, the historian of Peru, whom he had met while traveling on business on the road from Toledo toward "High Castile" (perhaps Burgos). This meeting between the English merchant and the *contador* Zarate, administrator of finances in the Viceroyalty of Peru, led to the English translation of Zarate's *Conquista del Perú*[14]. Although Nicholas only translated the first four books of this chronicle, he included an account of the *Mynes of Potosi, and how Captain Caravajall took it into his power*. Nicolas's translation, entitled *The strange and delectable historie of the discoveries and conquest of the provinces of Peru, in the South*

Sea (1581), is one of the best examples of the literary activity of the English merchant class at the end of the sixteenth century. The enthusiasm these books elicited in the Elizabethan merchants foreshadows the popular interest in geographical compendiums and translations of Spanish works on the Indies which accompanied Cromwell's expedition to the New World and capture of Jamaica in 1655. As it turns out, Cromwell's attack on the New Wold inspired the largest publications on Spain and America since the 1620s in England (Steele 1975: 63). The political agendas behind these publications speak to the enormous success, in seventeenth- and eighteenth-century France and the Netherlands, of Inca Garcilaso's oeuvre amid readers and booksellers.

Many other English translations of Spanish-American chronicles followed at the turn of the sixteenth century, along with books written by British corsairs and adventurers relating their achievements and hardships upon the coasts of the Peninsula or in the Spanish colonies. I have already alluded to the master figure among the historians of travel, Richard Hakluyt. An outstanding participant in the most active period of Elizabethan translation, Hakluyt not only established the canon of voyage, but also gave the Spanish chronicles of discovery their place next to the literary works, which were being translated at the same time by Sir Philip Sidney and others. Representing the Spanish influence in its fullest development, the second edition of Hakluyt's *Principal Navigations* (1588-1600) included 216 voyages and 378 supporting documents, which covered sixteen hundred years of travels (Helgerson 1992: 166). Besides English accounts of voyages to the coasts of the Spanish and Portuguese colonies, and letters from English residents in the Spanish peninsula, there are over fifty sections in this work which are translations from Spanish documents, letters intercepted by English ships, and personal interviews granted to Hakluyt by Spanish prisoners in England.

After Hakluyt's death in 1616, Samuel Purchas, who had already published travel literature with great success, continued Hakluyt's work. With more than 4000 pages, the four huge volumes of *Purchas his Pilgrimes*, published in 1625, constituted one of the largest publications in the English language to that date. *Purchas his Pilgrimes* contains translations from Antonio de Herrera y Tordesillas's *Historia general de las Indias*, from which Purchas extracted a general description of the New World; selections from José de Acosta's work; selected passages from Gonzalo Fernandez de Oviedo; extracts from the Codex Mendoza, produced in 1541-1542 by native scribes working in Mexico for the Viceroy of New Spain, Antonio de Mendoza; segments from López de Gómara's *History of the Indies*; as well as the inaugural accounts of Francisco de Xerez and Pedro Sancho, secretaries to Pizarro, regarding the events of Cajamarca. One of Purchas's most important contributions to the history of the New World was his publication of selected chapters from both parts of Inca Garcilaso's *Comentarios reales*. Because he had already published extensive extracts on Peru from Acosta, Purchas merely took from Garcilaso descriptions of Inca religion and society, including details on the murder of

Manco Capac and the rebellion of Tupac Amaru. Purchas's *Pilgrimes* thus remained the only source for Inca Garcilaso in English until Sir Paul Rycaut's translation in 1688.

These compilations of Spanish chronicles speak to the European fascination with Peru, exemplified by the continual translations of Inca Garcilaso's works that appeared between 1633 and 1745 in France and the Netherlands. In the seventeenth century, Peru was known as the principal source of income for the Spanish Crown, a land of exotic Indian civilizations which gave rise to the legend of El Dorado and to the fabulous wealth of Potosí. Along the coasts of Peru toward Panama sailed ships brimming with gold and silver of extraordinary valor. In this respect, Hakluyt was the first English writer to directly challenge Iberian claims in the New World. The hopes of his compatriots are resumed in his plans to occupy Magellan's Strait, the key to the treasures of both the East and the West Indies, a plan that proposed to transport a thousand cimarrons, who hated the Spaniards, to the Strait, as well as some English colonists, who would settle there. In this way, claimed Hakluyt (1967: vol. 1, 142), "we shal make subjecte to England all the golden mines of Peru and all the coste and tract of that firme of America upon the sea of Sur"[15]. Even before Drake's famous "voyage of exploration" in 1577, the immense wealth of Peru was already known through Cieza de León and Augustín de Zarate's works, which broadcast in Europe the news of Potosí. It is even possible that in 1550-1551 Sebastian Cabot was a principal party in an Anglo-French scheme for invading Peru by way of the Amazon, a scheme reported by Cabot himself to Charles V, in 1553, well after the event (Andrews 1982: 74).

Evidently, Hakluyt's translations not only conveyed vital information on the Spanish colonies in America but also revealed the political and economic agendas of English entrepreneurs, merchants, printers, and translators at the turn of the century. Merchants, in effect, were the driving force behind England's expansion, one characterized by the entry of English landowners into the world of trade and commercial investments (Helgerson 1992: 178). These political, religious, and economic plans on the part of the English fueled parallel militant activities through another form of early capitalist enterprise, book-publishing. As Lucien Febvre and Henri-Jean Martin remind us in their classic work on the impact of printing, *L'Apparition du livre*, print-capitalism not only created a new reading public in Europe, but also exploited each potential vernacular market through "a veritable 'international' of publishing houses" which surpassed national frontiers in their search for new markets" (1976: 122)[16]. Both in England and on the Continent, as we shall see, printers and book-publishers were instrumental in the production of travel books and translations of Spanish chronicles on the New World. The early modern publishing industry was a booming business that profited from the explosive interaction between capitalism, technology, and human linguistic diversity[17]. Such interactions also invoke the political agendas behind Inca Garcilaso's

European translations, which were frequently used by the supporters of the Black Legend against Spain[18]. Purchas's *Pilgrimes* not only offered the English readers their first taste of Garcilaso's history of ancient Peru, but also ended with a condensed version of Bartolomé de las Casas's *Brevísima relación de la destrucción de las Indias*, a work that ensured the continuation of the "Black Legend" against Spain in England. First published in Antwerp in 1578-1579, Las Casas's work became a best-seller which was soon translated into Flemish, French, English, German, and Latin in a few years, diffusing anti-Spanish sentiment in Europe.

3.4.2. *L'histoire des Yncas, Roys du Perou*

Las Casas, however, was not the only best-selling author in Europe on matters of America, for Inca Garcilaso also appears to have been an authentic success in France and the Netherlands, where he was continually translated and reedited between 1633 and 1745. The first part of the *Comentarios reales* appeared in France in 1633 through Jean Baudoin's translation, entitled *Le commentaire royal, or l'histoire des Yncas, Roys du Perou [...] Escrite en langue Peruvienne par l'Ynga Garcilasso de la Vega*. A prolific writer and translator, best known for his French version of Francis Bacon's Essays, Baudoin (1564-1650) moved in the literary circles of the French court[19]. In spite of his claim that Garcilaso's work was originally written in the "Peruvian language" (Quechua), one can give credit to Baudoin for noticing that the *Comentarios reales* is a recollection of legendary stories, myths, customs, and laws, translated by Inca Garcilaso from the Quechua language. Quechua, as we know, was the language which Inca Garcilaso imbibed with his mother's milk–"la lengua que mamé en la leche", as he repeatedly declares. In his dedication to Prince Louis de Bourbon, Baudoin praises this "very true history" which conforms with "the style and good sense of the author who wrote it". The Incas, claims Baudoin, not only excelled in their natural knowledge of morals and politics, but also in "the true institution of the Laws and customs of their Empire". Their admirable genius "met that of Plato, in order to form the idea of a perfect government, and to give the highest import to public tranquility". Baudoin soon followed with his translation of the second part of the *Comentarios reales*, entitled *Histoire des guerres civiles des Espagnols dans les Indes* (1650).

　　Both French versions of Garcilaso's histories of Peru experienced a tremendous success in early modern France and the Netherlands, where at least twelve editions of *Le commentaire royal (Histoire des Yncas)* and *Histoire des guerres civiles des Espagnols* ensued (Paris: 1633, 1650, 1658, 1672; Amsterdam: 1633, 1704, 1706, 1715, 1737, 1744, and 1745). In addition, Garcilaso's *La Florida del Inca*, which recounts the history of Hernando de Soto's tragic Florida expedition, was also translated into French and other languages in this period[20]. The fervor elicited by Garcilaso's masterpiece resulted in a revised edition of Baudoin's *Histoire des guerres civiles des espagnols dans les Indes*, published in Amsterdam in 1706. Its editor, Gerald Kuyper affirmed that he had been compelled to reprint Baudoin's translation in response to the incessant demands of the public. In effect, if the *princeps* edition of the *Comentarios reales* (1609) was, according to Kuyper, almost extinct, its French versions were also difficult to acquire, and their price was excessive, as demonstrated by the auctions where these books were sold. The editor, however, took great liberties with Baudoin's translation, which he considered obsolete: "j'ai crû devoir l'a faire retoucher, de peur qu'elle ne degoutât ceux qui ne peuvent souffrir un trop ancien langage" [I believed it was necessary to retouch it, fearing that it would disgust those who cannot bear an excessively ancient language] (1701: vol. 3, 3). Speaking to the aftermath of translation, the editor and the book-seller's comments also reveal his preoccupation with marketing. The readers will surely approve of his revisions, he claims, because of the comments some people made on the amendments he had introduced in his edition of *L'Histoires des Incas* (*ibid.*: 4).

This proliferation of translations raises some questions regarding why and how translations travel. Why, for instance, were Inca Garcilaso's texts translated again and again on the Continent? What was the agenda behind these translations? As Susan Basnett forcefully argues (1998: 123), translation always takes place in a continuum, never in a vacuum: "textual and extratextual constraints upon the translator" are real and always at work. The comments of the Dutch editor of *Histoire des Incas* and *Histoires de guerres civiles des Espagnols* bear out the truth of what Lawrence Venuti (1995: 308) has said about such constraints::

> Every step in the translation process–from the selection of foreign texts to the implementation of translation strategies to the editing, reviewing, and reading of translations–is mediated by the diverse cultural values that circulate in the target language, always in some hierarchical order.

Could we propose, then, that beyond the political and economic stakes that put in motion the works of Inca Garcilaso through Europe, his texts became a sort of "cultural capital"? I am referring to a capital which should not be equated with "capital" as it is used in economics. In the sense defined by Pierre Bourdieu, cultural capital is what you need to exhibit in order to belong to the "right circles" in the society in which you live. These were the texts that the bourgeoisie hurried to read from the seventeenth century on because the aristocracy had been reading them. As Bourdieu claims (1979: 251), every appropriation of a work of art, including a *bien culturel*–a cultural asset or good–is in itself a social rapport, a rapport of distinction; here Bourdieu cites E.H. Gombrich, who, in his *Méditations*, says that in sixteenth- and seventeenth-century Europe, the "opposition between the 'vulgar' and the 'noble' became one of the principal preoccupations of critics". Both in England and on the Continent, aesthetic choices, including reading preferences, what Bourdieu calls *"capital culturel objectivé"* [objectified cultural capital]–the product of accumulated history, in the form of books, articles, documents, theories or critiques of these theories, and conceptual systems–determined social qualities and differentiation (*ibid*.: 251). In seventeenth-century France, for instance, accounts of voyages to distant lands acquired an enormous popularity among the aristocracy and the intelligentsia, especially after the decade of 1630-1640, when editions of them multiplied. In 1663, Chapelain noted that people preferred travel books to romances, as evidenced by his own library which held more than one hundred volumes dedicated to America (Pillorget 1995: 1066). Consequently, if Inca Garcilaso's reputation for veracity as a historian remained uncontested for centuries, the fascination with the exotic culture and civil achievements of the Incas was also a factor of success. The history of the Incas frequently served as vehicle for social and economic criticism, while their government was often used as a model by French authors of utopias. Many French writers compared the marvels of distant countries with "l'état de nostre malheureuse France" [the state of our unfortunate France], as the lawyer Pierre Bergeron said in 1648 (Atkinson 1925: 163).

3.4.3. *The Royal Commentaries of Peru*

Some of these questions may be explored through the study of the English translation of Inca Garcilaso at the end of the seventeenth century, a translation that stresses both the concern with cultural difference and with the political and mercantile agendas involved in these translations. As mentioned earlier, the second half of the seventeenth century in England evidenced a revival of interest in the West Indies, inaugurated by Cromwell's capture of Jamaica in 1655, and continued by the raids of English privateers in 1665 and by the energetic bucanneer activities of the 1680s. Thomas Mun's *English treasure by forraign trade*, published in 1664, stands as an example of English mercantilist literature that reinforced the acquisitive urge of the privateers. In his Preface, which is cited by Steele (1975: 76), Munn claims that: "All the Mines of Gold and Silver which are as yet discovered in the sundry places of the world, are not of so great value as those of the West Indies which are in the possession of the King of Spain". The year 1664 also marked the extraordinary success of *The Indian Queen*, a play written by John Dryden with his brother-in-law Sir Robert Howard, based on one of the first French exotic novels and partly set in an imaginary Mexico and Peru. Dryden's sequel, *The Indian Emperor*, drawn from Las Casas and other Spanish chronicles extracted from Purchas, was an even greater success than its precursor: ten editions of the text appeared between 1667 and 1703. As demonstrated by Steele (*ibid*.: 76-78), the proliferation of editions of *The Indian Emperor* attests to the recovery of the printing trade in England after the plague of 1665 and the Great Fire of 1661, which destroyed presses, type, and paper, as well as human lives; some 3,550 books, in effect, were printed in England between 1666 and 1680, of which 253 were works on geography, travel, and navigation.

In addition, the foundation of the Royal Society in London, in 1662, influenced the nature and production of travel accounts, through the publication in its monthly journal *Philosophical Transactions*, from 1665 to 1667, of a collection of travelers'reports, which were later collected in a single volume. Other travel publications followed, such as John Ogilby's luxurious travel compendiums and collections on Africa, America, Asia, and Europe, lavishly illustrated with plates and maps. Partly based on Arnoldus Montanus's Dutch work, *De nieuwe en onbekende weereld*, Ogilby's *America* (1670, 1671) was one of the largest surveys on the Americas since Purchas's *Pilgrimes*, a monumental work that offered a superlative over-all account of early modern Brazil. If the 1670s in England witnessed revivals, not originality, as Steele argues (*ibid.*:82), the 1680s would see numerous publications describing the attacks on the Caribbean and on the Pacific coast by English buccaneers, such as the expedition of Captains Bartholomew Sharp and John Coxon against Puerto Bello in 1680, and the massive attack on Panama City and other coastal towns on the Pacific by seven ships initially commanded by Richard Sawkins and other buccaneers in 1681. The 1680-1681 expedition, then, became very well known, thanks to the publication of various buccaneers' journals, which were eventually combined with the English translation of Alexandre Exquemelin's *Bucanniers of America*. First published in Amsterdam in 1678, this best-seller was soon translated into German (1680), Spanish (1681) and English (1684), and went into a second English edition in 1685. The enormous success of these works had a bearing on other publications, such as *The voyages and adventures of Capt. Barth. Sharp*, edited by Philip Ayres in 1684, a work that documented John Cox's account of Bartholomew Sharp's raid on the isthmus of Panama.

These years also reflected an increasing appreciation of the English colonies in America, as attested by Richard Burton's popular *The English Empire in America* (1685), which went through six editions before 1728, and by Richard Blome's *The present state of his Majesties isles and territories in America* (1687). Likewise, a fresh translation of Hernando de Soto's expedition to Florida appeared in 1686, with a new title: *A relation of the invasion and conquest of Florida*. Emphasizing the current interest in books on America, its anonymous translator claimed that "the publick cannot have too many Histories of Expeditions of that nature. This is apparent enough by the many Relations of the Conquest of Peru and New-Spain" (1686: A3v). Such a statement speaks to the veritable boom in publications on the New World, which began in the 1650s, with Cromwell's attack on Jamaica, and continued, as we shall see, until the end of the century. The last translation of the reign of James II is that of Inca Garcilaso de la Vega, whose *Royal Commentaries* appeared in London in 1688.

The translator of this English version of the *Comentarios reales*, Sir Paul Rycaut (1629-1700), was a diplomat, traveler, prolific writer and translator of Dutch and Spanish descent, who spent most of his life abroad in Turkey, first as secretary to the embassy of Sir Heneage Finch, second earl of Winchilsea, in Constantinople, and later, as consul of the English Levant Company at Smyrna (now Izmir), where he remained for eleven years. A qualified diplomat and skilled negotiator, Rycaut is renowned for his works on the Turkish Empire, based largely on his own observations at the Porte. Upon his return to England in 1679, he engaged in intense literary activities, published several books on the Turks, among them *The Present State of the Ottoman Empire [...], illustrating the variety of habits among the Turks*, published in 1666, which included illustrations of Turkish costumes Rycaut had collected in Smyrna[21]. Likewise, his *History of the Turkish Empire from 1623 to 1677*, published in 1679–a record of civil, military, and commercial events in the Ottoman Empire, attuned to British interests–went through numerous editions and translations. Rycaut's ensuing *History of the Turks beginning with 1679 until the end of 1698*, published in 1699, also had various editions, as well as French and German translations.

A polyglot, Rycaut knew Latin, ancient and modern Greek, French, Italian, and Turkish, as well as Spanish, which he learnt in his youth at the University of Alcalá de Henares in Spain. Between 1652 and 1653, while his elder brother attempted to collect from the Spanish government a large debt owed to their family, Rycaut enrolled at the Spanish university and astonished the students with the elegance of his Latin. As an exercise to master Spanish, he translated into English the first part of *El criticón*, a popular novel by Baltasar Gracián, which he finally published in 1681 under the title of *The Critick*. In his preface to the reader, Rycaut recounts his sojourn at Alcalá de Henares, "where I had the Honour to be esteemed more for my skill in the Latin Tongue, and my Faculty in Poetry, than ever I had a Reputation for in my own University" (1681: 6). He claims that his attempt to translate Gracián, which he undertook "for my own Improvement by the Translation, [...] almost made me a Master of the Spanish Tongue"; years later, in revising his youthful translation, Rycaut felt that he had been "over affectionate to words, and Romantick Expressions" but that he had kept close to the sense: "I was a faithful even in those years to the Author whom I translated" (*ibid.*: 6).

His flair for translation and his acceptance among the intelligentsia in England were confirmed by an invitation to contribute to the "Dryden translation" of *Plutarch's Lives*, a massive work of scholarship published in 1683-1686 by Jacob Tonson, with the participation of forty-two scholars who translated the fifty individual lives from the Greek (Bracken and Silver 1995: 292-301). Rycaut chose the life of Numa Pompilius, which dealt with the laws and customs of early Romans. The five-volume edition of *Plutarch's Lives* was an ambitious undertaking, which went through various editions in the 1700s. Tonson, in fact, was one of the first publishers to use newspapers to advertise his books. His carefully edited luxurious editions often included impressive illustrations, such as the ones used in his 1688 edition of Milton's *Paradise Lost*, which contained splendid engravings by the John Baptist Medina. These drawings not only provided an important interpretation of the text, but also helped readers to have access to the complex work through visual images (*ibid.*: 294).

In 1685, Rycaut was commissioned by his own printer and bookseller, Christopher Wilkinson, to compose a translation of Inca Garcilaso's *Comentarios reales*, which was a best-seller in French. Significantly, the license for this English translation of Garcilaso, granted on 5 August 1685, coincided with the time of the success of the Exquemelin volumes on the buccaneers of America. If the interest in travel books and accounts of the Conquest of Mexico and Peru guaranteed the commercial prospects of a translation of Inca Garcilaso, the size of this work meant that the cost of production was to be shared amongst four booksellers–Christopher Wilkinson, Jacob Tonson, Richard Tonson, and Samuel Heyrick–a new practice that resulted in many large volumes coming out simultaneously from several printing presses (Steele 1975: 92). This joint venture for the publication of a folio volume on America, announced the beginning of the new era of travel literature in England at the turn of the eighteenth century.

Nevertheless, Rycaut's unexpected appointment in 1685 as chief secretary in Ireland, under lord-lieutenant Sir Henry Hide, second Earl of Clarendon, slowed down his work (Anderson 1991: 267). A letter to Christopher Wilkinson, written from Dublin Castle in May 1586, reveals that Rycaut was working on the translation of Inca Garcilaso "as often as I find the least leisure", sending home chapters to be printed by installments. Promising Wilkinson to send him "a good bundle" of sheets, as soon as "I come to the end of the 4th booke", Rycaut adds that, after this, "the matter will be easyer [...]; time and patience doe all the great things of this world"[22]. Rycaut completed the translation in 1687 and Inca Garcilaso's *Royal Commentaries* appeared in 1688, as a handsome illustrated folio of over a thousand pages, which was well received and quickly required a second impression (*ibid.*: 267). Again, only extracts from Garcilaso had been published in Purchas's *Pilgrimes*. Rycaut's large folio volume was the first separate edition of Inca Garcilaso in the English language.

A few words on Theodore de Bry are necessary at this point. In 1590, de Bry began his *Thesaurus of Travels to the West Indies* and, by 1634, the de Bry family–father and sons–had published fourteen volumes of the series called *America*, a collection of books that enjoyed an enormous commercial success in early modern Europe. Representing a Protestant iconography of the Discovery, and dedicated in part to contest the Spanish conquest of America, de Bry's work fueled anti-Spanish sentiment in Europe, showing the Spaniards as terrible oppressors, capable of acting in the New World as they had in the Low Countries. Through its vivid images depicting the customs of the Incas and the brutal encounter with the Spaniards, then, Rycaut's *Royal Commentaries* implicitly evoked the Black Legend of Spain. The impressive illustrations by de Bry would also have functioned as a marketing device that converted the book into a precious object even while reinforcing its points. Indeed, the haunting visual images of the Spanish conquest had been circulating in Europe for almost a century. Thirty years before, Milton's nephew, John Phillips, had translated the most famous English version of Las Casas's work, entitled *The Tears of the Indians* (1658), a version that reproduced, albeit in a reduced size, a few of de Bry's famous engravings. These plates lent visual impact to the image of the Spaniards, who "dismember the Indians both men and women, cutting off their ears, noses and hands, and that in so many places and regions, that it would be a tedious thing to relate them" (1656: 116)[23]. The move by the English publisher of Las Casas, in 1658, to provide visual background to the Dominican's text informs Rycaut and Wilkinson's use of the full-size engravings by de Bry in *The Royal Commentaries*. Although Rycaut was not particularly anti-Spanish, he stated, in his letter to the reader, that "God who is just and compassionate of the Creatures that he hath made, would not suffer these Cruelties to pass unpunish'd, but caused the Spaniards themselves to be instruments of his vengeance on each other". Dramatized by the sensational illustrations, this phrase recalls Las Casas's denunciations of Spanish cruelty in the New World. Coincidentally, the appearance of Rycaut's translation concurred with a new edition of Las Casas, significantly entitled *Popery truly display'd in its bloody colours* (1689).

*The Royal Commentaries*was dedicated to James II, the unfortunate Catholic King who reigned for only three years (1685-1689), and was deposed by his son-in-law, William of Orange, in the "Glorious Revolution" of 1688[24]. Rycaut's dedication calls on the king to take arms against the pirates and buccaneers in the New World:

> This translation, out of Spanish, having the name of *Royal Commentaries*, seems justly to claim a Title to your Majesty's gratious Favour [...]. And likewise, your Majesty's Dominions being adjacent & almost contiguous to the Countries which are the subject of this History, make your Majesty a party concerned in the Affairs of the New World, & so supreme an arbitrator in the government thereof that to suppress the robberies & insolence of certain pirates, who infest those coasts, your Majesty's Royal arms are called for as the most proper means and power to reduce them.

The call to arms against the robberies "of certain pirates, who infest those coasts" speaks to the recent expeditions to the New World by English, French, and Dutch privateers, which were highlighted, as we know, by a series of popular publications in 1684 and 1685. Given the tumultuous nature of events in England in 1688, the suppression of the buccaneers was rather a futile hope. Rycaut's preface focuses on the Indians of Peru, "a naked people, simple and credulous", who possessed "simplicity and good nature" and "uncorrupted Loyalty and Truth" (1688: A2v and 1r). The phrase, in fact, echoes the words of Jean Baudoin, the French translator of Inca Garcilaso, regarding the Incas.

One may ask what led Rycaut to accept the translation of Inca Garcilaso's monumental twin histories of the Incas and of the Spanish conquest of Peru. As a member of the Levant Company which–through its principal factories established at Constantinople, Aleppo, and Smyrna–held a monopoly on the Levant trade for 80 years, Rycaut was certainly committed to the expanding mercantile activities of the English merchants. On his return to England in 1578, "Consul Rycaut", as he was known, was elected to a seat on the Company's board of directors and for the next ten years exercised considerable influence on the company's policies. Yet Rycaut was also a sophisticated world traveler who was interested in the laws and customs of different peoples. From his many years of life in Constantinople and Smyrna he had acquired an understanding of the structure of Ottoman society and an expertise in analyzing the economic, aesthetic, and environmental factors that affect diverse cultures. His translation of the life of Numa Pompilius for the "Dryden translation" of *Plutarch's Lives*, attests to Rycaut's interest in the laws and customs of early Romans. He was, as Sir Steven Runciman has said, "almost alone among Western writers of the seventeenth and eighteenth centuries in showing such sympathy" for different cultures and religions (in Anderson 1991: 226)[25]. This openness and interest in different cultures connects Rycaut with prominent philosophical travelers, such as Montaigne, Rousseau, and Voltaire. More importantly, like Inca Garcilaso, Rycaut lived his life on the borderline between cultures, in the indeterminate temporality of the in-between that, according to Homi Bhabha (1994: 227), "has to be engaged in creating the conditions through which 'newness comes into the world'".

Steele has documented (1975: 151) the consistent presence of both the Spanish and French editions of Parts I and II of *Comentarios reales* in libraries of the period in England and on the Continent. Becoming established as important historical sources, the Spanish editions of Inca Garcilaso and Herrera y Tordesillas appeared continuously in book auctions in London and showed a steady upward trend in price until the eighteenth century. John Locke, who possessed the 1633 French translation of Inca Garcilaso, was inspired by Garcilaso's history of the Incas. In his *Two treatises of government*, published in 1690, Locke imagined "a state of nature in which men lived according to reason, unfettered by money, property, and intuitions of government" (in Steele 1975: 91). Locke's "Scholastic Philosophy of the Wilderness" presented a distorted vision of the New World; Garcilaso's insights into both the Spanish and the Amerindian worlds, which were lived and vital, endowed his work with an outlook of unusual breadth. Europeans were interested to learn from it that the New World, in Garcilaso's view, had also produced highly civilized and sophisticated societies which believed in the immortality of the soul and in the existence of an unseen God. Garcilaso's history of the Incas was often abridged and included in other travel books: in France, among others, Jean de Laet made use of it in his *Histoire de Nouveau Monde* (1640) and the *savant* Bernard de Fontenelle (1690) used Garcilaso as an example of the similarities between Greek and Amerindian myths (McCormack 1991: 106).

In England, the commercial success of *The Royal Commentaries* is suggested by the fact that this large folio volume soon went through a second impression. Rycaut's Incas, as well as his Turks, were to reappear in a great many English works of sociological or anthropological complexion (Anderson 1991: 267). Sir William Temple was one of the first English writers to include this information in various essays, also published in 1690. As various critics have indicated, moreover, Daniel Defoe's attempts to define human nature appear to be doubly indebted to Rycaut's translation, for Robinson Crusoe is believed to have several touches of the castaway sailor Pedro Serrano, who materializes in Book I of *The Royal Commentaries*, while Andrenio in *The Critik* is thought to have been the prototype for Man Friday (*ibid.*: 267).

Like Dryden, Rycaut believed that a good translation should be faithful to the author's sense, but not necessarily to his wording; accordingly, he did not attempt a literal translation of Inca Garcilaso[26]. Even though the translator omitted some material and summarized long passages in Inca Garcilaso, certainly Rycaut's text is far more readable today than any of its successors and the merits of his translations are beginning to be recognized once more. A sample comparison of Rycaut's translation of Garcilaso and that of Livermore, which is the best of the modern ones, reveals that, although Rycaut was not a literal translator, his rendition is quite clear and readable. The commercial success of *The Royal Commentaries* thus marks the beginning of the new era of travel literature that would flourish in England between 1689 and 1726 (Steele 1975: 93). The turn of the century, in effect, would attest to the great popularity of books of travel and general geography in England. Confirming this are the dispirited words of Anthony Ashley Cooper, the third Earl of Shaftesbury, in 1714: "Barbarian Customs, Savage Manners, Indian Wars, and Wonders of the Terra Icognita, employ our leisure Hours, and are the chief Materials to furnish out a Library" (1714: vol. 1, 344).

To conclude: the diverse translations of Inca Garcilaso published in early modern Europe speak to the spirit of transatlantic expansion that fomented these publications, as the eyes of English, French, and Dutch merchants, travelers, diplomats, book-publishers, and translators focused more and more on America as a place of mercantile enterprise and colonial endeavors. In England, the increased publication of travel literature marked the revival of English overseas activity. As J. J. Richetti has put it (1969: 161), "the travel book served the ideological needs of an emerging modern world". These ideological needs are evoked by Armitage's description (1995: 59) of the transatlantic expansion of England: "America moved from a marginal role in the English cosmographical histories to center stage as England asserted its *imperium* from Virginia and New England through the Caribbean and along the eastern seaboard of America and New Foundland to the Carolinas". That *The Royal Commentaries* appeared in the same years as the "Glorious Revolution" (1688) that ousted the Catholic King James II and brought the Dutch William of Orange to the English throne is suggestive. Staged by a powerful group of

English aristocrats, and backed by the merchants of the City of London, this almost bloodless revolution has been seen as a crucial Anglo-Dutch business merger that introduced the British to a numer of important Dutch financial institutions. Complementing the transatlantic thrust that led hundreds of English companies to carry goods to and from America and the Caribbean in the 1680s, the Anglo-Dutch merger not only allowed the British to operate more freely in the East but also announced the advent of England as Europe's dominant naval power in the 1700s (Ferguson 2002: 24).

Still, the interest in Inca Garcilaso's *Royal Commentaries* points to the curiosity elicited by exotic cultures and, concomitantly, to the staging of cultural difference in early modern Europe. As "the performative nature of cultural communication", translation, as Homi Bhabha says (1994: 228), is "language *in actu* (enunciation, positionality), rather than language *in situ* (*énoncé*, propositionality)". Accordingly, the sign of translation "continually tells, or 'tolls' the different times and spaces between cultural authority and its performative practices". The English and French translations of Inca Garcilaso invoke the different times and spaces between cultural authority and its performative practices in the age of imperial expansion. To return to Octavio Paz's definition of translation, with which I began this study, I suggest that the continuous translations of Inca Garcilaso's work emerge as a system of symptoms or metaphors that speak to the struggle to understand an ever expanding cosmos and, at the same time, to the battle for world supremacy that still haunts us today.

[1] The original reads thus:

> Cada uno ligeramente distinto del anterior: traducciones de traducciones de traducciones. Cada texto es único y, simultáneamente, es la traducción de otro texto. Ningún texto es enteramente original porque el lenguaje mismo, en su esencia, es ya una traducción: primero, del mundo no-verbal y, después, porque cada signo y cada frase es la traducción de otro signo y de otra frase. (1971: 9)

Henceforth, all English translations are mine, unless otherwise noted.
[2] Abravanel's work had already been translated into Spanish on three occasions: by the Jewish scholar Guedeliah Yahia (1568 and 1584) and by Carlos Montesa (1582). A noted Neoplatonic philosopher and writer, Judah or Jehudah Abravanel, or Abrabanel, had great influence among fifteenth- and sixteenth-century Hebrew intellectuals in Europe. See James Nelson Novoa's article in this volume and also Aurelio Miró Quesada (1971: 111-123).
[3] *La traduzion del Indio de los Tres Dialogos de Amor de Leon Hebreo, hecha de italiano al español por Garcilasso Inga de la Vega, natural de la gran Ciudad del Cuzco, cabeça de los Reinos y Provincias del Piru. Dirigidos a la Sacra Catolica Real Magestad del Rey don Felipe nuestro Señor*, En Madrid. En casa de Pedro Madrigal MDXC. I have used the facsimile edition by Miguel Burgos de Núñez (Seville: Padilla Libros-Quinto Centenario del Descubrimiento, 1989); the quotations come from Inca Garcilaso's letter to Maximiliano of Austria.
[4] On the role of translation in the work of Inca Garcilaso, see Susana Jákfalvi-Leiva.
[5] "Mi intención no es contradecirlos, sino servirles de comento y glosa y de intérprete en muchos vocablos indios, que como extranjeros en aquella lengua, interpretaron fuera de la propiedad de ella" (1960: vol. 1, 3). See also the translation by Harold V. Livermore (de la Vega 1987).

[6] "Yo he procurado traducir fielmente de mi lengua materna, que es la del Inca, en la ajena, que es la castellana [esta relación del origen de sus Reyes], aunque no la he escrito con la majestad de palabras que el Inca habló ni con toda la significación que de aquel lenguaje tienen [...]. Antes la he acortado, quitando algunas cosas que pudieran hacerla odiosa" (1960: vol. 1, 17).

[7] This leads Margarita Zamora to state that "the conquest and colonization of the New World is not a military struggle but a discursive one" (1988: 3).

[8] The historian Ambrosio de Morales praised Garcilaso's splendid rendition of León Hebreo from Tuscan into Castilian; see Asencio (1953: 583-593). Likewise, the defender of Góngora and author of *Apología de las Soledades*, Francisco Hernández de Córdoba, Abbot of Rute, eferred three times to Inca Garcilaso in his *Didascalia multiple* (1615); see Varner (1986: 303-304 and 350-351) and Barrenecha (1955: 261-263).

[9] In 1577-1580, Francis Drake completed his circumnavigation of the world, presenting a dazzling proof of the riches lying ahead in the New World. His compatriot Thomas Cavendish also returned from the coasts of Peru and New Spain (1586-1588) with a booty consisting of articles of silk, pearls, spices, gold and silver. See Quinn (1975: 17).

[10] See also Fitzmaurice-Kelly.

[11] It was not unknown in England that the English residents in Spain concealed their Protestantism. Hakluyt noted with disapproval that "the merchant in England cometh here devoutly to Communion and sendeth his son into Spain to hear Mass. These things are kept secret by the merchants" (1903-1906: 33-34).

[12] Monardes's *Historia medicinal de las cosas que se traen de nuestras Indias occidentales* (1565), first two parts, had further editions, 1580 and 1596, and was translated into Latin, Italian, and other languages. Among other works Frampton translated was *A description of the ports, creekes, bayes, and havens of the West Indies* (1578). He also translated Bernardino de Escalante, *Discurso de la navigation que los Portugueses hazen a los reinos y provincias de oriente, y de la noticia que se tiene de las grandezas del reino de la China* (1577). Frampton's English version was titled: *Discourse of the navigation the Portugales doe make*. See Donald Beecher's essay in this volume.

[13] Francisco López de Gómara, *The pleasant historie of the conquest of the West Indies* (1596); cited in Colin Steele (1975: 10). I am indebted to Steele's fine study for my views on seventeenth-century English publications on the New World.

[14] The anecdote is told in the dedication he wrote for this book (see 'Nicholas' in John Payne Collier). Nicholas also translated letters and reports, such as the *Newes lately come from the great kingdom of China* (1577), a version of a Spanish letter sent from Mexico to Spain.

[15] On the English geographers, see Hilgarth (2000: 370-378). Hakluyt believed that, once the flow of treasure from the New World was intercepted, Philip II's "Territories in Europe oute of Spaine [would] slide from him, and the Moores enter into Spaine it selfe, and the people revolte in every forrein territorie of his, and cutt the throates of the proude hatefull Spaniardes their governours" (1967: vol. 2, 246).

[16] See also the original (1958: 184) and Benedict Anderson's important study of nationalism.

[17] See Clair's history of printing and also Plomer's, which includes appendixes with the number of presses and workmen employed in the printing houses of London in Tudor and Restoration England.

[18] The term was coined by a conservative Spanish Crown official, Julián Juderías, in his book *La leyenda negra*, first published in 1914. Judería's book argued for the existence of a Black Legend that falsified Spain's past and, especially, her role in America.

[19] His career began as a "reader" for Marguerite de Valois, the estranged wife of the popular Henry IV (Henri de Navarre). At Marguerite's death in 1605, Baudoin passed to the service of Louis de Marillac, brother of the Minister of Justice Michel de Marillac, who opposed Cardinal Richelieu in his wars against Spain.

[20] The first Dutch edition of Baudoin's *Histoire des Yncas* (1633) included, in a second volume, a translation of *La Florida del Inca*. More translations of *La Florida del Inca* appeared in France and the Netherlands in 1670, 1685, 1709, 1711, 1731 and 1737.

[21] New editions appeared in 1668, 1670, and 1675, and the work was rapidly translated into French, German, and Polish. Rycaut also published a study of *The Greek and Armenian Churches* (1679), and another work, *Lives of the Popes* (1685). In September 1666, the Fire of London

María Antonia Garcés

destroyed almost the entire stock of *The Present State of the Ottoman Empire*–all but twenty two copies, according to Pepys, remained. In spite of this, the book was "much cried up" and remaining copies were avidly hunted by collectors and scholars. See Sonia P. Anderson's study, to which I owe part of my discussion on Rycaut's life and works.
[22] British Library, Lansdowne 1153 A, fol. 33, Rycaut to Christopher Wilkinson, 18 May 1686. My thanks to Anthony Puglisi for helping me to decipher this letter.
[23] Las Casas's translation was soon followed, in 1658, by Sir William D'Avenant's "Opera": *The cruelty of the Spaniards in Peru*.
[24] Married to Mary, the Protestant daughter of James II, William was recalled from Holland by the English Whigs who rose up against their Catholic King and his alliance with Louis XIV, staging a revolution in 1688 for a "free Parliament and a free Protestant religion". James II fled to France and, in January 1689, the Parliament declared the throne vacant and offered it to William and Mary conjunctly.
[25] Rycaut was one of the earliest defenders of intercommunion between the Orthodox Churches and the Church of England, a position already suggested by the preface to his *Greek and Armenian Churches*, which looks ahead to ecumenical union.
[26] In the nineteenth century, Sir Clements R. Markham justified his own translation of Inca Garcilaso by severely criticizing Rycaut in words that have been reproduced in every bibliographical entry to this translation: "The worthy knight", he said in his introduction, "had a very slight knowledge of the Spanish language, and he did not scruple to make wild guesses at the meaning of sentences, and to omit whole chapters" (de la Vega 1869: vol. 1, xvi). This perception is, of course, inaccurate.

References

Anderson, Benedict. 1991. *Imagined Communities: Reflections on the Origin and Spread of Nationalism*. New York, NY: Verso.
Anderson, Sonia P. 1989. *An English Consul in Turkey: Paul Rycaut at Smyrna, 1667-1678*. Oxford: Clarendon Press.
Andrews, Kenneth. 1982. 'On the Way to Peru: Elizabethan Ambition in America South of Capricorn' in *Terra Icognita* 14 : 61-75.
Armitage, David. 1995. 'The New World in British Political Thought: from Richard Hakluyt to William Robertson' in Karen Ordahl Kupperman (ed.) *America in European Consciousness: 1493-1750*. Chapell Hill, NC: University of North Carolina Press. 52-75.
Asencio, Eugenio. 1953. 'Dos cartas desconocidas del Inca Garcilaso' in *Nueva revista de filología hispánica* 7(3-4): 583-593.
Atkinson, Geoffroy. 1925(?). *Les Relations de voyages du XVIIe siècle et l'évolution des idées*. Paris: Librairie Ancienne Edouard Champion.
Barrenecha, Raul Porras. 1955. *El Inca Garcilaso en Montilla, 1561-1614*. Lima: San Marcos.
Basnett, Susan. 1998. 'The Translation Turn in Cultural Studies' in Susan Basnett and André Lefevere (eds) *Constructing Cultures: Essays on Literary Translation*. Cleveland, OH: Multilingual Matters. 123-140.
Bellini, G. 1982. *Storia delle relazioni letterarie tra l'Italia e l'America di lingua spagnola*. Milano: Cusalpino-Goliardica.
Bhabha, Homi. 1994. 'How Newness Enters the World: Postmodern Space, postcolonial times and the trials of cultural translation' in *The Location of Culture*. London: Routledge. 212-235.
Bourdieu, Pierre. 1979. *La distinction. Critique sociale du jugement*. Paris: Editions de Minuit.
Bracken, James K. and Joel Silver (eds). 1995. 'Jacob Tonson the Elder' in *The British book Trade, 1475-1700*. Vol. 147 of the *Dictionary of Literary Biography*. Detroit, MI: Bruccoli Clark Layman. 292-301.

Clair, Colin. 1966. *A History of Printing in Britain*. New York, NY and London: Oxford University Press.

Collier, John Payne. 1865. *A Bibliographical and Critical Account of the Rarest Books in the English Language, Alphabetically Arranged, Which During the Last Fifty Years, Have Come Under the Observation of J. Payne Collier*. 2 vols. London: Joseph Lilly.

Cooper, Anthony Ashley. 1714. *Characteristics of men, manners, opinions, times*. 2 vols. London.

D'Agostino, Alfonso. 1992. 'El Inca Garcilaso traductor de los *Dialoghi d'Amore* de León Hebreo' in *Del Tradurre*. Roma: Bulzoni. 59-75.

D'Avenant, Sir William. 1658. *The cruelty of the Spaniards in Peru: Exprest by instrumentall and vocall musick, and by art of perspective in scenes, &c. Represented daily at the Cockpit in Drury-Lane, at three after noone punctually*. London: Henry Herringman.

de la Vega, Garcilaso. 1625. *Observations of things most remarkable collected out of the first Part of the* Commentaries Royal, *written by the Inca G. de la Vega. The supplement of the History of the Incas, briefly collected out of the Authors second part. Book IV of* Hakluytus Posthumus or Purchas his Pilgrims (ed. Samuel Purchas). London.

–. 1633. *Le commentaire royal, ov L'Histoire des Yncas, roys dv Perv; contenant leur origine, depuis le premier Ynca Manco Capac, leur establissement, leur idolatrie, leurs sacrifices, leurs vies, leurs loix, leur gouuernement en paix et en guerre, leur conquestes [...] Escritte en langue peruuienne par l'Ynca Garcillasso de la Vega [...] & fidellement traduitte sur la version espagnolle par J. Baudoin* (tr. Jean Baudoin). Paris: A Courbé.

–. 1650. *Histoire des guerres civiles des Espagnols dans les Indes, causées par les souslévemens des Piçarres et des Almagnes, suivies de plusieurs désolations à peine croyables, arrivées au Peru par l'ambition et par l'avarice des conquérans de ce grand Empire* (tr. Jean Baudoin). Paris: chez Augustin Courbé et chez Edme Couterot.

–. 1688. *The royal commentaries of Peru, in two parts: the first part: treating of the original of their Incas or kings, of their idolatry, of their laws and government both in peace and war, of the reigns and conquests of the Incas [...]: the second part: describing the manner by which that new world was conquered by the Spaniards, also the civil wars between the Piçarrists and the Almagrians [...] and other particulars contained in that history / Written originally in Spanish by the Inca Garcilasso de la Vega; and rendred into English by Sir Paul Rycaut* (tr. Paul Rycaut). London: Printed by Miles Flesher for Jacob Tonson.

–. 1706. *Histoire des guerres civiles des Espagnols, dans les Indes, entre les Piççarres & les Almagres, qui les avoien conquises* (tr. Jean Baudoin). 2 vols. Amsterdam: G. Kuyper.

–. 1707-1711. *Histoire de la conquete de la Floride, ou, Relation de ce qui s'est passé dans le découverte de ce pays par Ferdinand de Soto. Composée en Espagnol par l'Inca Garcilasso de la Vega, & traduit en François par P. Richelet* (tr. Pierre Richelet). Paris: Chez Jean Musier.

–. 1869. *The First Part of the Royal Commentaries* (ed. Clements R. Markham). 2 vols. London: The Hakluyt Society.

–. 1960. *Comentarios reales de los Incas* (ed. Aurelio Miró Quesada). 2 vols. Caracas: Biblioteca Ayacucho.

–. 1987. *Royal Commentaries of the Incas* (tr. Harold V. Livermore). Austin, TX: University of Texas Press.

de Man, Paul. 1986. *The Resistance to Theory*. Minneapolis, MN: University of Minnesota Press.

de Soto, Hernando. 1686. *A relation of the invasion and conquest of Florida by the Spaniards, under the command of Fernando de Soto* (tr. anon). London: Printed for John Lawrence.

Ebreo, Leone. 1989. *La traduzion del Indio de los Tres Dialogos de Amor de Leon Hebreo, hecha de italiano al español por Garcilasso Inga de la Vega, natural de la gran Ciudad del Cuzco, cabeça de los Reinos y Provincias del Piru. Dirigidos a la Sacra Catolica Real Magestad del Rey don Felipe nuestro Señor, En Madrid. En casa de Pedro Madrigal MDXC*. Facsimile edition by Miguel Burgos de Núñez. Seville: Padilla Libros-Quinto Centenario del Descubrimiento.

María Antonia Garcés

Febvre, Lucien and Henri-Jean Martin. 1958. *L'Apparition du livre*. Paris: Albin Michel.

–. 1976. *The Coming of the Book. The Impact of Printing, 1450-1800* (tr. David Gerard). London: New Left Books.

Ferguson, Niall. 2002. *Empire: The Rise and Demise of the British World Order and Lessons for Global Power*. New York, NY: Basic Books.

Fitzmaurice-Kelly, James. 1910. *The Relations between Spanish and English Literature*. Liverpool: University Press of Liverpool.

Gracián, Baltasar. 1681. *The Critick, written originally in Spanish by Lorenzo Gracian, one of the Best Wits of Spain, and Translated into English by Paul Rycaut, Esq.* (tr. Paul Rycaut). London: Printed by T.N. for Henry Brome.

Hakluyt, Richard. 1903-1906. *The Principal Navigations Voiages and Discoveries of the English Nation by Richard Hakluyt* (ed. Walter Raleigh). Glascow, 1903-1906) Vol. 12.

–. 1967. *The Original Writings & Correspondence of the Two Richard Hakluyts* (ed. E.G.R. Taylor). 2 vols. Nendeln, Liechtenstein: Krauss Reprint Ltd.

Hebreo, León. See Leone Ebreo.

Helgerson, Richard. *Forms of Nationhood: The Elizabethan Writing of England*. Chicago, IL: University of Chicago Press.

Hernández, Max. 1993. *Memoria del bien perdido: Conflicto, identidad y nostalgia en el Inca Garcilaso*. Lima: Instituto de Estudios Peruanos-Biblioteca Peruana de Psicoanálisis.

Hilgarth, J. N. 2000. *The Mirror of Spain, 1500-1700*. Ann Arbor, MI: University of Michigan Press.

Jákfalvi-Leiva, Susana. 1984. *Traducción, escritura y violencia colonizadora: un estudio de la obra del Inca Garcilaso*. Syracuse, NY: Maxwell School of Citizenship and Public Affairs.

Juderías, Julián. 1954. *Leyenda negra: estudios acerca del concepto de España en el extranjero*. Madrid: Editora Nacional.

Las Casas, Bartolomé de. 1552. *Breuissima relacion de la destruycion de las Indias [...]*. Sevilla: Sebastian Trugillo.

–. 1656. *The tears of the Indians: being an historical and true account of the cruel massacres and slaughters of above twenty millions of innocent people, committed by the Spaniards in the islands of Hispaniola, Cuba, Jamaica, &c.: as also in the continent of Mexico, Peru, & other places of the West-Indies, to the total destruction of those countries / written in Spanish by Casaus, an eye-witness of those things; and made English by J.P.* (tr. John Phillips). London: Printed by J.C. for Nath. Brook.

–. 1993. *Brevísima relación de la destrucción de las Indias* (ed. Andre Saint-Lu). Madrid: Cátedra.

McCormack, Sabine. 1991. *Religion in the Andes*. Princeton, NJ: Princeton University Press.

Ortega, Julio. 2003. 'Transantlantic Translations' (tr. Christopher Conway) in *PMLA* 118(1): 25-40.

Paz, Octavio. 1971. *Traducción: literatura y literalidad*. Barcelona: Tusquets Editores, S.A.

–. 1992. 'Translations of Literature and Letters' (tr. Irene del Corral) in R. Schulte and J. Biguenet (eds) *Theories of Translation from Dryden to Derrida*. Chicago, IL: University of Chicago Press. 152-63.

Pillorget, René and Suzanne Pillorget. 1995. *France baroque, France classique: 1589-1715*. Paris: R. Laffont.

Plomer, Henry R. 1900. *A Short History of English Printing 1476-1898*. London: Kegan Paul, Trench, Trübner and Co..

Quesada, Aurelio Miró. 1971. *El Inca Garcilaso y otros estudios garcilasistas*. Madrid: Ediciones de Cultura Hispánica.

Quinn, David B. (ed.). 1975. *The Last Voyage of Thomas Cavendish (1591-92)*. Chicago, IL: University of Chicago Press.

Richetti, J.J. 1969. *Popular Fiction before Richardson. Narrative Patterns 1700-1739*. Oxford: Clarendon Press.

Steele, Colin. 1975. *English Interpreters of the Iberian new World from Purchas to Stevens: A Bibliographical Study. 1603-1726*. Valencia: The Dolphin Book Co., Ltd.

Underhill, John Garret. 1899. *Spanish Literature in the England of the Tudors* New York, NY: Macmillan.

Varner, John. 1986. *El Inca: The Life and Times of Garcilaso de la Vega*. Austin, TX: University of Texas Press.

Venuti, Lawrence. 1995. *The Translator's Invisibility: A History of Translation*. London and New York, NY: Routledge.

Zamora, Margarita. 1988. *Language, Authority and Indigenous History in the* Comentarios reales de los Incas. Cambridge: Cambridge University Press.

Section IV

Towards Art and Parody

4.1. Early Anglo-American Attitudes to Native American Languages

Randall C. Davis

A survey of several accounts of contact between English and Native Americans in the Early Modern Period reveals much about early instances of intercultural communication and Anglo-American attitudes towards Native languages. One prominent feature of many of the earliest English New World travel narratives–including those of Francis Drake's exploratory expedition and accounts of colonization by Thomas Harriot and Captain John Smith–is the relative lack of attention devoted to Native languages. English writers generally avoid discussion of the practical challenges in communication between English and Natives; indeed, English eloquence is frequently implied to make translation unnecessary. Most revealing, however, is the first extended English examination of a Native language, Roger Williams's *A Key into the Language of America* (1643), which acknowledges the formidable difficulties of communication that characterized early Anglo-Indian encounters. Though Williams generally accepted the conventional Anglo-American assumption of Native linguistic (and cultural) inferiority, he considered in greater depth than anyone before him the subtleties involved in mutual understanding between individuals of different cultures.
Keywords: Indian, language, Native American, Roger Williams, translation, travel.

By a number of measures the canon of American literature has expanded to include texts originally created in Native American languages. While Robert Spiller's long-standard *Literary History of the United States* (1946) had begun with European "reports and chronicles", both Emory Elliott's *Columbia Literary History of the United States* (1988) and Sacvan Bercovitch's *Cambridge History of American Literature* (1994) acknowledge at the outset the presence of a Native American oral tradition as part of a reconceived "American literature". Myra Jehlen asserts, in her contribution to the *Cambridge History* (1994: 37), that "[t]he people who already inhabited the North American continent had an old and richly developed oral literature". N. Scott Momaday (1988: 6) more boldly insists, "[t]he native voice in American literature is indispensable. There is no true literary history of the United States without it".

Most anthologies of American literature have followed suit, consistently including in their opening pages translations of Native American texts juxtaposed with European chronicles of exploration and colonization from the late fifteenth through the seventeenth centuries. Yet these translations of Native American texts invariably date from a much later period, from the nineteenth and–many of them–from the twentieth century[1]. There is good reason why these translations are so relatively recent: there are virtually no English-language translations of Native American oral literary texts from the early modern period. Indeed, Arnold Krupat's useful historical overview (1992: 3-32), "On the Translation of Native American Song and Story" *begins* in the mid *eighteenth* century. As William Clements (1996: 3) observes of prevalent Anglo-American attitudes through the nineteenth century, "[k]nowing what Indians were saying had practical, political import, but the artistic potential of such discourse was seldom acknowledged". Oddly enough, many of the most authoritative English-language translations of traditional (that is, pre-European contact) Native American texts are also among the most recent: that is, the furthest removed, in time, from the originals. The 1994 collection *Coming to Light* offers such "state of the art" translation–translation that is accompanied by contextual information regarding the translator, the storyteller, and the circumstances and particular features of oral performance. The theoretical framework–including, most importantly, the attitudes towards Native American languages and oral performances–that produces such translation has evolved only within the last century or so.

To illustrate this problem, we might examine what is generally considered the first English-language translation of a Native American literary text. Henry Timberlake's 1765 *Memoirs* offers what purports to be a translation of a Cherokee war song[2]. It reads in part:

> Where'er the earth's enlighten'd by the sun,
> Moon shines by night, grass grows, or waters run,
> Be't known that we are going, like men, afar,
> In hostile fields to wage destructive war;
> Like men we go, to meet our country's foes,
> Who, woman-like, shall fly our dreaded blows. (1927: 81)

We might debate about how useful this text is as an ethnographic document, but it is obvious that Timberlake created this translation on the model of the dominant contemporary English verse form–the heroic couplet. Timberlake approached the original Cherokee text (or a translated version of it, since Timberlake himself apparently knew little of the Cherokee language) as raw material to be reworked before it may serve as "literature"[3].

What about the early modern period, then? How are Native American languages treated in the early English-language accounts of intercultural contact? More broadly, how is the act of communication itself portrayed?

As numerous scholars have pointed out, many of the earliest European explorers and colonists of the New World perceived Native Americans in terms of what they lacked. Virtually all aspects of Native American cultures, including languages, were presumed to be inferior. "From the earliest encounters we can find scattered comments, and rather random collections of Indian words, sometimes reflecting particular beliefs about their Hebrew or Welsh connections, but almost always assuming that Indian languages were deficient or limited" (Murray 1991: 14). Indeed, this perceived linguistic deficiency was often cited along with other "evidence" of cultural inferiority to justify European claims to the Americas.

In what has become a fashionable trope for considering the earliest encounters between Europeans and Native Americans, Moffitt and Sebastián (1996: 103) claim that New World "lands and [...] native populations were not so much *discovered* as gradually *invented*". Europeans' pre-conceptions often determined perceptions; Europeans found (or rather, "invented") what they expected. Scholars are thus skeptical about many of the early European accounts of contact between Europeans and Native Americans since European chroniclers often seem so confident in what they report of Native Americans, including information purportedly derived from verbal communication, though they often acknowledge limited or no understanding of Native languages. Of course, one of the most famous examples is Columbus's "invention" of the cannibal. During his first voyage to the Caribbean, Columbus heard the Taino speak of the *canibas*, whom he understood to be a bellicose people living to the west (*ibid.*: 117)[4]. The perceived similarity between the sounds in "canibas" and "Khan"–as in *El Gran Can*–encouraged Columbus to believe that he had indeed arrived close to his intended destination–the East. Columbus's conception of the *canibas* was clearly influenced by his awareness of the anthropophagi, mythological man-eaters whose origins predate the classical era. Through Columbus's account, the word "cannibal" entered European vocabularies, coloring subsequent European conceptions of New World natives (and perhaps providing Shakespeare with the name for one of his most famous creations–Caliban).

Since England did not begin serious efforts at New World colonization until after other European nations, many of the Native Americans that English explorers first encountered had already seen Europeans, though they may not necessarily have acquired competence in European languages[5]. A particularly curious phenomenon is that many of the English accounts often describe instances of intercultural communication–sometimes involving rather abstract concepts–without explaining the method of exchange. One is left with perplexing questions about just how Anglo-American writers derived certain information–often presented with unwavering confidence–regarding Native Americans. The absence of such information has led a number of scholars to question the reliability of many of these accounts, supporting assumptions about the European "invention" of America. Indeed, one must carefully consider the particular circumstances under which these accounts were generated, including the probable motives of the writers.

The following study surveys several accounts of contact between English and Native Americans from the late sixteenth through mid seventeenth century, focusing on instances of intercultural communication and what they reveal about early Anglo-American attitudes towards Native languages.

One particularly intriguing early account of Sir Francis Drake's celebrated 1577-1580 circumnavigation of the globe was a twelve-page pamphlet printed by Richard Hakluyt in 1595 or 1596 and designed for insertion in the 1589 edition of *Principal Navigations*. The author is unknown;

some have speculated that it may have been Hakluyt himself drawing upon his conversations with Drake and other members of the expedition (Kelsey 1988: 179). Regardless, Hakluyt's version has become one of the best-known and often-reprinted accounts of the voyage.

According to the Hakluyt narrative, many of the Native Americans Drake encountered were already familiar with Europeans. Though the account doesn't specify (1972: 176-177), one may assume that Drake's crew used Spanish to communicate with the natives they met in present-day Brazil and Chile; the chronicler notes that in both instances, the crew were mistaken for Spaniards. Spanish was not a possibility, however, for the natives the *Golden Hind* encountered in present-day California (most probably San Francisco Bay), had apparently never seen Europeans. Hakluyt's chronicler writes: "When they came unto us, they greatly wondered at the things that we brought, but our general (according to his natural and accustomed humanity) courteously entreated them, and liberally bestowed on them necessary things to cover their nakedness, whereupon they supposed us to be gods, and would not be persuaded to the contrary" (*ibid.*: 180). In the absence of any more explicit information about communication, one can only wonder what provoked this assumption about the natives' beliefs, beyond the Europeans' unquestioning sense of superiority.

Hakluyt's chronicler continues:

> After they were departed from us, they came and visited us the second time, and brought with them feathers and bags of tobacco for presents: and when they came to the top of the hill (at the bottom whereof we had pitched our tents) they stayed themselves: where one appointed for speaker wearied himself with making a long oration, which done, they left their bows upon the hill, and came down with their presents.
>
> In the meantime the women remaining on the hill, tormented themselves lamentably, tearing their flesh from their cheeks, whereby we perceived that they were about a sacrifice. In the meantime our general with his company went to prayer, and to reading of the Scriptures, at which exercise they were attentive, and seemed greatly to be affected with it. (*ibid.*: 181)

In this remarkable episode the two groups talked at or talked towards one another, but it is questionable what was actually communicated. The chronicler does suggest that the natives were responsive to English religious discourse, though he offers little support for his claim. The chronicler may have been predisposed to observe (or invent) such an effect, however, since European imperialism was invariably publicized in part as an attempt to bring Christianity to the heathen.

Along similar lines, the chronicler next describes a ceremony in which the native "king" ritually defers to Drake:

> They made signs to our general to sit down, to whom the king, and divers others made supplications, that [Drake] would take their province into his hand, and become their king, making signs that they would resign unto him their right and title of the whole

land, and become his subjects. [...] Wherefore in the name, and to the use of Her
Majesty [Drake] took the sceptre, crown, and dignity of the said country [which Drake
dubs "New Albion"] into his hands. (*ibid.*: 182)

In addition to fantastically expressive sign language, we should note in this
passage how the chronicler naturally attributes English terms and European
concepts (such as *king, title, subjects*) to an imagined native perspective.
English eloquence makes translation unnecessary; native and English are
depicted as "on the same page", as it were, as the natives are presumed to
subordinate themselves happily to English rule.

The next example involves an expedition shortly after Drake's circling
of the globe. Thomas Harriot was an employee of Sir Walter Raleigh assigned
to assess the profitability of a New World English colony. Scholars are
uncertain whether Harriot was among the initial group of explorers in 1584, but
he definitely traveled with the second expedition in 1585. After Harriot's return
to England in late summer of 1586, Raleigh turned to Harriot for help in
advertising his colonial venture, hoping to lure potential investors. Harriot's
Briefe and True Report of the New Found Land in Virginia was first published
in 1588 and was subsequently reprinted in Hakluyt's *Principal Voyages*.
Unfortunately for Raleigh, the promotional effect of Harriot's book was more
than offset by the troubling news of the lost colonists. Yet *A Briefe and True
Report* remains one of the most significant sixteenth-century English works on
the New World, particularly its native inhabitants.

In this work, Harriot emphasizes Native Americans' lack of literacy
(1972: 25-26), but he recognized the importance of communicating with them
and he learned the Algonquin language from Manteo and Wachese, two natives
from Croatoan and Roanoke who had returned to England with Arthur
Barlowe's first voyage in 1584 (Oberg 1999: 27-28). Harriot may have even
intended to publish a linguistic study of Algonquin[6]. *A Briefe and True Report*
provides more detailed information about non-material culture than many
contemporary reports, suggesting, as Myra Jehlen notes (1994: 63), that Harriot
was "interested in the Indians for their own sake". *A Biefe and True Report*
includes Latin-alphabet transcriptions of a number of Algonquin terms,
especially for items with no English-language equivalents. Harriot observes
(*ibid.*: 26), for example, that "[t]hey think that all the gods are of human shape,
and therefore represent them by images in the forms of men, which they call
Kewasowok, one alone is called *Kewas*. Them they place in houses appropriate,
or temples, which they call *Machicomuck*, where they worship, pray, sing, and
make many times offerings unto them". The transcription of Algonquin terms
alone is tacit acknowledgment of a perspective different from the Europeans',
one which it might pofit the Europeans to understand, if only by rendering them
better armed to colonize.

Probably the most famous early English accounts of intercultural
contact are Captain John Smith's several publications describing his
experiences in Jamestown. Smith was among the first group of English

colonists who arrived in Jamestown in April 1607, remaining in Virginia until a powder burn forced him to return to England in October 1609. Smith's narratives are best known for introducing Pocahantas to Anglo-American literature, though variations in his accounts have led many scholars to question what really may have happened. Like Harriot's, Smith's motives were to promote the colonial endeavor, yet unlike Harriot, Smith also had the motive (perhaps it was his primary one) to promote himself: Smith as swashbuckling hero remains front and center throughout his narratives.

Smith's narratives–including *A True Relation of Such Occurrences and Accidents of Note as Hath Happened in Virginia* (1608), *A Map of Virginia, with a Description of the Country* (1612), and *The General Historie of Virginia, New England, and the Summer Isles* (1624)–include, as does Harriot's *Briefe and True Report*, a number of transcriptions of Algonquin words. Indeed, Smith announces (1986: vol. 1, 136) at the beginning of *A Map of Virginia*, "[b]ecause many doe desire to knowe the maner of their language, I have inserted these few words", subsequently listing over 70 Algonquin terms with their English translations. This list–including Smith's prefatory note–is reprinted *verbatim* at the end of Book II of *The General Historie*. As Barbour has observed (*ibid.*: vol. 1, 139), Smith may have been influenced–perhaps may have even copied from–a similar word list compiled by Harriot that may have been circulating in manuscript. Smith's rhetorical purpose in inserting transcriptions of Algonquin terms into his text seems to be, however, to bolster his own authority: "Indian words bespeak his special knowledge, gained from firsthand experience, and are therefore essential to the authoritative self that [Smith's works] would fashion" (Spengemann 1994: 80).

Despite the inclusion of Native terms, Smith acknowledges that he was no adept in the Algonquin language, an admission that would seem to cast some doubt on his professed powers of communication. In the following episode from the section of *The General History* describing his captivity by the Powhatans (which is considerably–and thus suspiciously–expanded from the 1608 *True Relation*), Smith shows his captors a compass.

> Much they marvailed at the playing of the Fly and Needle, which they could see so plainely, and yet not touch it, because of the glass that covered them. But when he [that is, Smith himself] demonstrated by that Globe-like Jewell, the roundnesse of the earth, and skies, the sphaere of the Sunne, Moone, and Starres, and how the Sunne did chase the night round about the world continually; the greatnesse of the Land and Sea, the diversitie of Nations, varietie of complexions, and how we were to them Antipodes, and many other such like matters, they all stood as amazed with admiration. (1986: vol. 2, 147)

As in the Drake narrative, the eloquence of the English speaker is assumed to transcend any practical difficulties of translation (Cheyfitz 1997: 81-82).

By far the most significant Anglo-American work of the early modern period involving Native languages is Roger Williams's 1643 *A Key into the Language of America*, a work that Lyle Campbell (1997: 34) identifies as "an important early contribution to American Indian linguistics". Fluent in Latin, Greek, and Hebrew, Williams had learned the language of the Narragansett Indians to whom the Puritan outcast had fled in 1636. The book is thematically organized with a table of contents for easy reference to such subjects as salutations (appropriately the first chapter), numbers, travel, trading, and money (including a note on exchange rates of wampum and English coins). Williams places the Native term on the left side of each page with English translations on the right. Interspersed liberally throughout the book are miscellaneous observations about various features of Narragansett culture. Indeed, these observations are so extensive that some have considered *A Key* the first Anglo-American work of Native American ethnography. Notably absent from these observations, however, is any but the briefest hint of a native oral narrative or poetic tradition. No doubt the structure of the work is partly responsible: Williams's subject for each chapter seems primarily driven by the practical contexts in which he imagines the English and Narragansett would interact. These don't include storytelling.

Williams doesn't depart from the conventional Anglo-American assumption of Native linguistic (and thus cultural) inferiority. In the preface to the *Key*, he points out (*ibid.*: A4) that the Natives "have no *Clothes*, *Bookes*, nor *Letters*, and conceive their *Fathers* never had; and therefore they are easily perswaded that the *God* that made *English* men is a greater *God*, because Hee hath so richly endowed the *English* above *themselves*". Indeed, in his chapter on Narragansett religion–probably the best-known portion of the book–Williams purports to recreate an exchange between two Native men on the relative merits of the Native and English belief. The subject is the fate of the soul after death. One Indian maintains

> [...] Our fathers have told us, that our soules goe to the *Southwest*.
>   The *Sachim* answered, But how doe you know your selfe, that your soules goe to the *Southwest*; did you ever see a soule goe thither?
>   The Native replyed; when did he (naming my selfe) [Williams] see a soule goe to Heaven or Hell?
>   The *Sachim* againe replied: He hath books and writings, and one which God himselfe made, concerning mens soules, and therefore may well know more than wee that have none, but take all upon trust from our forefathers. (*ibid.*: 137)

Despite such assumptions about the superiority of English literacy, the project of the *Key* itself apparently testifies to Williams' belief in the importance for the English to learn something of native languages[7].

More than many other Anglo-American works, Williams's *Key* acknowledges the challenges of communication. Rather than the awed, but purportedly comprehending Indians of the Drake and Smith narratives, Williams's natives struggle with certain concepts, for Williams considers in greater depth the difficulties and subtleties involved in mutual understanding between individuals of different cultures. Thus he observes:

> In the Nariganset Countrey [...] a man shall come to many Townes, some bigger, some lesser, it may be a dozen in 20. miles Travell.
> Observation
> Acawmenoakit *Old England*, which is as much as from *Land on t'other side*: hardly are they brought to believe that the Water is three thousand English mile over, or thereabout. (*ibid.*: 3-4)

Conversely, Williams confesses his own inability fully to understand the dialect of a neighboring band. He states (*ibid.*: 20) that he "once travelled to an Iland of the wildest in our parts [...] I was alone [...] and little could I speake to them to their understanding especially because of the change of their Dialect, or manner of Speech from our neighbors". The *Key* admits what previous accounts often ignored–the practical difficulties involved in intercultural communication.

One of the most notable features of Williams's book is how it records ways in which the Narragansetts' language had adapted to the European presence. Thus Williams includes, in his chapter on war (*ibid.*: 184), the terms "Peskcunk: A Gunne" and "Saupuck: Powder". He also includes several Narragansett neologisms that were derived from English. He notes (*ibid.*: 152), for example, that "[t]he *Indians* are ignorant of *Europes* Coyne; yet they have given a name to ours, and call it *Moneash* from the *English* Money". Likewise, he glosses (*ibid.*: 185) the Narragansett "Shottash" as "Shot; A made word from us, though their Gunnes they have from the *French*, and often sell many a score to the *English*, when they are a little out of frame or Kelter". Such details perhaps suggest a depth to the Narragansett language, a resilience or flexibility little hinted at in other treatments of native speech.

Though Williams's *Key* seems obviously intended to assist intercultural communication, it is difficult to imagine its actual use as a linguistic guide. The first edition was printed in London in 1643; a second edition was not published until the 1790s by the Massachusetts Historical Society. I have discovered no contemporary testimonies of the *Key* being used for its apparent design. Indeed, there are features of the work that suggest an intent beyond that of training English speakers to converse with the Narragansett. By his own account, Williams composed the work on his return to England in 1643 as an aid to his memory: "I drew the *Materialls* in a rude lumpe at Sea, as a private *helpe* to my owne memory, that I might not by my present absence *lightly lose* what I had so *dearely bought* in some few yeares *hardship*, and *charges* among the *Barbarians*" (*ibid.*: A2). In addition to spurring Williams's memory, *A Key* may have also been instrumental, as Henry Chupack points out (1969: 69-70), in his securing the charter for Rhode Island. Several members of Parliament signed a letter that Williams was to present to the Bay colony that emphasized his "great industry and travail in his printed Indian labours" (in Chupack, *ibid.*: 70).

Whatever Williams's motives in publishing *A Key into the Language of America,* the work remains the most extensive Anglo-American treatment of a Native American language of the early modern period. Yet the *Key*, like Williams himself, was essentially an anomaly. Though Daniel Gookin and John Eliot would in subsequent years perform more systematic study of Native languages, their purposes were much narrower; both were interested solely in Anglo-American instruction of Natives. It would still be quite some time before English language writers would be truly interested in what Native Americans had to say.

[1] This typical placement of translated Native American texts begs the question of how they should be dated. To consider one example–the first literary text in Volume A of *The Norton Anthology of American Literature* (sixth edition) is "The Iroquois Creation Story". No author is attributed. The introductory headnote, however, identifies the translator as David Cusick, who included this text in his 1827 *Sketches of the Ancient History of the Six Nations*. Editors' footnotes suggest a number of instances in which Cusick's translation may have been influenced by Judeo-Christian belief–whether directly from Cusick or from Cusick's unnamed source is impossible to say. One might plausibly argue that this text would be more accurately placed with other works of the nineteenth century rather than in a section titled "Literature to 1700".

[2] As a member of the Virginia Militia during the French and Indian War, in 1761 Timberlake had undertaken a mission to negotiate peace between the Cherokee and the British and the American colonists. In 1765 Timberlake sought to capitalize on his experiences among the Cherokee by publishing *The Memoirs of Lieut. Henry Timberlake*.

[3] Of course, the most famous example of such "polishing" in American literature is Henry Wadsworth Longfellow's 1855 *Song of Hiawatha*. In this popular poem, Longfellow freely reworked material from Henry Rowe Schoolcraft's *Algic Researches*–conflating features of distinct Native American oral traditions–using a meter adapted from the Finnish epic *Kalevala*.

[4] Eric Cheyfitz (1997: 41) suggests that Columbus may have misheard the word *carib*.

[5] As Cheyfitz has observed (1997: 63), Native Americans were far more often translators of European languages than Europeans were of native languages.

[6] Hulton records that Harriot's manuscript notes "on this subject" –now lost–"were still extant in 1684" (Harriot 1972: ix).

[7] As David Murray (1991: 14) observes, though, the book resembles "a modern phrasebook which allows one to 'get by' in a language rather than pay attention to the properties of the language itself". For example, there is no discussion of grammar or syntax.

References

Bercovitch, Sacvan. See Myra Jehlen.

Campbell, Lyle. 1997. *American Indian Languages: The Historical Linguistics of Native America*. New York, NY: Oxford University Press.

Cheyfitz, Eric. 1997. *The Poetics of Imperialism: Translation and Colonization from* The Tempest *to* Tarzan. Philadelphia, PA: University of Pennsylvania Press.

Chupack, Henry. 1969. *Roger Williams*. New York, NY: Twayne.

Clements, William M. 1996. *Native American Verbal Art: Texts and Contexts*. Tucson, AZ: University of Arizona Press.

Cusick, David. 1827. *Sketches of Ancient History of the Six Nations*. Lewistown, NY.

– (tr.). 2003. 'The Iroquois Creation Story' in Nina Baym (ed.) *The Norton Anthology of American Literature*. Vol. A. New York, NY: W.W. Norton. 19-23.

Hakluyt, Richard. 1972. *Voyages and Discoveries* (ed. Jack Beeching). New York, NY: Penguin.

Randall C. Davis

Harriot, Thomas. 1972. *A Briefe and True Report of the New Found Land of Virginia* (ed. Paul Hulton). New York, NY: Dover.
Jehlen, Myra. 1994. 'The Natural Inhabitants' in Sacvan Bercovitch (ed.) *The Cambridge History of American Literature*. Vol. 1. New York, NY: Cambridge University Press. 37-58.
Kelsey, Harry. 1998. *Sir Francis Drake: The Queen's Pirate*. New Haven, CT: Yale University Press.
Krupat, Arnold. 1992. 'On the Translation of Native American Song and Story: A Theorized History' in Brian Swann (ed.) *On the Translation of Native American Literatures*. Washington, DC: Smithsonian Institution Press. 3-32.
Moffitt, John F., and Santiago Sebastián. 1996. *O Brave New People: The European Invention of the American Indian*. Albuquerque, NM: University of New Mexico Press.
Momaday, N. Scott. 1988. 'The Native Voice' in Emory Elliott (ed.) *Columbia Literary History of the United States*. New York, NY: Columbia University Press. 5-15.
Murray, David. 1991. *Forked Tongues: Speech, Writing and Representation in North American Indian Texts*. Bloomington, IN: Indiana University Press.
Oberg, Michael Leroy. 1999. *Dominion and Civility: English Imperialism and Native America, 1585-1685*. Ithaca, NY: Cornell University Press.
Smith, John. 1986. *The Complete Works of Captain John Smith* (ed. Philip L. Barbour). 3 vols. Chapel Hill, NC: University of North Carolina Press.
Spengemann, William C. 1994. *A New World of Words: Redefining Early American Literature*. New Haven, CT: Yale University Press.
Spiller, Robert Ernest, *et al.* 1946. *Literary History of the United States*. 2 vols. New York, NY: Macmillan.
Timberlake, Henry. 1927. *The Memoirs of Lieut. Henry Timberlake 1756-1765* (ed. Samuel Cole Williams). Johnson City, TN: The Watauga Press.
Williams, Roger. 1997. *A Key into the Language of America* (ed. Howard M. Chapin). Bedford, MA: Applewood Books.

4.2. "Where the devil should he learn our language?"–Travel and Translation in Shakespeare's *The Tempest*

Jack D'Amico

In *The Tempest* Shakespeare explores a New World axis of translation, naming, and cultural exchange between the islander Caliban and the Italians who visit the play's island. Shakespeare sets up another axis that stretches from Prospero's northern Italian city, "fair Milan", to the Kingdom of Naples in the south of Italy and to Tunis in North Africa. The works of Machiavelli, moreover, inform an examination of the connections between translation and the founding of new regimes. In this context, translation includes the figurative shifts in understanding that accompany the founding of a new political regime, or the establishment of a new social order.
Keywords: Caliban, language, Machiavelli, Shakespeare, *The Tempest*, translation, travel.

The line quoted in the title of this paper (2.2.65-66) picks up a meta-theatrical device employed by Shakespeare, who draws attention to a basic convention of theater–the fictive experience on the play's island, wherever it might be, will be represented to the audience in "our" language[1]. At its most obvious level the joke is that Stephano, the shipwrecked, drunken, Neapolitan butler, expresses surprise to hear Caliban, the native islander, speaking Italian, a language represented in the play by "our" English. Other "subtleties o' th' isle" (5.1.124) follow[2]. Stephano's imprecation, "how the devil", reminds us that Caliban, according to Prospero, was "got by the devil himself" upon the witch Sycorax, Caliban's "wicked dam"[3]. And it was apparently from the magus Prospero and his daughter Miranda, not from the devil or Sycorax, that Caliban learned the language he speaks on the island stage.

There is something magical, or devilish in the work of translators who can turn strange creatures into beings we understand. The tension between division and identification makes translation, when considered in the broad sense, central to the most important dramatic moments in the play, most notably Prospero's decision to choose the virtue of forgiveness over vengeance when he identifies his enemies as one of his kind (5.1.23) and acknowledges that the "bastard" Caliban is someone who shares more than his language: "this thing of darkness I / Acknowledge mine" (5.1.275-277).

4.2.1. Part One

In this late play, Shakespeare examines the complex political, cultural, and psychological import of the possessive "our" as it relates to language. In the second scene of the play Miranda describes how she pitied Caliban and "Took pains" as she says, "to make thee speak, taught thee each hour / One thing or other. When thou didst not, savage, / Know thine own meaning, but wouldst gabble like / A thing most brutish, I endowed thy purposes / With words that made them known" (1.2.354-359). What do we make of "gabble?"[4]. We know that Sycorax was banished to the island pregnant with her demi-devil son, that she gave birth to Caliban there, or as Prospero puts it, "she did litter here, / A freckled whelp, hag-born" (1.2.282-283). Savage, half-animal, but teachable, Caliban had learned something from his mother, though not, apparently, a language that could be translated. He has purposes but no words to go with them, or none that "we" would recognize.

In the scene where Caliban encounters Stephano, he is introduced to the "celestial liquor" Stephano has salvaged from the shipwreck. This drink surpasses the "Water with berries in't" (1.1.335) that Prospero gave him in their first meeting many years before. More than a bit inebriated, Caliban asks if Stephano has not "dropped from heaven". The witty butler replies, "Out o' th' moon, I do assure thee. I was the man 'i th' moon when time was" and Caliban recalls something else from his past: "My mistress showed me thee, and thy dog and thy bush" (2.2.134-138). Since Caliban was on the island twelve years before Prospero and Miranda arrived, and since we do not know when Sycorax died, it is possible to read this reference to his "mistress" as a recollection of something his mother taught him. The use of the term mistress, however, stands out because Caliban otherwise uses the pejorative word "dam" for his dear mom, a word Shakespeare consistently associates with the devil or four-legged creatures. The language Caliban has learned from Prospero and Miranda brings with it a translation of his own past. Under the influence of Stephano's liquor, however, Caliban perhaps remembers his mother as teacher rather than witch. Prospero always represents Sycorax as his antithesis, the evil female identified with all things abhorrent–the "abhorred commands" she gave Ariel and the "Abhorred slave" she littered on the island (1.2.273, 352). The subtleties of translation return, however, when Shakespeare injects Golding's translation of Medea's incantation from Ovid (*Metamorphoses* VII.197-209) into Prospero's speech abjuring his rough magic (5.1.33-57). Just as Prospero, the good magician, has something to recant, it may be that Sycorax, the evil witch, had something decent to offer her "freckled whelp" of a son. If nothing else, her name has survived, with the name of her god "Setebos" (1.1.374), the god Caliban continues to swear by, as in act five when he sees the court party and exclaims "O Setebos, these be brave spirits indeed" (5.1.261). Shakespeare mixes the Algerian provenance of Sycorax with the Patagonian derivation of a name that, like translation itself, connects distant worlds and cultures.

So it is possible to think of Caliban as speaking a language which sounded like gabbling to Prospero and Miranda, or a language which Prospero needed to suppress rather than translate as he established his temporary residence on the island. Caliban recalls the happier period when Prospero "made much of" him and taught him how "To name the bigger light and how the less" (333-335). Naming the moon is part of his acquisition of language itself, or of "our" language in place of what he may have known before. As he acquires an ability to make his "purposes" known, Caliban describes "the qualities o'th 'isle" (1.2.338) needed for survival. And we learn that eventually he revealed a procreative purpose that Prospero would rather not acknowledge. As the magus who controls Ariel, Prospero hardly requires knowledge of the island to survive, but Caliban's recollection of their first exchange recalls a period of mutual dependence. That balance has been lost. Though the island is never named, Caliban's acquisition of "our" language on "his" island causes discontent: "You taught me language, and my profit on't / Is I know how to curse" (1.2.364-365)[5]. With the memory of his mother's name and the name of her god comes a sense of possession; that residue has not been wiped away. Or to put it in Prospero's terms, Caliban's education has not been completely successful, "our" language has not fully reshaped, or translated, his past.

Prospero calls himself Miranda's "schoolmaster" (1.2.172) and we have to assume that he was Caliban's first teacher, since Miranda was only three years old when they arrived on the island. But it is Miranda who says that she taught Caliban "each hour / One thing or other" (1.2.356). Therefore, she might have been the schoolmistress, or "mistress" who taught Caliban to identify the man in the moon and who replaces Sycorax and Setebos. If Miranda is the "mistress", the process of learning "our" language puts Caliban in touch with things above the earth, with the moon and with Miranda, called a "cherubim" (1.2.152) by Prospero and a "goddess" by Ferdinand (1.2.422). If "mistress" refers to Miranda, the romantic connotation of the term relates it to the event which has poisoned his relationship with Miranda and Prospero–Caliban's attempt, as Prospero says, to "violate / The honour of my child" (1.2.346-347). We know the old joke about learning a language in bed, preferably with a goddess rather than a witch. Prospero sees Caliban as a deformed creature who perverts, or mistranslates what he is taught: "A devil, a born devil, on whose nature / Nurture can never stick" (4.1.188-189). And Stephano's expression "how the devil" suggests something devilish not in Caliban's pedigree but in the very ability of such a creature to learn our language, or something devilish in those who taught him–what the devil could they have been thinking? The process by which Caliban's purposes were translated into articulate speech combines things celestial and devilish.

No devilish mistranslation gets in the way of the young lovers. Miranda sees Ferdinand as "A thing divine" and he, in turn, calls her a "goddess" (1.2.419, 422). They speak the same language. "My language! Heavens!" exclaims Ferdinand when Miranda identifies herself as "No wonder, sir, / But certainly a maid" (1.2.428-429). Later she becomes the mistress he serves (3.1.6). In a pattern reminiscent of *Romeo and Juliet*, Shakespeare gives Ferdinand a more conventionally courtly style of speech (3.1.39) that contrasts with Miranda's maidenly directness: "Hence, bashful cunning" (3.1.81) she says as she prepares to propose. Just as Caliban operates on a linguistic and social level with the commoners Stephano and Trinculo, Miranda meets her social and linguistic match in Ferdinand. But Shakespeare also complicates the picture. He gives Caliban a range of speech that extends toward the heavens, best represented by his dreaming of clouds that open to show riches (3.2.141), and undercuts the courtly circumlocutions Ferdinand brings with him to the island with Miranda's directness. "Do you love me?" (3.1.67) she asks, sending the Neapolitan prince off on another round of protestations.

And other, more serious differences lurk within the language the lovers share. When Ferdinand says that he is "the best that speak this speech / Were I but where 'tis spoken" (1.2.430) he assumes that his father is drowned and that he has inherited the Kingdom of Naples. In the social, political, and linguistic hierarchy, he is "the best". And yet his father, once best, conspired to exile Prospero and to destroy the very "goddess" the son now worships. Though ignorant of his father's transgression, Ferdinand speaks his language and that language carries with it the political and cultural assumptions of place, of Naples and of his place at the top of Neapolitan society. Nearer the bottom of that social hierarchy, Stephano parodies the roles of Alonso and Ferdinand when he accepts Caliban's "suit" to kill Prospero, take Miranda, and rule the island. Stephano imagines himself elevated: "His daughter and I will be king and queen–save our graces!–and Trinculo and thyself shall be viceroys" (3.2.103-105). Travel itself often triggers a kind of imaginative translation that produces a new self, but that does not work for Stephano, who ends up worse than he began, not Stephano "but a cramp", and if king of the isle, "a sore one then" (5.1.286-289). And Ferdinand has an important lesson to learn about what is best. When in act five Ferdinand explains that the betrothal to Miranda has given him a second life and made Prospero his second father, Alonso makes a statement that carries with it a powerful recognition of what is less than morally best in his relationship to Miranda, for he is her second father, but as he says, "O, how oddly will it sound that I / Must ask my child forgiveness" (5.1.197-198).

Shakespeare understands that the encounter with "our" language in a strange place arouses suspicion and wonder. That heady experience can mask, or exacerbate differences. I recall my own experience teaching in Naples many years ago when my attempts to assist lost American tourists near *spacca Napoli* by speaking "our" language fell on deaf ears. Speaking a broken tongue which was the closest they could get to Italian they would respond–"no speak Italian". It did not help to point out that I was not speaking Italian. Travel transports us to a place of linguistic tricks and wonders. Like Stephano, the American tourists anticipated trouble: "Do you put tricks upon's with savages and men of Ind?" (2.2.56) and fake Americans? But I cannot be too smug because I experienced another version of this commedia dell'arte *lazzo* when I met an ex-patriot African American soldier who had stayed on in Naples. I too could not credit my ears–where the devil should he learn my grandmother's language?

Exchanges of one kind or another persuade us that translation, however strange, is not a trick; exchange makes it possible for the traveler and islander to trust and understand one another. When Miranda opens "the fringéd curtains" of her eyes to look at Ferdinand, Prospero editorializes on what the audience would observe: "At the first sight / They have changed eyes" (1.2.441-442). Here "changed" means interchanged. After he has identified Caliban as a speaker of "our" language, Stephano says that his liquor "will give language to you, cat" (2.2.79). The liquor will loosen Caliban's tongue, but it will also initiate a complex process of exchange. By sharing liquor, song, and dance, Caliban and the Neapolitan travelers overcome their initial fears and begin to trust one another, though Ariel can easily undermine that trust when he mimics Trinculo's voice to disrupt Caliban's conspiracy (3.2.43).

Caliban's "translation" from a "cat" to someone who speaks our language implies, among other things, a shared identity. When Trinculo discovers Caliban he recalls another voyage he once made: "Were I in England now, as once I was, and had but this fish painted, not a holiday-fool there but would give a piece of silver. There would this monster make a man–any strange beast there makes a man" (2.2.27-30). Shakespeare plays on "make" in the sense of make your fortune and "make" in the sense of pass for a man. The Neapolitan clown puts himself above both the fish he discovers and the customers, those holiday fools in the London audience who, like Caliban, pass for humans[6]. Before he can take possession of Caliban, however, the impending storm forces a comic identification of the fool and the fish when Trinculo seeks protection under Caliban's cloak: "Misery acquaints a man with strange bedfellows" (2.2.38). Trinculo and Caliban become, to Stephano's eyes, a four-legged beast, or monster, which speaks two languages: "His forward voice now is to speak well of his friend, his backward voice to utter foul speeches and to detract" (2.2.89-91). This Rabelaisian creature is man–it is Caliban who can both curse and extol the musical delights of the island (3.2.135-143). The traveler typically assumes that a shared language comes from the forward voice that speaks well of us. But we know that among the first things translated by those who begin to share a language are the terms of and for the backside. That backward voice might be the devil's, but it is also the familiar source of vulgar sounds and potent animal forces that travelers and islanders share.

Whatever else she may have been, Sycorax had her own language and the power of sorcery (1.2.273). She is identified with the city of Algiers and is, perhaps, meant to be associated with the Islamic sphere of military power and economic expansion that extended along the northern coast of Africa[7]. The travelers do not encounter the world of Sycorax or of Islam, but their experience on the island is strange enough to shake the cultural assumptions they have imbibed with their language. The most noteworthy example of translation in the play, Gonzalo's speech on plantation of the island, draws on John Florio's translation of Montaigne. In his essay 'Of the Caniballes', Montaigne (1910: vol. 1, 220) makes translation itself a key issue when he examines the preconceptions and confusions that prevent Europeans from understanding the behavior of the seemingly barbarous inhabitants of the new world. In the famous passage paraphrased by Shakespeare[8], Gonzalo follows

Montaigne's intellectual journey back to a golden age of innocence, a journey that proceeds by contraries: "I'th'commonwealth I would by contraries / Execute all things" (2.1.148-149). In a variation on Miranda's teaching, these contraries remove the link between destructive "purposes" and the very "words" or names whose accretion has driven innocence from the language of our iron age. Gonzalo would have "no name of magistrate" and in his utopia "Letters should not be known" (2.1.150-51), so that the record of our language, especially the link between words and destructive purposes, would be wiped clean. It is an innocent dream–to remove the words and instruments of evil.

We know that the inhabitants of Gonzalo's imagined plantation would not speak the language of Antonio and Sebastian, nor would "our" language survive where names and things are so radically altered. Gonzalo leads those who will listen to him on an intellectual journey back to a golden age, while Prospero forces his enemies to endure a traumatic stripping away of their very will to live. He too works by contraries, taking the mind on a journey back to a kind of primal ooze before its reason can be restored: "Their understanding / Begins to swell, and the approaching tide / Will shortly fill the reasonable shore / That now lies foul and muddy" (5.1.79-82)[9]. But unlike Gonzalo's imagined voyage into a new relationship between words and purposes, Prospero returns to our language, to the humanity he shares with even his enemies, to the simple pulse of "flesh and blood" (5.1.114). Though his knowledge of the conspiracy causes Sebastian to exclaim, "The devil speaks in him" (5.1.129), Prospero speaks as we do. When he steps forward to address the audience at the end of the play to beg our indulgence he speaks our language.

4.2.2. Part Two

The second part of this essay examines the political implications of travel and translation in *The Tempest*, with particular reference to the role played by translation, or by a ruining of language and custom, in conquest (Lowenthal 1997: 21-70). The political context requires that we use the terms travel and translation metaphorically. For example, the island of the play is the meeting point of three voyages that force us to rethink what we mean by travel, a term that connotes freely chosen movement undertaken for recreation or edification. Prospero, and his daughter Miranda, and Sycorax, pregnant with Caliban, are exiles from Milan and Algiers respectively. They "travel" under duress. The Neapolitan court has traveled in a more conventional sense to Tunis for the marriage of King Alonso's daughter Claribel to the King of Tunis (1.2.232). While the devilish Sycorax invokes the threat of the Barbary corsairs of Algiers, the King of Tunis represents a North African ally.

Prospero's "travels" begin with a thinly disguised assassination orchestrated by Alonso: "In few, they hurried us aboard a bark, / Bore us some leagues to sea, where they prepared / A rotten carcass of a butt, not rigged, /

Nor tackle, sail, nor mast–the very rats / Instinctively have quit it" (1.2.144-148). The two forms of travel are linked–a combination of Prospero's "prescience" and fortune conspire to bring Prospero and Miranda back to Milan, where their twelve years of travel will be completed with the dynastic union of Milan and Naples. The return voyage from a wedding in Tunis blends with a return voyage to a wedding in Naples. By means of these voyages, Shakespeare creates an imaginary political sphere that extends from Milan in northern Italy to the Tunisian capitol in North Africa, an expanse that includes many varieties of language and customs. The middle voyage of Sycorax and Caliban remains unresolved in the play. Sycorax dies and Caliban, though he will "seek for grace" (5.1.295), is not explicitly included in the return to Naples; he has the much desired freedom he thought he had found in Stephano–freedom to remain on the island, or to return to Algiers, if he can build a boat.

The play frames Prospero's decision to forgive his enemies as a response to the suffering of "the good old Lord Gonzalo" (5.1.15), the very courtier Alonso made "master" of the nefarious "design" whose purpose was to eliminate Prospero and secure Antonio's position as a new prince indebted to Naples. My use of the phrase "new prince" derives from Machiavelli's *Prince*, though the machinations of the Italian princes in Shakespeare's play are, in many ways, un-Machiavellian. Alonso, for one, has put a good man in charge of the assassination[10]. Gonzalo follows his prince's orders, but out of his "charity" provides Prospero with food, water, garments, and the "volumes" Prospero prized above his dukedom (1.2.162-168). We are never told how Prospero, with books, but without tackle, sail, or mast, managed to get the sinking boat to the island. Was it magic from the books, the divine intercession of the "cherubin" Miranda, or luck that guided his travels? But Gonzalo's charity contributes to Prospero's survival and in time undermines Alonso's Machiavellian design, though in an unexpected way it does secure a longer-lasting alliance between the two cities by means of the marriage of Miranda and Ferdinand.

If we consider the political implications of these events, we might say that, on the one hand, Gonzalo does not conform to the high standards set by Baldassare Castiglione in *The Book of the Courtier*, where Sir Frederick maintains that a courtier called upon by his lord to carry out an immoral act should withdraw from the service of that lord (1928: 112-113). On the other hand, looking to chapters three and five of Machiavelli's *Prince*, we have to conclude that Alonso's political design, even without Gonzalo, would fall short of Machiavelli's recommendations for expansion. In chapter three, Machiavelli says of states that are annexed that they "are either of the same province and the same language, or they are not". In the former case, especially when they are not accustomed to living free, "it is enough to have extinguished the line of the prince who ruled over them, because, if former conditions are maintained and there are no differences in customs, men live quietly [...]" (1980: 12-13)[11].

Alonso adds Milan as a "member" to his state. Milan and Naples belong to one province, Italy; they share a language and some customs. However, Shakespeare represents Milan as a city accustomed to living under a prince who has earned the love of his subjects, as Prospero recalls when he indicates that "the love my people bore me" prevented his outright murder (1.2.141). We have the impression that it was, in Machiavelli's sense, a city living in liberty. Alonso, the more aggressive king, does not extinguish the line of the former ruler, as Machiavelli says the conqueror must; he leaves conditions in Milan generally unchanged by employing Antonio as a surrogate. Fearful of Prospero's popular support and unable to "set / A mark so bloody on the business" by destroying the duke and his daughter, Alonso takes the kind of middle way that Machiavelli generally rejects when he "With colours fairer painted their foul ends" (1.2.141-143). Alonso's attempt to replace the bloody mark of outright murder with a painted show, the sea "business", does not accomplish its purpose because Gonzalo is a genuinely "fair" person, not the man for this "foul" design.

From a strictly Machiavellian point of view, Alonso's actions are severely compromised because he does not extinguish the ruling family. The implications of this mistake are born out in the play when Shakespeare shows us Antonio instigating a conspiracy to assassinate Alonso. A man who seeks to "extirpate" or "supplant" a ruler must, as these words suggest, use violence to uproot (see 1.2.125, 2.1.272 and 3.3.70). And when annexing a state accustomed to political liberty, even extirpating the ruling family is not enough. As Machiavelli develops his argument in chapter three (1960: 18; 1980: 13), he asserts that to hold states accustomed to living freely under their own laws, the prince must either ruin them, or go there to live. Though chapter five focuses on states that differ in language and customs, Machiavelli makes a statement relevant to Alonso's annexation of Milan:

> And whoever becomes the master of a city accustomed to living in liberty, and does not destroy it–he waits to be destroyed by it. For it always has as a refuge in rebellion the name of liberty and its ancient orders, which are never forgotten either through length of time or through benefits[12]. (1980: 30)

Machiavelli constructs a typical either or dilemma, underlined by the rhetorical balance and antithesis of "disfaccia" and "disfatto". And destruction means more than ruining buildings. Given what Machiavelli says about the nobles in chapter four, we can safely conclude that the unmaking of a city's laws and orders would require the removal of the old ruling class, and with it the very memory of the former state; ruin would alter language itself, extinguishing family names and the name of liberty. Alonso's reluctance to shed Prospero's blood shows that he is not capable of this kind of radical action. As a consequence, he is in danger of being destroyed ("disfatto") by Antonio and by Prospero.

Prospero's survival reflects Machiavelli's belief that a prince can find no greater security than the love of his people (1980: 19). However, Shakespeare shows the danger of failing to back up that popular support with vigilance and military power when Antonio, a Renaissance Synon, opens the gates of Prospero's Milan (1.2.130) and launches his brother on a voyage of exile[13]. In a sense Shakespeare reconfigures the Italian Renaissance opposition between Florence, a republic, and Milan, a tyranny; his Milan becomes the city accustomed to living in liberty under Prospero and Naples, led by the ambitious Alonso, the state that more closely resembles a tyranny. Though their language is technically the same, the cultural distance between Milan and Naples approximates the difference of customs and orders that, according to Machiavelli, requires that a prince choose between ruining the conquered state or going there to live. Machiavelli cites "what the Turk has done in Greece" as an example of conquest overcoming differences of "language, customs and orders" by going there to live, but he does not spell out how these differences, which would include religion, will be negotiated (1980: 13; 1960: 19). If Alonso had treated Milan as a fundamentally different state, in accordance with Machiavelli's principles he should have either ruined the city and imposed a new form on it, or have collapsed the distance between Milan and Naples by identifying his interests with the interests of the conquered city. The two cities are not total opposites–Naples has its Gonzalo and Milan its Antonio, the expansionist king turns out to be a man not without a conscience and the beloved duke ends the play asking to be relieved by prayer.

But for Shakespeare, political difference, even within a city state, implies a fundamental difference that he represents as metaphorical travel, or distancing, and as translation, or a reshaping of language. The "travels" of Prospero and Miranda began when Prospero "cast" the government of Milan on his brother Antonio and to the state "grew stranger, being transported / And rapt in secret studies"(1.2.75-77). The word "transported" refers to Prospero's intellectual voyage, but as Stephen Orgel points out, in a note to his edition of the play (1987: 105), "Prospero describes his studies as a prefiguration of his abduction and dispatch to the island". The marriage of Miranda and Ferdinand promises to reduce, if not eliminate, the differences between the two political regimes, one founded in freedom and philosophy and the other in ambitious expansion. Whether Miranda will reside in Naples, or Ferdinand in Milan, we are to assume that differences will be reconciled in the playful spirit of comedy and of the chess match the betrothed couple is discovered playing in act five.

The potential for the radical political and linguistic transformation represented by Machiavelli's use of the term "ruin" resides with the two brothers, Prospero and Antonio. When Prospero recounts the events that led up to his brother's betrayal, he describes the metaphorical birth of a second, evil nature: "I thus neglecting worldly ends [...] in my false brother / Awaked an evil nature, and my trust, / Like a good parent, did beget of him / A falsehood in its contrary as great / As my trust was" (1.2.89-96). This monstrous creation is not unlike the monster Stephano encounters, the creature with a forward voice that speaks well and a backward voice that utters foul speeches (2.2.89-90). Antonio changes the language or the tune sung at court under his new rule when, as Prospero says, he "new created / The creatures that were mine, I say, or changed 'em / Or else new formed ' em" (2.2.81-83). Political rule becomes equated with a god-like power to create and shape subjects, who are the "creatures" of the ruler[14]. The founding of Prospero's Milan in liberty and philosophical studies undergoes a change, though we are not told what the state was like under Antonio's twelve-year rule. Perhaps we are meant to imagine a state more like the historical Milan of the Visconti and Sforza tyrants.

Despite this dangerous potential, Antonio does not emerge as the founder of an aggressively expansionistic state; he continues to play the role of a subordinate allied to the Neapolitan court. Antonio is a prince who knows how to take advantage of, but is also limited to occasion. However, the opportunity for a more ambitious step opens up to him on the island. As Antonio says to Sebastian when inciting him to assassinate Alonso: "Th' occasion speaks thee, and / My strong imagination sees a crown / Dropping upon thy head" (2.1.207-209). Their exchange plays on the related metaphors of language, birth, and performance. Antonio plays the schoolmaster and political midwife who will teach Sebastian the "sleepy language" of ambition, a language that requires him to wake and to kill his brother.

As ruler of the island Prospero had, like Antonio, new created the creature Caliban by giving him language. Prospero also translated the groans of Ariel, imprisoned in a pine by Sycorax, into a form of contracted service that must be performed "To th' syllable" (1.2.501). The most god-like power Prospero abjures by the end of the play is the power to "command" graves to open and release their sleepers (5.1.48-49). The one who calls the tune shapes human beings at court, or on the island, where Ariel becomes the spectacular instrument Prospero uses to control his adversaries. Both brothers have the power to create and to ruin.

Travel plays an important role in Prospero's attempt to transform and to new create his enemies, as Antonio had reshaped the creatures that were once Prospero's subjects. Before Ariel appears as harpy, the court party encounters what the stage direction calls "*several strange shapes, bringing in a banquet*". The strange, yet articulate gestures of the "shapes" move even the cynical Antonio to credit his eyes and to alter his opinion of the notorious exaggerations of travelers: "Travellers ne'er did lie, / Though fools at home condemn 'em" (3.3.26-27). Travel challenges conventional beliefs and it can in some, though not all cases, reshape character (Marienstras 1985: 171). Punished with the apparent loss of his son, Alonso hears the moral language of destiny in the tempest, which has been effectively translated for him by Ariel: "Methought the billows spoke and told me of it, / The winds did sing it to me, and the thunder– / That deep and dreadful organpipe–pronounced / The name of Prosper. It did bass my trespass" (3.3.96-99). The boatswain's line takes on added significance: "What cares these roarers for the name of king?" (1.1.16). These powers do not bow to the political authority of a king. And it is this message which sends Alonso on what might be his last voyage: "Therefore my son i'th' ooze is bedded, and / I'll seek him deeper than e'er plummet sounded, / And with him there lie mudded" (3.3.100-102). We know that this perspective was created by Prospero, who confronts the travel-weary courtiers with a fiction (Ferdinand, Prospero, and Miranda are all strangely alive) designed to arouse remorse.

On the other hand, Antonio's experience on the island does not change him; he continues to reject the moral perspective advanced by Prospero–or at least that is the conclusion I draw from the fact that he remains silent at the end of the play when we might expect some expression of remorse. However, with his enemies "distracted" (5.1.12), Prospero alone has the power that Machiavelli says can reshape a city and with it the political memory of its citizens[15]. But rather than its destruction, Shakespeare's comedy moves toward a more conventional recovery of an old order purged of its more aggressive political ambitions.

The "good old Lord Gonzalo" provides a characteristically optimistic summary of the play's travels when he proclaims, "set it down / With gold on lasting pillars: in one voyage / Did Claribel her husband find at Tunis; / And Ferdinand, her brother, found a wife / Where he himself was lost; Prospero his dukedom / In a poor isle, and all of us ourselves / When no man was his own" (5.1.208-213). Gonzalo memorializes a voyage of discovery and recovery. Prospero will finally achieve the safe retirement he first sought when he cast the government on his brother. The play's allusions to the *Aeneid* are reminders of how much Prospero is not like Aeneas, the tempest-tossed exile who meets Dido, founder of Carthage, on his way to found Rome (I.418-586). What could be more unlike Aeneas and the "Widow Dido" (2.1.77) than Prospero's relationship to the witch Sycorax, safely dead before she might have even thought about seducing the duke into a longer sojourn on the island. Only his affection for Ariel might make him an exile, but that affection serves his love for Miranda and that love points back to Milan. Prospero is not the founder of a new state. Nor does Prospero "find" himself in the guise of a philosopher who might make a cell, or cave, a new world apart from the courtly intrigues of Milan. He withdraws from the court, but cannot exchange the court for the island; as father, or philosopher, he still needs the city, though not the government of it.

So Prospero finds on the island what he, ironically, sought in the library–a variation on the freedom Ariel too seeks. He now has the freedom to pursue his studies with the government cast on the consorts Ferdinand and Miranda, who promise to be more trustworthy than his brother. The political implications of the extended alliance between Milan, Naples, and Tunis are hinted at but never spelled out in the play. How will the two powers negotiate differences of language, customs, orders, and the religion Shakespeare never mentions? After the shipwreck and apparent drowning of Ferdinand, heir to the Neapolitan crown, Alonso feels only the loss that has resulted from his voyage to North Africa (2.1.108-212). But there must have been some potential gain that inspired the original union of two kingdoms, making it important for Claribel to "find" her husband at Tunis.

Sebastian's criticism of his brother's ambitious movement outside of Europe alludes to permanent racial, or ethnic separation: "Sir, you may thank yourself for this great loss, / That would not bless our Europe with your daughter / But rather loose her to an African" (2.1.124-126). Sebastian juxtaposes "our Europe" and "an African", the proper choice that would "bless" the union and this one where she is lost. Since it is Claribel who, according to Sebastian, reluctantly goes to Tunis, it would appear that Tunisian customs and language will take precedence in the marriage and might do so in the alliance. But Alonso's power either overcame, or did not need to bother with his daughter's supposed sensitivity. Travel and marriage imply translation in the broadest sense, a linguistic, economic, and political interplay between the two states that promises some advantage to both kingdoms, though the final balance of power remains unresolved. Whatever else it may mean, the allusion to "widow Dido's time" (2.1.77) suggests that Shakespeare was thinking of the ebb and flow of political and linguistic dominance in the Mediterranean over a long period of time. And the play's allusions to the New World implies that the same forces will be at work across the Atlantic.

Machiavelli bluntly describes the necessity to ruin a city in order to provide the foundation for a new state; in Shakespeare's play, the tension between different cultures and languages gives way to the conventions of comedy, which from our perspective are the conventions of travel and translation. Sebastian describes potential difficulties in the marriage of Claribel to the King of Tunis, but comedy would have us believe that the wrangling of politics and marriage can be reconciled in a kind of chess game where the rules are the same for both players. However we interpret the exchange between Miranda and Ferdinand about playing false and wrangling at chess (5.1.172-174), we have to assume that the spirit of love will close the distance between Milan and Naples, with warfare reduced to the symbolic level of a chess match. Obviously, those rules did not apply on the island as regards the exchange between Miranda and Caliban.

At the play's conclusion Prospero says that he will retire to Milan "where / Every third thought shall be my grave" (5.1.311-312) and in the Epilogue, stripped of his magician's robes, he appears to us as a man who can neither ruin nor create. His options are to be confined to the island "Or sent to Naples" (5), a variation on Machiavelli's "go there to live". The magician's power he abjures can ruin a city, as we see when Prospero temporarily destroys the consciousness of his enemies before releasing them, as he in turn asks to be released by the audience. We are brought back to the moment where Prospero must choose between identification with his kind and the distance from them required for vengeance. Unleashing the power to ruin requires that one equate differences of language, customs, and orders with differences of kind; they cannot be translated, they have to be removed. On the other hand, the conqueror who relinquishes the power to ruin and "goes there to live" relies on the indulgence of higher powers, on the freedom to travel back to a library, and on the protection of a daughter. We leave Prospero to his final voyage, confident that he is no Lear.

[1] The island setting has been located somewhere between Naples and the north coast of Africa, or beyond the pillars of Hercules, imaginatively if not geographically appended to the New World. Useful selections and summaries of the extensive criticism are found in Vaughan and Vaughan (1997), Hulme and Sherman (2000), Graff and Phelan (2000) and Murphy (2001).

[2] See Stephen Orgel's Introduction to *The Tempest* (1987) and also Stephen Greenblatt (1990: 24-32). All references to *The Tempest* are from the Arden edition by Vaughan and Vaughan (1999); all other references to Shakespeare are from *The Arden Shakespeare* (1998).

[3] See 1.2.321 and 374, 3.2.101, 4.1.187 and 5.1.272-273.

[4] In *Twelfth Night*, Malvolio says of the inebriated singing of Sir Toby, Sir Andrew and the Clown, "Have you no wit, manners, nor honesty, but to gabble like tinkers at this time of night?" (2.3.87-89). In *All's Well That Ends Well*, the invented nonsense used to befuddle Parolles is "choughs' language, gabble enough" (4.1.19-20). In both contexts Shakespeare uses the word for something that sounds like language but is incoherent and incomprehensible.

[5] On this vexed theme, see Eric Cheyfitz (1997: 142-172).

[6] See Alden T. Vaughan (2000: 49-59).

[7] On Tunis and North Africa, see Barbara Fuchs (1997: 45-62), Jerry Brotton 1998: 23-42), Richard Wilson (1997: 333-357), Marjorie Raley (1997: 95-119), David Scott Kastan (1997: 91-103), and Robin Kirkpatrick (2000: 78-96).

[8] On the spirit of the relationship between Shakespeare and Montaigne, see Alan De Gooyer (2001: 509-531).

[9] Alonso imagines his son bedded in the foul "ooze" where he will drown himself and with his son "there lie mudded" (3.3.100-102).

[10] On this subject, see Barbara Tovey (1983: 300-302) and Geraldo U. de Sousa (1999: 170-171).

[11] The key passage, in the original, reads thus: "[...] et a possederli securamente basta avere spenta la linea del principe che li dominava. [...]" (1960: 18).

[12] In the original: "E chi diviene patrone di una città consueta a vivere libera, e non la disfaccia, aspetti di esser difatto da quella [...]" (1960: 29). Machiavelli describes ruin, destruction, dispersion, the extinction of the ruling class and of citizens and eradication of the very memory of the city's institutions, using such terms as *ruinarle, disfare, disfaccia, disfatto, disuniscano, dissipano, dimenticare,* and *spegnerle.*

[13] See *Aeneid* II, 255. On Shakespeare and Virgil, see John Pitcher (1984: 193-215), Robert Wiltenburg (1987: 159-168), Donna B. Hamilton (1990), Robin Headlam Wells (2000: 69-84), and Barbara A. Mowat (2000: 27-36).

[14] See Orgel's note to 1.2.156-157 (1987: 109).

[15] On Machiavelli and memory, see Jack D'Amico (1991: 24-25).

References

Brotton, Jerry. 1998. '"This Tunis, sir, was Carthage": Contesting Colonialism in *The Tempest*' in Ania Loomba and Martin Orkin (eds) *Post-Colonial Shakespeares*. New York, NY: Routledge. 23-42.

Castiglione, Baldassare. 1928. *The Book of the Courtier* (tr. Sir Thomas Hoby). New York, NY: Dutton.

Cheyfitz, Eric. 1997. *The Poetics of Imperialism: Translation and Colonization from* The Tempest *to* Tarzan. Philadelphia, PA: University of Pennsylvania Press.

D'Amico, Jack. 1991. 'Machiavelli and the Perspective of Memory' in *Machiavelli Studies* 4: 17-37.

De Gooyer, Alan. 2001. '"Their senses I'll restore": Montaigne and *The Tempest* Reconsidered' in Murphy (2001): 509-531.

De Sousa, Geraldo U. 1999. *Shakespeare's Cross-Cultural Encounters*. New York, NY: St. Martin's.

Fuchs, Barbara. 1997. 'Conquering Islands: Contextualizing *The Tempest*' in *Shakespeare Quarterly* 48(1): 45-62.

Graff, Gerald and James Phelan (eds). 2000. *The Tempest: A Case Study in Critical Controversy*. Boston, MA: Beford.

Greenblatt, Stephen J. 1990. *Learning to Curse: Essays in Early Modern Culture*. New York, NY: Routledge.

Hamilton, Donna B. 1990. *Virgil and* The Tempest: *The Politics of Imitation*. Columbus, OH: Ohio State University Press.

Hulme, Peter and William H. Sherman (eds). 2000. *The Tempest and Its Travels*. Philadelphia, PA: University of Pennsylvania Press.

Kastan, David Scott. 1997. '"The Duke of Milan / And His Brave Son": Dynastic Politics in *The Tempest*' in Vaughan and Vuaghan (1997): 91-103.

Kirkpatrick, Robin. 2000. 'The Italy of *The Tempest*' in Hulme and Sherman (2000): 78-96.

Lowenthal, David. 1997. *Shakespeare and the Good Life: Ethics and Politics in Dramatic Form*. Lanham, MD: Rowman & Littlefield.

Machiavelli, Niccolò. 1960. *Il Principe e Discorsi* (ed. Sergio Bertelli). Milan: Feltrinelli.

–. 1980. *The Prince* (tr. Leo Paul S. de Alvarez). Irving, TX: University of Dallas Press.

Marienstras, Richard. 1985. *New Perspectives on the Shakesparean World* (tr. Janet Lloyd). New York, NY: Cambridge University Press.

Montaigne, Michel Eyquem de. 1910. *Montaigne's Essays* (tr. John Florio). 3 vols. New York, NY: Dutton.

Mowat, Barbara A. 2000. '"Knowing I loved my books": Reading *The Tempest* Intertextually' in Hulme and Sherman (2000): 27-36.

Murphy, Patrick M. 2001. *The Tempest: Critical Essays*. New York, NY: Routledge.

Orgel, Stephen. See William Shakespeare (1987).

Pitcher, John. 1984. 'A Theatre of the Future: The *Aeneid* and *The Tempest*' in *Essays in Criticism* 34(3): 193-215.

Raley, Marjorie. 1997. 'Claribel's Husband' in Joyce Green MacDonald (ed.) *Race, Ethnicity, and Power in the Renaissance*. Madison, WI: Fairleigh Dickinson University Press. 95-119.

Shakespeare, William. 1987. *The Tempest* (ed. Stephen Orgel). New York, NY: Oxford University Press.

–. 1998. *The Arden Shakespeare: Complete Works* (eds Richard Proudfoot *et al.*). Walton-on-Thames: Thomas Nelson.

–. 1999. *The Tempest* (eds Virginia Mason Vaughan and Alden T. Vaughan). The Arden Shakespeare, Third Series. London: Thomson Learning.

Tovey, Barbara. 1983. 'Shakespeare's Apology for Imitative Poetry: *The Tempest* and *The Republic*' in *Interpretation: A Journal of Political Philosophy* 11(3): 275-316.

Vaughan, Virginia Mason and Alden T. Vaughan (eds). 1997. *Critical Essays on Shakespeare's The Tempest*. New York, NY: Cambridge University Press.

Vaughan, Alden T. 2000. 'Trinculo's Indian: American Natives in Shakespeare's England' in Hulme and Sherman (2000): 49-59.

Wells, Robin Headlam. 2000. 'Blessing Europe: Virgil, Ovid and Seneca in *The Tempest*' in Michele Marrapodi (ed.) *Shakespeare and Intertextuality: The Transition of Cultures Between Italy and England in the Early Modern Period.* Rome: Bulzoni. 69-84.

Wilson, Richard. 1997. 'Voyage to Tunis: New History and the Old World of *The Tempest*' in *ELH* 64(2): 333-357.

Wiltenburg, Robert. 1987. 'The *Aeneid* and *The Tempest*' in *Shakespeare Survey* 39: 159-168.

4.3. Tamburlaine: the Migration and Translation of Marlowe's Arabic Sources

Howard Miller

Christopher Marlowe's character, Tamburlaine the Great, bears some uncanny similarities to the historical Timur as he was portrayed in Arabic accounts. These similarities may well be the results of the keenness of Marlowe's insight, of the extraordinary fertility of his imagination. However, what remains to be considered is the possibility that Marlowe, while he was a student at Cambridge, might have studied with scholars of Hebrew and Arabic, converted Jews who had migrated to England and who would have been able to make the historical Timur accessible. In particular, scholars such as Phillip Ferdinand or, more likely, Franciscus Raphelengius, would have known Timur through the most authoritative texts of the time. Did these traveling translators, who would have known, for example, Ibn 'Arabshah's biography of Timur, somehow convey their knowledge to Marlowe, who then used it in order to create his Tamburlaine? The textual similarities are provocative indeed; they suggest that Marlowe's great creation might be, at least in part, the result of travel and translation.
Keywords: Arabic, Ibn 'Arabshah, Marlowe, Tamburlaine, Timur, translation, travel.

By the end of the sixteenth century, when Christopher Marlowe wrote his *Tamburlaine* plays, most Western accounts of the Central Asian tyrant had become little more than myths which, in the words of Vivien Thomas and William Tydeman (1994: 70), "supplied a graphic case history through which to validate the legitimacy of relentless aspiration, deplore the vagaries of Fortune's favours, or regret absolute ruthlessness inseparable from martial power". The story of the historic Timur had grown into a "moralized saga for Western christendom" (Battenhouse 1941: 137) which had "drawn to itself various elements of the Romance tradition" (Godschalk 1974: 103). In other words, Europe's Tamburlaine bore only a passing resemblance to Asia's Timur.

Yet, despite this, most scholars have conceded that Marlowe was able to go beyond the moralized, didactic, heavy-handed and often incorrect material to produce a believable Asian tyrant, one that bore a great deal of resemblance to Timur himself. Exactly what allowed him to do so is impossible to prove with any certainty; but as I hope to show, it is possible that Marlowe's uncannily true vision of the tyrant came to him because of a knowledge of Arabic that he might have gained through his studies at Cambridge, a knowledge made possible by the presence of Jewish scholars who had migrated there. First, however, a brief consideration of the main sources is in order.

Although most sixteenth century Western accounts of Tamburlaine were lacking in historical verity, there did exist a number of important Eastern biographies and firsthand accounts of the historical Timur, a few of which actually circulated on the edges of Europe. (Henceforth, for clarity's sake, I will refer to the historical figure as Timur, and the subject of the Western biographies and Marlowe's play as Tamburlaine.) These accounts of the historical Timur, many of which are carefully-researched, nearly contemporaneous histories of Timur's career, appear in Armenian, Bulgarian, Georgian, Greek, Latin, Italian, Spanish, Turkish, Uigar, Persian, and Arabic.

Among the eastern sources, two of the most often cited by modern historians, are the "official" Persian biographies of Timur, both of which are titled *Zafar Nama* ("Book of Victories"). The first *Zafar Nama*, ordered by Timur from court historian Nizam ad-Din Shami, was presented to Timur before his death in 1405. Following the official dictates that a history of Timur's reign should be written in a simple, unpretentious style, Nizam ad-Din used the court records to prepare a concise history of Timur's military campaigns. The second *Zafar Nama* appeared in 1424. It too was written by a Timurid court historian, Sharaf ad-Din 'Ali al-Yazdi. Ornate and wordy in the extreme, this second *Zafar Nama* was a reworking of the first, with material that Sharaf ad-Din added. Of the contemporaneous biographies, Sharaf ad-Din's is the most detailed. Unfortunately it is also the most consistently flattering of Timur, going so far as to turn his very infrequent military setbacks into victories. Sharaf ad-Din's *Zafar Nama* was the first of the two to appear in a European language, French, in 1722.

Another source, unlikely to have been familiar in the West but nonetheless pregnant with meaning and possibility, recounts the meeting of Timur and the great Arab philosopher and historian, Wali ad-Din 'Abd ar-Rahman Ibn Khaldun. Timur, who was almost as devoted to philosophical disputation as he was to conquest, instigated the meeting when he learned of Ibn Khaldun's presence in the city of Damascus, captured by the tyrant in 1401. (The indispensable record of this meeting, from Ibn Khaldun's own account, has been edited and translated by Walter Fischel under the title, *Ibn Khaldun and Tammerlane*.) For his part, Ibn Khaldun, who had once met the Spanish king, Pedro the Cruel, was less than eager to meet with the conqueror of the Eastern world. According to the accounts in Ibn Khaldun's autobiography, *at-Ta 'rif,* the historian met with Timur on 35 separate occasions over the 48 days immediately following the fall of Damascus in 1401. Ibn Khaldun was treated kindly by Timur, and the pair, speaking through a translator, discussed religion, heroes in history, including Alexander and the Caesars, the geography and history of Spain and the Maghrib, and the disposition and security of some of the more noteworthy captives taken in Damascus. At the end of the meetings, Ibn Khaldun, who found Timur to be intelligent and courteous, was allowed to return home to Cairo. In fact, during the meeting Timur offered to buy a mule from Ibn Khaldun, a mule which was quickly offered up as a gift to the Conqueror of the World. Later, as Ibn Khaldun was leaving Damascus on his way home to Cairo, presumably on a rented ass, an emissary from Timur caught up with the historian and gave him a small purse of gold, one which exactly equaled the value of the mule that had been given to Timur.

What makes this meeting between Timur and Ibn Khaldun at once important and frustrating is the reputation of Ibn Khaldun himself. He was, according to George Sarton (1948: vol. 3, 1775-1776), "the greatest theoretician of history, the greatest philosopher of man's experience, not only of the Middle Ages, but the whole period extending from the time of the great classical historians down to that of Machiavelli, Bodin and Vico". And Arnold Toynbee (1935: vol. 3, 322) called Ibn Khaldun's monumental work of historical philosophy, *Muqaddimah*, "the greatest book of its kind that has ever yet been created by any mind in any time or place". So the importance of the record left by Ibn Khaldun of his meeting with Timur at Damascus cannot be overestimated. Yet, it is precisely the reputation of Ibn Khaldun that makes this account problematical. Phillip Hitti (1968: 254) would note that "[h]is meteoric career flashed across the North African firmament leaving hardly a glare behind". In other words, Ibn Khaldun had no immediate predecessors and left no immediate successors. After his death in 1406, his reputation and his works were quickly forgotten by the Arabs, whose high culture was in decline, and were virtually unheard of among the Europeans, who had not yet begun their Renaissance. Not until the early decades of the nineteenth century was his importance recognized by European Orientalists and historians, and thus an important account of Timur was unknown in the West.

Oddly enough, one of the first times Ibn Khaldun's name appears in a western book is in Jacob Golius's 1638 Latin translation of an Arabic biography of Timur, one written by Ahmad bin Muhammad bin 'Arabshah, in the early fifteenth century. This work, titled *'Aja'ib al-maqdur fi nawa'ib Timur*, is considered one of the highlights of late-Classical Arabic literature.

Like Ibn Khaldun's meeting with Timur, Ibn 'Arabshah's *'Aja'ib al-maqdur* is a result, albeit an indirect one, of the tyrant's conquest of Damascus in 1401. It was the regular custom of Timur to remove the majority of the scholars, craftsmen and artists, from whatever city he conquered, to Samarkand, where they would be required to work to the greater glory of Timur and his Central Asian capital. Included in the forced migration from Damascus was Ibn 'Arabshah, then the twelve-year-old-son of a well-known religious scholar. The young Damascene was trained as a clerk, fluent in Turkish, Persian, and his native Arabic, by the officials of Timur's court. Eventually, after the death of Timur in 1405, Ibn 'Arabshah made his way to Adrianople, where he entered service with Sultan Muhammed I, the son and successor of the Turkish Sultan Bayazid as a confidential secretary. According to Clement Huart,

> [t]he Sultan received him with great honor, took him into his own service. [...] He commissioned him to translate Persian and Arabic books into Turkish, made him his private secretary, and employed him to keep up Arabic, Persian, and Turkish correspondence with foreign courts. (1966: 364)

With the death of Muhammed I in 1421, Ibn 'Arabshah returned to his native Damascus, where he led a contemplative life and dedicated himself to editing his works. The *'Aja'ib al-maqdur* is most likely the product of the period between 1411, when Ibn 'Arabshah entered service with Muhammed I, and 1428, when the author left Damascus on a pilgrimage to Mecca, after which he settled in Cairo where he died in 1450.

In comparison to other Eastern histories of Timur, most of which are hagiographic pieces written by Timurid court historians, Ibn 'Arabshah's account is unstintingly hostile towards its subject. In the words of Edward Sokol (1977: 261), it "pulses with hatred". Filled with invective, with chapter titles such as "An account of what happened to that bastard Timur in Subzuar with Sharif Muhammed, a leader of a band of immoral men" (1986: 74)[1]. The *'Aja'ib al-maqdur* is obviously Ibn 'Arabshah's literary revenge on the destroyer of Damascus. It is also a revenge of sorts for the author's patron, Muhammed I, whose father Bayazid I (Bajazeth in Tamburlaine) was captured by Timur at the Battle of Ankara in 1402. However, despite Ibn 'Arabshah's great hatred of Timur, which is evident throughout his work, he "does not deny Timur his high intellect, organizational talent, or military genius" (Sokol 1977: 261). And although Ibn 'Arabshah passionately hates Timur, he still shows concern for historical truth. He is careful to use official records, eyewitness reports, and the work of other historians to build his case against the tyrant, presenting both Timur's horrifying cruelty and his gracious generosity. Because of this, the *'Aja'ib al-maqdur* is an important check on the official, fawning Timurid histories, and an important source for modern historians.

Less certain than the value of Ibn 'Arabshah's biography to modern historians is its position in the development of the fifteenth and sixteenth-century Western European accounts of Tamburlaine. Since the first translations of this work into a European language did not appear until Golius's Latin version of 1638, and Pierre Vattie's 1658 French edition, the direct transmittal of Ibn 'Arabshah's history of Timur to Marlowe is considered highly unlikely. For this reason, Ibn 'Arabshah's biography is generally, and with seeming justification, ignored by literary scholars in the search for the sources of Marlowe's *Tamburlaine* plays. Yet, when closely examined in conjunction with Marlowe's probable sources, and the plays themselves, the *'Aja'ib al-maqdur* reveals a number of intriguing similarities with the play; similarities that do not exist between the play and its most frequently cited probable sources. Chief among these similarities is a surprising congruency between the physical appearance and character of Marlowe's Tamburlaine and Ibn 'Arabshah's Timur. Likewise, a handful of incidents surrounding the capture of the Ottoman Turkish sultan Bajazeth, an event that occurred in 1402 in real life, and Act III in Marlowe's play, are strikingly similar. What becomes clear when the *Tamburlaine* plays are laid alongside Ibn 'Arabshash's earlier Arabic work is that Marlowe has selected many incidents and details from his probable Western sources that most likely have their bases in Ibn 'Arabshah's *'Aja'ib al-maqdur*.

Roughly the first four-fifths of *'Aja'ib al-maqdur* is taken up with a chronological retelling of Timur's military campaigns and diplomatic intrigues.

The final sections of the book, which are a detailed study of Timur's person and character, begin with the chapter entitled, "fi sufat timur al-badi'a wa ma jubala 'alihi min sajiha wa tabi'ha"(1986: 450), or "Of the Wonderful Gifts of Timur and his Nature and Character" (1936: 295). The physical description that begins this chapter is perhaps the most often quoted passage from Ibn 'Arabshah's work:

> Timur was tall and of lofty stature as though he belonged to the remnants of the Amalekites, big in brow and head, mighty in strength and courage, wonderful in nature, white in colour, mixed with red, but not dark, stout of limb, with broad shoulders, thick fingers, long legs, perfect build, long beard, dry hands, lame on the right side, with eyes like candles, without brilliance, powerful in voice; he did not fear death [...]. (1936: 295)

Compare the specific details of Ibn 'Arabshah's description of Timur with Marlowe's Tamburlaine[2]:

> Of stature tall, and straightly fashionèd,
> Like his desire lift upwards and divine;
> So large of limbs, his joints so strongly knit,
> Such breadth of shoulders as might mainly bear
> Old Atlas' burthen; 'twixt his manly pitch,
> A pearl, worth more than all the world, is placed
> Wherein by curious sovereignty of art
> Are fixed his piercing instruments of sight,
> Whose fiery circles bear encompassèd
> A heaven of heavenly bodies in their spheres,
> That guides his steps and actions to the throne,
> Where honor sits invested royally:
> Pale of complexion, wrought in him with passion,
> Thirsting with sovereignty and love of arms;
> His lofty brows in folds do figure death,
> And in their smoothness amity and life;
> About them hangs a knot of amber hair,
> Wrappèd in curls, as fierce Achilles' was,
> On which the breath of heaven delights to play,
> Making it dance with wanton majesty.
> His arms and fingers, long, and snowy
> Betokening valor and excess of strength–
> In every part proportioned like the man
> Should make the world subdued to Tamburlaine. (*Part One*: 2.1.7-30)

Both the fictional Tamburlaine and the historical Timur are tall. Both are broad shouldered, stout limbed, large browed, and have a pale complexion infused with red. And both have eyes that glow from within.

The physical resemblance between the 'Arabshah's historical and Marlowe's fictional Tamburlaine is striking. But as W. L. Godschalk (1974: 106) has cautioned, "the judicious source hunter must be skeptical of finding a unique source for Marlowe's conventional description of his Scythian warrior as tall, broad shoulderd, and fiery eyed". Many of the European versions of the Tamburlaine story contain the tall, broad-shouldered, fiery-eyed Scythian. Audiences expect their world-beaters to be physically imposing men, and in Tamburlaine they are not disappointed. Yet this belief in a completely conventionalized account ignores Ibn 'Arabshah's first-hand account of Timur. It is unlikely that Ibn 'Arabshah, an unremittingly hostile biographer, would go out of his way to make his hated subject more appealing by improving his appearance. And lest we forget, Ibn 'Arabshah, as a member of the court in Samarkand, has an advantage that Marlowe's sources do not; he has seen Timur. Indeed, when Soviet archeologists opened Timur's tomb in 1941, they found the body inside to be of a man of above average stature, around 5'10" tall, broad shouldered, lame on the right side, with, oddly enough, a hank of red hair still attached to his desiccated skull.

Like the physical description, the details of Timur's parentage and early life are another area of congruence. Marlowe's Tamburlaine proclaims his low parentage as a badge of honor, "I am a lord, for so my deeds shall prove, / And yet a shepherd by my parentage" (*Part One*: 1.2.34-35). This belief in Tamburlaine's low birth is presented by many of Marlowe's possible sources. And it is also exactly in keeping with the version of Timur's youth found in Ibn 'Arabshah:

> He and his father were shepherds, belonging to a mixed horde, lacking either reason or religion [...] he himself from his youth excelled in keenness of intellect and strength; but because of poverty began to commit acts of brigandage [...]. (1936: 1-2)

Despite this low birth, both the young Timur and Tamburlaine are possessed of amazing powers of persuasion and outlandish visions of world conquest. Ibn 'Arabshah's Timur convinces his young outlaw friends to swear an oath of allegiance, telling them that he is destined to be "Lord of the Stars and Master of the Kings of the age" (*ibid*.: 4). Likewise, Marlowe's Tamburlaine convinces Theridamas, who is at the head of a thousand armed horsemen, to turn traitor and join him in his conquest of the world. When Theridamas acknowledges Tamburlaine's ability to persuade–"Won with thy words, and conquered with thy looks" (*Part One*: 1.2.228)–he is asserting Tamburlaine's ability as surely as Ibn 'Arabshah asserts Timur's persuasive ability.

Just as the manner of their beginnings is similar, so too is the manner of their deaths. Both Timur and Tamburlaine go to their deaths still thinking, not of what they had conquered, but of what they would leave unconquered. As Tamburlaine is dying, he orders a map brought to him, so that he may "see how much / Is left for me to conquer all the world", and it is during this scene that his famous lament is made: "And shall I die, and this unconquerèd?" (*Part Two*: 5.3.124-125, 151). This scene, which is without precedent in Marlowe's sources, could well have been lifted from Ibn 'Arabshah's life of Timur. The historical Timur died, at the age of seventy, of a fever contracted while crossing a frozen Central Asian river in the middle of a particularly cold winter. He had begun what he hoped would be the conquest of China–a wildly audacious undertaking, considering not only the logistics involved, but also the size of the Ming Dynasty Middle Empire. Both Tamburlaine and his historical predecessor Timur are, at their deaths, still possessed of the ambition which led them to subjugate a goodly portion of their worlds. Although, Ibn 'Arabshah's Timur does not openly lament what he has left unconquered, there is no doubt in the mind of the reader that he is still driven by a lust for conquest.

Another interesting congruency between Tamburlaine and the historical Timur is revealed in their attitudes towards their impending deaths. Marlowe shows his central character raging against the unseen deity who would end his life:

> What daring god torments my body thus,
> And seeks to conquer mighty Tamburlaine?
> Shall sickness prove me now to be a man,
> That have been termed the terror of the world?
> Techelles and the rest, come, take your swords,
> And threaten him whose hand afflicts my soul.
> Come, let us march against the powers of heaven,
> And set black streamers in the firmament,
> To signify the slaughter of the gods.
> Ah, friends, what shall I do? I cannot stand.
> Come carry me to war against the gods
> That thus envy the health of Tamburlaine. (*Part Two*: 5.3.42-53)

Ibn 'Arabshah says that Timur, seized in the throes of his final illness, "ceased not to oppose fate and wage war with fortune and obstinately resist the grace of God Almighty, wherefore he could not but fail and endure the greater punishments for wickedness" (1936: 232). Both Ibn 'Arabshah and Marlowe show their central characters engaged in a final unwinnable war against God. Both have beaten and humiliated every earthly foe, including the mighty Ottoman Sultan, yet they are unable to escape the final reckoning. They try desperately to turn Death into another contest winnable by force of arms. But at the end Tamburlaine recognizes that Death, not Tamburlaine, is the "monarch of the earth" (5.3.216). And for Timur, "the butler of death gave him to drink a bitter cup and soon he believed that which he had resolutely denied [...]" (1936: 232).

With a few notable exceptions and a good deal of dramatic license, the incidents portrayed as historical events in *Tamburlaine, Part One* follow the course of history as relayed by the various Eastern accounts. Perhaps the most important event that appears in Marlowe's likely sources, in *Tamburlaine*, and in *'Aja'ib al-maqdur* is the defeat and capture of the Ottoman Sultan at the Battle of Ankara in 1402. It is Tamburlaine's greatest victory, as Bajazeth is his most worthy opponent. In the play, the events that lead up to the battle are a dramatic invention. Marlowe represents a confrontation first between Tamburlaine and Bajazeth and then between Zenocrate and the Sultan's wife, Zabina, by having the characters come on stage together and verbally exchange taunts.

While this seems like a complete Marlovian invention, there does seem to be a precedent of sorts in *'Aja'ib al-maqdur*. Ibn 'Arabshah records an exchange of letters, filled with wordy threats and high boasting. Timur's letter enrages the Ottoman Sultan because Timur has disrespectfully written to him as an equal. The Turk's reply is wordy and dismissive: "I know that this speech will rouse you to invade our countries: but if you should not come, may your wives be condemned to triple divorce [...]" (1936: 173). Ibn 'Arabshah also records Timur's reply and the reason for his high anger and subsequent invasion: "The son of Othman is mad, for he was prolix and sealed the purpose of his letter with the mention of women" (*ibid.*: 173). While Marlowe's version of the exchange of insults is more dramatic and immediate, Ibn 'Arabshah's exhibits the same spirit of verbal conflict.

The results of the battle between Bajazeth and Tamburlaine are in some respects a near mirror image of the historical results as recounted by Ibn 'Arabshah. In the play, Tamburlaine captures Bajazeth and Zabina, locks them in a cage and treats them like animals (*Part One*: 4.2.1-126). Rather than submit to continued humiliation at the hands of the hated Tamburlaine, the Turk and his wife commit suicide (*ibid.*: 5.1.286-320). By comparison, Ibn 'Arabshah's account of Timur's treatment of Bayazid is similar to Marlowe's fictional reconstruction. (Of course there is no Zabina and no Zenocrate. Like most Muslim rulers both Timur and Bayazid were polygamous. And Zenocrate's historical antecedents have long been sought in Marlowe's likely sources, with little success. She seems to be a complete invention of Marlowe's. This is likewise true for Zabina.) Instead of a single wife each, what Ibn 'Arabshah presents is a host of nameless concubines and wives for both men. However, he does show Timur exacting his revenge for Bayazid's mention of women by shaming the Turk's wives and concubines. Timur orders a great feast and has the shackled Bayazid brought to it, seating him in a place of honor. When the wine was served,

> Ibn Othman saw that the cupbearers were his consorts and that all of them were his wives and concubines; then the world seemed black to him and he thought the likeness of the agonies of death sweet and his breast was torn and his heart burned [...]. (1936: 188)

In addition to the horror of seeing his wives and concubines treated like serving wenches, Bayazid is locked in an iron cage and publicly mocked by Timur (*ibid.*: 188).

The matter of the iron cage is an interesting one. Samuel Chew gives a good accounting of its use in the various stories–an accounting that stresses the inaccuracy of the iron cage story:

> Pope Pius II first gave currency to this story in western Europe in his *Asiae Europaeque Elegantissima descriptio*, 1534. Thereafter it became one of the most popular incidents in European accounts of the Scythian conqueror. Joseph von Hammer-Purgstall argued long ago (*Geschichte des Osmanischen Reiches,* Pest, 1827, I, 317f.) that the legend

owed its origin to a misunderstanding of the Turkish word 'kafes' which may mean
either a litter or a cage. (1937: 469)

The idea, generally accepted by most scholars, that the provenance of the iron
cage rests on a dubious piece of translation flies in the face of Ibn 'Arabshah:
Bayazid "had been shut in an iron cage at the camp of Timur, which Timur did
only for revenge [...]" (1936: 197). This tidbit, supplied almost in passing by
Ibn 'Arabshah, and unknown in most of the usual eastern sources, would
appear to be the earliest mention of the Sultan's confinement in a cage. It is
unlikely that Ibn 'Arabshah, who was a skilled translator of Turkish, Persian,
and Arabic (noted for having translated a number of Arabic classics into
Turkish for the library of the Sultan Muhammed I), would have mistaken *litter*
for *cage*.

In addition to the confinement of the defeated Turkish Sultan in an
iron cage, there are certain other incidents and facts that seem to have their
genesis in Ibn 'Arabshah, and that seem to have a certain staying power
through successive Western retelling. Of course, the physical description of
Timur, especially the fiery eyes; the destruction of a group of innocent
supplicants outside the walls of a besieged city; the complex relationship with
God–at once His servant and His curse; even Ibn 'Arabshah's didactic tone and
incessant moralizing, have found their way into European accounts of
Tamburlaine.

Although the search for Marlowe's sources has focused almost
exclusively on the Western accounts nearest to him in time, the possibility that
Marlowe had some access to primary Eastern historical material cannot be
discounted. The first critic to suggest this was Hugh Dick, who in 1949 traced
a possible connection between Marlowe and Richard Knolles, the author of a
work entitled *The Generall Historie of the Turkes*, published in London in
1603. Dick (1949: 154-166) makes this connection through Sir Roger
Manwood of Kent, an important figure around Marlowe's hometown of
Canterbury who was well known by both Marlowe and Knolles. What makes
this possible connection so interesting is that Knolles's *Generall Historie* is a
compilation and distillation, in English, of a number of the Tamburlaine
narratives. Dick hypothesizes that Knolles, who undoubtedly spent a great deal
of time working on his history–twelve years according to Samuel Chew (1937:
112)–may have been able to introduce Marlowe to the Eastern stories on which
the European histories are based.

A second possible connection has been suggested as well. Godschalk
(1974: 145) points out a series of strong parallels between the texts of
Tamburlaine the Great, Part Two and *Histoire du grand Tamerlanes,* by Jean
Du Bec-Crespin, first published in 1594. Du Bec-Crespin's story of
Tamburlaine was supposedly translated from Arabic into French by "Alhacen",
an Arab whom Du Bec-Crespin supposedly met in the Near East sometime
before 1578. Godschalk's theory about how these parallels came about is
explainable by two possibilities:

Howard Miller

(1) Marlowe consulted the same basic material as did Du Bec, or (2) Marlowe read Du Bec's account before writing 2 Tamburlaine and probably after writing Part One. The first possibility cannot be disproven, and it may well be that Du Bec is retelling eastern stories of Emir Timur which were gaining currency in late sixteenth-century Europe. (*ibid.*: 145)

For the second possibility, Godschalk provides a more speculative theory. If Du Bec's translated Eastern account was available in manuscript during the late 1580s, it is possible, according to Godschalk (*ibid.*: 146), that Marlowe, who traveled to France on a secret mission for Elizabeth's government, came in contact with it. Godschalk admits that his theory is difficult to verify. "Whether he met Du Bec while in France or had a chance to read his manuscript history, we have no right to guess–but Marlowe's shadowy journey allows us to entertain the possibility" (*ibid.*: 146). Of course even if Marlowe had come in contact with Du Bec's history of Tamburlaine, there is some question about whether it is an authentic Eastern history or merely an invention of Du Bec's imagination.

A third possibility, however, one that has not yet been fully explored by scholars, lies in the fact that Edward VI decreed in 1549 that Hebrew should be an important part of the course of study for the Master of Arts degree at Cambridge. "The Master of Arts, after the time of his regency had elapsed, was required, unless intending the study of law or medicine, to devote his attention solely to theology and Hebrew" (Mullinger 1888: vol. 2, 111). Although completely uncommented upon by his biographers, it seems likely that Marlowe, who took the M.A. in March of 1587, studied Hebrew. Of course, the fact that he probably studied Hebrew does not in itself establish a conclusive link to any Eastern account of Timur. More persuasive of a possible link between Marlowe and the stories of the east, however, are the personal histories of the men who taught Hebrew at Cambridge–the men with whom Marlowe would have studied.

Cecil Roth (1964: 146) notes that beginning in about 1540, when the first Regius professor of Hebrew was named for Cambridge, "a few Jews by birth (generally converted) began to haunt the purlieus of the universities". One of the most intriguing of these converted Jews, and one of the few instructors of Hebrew mentioned by name in the various histories of Cambridge, is Phillip Ferdinand. According to the *Encyclopaedia Judaica* (Roth 1972: vol. 6, 1227), Ferdinand was born in Poland in 1555, lived for some time in Constantinople, converted to Catholicism and then Protestantism, and then finally made his way first to Oxford and then to Cambridge, teaching Hebrew in both places. He was later appointed professor of Hebrew and Arabic at Leiden University in 1599, a post he filled until his death in 1601 (Brugman 1979: 202). His stint as a student of languages in Constantinople, a city then under Ottoman rule, would have undoubtedly placed him in contact with Eastern historians and translators familiar with works such as Ibn 'Arabshah's *'Aja'ib al-maqdur fi nawa'ib*

Timur. And the oral transmission of this information to a diligent student, one with a particular interest in a figure of the East, would have been the most natural thing.

Phillip Ferdinand, however, who appeared at Cambridge in the mid-1590s, was perhaps a few years too late to have instructed Marlowe, but the record of another possible tutor, Franciscus Raphelengius, may be closer to the mark. Raphelengius, who is famous as a bookseller and printer, and recognized as a pioneer of Arabic instruction at Leiden, "spent some time in Cambridge", apparently in the early 1580s; appointed to teach Hebrew at Leiden in 1586, he also gave instruction in the elements of Arabic (Brugman 1979: 202). (Hebrew was often studied in conjunction with Arabic, since it was thought that the second language would help in understanding the first.) That Raphelengius filled a similar purpose at Cambridge seems likely. And it is likely that Marlowe, who probably did not know much, if any, Arabic, did study Hebrew with converted Sephardic Jews who knew Arabic. A direct connection between Marlowe and either Raphelengius, Ferdinand, or a third, unknown instructor of Eastern languages has not been made, but the possibility that one existed is a real one. Such a connection would provide yet another possible method through which Marlowe could have received information about the Eastern version of the life of Timur. From scholars such as Ferdinand and Raphelengius, Marlowe could have heard stories of Timur taken from the primary texts, stories that would make their way, eventually, into his Tamburlaine plays.

Many modern critics have commented favorably on Marlowe's reputation as a scholar, and he most certainly read many of the available accounts of the *vita tamerlani*. When Marlowe studied the various accounts of Tamburlaine he encountered a mare's nest of contradictory facts and blatant moralizing. As a dramatist he was free to pick out those items that seemed to him the most accurate, and reject those that didn't meet his needs. In some instances, if the facts didn't suit his temperament or his conception of what an oriental despot should be like, he rejected them and invented more suitable ones. That Marlowe went through this selection process is proven by his rejection of Timur's lameness. Even though many of his potential sources commented on Timur's injury, Marlowe makes a conscious effort to exclude it from his play, apparently because he believed it would make his Tamburlaine less impressive.

Combine Marlowe's scholarship with a series of texts that contain various levels of truth and his desire to produce a play about the getting and legitimizing of power, and it becomes possible to see how Marlowe could begin to match the Oriental original. His selections, such as his rejection of Timur's lameness in favor of physical perfection, obey a certain sophisticated logic. He selected those facts that allowed him to create a self-made man–a character who usurps the existing order and establishes a new order. Because Marlowe favored complexity over simplicity, his object was to make Tamburlaine simultaneously as attractive and as odious as possible. Perhaps, as Roy Battenhouse and others suggest, he was guided in this selection process by the thinking of Machiavelli, or perhaps he was guided by his own knowledge of the demons that drive the human psyche. In either event, Marlowe chose from his sources many incidents that had a basis in actual history. The resulting character–a wholly believable, if somewhat stylized, world conqueror, a man able to stride onto the stage and "hold the Fates bound fast in iron chains" (*Part One*: 1.2.174)–came to life because of his creator's extraordinary imagination. But if Marlowe had no knowledge of the Arabic texts–that is, if Ferdinand and Raphelengius and other scholars had not migrated to England to teach Hebrew and Arabic–would Marlowe's imagination have flourished in quite the same way?

[1] All translations from the original are my own. Henceforth, however, I shall quote mainly from John Herne Sanders's translation of this work.

[2] All references to Marlowe's plays will come from the editions edited by Fraser and Rabkin.

References

Battenhouse, Roy. 1941. *Marlowe's Tamburlaine: A Study in Renaissance Moral Philosophy*. Nashville, TN: Vanderbilt University Press.

Brugman, J. 1979. *Arabic Studies in the Netherlands*. Leiden: E. J. Brill.

Chew, Samuel. 1937. *The Crescent and the Rose: Islam and England during the Renaissance*. London: Oxford University Press.

Dick, Hugh G. 1949. 'Tamburlaine Sources Once More' in *Studies in Philology* 46: 154-166.

Fischel, Walter J. 1957. *Ibn Khaldun in Egypt*. Berkeley, CA and Los Angeles, CA: University of California Press.

Godschalk, W. L. 1974. *The Marlovian World Picture*. The Hague: Mouton.

Hitti, Phillip K. 1968. *Makers of Arab History*. New York, NY: St. Martin's Press.

Huart, Clement. 1966. *A History of Arabic Literature*. Beirut: Khayats.

Ibn 'Arabshah, Ahmed. 1936. *Tamerlane or Timur the Great Amir* (tr. John Herne Sanders). London: Luzac & Co.

–. 1986. *'Aja'ib al-maqdur fi nawa'ib Timur*. Beirut: Musasat ar-Rasala.

Ibn Khaldun. 1952. *Ibn Khaldun and Tammerlane* (ed. Walter J. Fischel). Berkeley, CA and Los Angeles, CA: University of California Press.

Knolles, Richard. 1603. *The Generall Historie of the Turkes*. London.

Marlowe, Christopher. 1976. *Tamburlaine the Great, Part One and Tamburlaine the Great, Part Two* in Russell A. Fraser and Norman Rabkin (eds) *Drama of the English Renaissance I: The Tudor Period*. New York, NY: Macmillan Publishing Co., Inc. 207-261.

Mullinger, James Bass. 1888. *A History of the University of Cambridge*. 3 vols. London: Longman's, Green, and Co.

Roth, Cecil. 1964. *A History of Jews in England*. Oxford: Clarendon Press.

– (ed.). 1972. *Encyclopaedia Judaica*. 16 vols. Jerusalem: Keter Publishing House.

Sarton, George. 1948. *An Introduction to the History of Science*. 3 vols. Baltimore, MD: Johns Hopkins University Press.

Sokol, Edward D. 1977. *Tammerlane*. Lawrence, KS: Coronado Press.

Thomas, Vivien and William Tydeman (eds). 1994. *Christopher Marlowe: The Plays and Their Sources*. London and New York, NY: Routledge.

Toynbee, Arnold. 1935. *A Study of History*. 12 vols. London: Oxford University Press.

4.4. Travel and Pseudo-Translation in the Self-Promotional Writings of John Taylor, Water Poet

Joanne E. Gates

Known mainly for having written about his walking tours, John Taylor was also a kind of translator, or at least he pretended to be one. This he did several times, in self-promotional printing escapades. The works he produced in this way are clearly parodic. His replication of the "Persian" of Thomas Coryate is obviously doggerel Latin. In the guise of Coryate, Taylor boasts that he spoke Italian to a Mohammedan in India and that he is supplying the English translation of the Italian. These are just some of his ploys. Taylor's promotion of travel within Britain, while a paramount concern in evaluating his output, can be seen better in light of his manipulation of dual language strategies as a tactic in his satire upon the more highly educated English travelers. An examination of his works suggests that Taylor evolved from a mere common-man versifier, amusing himself with his derisive put-down of the educated and foreign-land-traveling, learned writers to a writer of genuine talent, dextrously allusive and able to shift tone and intention while spinning out rhyming couplets *ad infinitum*.
Keywords: parody, John Taylor, Thomas Coryate, translation, travel, Utopian.

John Taylor, boatman on the Thames, has been recognized primarily as a cataloguer of places he visited on his walking tours. His self-promotional printing escapades include his tactic of soliciting subscriptions to support his travel publications. His short pamphlets and compendiums on various subjects (a bawd, a whore, a thief, the escapades of a twelve-pence, the uses of hemp) appeared through the early half of the seventeenth century, beginning with his autobiographical *The Sculler,* in 1612. In 1630 he oversaw the Folio of his collected works, which John Chandler, his most recent editor, reminds us (Taylor 1999: vii), carries Taylor's boast that he employed four printing presses. In this recent collection of Taylor's walking tours, his twelve journeys within Great Britain are separated from the rest of his works. Chandler identifies only two journeys–one to Hamburg (1616) and another to Prague during the Bohemian wars (1620)–that had foreign destinations. Indeed, for Taylor, the literary manifestations of foreign travel became objects of parody; he found a particular target in his countryman, Thomas Coryate.

Coryate, sometimes described as a jester at court, was known for his 'macaronicks', his witty and extemporaneous epigrams in Latin and Greek (Nicholl 1999: 3 of 13). Yet when he traveled across Europe and wrote out a detailed account for publication, he could not get it published without endorsements. Michael Redmond (1998: 125-126) states that Prince Henry demanded some preliminary tributes in the form of prefatory verses by others, partly to stay in line with the foreign decadence warned against in Roger Ascham's *The Schoolmaster* (1570), partly because Henry resented James's attempts to marry him to an Italian papist. When the over-witty tributes in verse became instead a mocking praise, Coryate was forbidden to excise them. Ben

Jonson, Henry Peacham, Inigo Jones, John Donne, and many others exaggerated upon the foolish figure at court because Coryate's inflated polyglot style was so easy to imitate. Taylor's own mockery of those "tributes", however, and his parody of Coryate himself, constitute what I maintain is a clever appropriation, meant to develop his Anglophile persona. Taylor's shift into publication was not solely motivated by a desire to attack Coryate. Like Will Kempe, he staged a journey; then the circulation of its account popularized him as writer. That Chandler includes *Voyage in a Paper Boat from London to Queenborough* is a reminder that Taylor's self-promotion had its roots in Will Kempe's *Nine Daies Wonder* (1600). (Both the Morris-dancing Kempe and Taylor were beset with crowds who came out to see their spectacles; Taylor's welcoming party shredded his boat for souvenirs while he was off feasting. Yet the paper boat incident is not simply derivative; it is an inset in his longer work, *The Praise of Hemp-Seed,* Taylor's over-ambitious catalogue of the uses of hemp[1].) To assume, however, as Chandler does by focusing on his English voyages, that Taylor excluded any consideration of foreign influences is to under-emphasize how Coryate–as representative popularizer of foreign travel–also allowed Taylor a perfect target for developing a unique satirical voice.

Taylor's loyalty was to all things British. This would cause him to denounce beer–for its foreign ingredient of added hops–in favor of English ale, and it enabled him to put in rhyme his elegy for Prince Henry and a History of English Kings. By the 1630s and 40s, he warns against what he considers horrendous threats to the monarchy. Yet his full body of work leaves a legacy that is rich with culture and language of England as a center of publishing by the plebeians of their time. If Taylor is exemplary of a grammar-school educated writer, he is one who, like Shakespeare, cultivated noble patronage, knew his classics-in-translation well, peppered his own work with borrowings from others, personalized his sense of Empire, and experimented with the richness of an English language whose verbal acrobatics derived from its affinities with other languages, those classical or those invented, those that sounded exotic, and those whose fake forms and declensions afforded clever sounding insults.

Perhaps deceptive in Chandler's enumeration of only the two foreign voyages is the manner in which Taylor's lampooning of Coryate depended upon the tactics of pseudo-translation. Bernard Capp (1994: 54) states that Taylor latched on to the device of a "Utopian" language first employed by a mock tribute printed in *Coryat's Crudities*. In this, his first book, Coryate prefaced his travels across Europe with more than a hundred pages of padding: verses written by others to welcome the travel account. Coryate's inflated sense of himself was mentioned by Taylor in 1612, in his first pamphlet, *The Sculler*. Later in the year, Taylor constructed a pamphlet whose entire purpose was to mock Coryate's commendatory verses, *Laugh and Be Fat*. In 1613, not satisfied with this appropriation, Taylor wrote a mock elegy in which he assumed Coryate's death (subtitled *Coriats Funerall Epicedivm*), only to revive him, later in the same year, in *The Eighth Wonder of the World, Or Coriats Escape From His Supposed Drowning*. When, in 1616, a thin pamphlet, *Greeting from the Court of the Great Mogul*, appeared, with Coryate depicted riding an elephant, Taylor knew he had occasion to parasitize him again; he responded to this pamphlet, therefore, with his own printing of a subsequent Coryate letter, one that is tempting to read as pure parody, but becomes even more curious if we accept that Taylor merely appended prefatory and concluding verses–some 200 lines in rhyming couplets–to Coryate's farthest missive from India. This pamphlet–which I will call the second Coryate letter, published in quarto in 1618, and republished in Taylor's 1630 Folio, without the illustration of Coryate being borne on a camel and led by a black servant–should interest us especially for how translation negotiated travel and the perceptions of travel in the beginning of the seventeenth century. The letter proper, *Master Thomas Coriats Commendations to His Friends in England*, which Taylor quipped was Coryate's prose–"he did make it / And who dares claime it from him, let him take it" (1967a: vol. 2, 240)[2]–includes a speech in transliterated Persian delivered in Agra, together with Coryate's own translation of it, and the English version of a speech Coryate claims he delivered in Italian to the Mogul of Moltan (*ibid.*: 243-250). What induced Taylor to sponsor this unique document, given his previous derision of Coryate? I maintain that Taylor seemed never to exhaust his indebtedness to Coryate for instigating his career. Indeed, a careful tracking of the dates of the early publications verifies that Taylor initially made his name in print from this strategy of making fun of the university wit who claimed he had walked nearly 2,000 miles in a single pair of shoes.

    Thomas Coryate himself wanted to be identified by his family seat, Odcomb Hill, and he alone is not without deserving stature as a subject appropriate to a volume on travel and translation. His *Crudities* were published in a 1905 Glasgow reissue and images of the 1611 edition have been made available on line at the University of Michigan's Early English Books site[3]. Yet Taylor, when the published version of the travelogue appeared in 1611, prefaced by its more than one hundred pages of panegyrick verses, saw the buzz over the book, apparently even in the bookstalls at St. Paul's, and took aim at the self-inflation of this man who was already known as a pompous fool at court. Taylor repeatedly made fun especially of the fact that the dedicatory verses were written not merely in English, but in the languages of the learned, Latin and Greek. One verse tribute, that of Henry Peacham, purports to be in the "Utopian" and this gave Taylor the occasion to make up gibberish and nonsense verse, feigning the language not only of Utopia but also of "Bermooda" and of other places. Later in his career, Taylor would perpetuate the fascination for translation by mocking it, even when it was clear that the voice and attitude of a piece could be none other than Taylor's own. (For example, Taylor made up a lecture, *A Tale of a Tub* (1641), by an "Inspired

Brownist, and most upright Translator" (1967b: 1), in order to satirize the Brownists and other Roundheads in a subsequent pamphlet, *A Full and Compleat Answer Against the Writer* (1642), in which, under the guise of yet another pseudonym, he speculates that the author of the first is actually John Taylor. The first pamphlet's elaborate title page claimed authorship by "Myheele Mendsoale" yet "Written by J.T." The responding pamphlet is authored "By Thorny Ailo, Annagram" (1967b: 1), an obvious visual puzzle alluding to the way Taylor often printed his name, Iohn Taylor.)

In *The Sculler*, his first connection in print to Coryate, Taylor is primarily dismissive. He addresses several notables. He honors his "deere and respected friend, Maister Beniamin Johnson" at the beginning and addresses the last of his dedications "To Tom Coriat" with these seven couplets:

> What matters for the place I first came from
> I am no Duncecomb, Coxecomb, Odcomb *Tom*
> Nor am I like a wool-pack, cram'd wth Greek,
> *Venus* in *Venice* minded to goe seeke;
> And at my backe returne to write a Volume,
> In memory of my wits *Gargantua* Colume.
> The choysest wits would neuer so adore me;
> Nor like so many Lackies run before me,
> But honest *Tom,* I enuy not thy state,
> There's nothing in thee worthy of my hate;
> Yet I confesse thou hast an excellent wit:
> But that an idle braine doth harbour it.
> Foole thou it at the Court, I on the Thames,
> So farewell Odcomb *Tom,* God blesse King *James*. (1967a: vol. 3, 499)

As yet, Taylor is merely distancing himself from Coryate, but within the year, he would follow this first mention with a fully blown imitation of the dedicatory verses. As centerpiece, he appropriated the style of Henry Peacham's contribution to the original Coryate volume, in which he which makes up the following lines "In the Utopian Tongue":

> Ny thalonin ythsi Coryate lachmah babowans
> O Asiam Europam Americ-werowans
> Poph-himgi Savoya, Hessen, Rhetia, Ragonzie
> France, Germanien dove Anda-louzie
> Not A-rag-on ô Coryate, ô hone vilascar
> Einen tronk Od-combe ny Venice Berga-mascar.
>   Explicit Henricus Peachum. (1905: vol. 1, 115)

Peacham, who also receives credit for the sketch of Coryate's famous sandals, introduced the example of Utopian as a mock tribute in something resembling doggerel Latin. But immediately afterwards, in *Laugh and Be Fat*, Taylor imitated the "Panegyrick Verses" which had inflated Coryate's original *Crudities*. Andrew McRae (1998: par. 11), citing Strachan, reminds us that "Jonson [...] was a central figure in the project of packaging the *Crudities* as carnivalesque, and presenting Coryate as a buffoon"; the project, says McRae, apparently had the sanction of Prince Henry, but not of Coryate (see also Michael Strachan 1962: 124-125). Coryate himself is at pains to distance himself from the most insulting characterizations. This is especially obvious in *Coryats Crambe*, where he appeals to those who misrepresent him as "ass": he meant, he explained, that when he employed an ass to carry books to give to Noblemen at court, his Latin inscription, "in faire Capitall Romane Letters", reading "Asinus portans mysteria", should allude to one of "Alciats Emblemes", which identified "an Ass that carried the Image of the goddesse Isis"[4]. The qualified enthusiasm with which Coryate accepts these prefatory verses is most evident in the manner in which he footnotes a misleading humiliation by Inigo Jones. Coryate claims misrepresentation in the panegyrics; yet, rather than delete or reject Jones's dedicatory verses, he underscores their misrepresentation with a footnote. Jones is clearly belittling Coryate by assuming he made his way into the Venetian brothels:

> Yet he undaunted slipt into the stewes
> For learnings cause; and in his Atticke rage
> Trod a tough hen of thirty yeares of age. (1905: vol. 1, 64)

But, adjacent to the last line, Coryate adds a lettered note and prints in the margin: "Believe him not Reader: Reade my Apology in my discourse of the Venetian Cortezans, page 270" (*ibid.*: 64). Coryate wants us to turn to page 270 (which would be 1905: vol. 2, 408) to get the full account. He claims there that he questioned the Cortezans for his information but never consorted with them.

Coryate's nature was to be oversensitive to some of the lampooning but oblivious to other parts of it. A brief taste of his own prose serves to illustrate. In *Greeting from the Court of the Great Mogul*, Coryate, while explaining how his family seat connects to his Eastern voyage, exposes his awareness that his pointy head is also his trademark:

> Yea, I hope my generall countrie of *England*, shall one day say, that *Odde-combe*, for one part of the word, may truelie be so called: (for *Odde-combe* consisteth of two words, odde, & combe, which latter word in the olde Saxon tongue signifieth besides the vertical point of a cocks head, the side of a Hill, because the east side of the hill wheron *Od-combe* standeth, is very conspicuous, and seen afar off in the Country Eastward) for breeding an odde man, one that hath not his peere in the whole kingdome to match him. (1968: 5)

Taylor, throughout his *Laugh and Be Fat*, which bears the subtitle *A Commentary Upon the Odcombyan Banket*, lampoons the commendatory verses with imitations of them. They are ascribed to what seem to be a few made-up names–"Pricksong" (1967a: vol. 2, 234), "Againe", and "This man hath a Greeke name" (*ibid.*: 236) (there are two such in Coryate's collection of worthies)–but include also Taylor's acknowledged "paraphrase" of known luminaries, Ben Jonson, John Donne, Michael Drayton, Inigo Jones and

Peacham himself, with the Utopian Tongue replicated (*ibid.*: 231-237). Here is where we see the direct association with Peacham's tactic, for "Henricus Peacham" is represented by both English and "Utopian Tongue" verses. Taylor's version of Peacham's Utopian, in his satire on Coryate in *Laugh and Be Fat,* reads:

> Thoytom Asse Coria Thshrump codsheadirustie,
> Mungrellimo whish whap ragge dicete tottrie,
> Mangelusquem verminets nipsem barelybittimsore
> Culliandolt trauellerebumque, graiphone trutchmore.
> Pusse per mew (Odcomb) gul abelgik foppery shig shag
> Cock a peps Comb sottishamp, Idioshte momulus tag rag. (*ibid.*: 237)

The very beginning, then, of Taylor's *Laugh and Be Fat* sets the context for his purpose. He restates what he claimed in *The Sculler,* that he is no Odcomb.

Taylor's use of the "Utopian" next appears in his "Epitaph" for Coryiat/Odcomb, first published in 1613. This is not merely a premature announcement of Coyrate's death. Here, appended to *Odcombs Complaint: Or, Coriats Fvnerall Epicedivm,* is Taylor's version of the epitaph in "the *Barmooda* tongue", which demonstrates the extremity of his lampooning. The seven lines of verse are printed in black type and, says Taylor, guiding his readers, "must be pronounced / *with the accent of the grunting /* of a hogge". The verses begin "Hough, gruntough wough Thomough". The text indicts "Odcough" for his "Callimogh gogh whobogh Raga- / mogh demagosgogh palemogh" (*ibid.*: vol. 1, 221-222). (Even this hog association can be traced to a printed oration in *Coryats Crambe* (1611: Sig. F1r), where Coryate invokes Livy to allude to a Roman practice of a Herald of arms striking a Hog. The symbolic action signifies a willingness to be smitten by Jove if alliances of friendship are violated.) Taylor claims he has translated this "Barmoodan" into the "Utopian"–a nonsense verse with hints of Latin–and then into English. Phrases in his "Utopian" read "Confabuloy Odcumbay Prozeugmolliton tymorumynoy"; then this, in English becomes a bland but still dismissive version of the Epitaph, "*Odcum* produc'd him; many Nations fed him, / And worlds of Writers, through the world have spred him" (1967a: vol. 1, 222). The final section of *Odcombs Complaint* consists of six sonnets, in doggerel fashion. The last reads:

> Sweet *Semi-circled Cynthia* plaid at maw,
> The whilst *Endimion* ran the wild-goose chase.
> Great *Bacchus* with his Cros-bow kild a daw,
> And sullen Saturne smil'd with pleasant face.
> The nine-fold Bugbeares of the Caspian lake,
> Sate whistling *Ebon* horne-pipes to their Ducks,
> *Madge-howlet* straight for ioy her Girdle brake,
> And rugged Satyrs friskd like *Stagges* and *Bucks.*
> The vntam'd tumbling fifteene footed Goat,
> With promulgation of the Lesbian shores,
> Confronted *Hydra* in a sculler Boat,

> At which the mighty mountaine *Taurus* rores,
> Meane time great *Sultan Soliman* was borne,
> And *Atlas* blew his rustick rumbling horne. (*ibid.*: 223)

Here the sonnets suggest to me the flavor of Shakespeare's Touchstone, mocking the serious tone of his betters, able to rhyme in any manner or form. And Taylor's conclusion boasts:

> If there be any Gentlemen, or others that are desirous to be practitioners in the *Barmoodo* and *Vtopian* tongues: the Professor (being the Authour hereof) dwelleth at the Old Swanne neere London Bridge, who will teach them (that are willing) to learne, with agility and facility. (*ibid.*: 223)

Taylor will return to this strategy of advertising himself as expert translator of the made-up language when he pens *Sir Gregory Nonsence*.

I find, in fact, that Taylor grew to cherish his chances to dedicate books of travel to Coryate. For instance, when Taylor writes up his own escapade of foreign travel, in his trip to Germany (1616), his invocation on his preface page is to Coryate. To me, Taylor is appropriating the popularity of foreign travel pamphlets at the same time that he mocks Coryate for his arrogance in foreign lands. Nor is Taylor shy about trying out alternatives to his pseudo-translation. In one section of *The Nipping or Snipping of Abvses: Or, The Wooll-gathering of Wit*, which functions as a direct satirizing of King James's *A Counterblast to Tobacco* (1604), Taylor appends to his advice about tobacco a few lines in a "mock" foreign tongue. Where James in his 1604 *Counterblast* is firmly yet diplomatically suggesting moderation, Taylor suggests a tactic of retaliation: he wants England to trade tobacco to enemies of the English state so that their excessive use of it will incapacitate them. Yet he claims he has an authentic document that could speak more to the issue. Typical of his contextual tactics, he arranges a prefatory remark which makes the pseudo-foreign snippet both a happenstance and calculated tactic:

> *Certaine verses written in the Barbarian tongue, dropt out of a Negroes pocket, which I thought good to insert, because they tend to the honour of Tobacco.* (*ibid.*: vol. 2, 391)

Then Taylor inserts his language antics:

> Vaprosh fogh stinkquash flauorumques fie fominoshte.
> Spitter spawlimon, loatherfo hem halkish spiwriboshte,
> Mistrum fog smoakrash, choakerumques olifa trish trash.
> Dam durticuu belchum, contagioshte vomitroshe:
> Whifferum, puffe gulpum, allisnuff huff fleaminonodish,
> Rewmito contaminosh diabollish dungish odorish. (*ibid.*)

This, of course, is the culmination of a blatant hyperbole of James's argument and invites reading as not only parody but ultimate tribute to the foresight of James. Earlier in the same publication, he clarifies his stance on true English poetry by invoking "Tom Coriat" again, claiming that Coryate's propensity for foreign phrases disqualifies him from any contest for authentic native poetry. The first of Taylor's two acknowledged travels to foreign lands deserves mention because it whetted his appetite for more of Coryate. In 1616, he traveled to Hamburg. It was a brief excursion: "three weeks, three days, three hours." Taylor's dedicatory page is a fantastical yet endearing tribute to Thomas Coryate, his predecessor, whom he addresses thus:

> To the Cosmographicall, Geographical describer, Geometricall / *measurer*; *Historiographicall Calligraphicall Relater and Writer*; / Enigmaticall, Pragmaticall, Dogmaticall Obseruer, Ingrosser, Surueyer / and Eloquent Brittish Graecian Latinist, or Latine Graecian Orator, the / *Odcombyan Deambulator, Perombulator, Ambler, Trotter, or un-* / tyred Traueller, Sir THO: CORIAT, Knight of *Troy*, and one of the dearest darlings to the blind Goddesse Fortune. (*ibid.*: vol. 3, 560)

Taylor's purpose becomes clear: he wants Coryate's return because the Latinate traveler can be fuel for further publishing ventures. Despite the front-page antics, Taylor's factual descriptions are quite informative. He is struck by harsh punishments meted out, indeed witnesses some hangings, and describes the scheme by which one prostitute turns another's customer in to the police in order to get a cut from the proceedings. However, he also embeds his fairly detailed itinerary with some linguistic gymnastics in an attempt to "translate" a quack doctor's speech which he cannot himself understand. One will recognize the parallels between Taylor's description of the performance artist he encounters at Hamburg and Ben Jonson's Volpone, disguised as mountebanck doctor:

> This fellow beeing clad in an ancient doublet of decayed Satin, with a Spruce Leather Ierkin with Glasse buttons, the rest of his attire being correspondent, was mounted vpon a Scaffold, hauing shelfes set with Viols, Gallipots, Glasses, Boxes, and such-like stuffe, wherein as he said, were Waters, Oyles, Vnguents, Emplasters, Electuaries, Vomits, Purges, and a world of neuer heard of Drugs; and being mounted (as I said) he & his man begin to proclaime all their skill and more, hauing a great number of idle and ignorant gazers on, he began as followeth (as I was informed by my Interpreter, for I vnderstood not one word he spake.) (*ibid.*: 568)

Taylor then constructs and quotes the English of what he heard:

> I *Iacomo Compostella*, Practioner in Physick, Chyrurgery, and the Mathematics, beeing a man famous through Europe, Asia, Affricke, and America, from the Orientall exhaltation of *Titan*, to his Occidentall declination, who for the Testimony of my skill, and the rare cures that I haue done, haue these Princes hands and seales; as first the great *Cham* of *Tartaria*, in whose Court, onely with this water which is the Elixar of Henbane, diastracted in a Diurnall of Egredients Hippocratonticke, Auicenian, and Catarackt, with this did I cure the great Dutchesse of *Promulpho*, of the cramp in her tongue: and with this Oyle did I restore the Emperour *Gregory Euanowich*, of a Convulsion in his Pericranion. From thence I trauailed through *Slauonia*, where I met with *Mustapha Despot* of *Serula*, who at that time was intolerably vexed with a *Spasmus*, so that it often droue him into a Syncope with the violent obstructions of the

conflagerating of his veines. Onely with this precious Vnguent being the Quintessence of *Mugwort,* with *Auripigmenty* terragrophicated in a Limbecke of Chystalline translucency, I recouered him to his former health, and for my reward I had a Barbary Horse with rich Caparisons, a Turkish Semitar, a Persian Robe, & 2000. Hungarian Ducats.

Besides, here are the hands and Seales of *Potohamacke, Adelantado* of *ProZewgma,* and of *Gulch Flownderscurfe* chief Burgomaster of *Belgrade,* and of diuers Princes and estates, which to auoid tedious prolixity I omit. But good people if you or any other bee troubled with Apoplexies, Palsies, Cramps, Lethargies, Cataracks, Quinsies, Tisicks, Pleurisies, Coughs, Headaches, Tertian, Quartan, and Quotidian Agues, burning Feauers, Iaundizes, Dropsies, Collicks, Illiaca passio's, the Stone, the Strangury, the Poxe, Plague, Botches, Biles, Blanes, Scabs, Scrurfs, Mange, Leprosies, Cankers, Megrims, Mumps, Fluxes, Meazels, Murreins, Gouts, Consumptions, Toothach, Ruptures, Hernia Aquosa, Hernia Ventosa, Hernia Carnosa, or any other maladie that dares afflict the body of man or woman, come and buy while you may haue it for money, for I am sent for speedily to the Emperour of *Trapezond,* about affaires of great importance that highly concernes his royall person. (*ibid.*: 568-569)

Taylor concludes in his own voice:

Thus almost two houres did this fellow with embost words, and most laborious action, talke and sweat to the people, that vnderstood no more what he said, then he himselfe undersood himselfe. And I thinke his whole takings for simple compounds did amount in the totall to 9. pence sterling. (*ibid.*: 569)

Most curious and most pertient to the theme of this volume is the second letter authored by Coryate but printed by Taylor. So hyperbolic and comic are Taylor's antics when parodying the mountebank that one is tempted to read his claim of printing an authentic Coryate letter as a tongue-in-cheek invention, verisimilitude that anticipates *Gulliver's Travels*, even. But the facts of Coryate's residence in foreign courts suggest otherwise. According to my colleague Howard Miller (another contributor to this volume), Coryate's Persian is a rough, but *very* rough, translation of the English printed with it. Coryate claims to have stayed his travel for months in order to learn the new language[5]. Coryate prefaced the Persian passage with the comment that he hopes his mother would at least show it to the clergy in his home parish, no doubt intending that its "novelty" be seen as something like a Rosetta Stone of his polyglot travels. Why, though, did Taylor reprint the entire pamphlet in his Folio? Quite likely, he expected the reprint, seen in the context of his full body of work, to be read as his ultimate jibe at the far-ranging traveler. For Taylor, it proved his point that Coryate was his own best imitator. Moreover, Taylor admits, in his prefatory verses, that he is enamored of Coryate's stance in defense of his Christian religion in a hostile environment. By surrounding the Coryate letter with verses of his own, Taylor managed simultaneously to parody and to perpetuate the status of the author of the earlier India letter, *Greeting From the Court of the Great Mogul* (originally 1616). With his prefatory verses, Taylor cleverly exposed more of Coryate's pomposity. Coryate himself, meanwhile, gained prestige for his record of distant travel, for

Joanne E. Gates

his transcription of the Persian and for the clever antics he boasts of when he speaks Italian to a Mohammedan in front of a body of two hundred. Writing back to his mother in England, Coryate claims that if they had known what he was saying or if he had addressed the remarks to a Muslim in his own country, he would have been killed.

What we have here, seen in the frame of Taylor's introduction, is the merging of sympathies between two who had been greatly at odds. For us, jaded by further centuries of bad rhymes and by Wordsworth's call to reject heroic couplets as the pinnacle of expression, it seems that Taylor's ragged rhymes are meant to belittle Coryate; yet Taylor welcomes his countryman's voice. Whereas Coryate appended to the earlier letter a short note addressed to his mother, he addressed the second letter primarily to her. Taken as a whole, the Coryate sections might be read as his bleak hope of finding ways to keep begging for sustenance until he can get to Constantinople and send back some "favors". Apostrophizing Coryate, in a brief passage entitled 'A SHORT DESCRIPTION OF THE LONGING / desire that AMERICA hath to entertaine this / vnmatchable Perambulator', Taylor begs,

> *America*, A merry K, *Peru,*
> Vnhappy all in hauing not thy view:
> *Virginia* of thy worth doth onely heare,
> And longs the weight of thy foot-steps to beare:
> Return thee, O returne thee quickly than,
> And see the mighty Court of *Powhatan;*
> [...]
> These Letters following, which thou didst subscribe
> Vnto thy Mother and th' *Odcombian Tribe,*
> Declare thy Art, and also whence thou art,
> And whence, from thence thy purpose is to part.
> Thy learn'd Oration to the mighty *Mogull,*
> All men thereby may see if thou beest no gull,
> Tis so compactly and exactly writ,
> It shewes an extraordinary wit.
> For write thou what thou please, ('tis thy good lot)
> Men like it, though they vnderstand it not. (*ibid.*: vol. 2, 241)

In 1620, Taylor prints his *Travels to Bohemia, or Travels from the Cittie of London to the Cittie of Prague.* While it appears that most of the account is factual and corresponds to specific diary dates, Taylor is not hesitant to point out great wonders with wild hyperbole. His description of the tun, originally constructed for wine at the chapel of the Bishop of Halverstadt, seems to echo Coryate's description of the tun at Heidelberg, but Taylor boasts that he viewed and sent his servant to crawl inside one twice the size of the Heidelberg tun, this bigger one now unused except as a tourist trap. One cannot avoid the suspicion that Taylor's one-upmanship, his appropriating of Coryate's exploration of the tun–celebrated in a well-known woodcut in Coryate's volume–also proves that their two sympathies merged.

276

In 1622, Taylor again invoked his Utopian–this time, however, not to reproduce the doggerel Latin of his earlier displays, but to purport to be "translator" of *Sir Gregory's Nonsence*'s spoutings. It is as thin a disguise as his earlier pretend foreign verses, but now Taylor is in his element as self-promoter. My original interest in Taylor included my supposition that *Sir Gregory Nonsence* might function as a centerpiece of evidence that Taylor's Englishness is forged by his own rustic substitution of travel with pseudo-translation. Frederick Waage (1973: 589-601) has analyzed this text culturally and linguistically, and Emma Renaud (1995: 37-55) argues that it is the origin of English nonsense verse. I certainly concur. In the end, what is most conspicuous about Taylor's works is his assurance of ability, his confident and winning verbal dexterity. With this assurance, he displays himself as self-educated writer and derides foreign influences, lacing his lines instead with subtle allusions to the works of another of his fellow countrymen, William Shakespeare.

For a final taste of Taylor, I must not leave out *Drinke and Welcome*. Like his pretend translation of *A Tale of a Tub*, the pamphlet that would parody Roundheads a few years later, this 1637 publication is a variation on his linguistic hijinks and author identity. The title page alone (1967c: 1) is a self-promotional essay, for it purports to be Taylor's translation of a brewer of Lubek:

Drinke and welcome:
or the
Famovs Historie
of the most part of Drinks, in use
now in the Kingdomes of *Great Brittaine*
and *Ireland*; with an especiall declaration
of the potency, vertue, and operation
of our *English* ALE.

With a description of all sorts of Waters, from the
Ocean sea, to the teares of a Woman.

As also,
The causes of all sorts of weather, faire or foule,
Sleet, Raine, Haile, Frost, Snow, Fogges, Mists,
Vapours, Clouds, Stormes, Windes,
Thunder and Lightning.

Compiled first in the high Dutch tongue, by the
painefull and industrious *Huldricke Van Speagle*, a
Grammaticall Brewer of *Lubeck*, and now most Learnedly
enlarged, amplified, and Translated into English
Prose and Verse.

By IOHN TAYLOR

One soon discovers that the "high Dutch" is mere façade: Taylor promptly expresses derision for hops, which–though their use in England had been established for 100 years–are, in his mind, still resented as the "foreign" ingredients that distinguish beer from true English ale. Lest anyone miss that it is Taylor himself speaking, his summary in verse is blatantly self referential; he drops his guise of translator of a foreigner's observations and speaks as himself. Parenthetically, it is ironic to note that Coryate died without seeing his Odcomb Hill after Taylor last addressed him and encouraged his return. Nicholl reminds us that the account of his death survives only in Edward Terry's *A Voyage to East India* (1655). Coryate wandered into the English enclave at Surat already sick from dysentery, begged for some English sack, drank a moderate amount of it, and within days fell dead, in December 1617 (Nicholl 1999: 10-11). John Taylor seems never to have learned the details of Coryate's death, yet as late as 1638, in *Bull, Beare, and Horse, Cut, Curtaile, and Longtaile,* was elaborating upon his original dispute with him. He appended to the gossip section at the end of *Bull, Beare, and Horse* an account of Coryate's complaint to King James and the clever sets of couplets he claims as answer to the King (1967d: 47-49). That we have, through Taylor's obsession with him, Thomas Coryate's Persian and Italian speeches, adds some detail to those last months. Twenty years later, it was Taylor who was able repeatedly to navigate his way through the English publishing world, rejecting Latin and Greek, yet pretending foreign translation as a joke. Typical of his cataloguing impulses, in his conclusion to *Drink and Welcome*, he summarizes his delineation of drinks:

> So I (a Water-man) in various fashions,
> Have wroate a hotchpotch here of strange mutations,
> Of ancient liquors, made by *Liber Pater,*
> Of drinkes, of Wines, of sundry sorts of Water:
> My Muse doth like a Monkey friske and frigge,
> Or like a Squirrell skip, from twigge to twigge:
> Now sipping *Sider,* straightway supping *Perry,*
> *Metheglin* sweet, and *Mead,* (that makes her merry)
> With *Braggot,* tharein teach a Cat to speake,
> And poore *Pomperkin* (impotent and weake)
> And lastly (as the chiefe of all the rest)
> She tipples *Huff-cap Ale,* to crowne the feast,
> Yet now and then in *Beere* and *Balderdash*
> Her lips she dips; and cleane her entrailes wash:
> And ending, she declares *Sack's* mighty power,
> Which doth time, coyne, wit, health, and all devoure,
> Not by the mod'rate use, but by th' abuse
> Which daily is in universall use.
> For *Rhenish, Claret, White,* and other Wines
> They need not the expression of my lines;
> Their vertue's good, if not commix'd impure
> And (as they're us'd) they may both kill or cure.

Through drinks, through wines, and waters, I have run,
And (being dry and sober) I have

DONE. (1967c: 26)

Whether or not Taylor knew the facts of Coryate's death, of his collapsing after he asked for a little English sack (still yet to be published in the Terry volume), these lines might be read as Taylor's good-humored reproach to Coryate. Taylor asserts pride that his Muse does not speak to him in Latin epigrams. The thorough appropriation of Coryate's legend as foreign traveler has turned John Taylor into a true English original, a gymnast with his own language, a self-promoter whose continuous output matured a London printing industry and continues to invite scholarly attention.

[1] This work is now available on the Internet in an old spelling edition. See Taylor (2002).

[2] Where not otherwise noted, all Taylor citations are from the Spenser Society edition of his works, reprinted by Burt Franklin. These reprints include both the pagination of the original publications and a modern pagination. I shall refer only to the latter.

[3] The Glasgow edition reproduces the original pagination in the margins but also provides its own: I shall refer only to the latter. Further evidence of Coryate's lasting stature: Woodcuts that accompany his India book have recently been featured in an Australian university library's rare book exhibit; he is credited with introducing the fork to the English, for noting the Jewish enclave in Venice as "ghetto", and for titillating English readers with his factual description of Venetian brothels. See the exhibit catalogue, edited by Richard Overell.

[4] This passage is on the fourth to the last page (pages are unnumbered).

[5] On this matter see Nicholl (1999: 10-11), who cites Edward Terry's *A Voyage to East-India*. The relevant passage in Terry is quoted at length in the Publishers' Note to *Coryate's Crudities* (1905: vol. 1, x-xi).

References

Capp, Bernard (ed.). 1994. *The World of John Taylor the Water-Poet, 1578-1653.* Oxford: Clarendon Press.
Coryate, Thomas. 1611. *Coryats Crambe, or His Colwort Twise Sodden, and Now Served in with other Macaronicke Dishes, as the Second Course to his Crudities.* London: William Stansby.
–. 1905. *Coryat's Crudities.* 2 vols. Glasgow: James MacLehose and Sons.
–. 1968. *Greeting From the Court of the Great Mogul.* Reprint of the 1616 edition (Yale Benecke copy). English Experience No. 30. New York, NY and Amsterdam: Da Capo Press.
Kempe, Will. 2002. *Nine Daies Wonder* (1600) (ed. Richard Bear). On line at *Renascence Editions*: http://darkwing.uoregon.edu/%7Erbear/kemp.html (consulted 29.07.2005).
McRae, Andrew. 1998. '"On the Famous Voyage": Ben Jonson and Civic Space' in *Early Modern Literary Studies* 4(2) [Special Issue 3]: 1-31 paragraphs. On line at http://www.shu.ac.uk/emls/04-2/mcraonth.htm (consulted 29.07.2005).
Nicholl, Charles. 1999. 'Field of Bones' in *London Review of Books* 21(17): 13- page printout. On line at on line at http://www.lrb.co.uk/v21/n17/nich02_.html (consulted 29.07.2005).
Overell, Richard (ed.). 1999. *Travel in the East.* Rare Books Exhibition. Monash University Library. The catalogue is available for sale. A summary of it may be viewed on line at http://www.lib.monash.edu.au/exhibitions/fareast/xeastcat.html (consulted 2.08.2005).

Redmond, Michael J. 1998. "'I have read them all": Jonson's *Volpone* and the Discourse of the Italianate Englishman' in Michele Marrapodi and A.J. Hoenselaars (eds) *The Italian World of English Renaissance Drama: Cultural Exchange and Intertextuality.* Newark, NJ and London: University of Delaware Press. 122-140.

Renaud, Emma. 1995. 'A Precursor of Nonsense: John Taylor, The Water Poet' in *Cahiers Elisabethains* 48: 37-53.

Strachan, Michael. 1962. *The Life and Adventures of Thomas Coryate.* London: Oxford University Press.

Stuart, James. 1604. *A Counterblaste to Tobacco.* Orig. 1604. 13 double page sheets. Facsimile available at University of Michigan's Early English Books Online, at http://eebo.chadwyck.com/home (consulted 2.08.2005).

Taylor, John. 1630. *All the Workes of Iohn Taylor the Water-Poet.* London: Iames Boler.

–. 1967a. *Works of John Taylor the Water-Poet Comprised in the Folio Edition of 1630.* 3 vols. New York, NY: Burt Franklin. Rpt. of London: Spenser Society, 1869.

–. 1967b. *Works of John Taylor the Water Poet Not Included in the Folio Volume of 1630: First Collection.* New York, NY: Burt Franklin. Rpt. of London: Spenser Society, 1870.

–. 1967c. *Works of John Taylor the Water Poet Not Included in the Folio Volume of 1630: Second Collection.* New York, NY: Burt Franklin. Rpt. of London: Spenser Society, 1873.

–. 1967d. *Works of John Taylor the Water Poet Not Included in the Folio Volume of 1630: Third Collection.* New York, NY: Burt Franklin. Rpt. of London: Spenser Society, 1876.

–. 1999. *Travels Through Stuart Britain: The Adventures of John Taylor, The Water Poet* (ed. John Chandler). Gloucestershire: Alan Sutton Publishing, Ltd.

–. 2002. *The Praise of Hemp-Seed* (ed. Joanne E. Gates). On line at *Renascence Editions*: http://darkwing.uoregon.edu/~rbear/taylor1.htm (consulted 2.08.2005).

Waage, Frederick O. 1973. 'John Taylor (1557-1654) and Jacobean Popular Culture' in *Journal of Popular Culture* 7: 589-601.

Name Index

Index